Best Practices in International Business

MICHAEL R. CZINKOTA
Georgetown University

ILKKA A. RONKAINEN
Georgetown University

Harcourt College Publishers

Fort Worth Philadelphia San Diego New York Orlando Austin San Antonio
Toronto Montreal London Sydney Tokyo

0015209

Publisher	Mike Roche
Acquisitions Editor	Tracy Morse
Market Strategist	Beverly Dunn
Developmental Editor	Kerri Jones
Project Manager	Andrea Archer

Cover image: Elm Street Publishing Services, Inc.

ISBN: 0-03-028721-9

Library of Congress Catalog Card Number: 00-105659

Copyright © 2001 by Harcourt, Inc.

All rights reserved. No part of this publication may be reproduced or transmitted in any form or by any means, electronic or mechanical, including photocopy, recording, or any information storage and retrieval system, without permission in writing from the publisher.

Requests for permission to make copies of any part of the work should be mailed to: Permissions Department, Harcourt, Inc., 6277 Sea Harbor Drive, Orlando, Florida 32887-6777.

Portions of this work were published in previous editions.

Copyrights and acknowledgments begin on page 358, which constitutes a continuation of the copyright page.

Address for Domestic Orders
Harcourt College Publishers, 6277 Sea Harbor Drive, Orlando, FL 32877-6777
800-782-4479

Address for International Orders
International Customer Service
Harcourt College Publishers, 6277 Sea Harbor Drive, Orlando, FL 32887-6777
407-345-3800
(fax) 407-345-4060
(e-mail) hbintl@harcourtbrace.com

Address for Editorial Correspondence
Harcourt College Publishers, 301 Commerce Street, Suite 3700, Fort Worth, TX 76102

Web Site Address
http://www.harcourtcollege.com

Harcourt College Publishers will provide complimentary supplements or supplement packages to those adopters qualified under our adoption policy. Please contact your sales representative to learn how you qualify. If as an adopter or potential user you receive supplements you do not need, please return them to your sales representative or send them to:

Attn: Returns Department, Troy Warehouse, 465 South Lincoln Drive, Troy, MO 63379.

Printed in the United States of America

0 1 2 3 4 5 6 7 8 9 039 9 8 7 6 5 4 3 2 1

THE HARCOURT COLLEGE PUBLISHERS SERIES IN MANAGEMENT

Anthony, Perrewé, and Kacmar
Strategic Human Resource Management
Third Edition

Bereman, Lengnick-Hall, and Mark
Compensation Decision Making: A Computer-Based Approach
Second Edition

Bergmann, Scarpello, and Hills
Compensation Decision Making
Fourth Edition

Boone and Kurtz
Contemporary Business
2000 Update

Boone and Kurtz
Contemporary Business
Ninth Edition

Bourgeois, Duhaime, and Stimpert
Strategic Management: A Managerial Perspective
Second Edition

Carrell, Ebert, and Hatfield
Human Resource Management: Strategies for Managing a Diverse Global Work Force
Sixth Edition

Costin
Strategies for Quality Improvement: TQM Reengineering & ISO 9000
Second Edition

Costin
Managing in the Global Economy: The European Union

Costin
Economic Reform in Latin America

Costin
Readings in Strategy and Strategic Management

Czinkota and Ronkainen
Best Practices in International Business

Czinkota, Ronkainen, and Moffett
International Business
2000 Update

Czinkota, Ronkainen, and Moffett
International Business
Fifth Edition

Czinkota, Ronkainen, Moffett, and Moynihan
Global Business
Third Edition

Daft
Leadership: Theory and Practice

Daft
Management
Fifth Edition

Daft and Marcic
Understanding Management
Third Edition

Daft and Noe
Organizational Behavior

DeSimone and Harris
Human Resource Development
Second Edition

Dilworth
Operations Management
Third Edition

Gatewood and Feild
Human Resource Selection
Fifth Edition

Greenhaus, Callanan, and Godshalk
Career Management
Third Edition

Harris
Human Resource Management
Second Edition

Hodgetts
Modern Human Relations at Work
Seventh Edition

Hodgetts and Kuratko
Effective Small Business Management
Seventh Edition

Holley and Jennings
The Labor Relations Process
Seventh Edition

Holt
International Management: Text and Cases

Kuratko and Hodgetts
Entrepreneurship: A Contemporary Approach
Fifth Edition

Kuratko and Welsch
Strategic Entrepreneurial Growth

Lesser
Business Public Policy and Society

Oddou and Derr
Managing Internationally: A Personal Journey

Robbins
Business.today

Ryan, Eckert, and Ray
Small Business: An Entrepreneur's Plan
Fifth Edition

Sandburg
Career Design Software

Sandburg
Discovering Your Business Career CD ROM

Vecchio
Organizational Behavior: Core Concepts
Fourth Edition

Vietor & Kennedy
Globalization and Development: Cases in National Economic Strategies

Weiss
Business Ethics: A Stakeholder and Issues Management Approach
Third Edition

Zikmund
Business Research Methods
Sixth Edition

To Susan, Sanna, and Alex
—IAR

To Ilona and Margaret Victoria
—MRC

is

A Harcourt Higher Learning Company

Now you will find The Dryden Press' distinguished innovation, leadership, and support under a different name . . . a new brand that continues our unsurpassed quality, service, and commitment to education.

We are combining the strengths of our college imprints into one worldwide brand: Harcourt

Our mission is to make learning accessible to anyone, anywhere, anytime—reinforcing our commitment to lifelong learning.

We are now Harcourt College Publishers.
Ask for us by name.

One Company
"Where Learning
Comes to Life."

www.harcourtcollege.com
www.harcourt.com

TABLE OF CONTENTS

INTRODUCTION

PART ONE NEW REALITIES OF THE GLOBAL MARKETPLACE 9

PART TWO ENVIRONMENTS 33

0015209

PART FIVE ORGANIZATION AND IMPLEMENTATION 247

PART SIX MARKET SPECIFICS 291

PART SEVEN THE FUTURE 339

GLOBALIZATION: AN INTRODUCTION AND ASSESSMENT OF REALITIES AND STRATEGIES

Michael R. Czinkota and Ilkka A. Ronkainen

Georgetown University

Globalization, the integration of economies around the world, has become a dominant influence on governments, firms, and individuals in the past ten years. While the phenomenon is not a new one, recent developments in opening of markets and free trade have sparked debate on its merits. The fastest globalizing nations have indeed enjoyed rates of economic growth up to 50 percent higher than those that have been integrating the world economy more slowly (Global Business Policy Council, 2000). These same countries have also improved in terms of political freedoms as well as benefits derived from increased social spending as witnessed in increases in life expectancy, literacy rates, and overall standard of living. At the same time, critics are pointing to a widening gap between the well-to-do and the poor and to the impact of free trade and investment on employment and the environment.

The new landscape of international business in the twenty-first century is shaped by interlinkages at every possible level. Regional groupings between nation-states have driven the dramatic increases in trade and investment. The benefits of free trade and stable exchange rates are available only if countries are willing to give up some measure of independence and autonomy in decision making. Economic integration is no longer characterized just by free movement of goods, services, labor, and capital across borders, but also by the development of common institutions, such as the European Central Bank and the euro.

The world marketplace is too large and the competition too strong for even the largest multinationals to do everything independently. Technologies are converging, making the cost and the risk of both goods and market development even greater. Partly as a reaction and partly to exploit the free-trade developments, management in firms has become more pragmatic about what it takes to be successful in global markets. The resulting strategic alliances with suppliers, competitors, and companies in other industries have also provided local companies new access to the world marketplace.

Linkages have also become intense at the individual level. The number of Internet hosts has grown from 9 million in 1993 to 72 million in 2000. A total of 304 million people were estimated to be online in 2000 with explosive growth expected from new, and increasingly more affordable, computer and telecommunication technologies. Advances in transportation and ease of travel allow consumers to experience new markets and products in person.

Globalization has been associated typically with large-scale multinational companies from the industrialized world. However, sheer size is no longer a buffer against competition in markets where customers are demanding specialized and customized products that draw from worldwide best practice. With the advent of electronic process and technology and the opportunities associated with e-business, these so-called mininationals are able to compete on price and quality—often with greater flexibility. By taking advantage of today's open trading regions, they can serve the world from a handful of manufacturing bases, sparing them from the necessity of building a plant in every country. Developments in information technology allow for access to data throughout the world, which in turn enables them to run inexpensive and responsive sales and service operations across languages and time zones. Increasingly, companies from emerging markets are establishing operations in developed markets independently or as part of strategic alliances.

With these issues in mind, this collection of twenty-three articles has been compiled to cover the current issues related to international business practice in the twenty-first century: the new realities of globalization, the changed environments in which firms will have to operate, subsequent market-development strategies, the changes evident in different functional areas, as well as the challenges faced by implementing strategies under the new circumstances. Given that globalization will not mean worldwide standardization, a number of region-specific issues will be raised, and the book will close with an assessment of future trends.

GLOBAL REALITIES

This collection begins with a focus on global realities. The first part defines the parameters of the global marketplace, and the second part focuses on the environmental opportunities and challenges that emerge from globalization.

NEW REALITIES OF THE GLOBAL MARKETPLACE

The first article, by Fraser and Oppenheim, presents the process by which the world's economy is transformed from a set of national and regional markets into a new set of markets that operate without regard to regional or national boundaries. Whereas globalization in the 1990s was largely a phenomenon of the developed markets of North America, Western Europe, and Asia, the process has quickened to include an increasing number of emerging markets. In terms of industry-markets, even governmental procurement is being liberalized, thus allowing nonlocal players to expand into the sector. The next article, by Mazur, argues that the forces behind globalization may not be sustainable if it happens at the expense of labor rights, the environment, and social standards. The argument is made that these issues need to be built into trade accords (for example, the World Trade Organization or the Free Trade Area of the Americas) and into the agendas of international financial institutions (such as the World Bank and the International Monetary Fund).

ENVIRONMENTS

Governments have been forced to realize that it is increasingly difficult to distinguish between domestic economic activity from international events and decisions made elsewhere in the world. Given the benefits to be derived from international business, governments are eager to take advantage of the opportunities but may at the same time also have to accept the negative consequences of increased market openness. The article by Czinkota analyzes the role of export assistance by exploring the dimensions that make exports different from other economic activities. Effective export assistance efforts by governments are those with clarity of purpose and tightness of focus; they are coordinated and built on exporter strengths.

While it is commonly agreed that export promotion is a critically important activity by a government, export controls are less so. In the next article, Czinkota and Dichtl discuss the use of export controls as economic and foreign policy tools. With today's new political realities (such as the end of the Cold War, the increased availability of high-technology products, and the rapid dissemination of information and innovation), the support for export controls has decreased. The foundation of a new, multilateral export control regime is presented, together with a discussion of the effect of export controls on the competitiveness of firms.

The final years of the 1990s witnessed a number of financial crises. The devaluation of the Mexican peso in 1994 served as a harbinger of things to come. The Asian crisis of July 1997, the Russian ruble's collapse in August 1998, and the fall of the Brazilian real in January 1999, all provided international businesses new challenges in their operations, not only in those countries but worldwide. The article by Brealey outlines the basics of how to prevent such crises, and, should they occur, how to resolve them.

The 1990s also found governments struggling to adjust economic regulation to a new global medium: the Internet. In the three megamarkets of the world, the debate is on the degree of regulation and legislation that should be imposed on e-business.

The article by Vander Weyer proposes the minimum interference by the public sector to reap the promised opportunity to its full potential.

As the number of environments in which the manager and the firm have to operate increases, so do the challenges in terms of responsible decision making. In the fifth article, Stajkovic and Luthans focus on ethical standards in international business and emphasize that paying attention to cultural variations is important because the potential for costly misconceptions and errors increases substantially when international managers interact with partners whose values, beliefs, and behavioral patterns are different from their own.

One of the controversies surrounding globalization is the environmental impact of increased industrialization and consumption. In this part's final article, Chan discusses the changing environmental attitudes in the world's largest emerging market, China.

GLOBAL STRATEGY

The challenge of globalization to managers is how to exert leverage on corporate capabilities around the world so that the company as a whole is greater than the sum of its parts (Maruca, 1994). Capabilities, regardless of their origin, will have to be leveraged in all the operations worldwide. Issues are highlighted in three parts: market entry and development, the adjustment of different functional areas to globalization, and how global strategy implementation should take place.

STRATEGIES OF ENTRY AND OPERATIONS

Gupta and Govindarajan outline in the first article of this part why globalization has ceased to be an option for companies and has become a strategic imperative for virtually any type or size of business. Growth is a must if a company is to remain viable; in many cases, growth can be had only by constantly seeking new markets.

Given the mature nature of the developed-country-markets, emerging markets are increasingly focused on. At the same time, companies in these new markets are looking for partners to secure their entry into world markets. In the second article, Adarkar et al. outline the challenges faced in alliances between developed and emerging market companies (in countries such as Vietnam) and how a win-win situation from all parties' point of view can be reached.

One of the myths of globalization is that local companies will lose to the more-powerful multinationals. However, local firms can be contenders by offering a difference in local alternatives (such as cultural goods). According to the last article in this part, by Ger, local companies must investigate the areas ignored by the multinationals, such as the local context, the urban and rural poor, and small local markets (possibly with similar conditions across markets so that they themselves can also pursue "global strategies").

FUNCTIONAL AREAS

Given the rapid changes in the environment, the competencies that companies exploit must also adjust. For a company to have a sustainable long-term competitive advantage, it has to cater to a real customer need in a way that cannot be easily copied or imitated, and has to do so across a wide variety of markets (Prahalad and Hamel, 1990). In the first article of this part, Mascrenhas, Baveja, and Jamil point out that leading companies are constantly changing their competencies in anticipation of emerging business conditions. A shift is occurring in relative emphasis from internal technological competencies towards external relationship competencies, which are difficult to replicate by competition.

At the same time, the requirements as far as cultural expertise is concerned, for example, are considerable. The marketing challenges, in particular, heighten in importance. The article by Kenneth Simmonds outlines the common pitfalls such as poor selection of markets, underestimation of competition, misunderstanding of customer differences, entry at the wrong price, and selecting inappropriate partners. In addition, many managers fail to contemplate what expansion in any one market will imply to the overall strategy and presence of the firm worldwide.

One of the bottlenecks of global expansion is the scarcity of qualified managers. With the growth of a knowledge-based society along with the emergence of new types of country-markets, managers have to take the development of human resources as a basis for a competitive advantage very seriously. In the next article, Quelch and Bloom outline how a cohesive network of managers can be developed to identify and leverage best practice worldwide. Assignments abroad today mean an integral part of a manager's development and advancement.

This part closes with an article that acknowledges the importance of infrastructure development in globalization. Projects that relate to power and transportation cannot necessarily be funded with the traditional methods to lead to superior financial execution and greater value creation. Esty outlines the benefits of project finance to fund large-scale capital projects.

ORGANIZATION AND IMPLEMENTATION

The next part includes contributions on the implementation of global strategies. Globalization is a change process that may go against the very grain of existing power structures, the needed skill levels or infrastructures, or may be threatening to those in present structures. Furthermore, the not-invented-here syndrome may emerge if strategy formulation has not included implementor input during the planning process. In general, as shown by the first article by Theuerkauf, Ernst, and Mahini, successful companies coordinate their decision making globally, with more central direction than their less-successful counterparts. Furthermore, they work as global networked organizations wherein the transfer of critical capabilities is a given as shown by Conn and Yip in the next article.

New initiatives not only can emerge from headquarters or from the home country of the firm, they also need to be encouraged from the field. Birkinshaw and Fry discuss some of the corporate barriers that need to be maneuvered to give local initiatives a chance not only in individual country markets but for regional or worldwide use.

GLOBAL MARKET DEVELOPMENT

Globalization is not standardization: market-specific differences will always exist, but they need to be approached not as problems but as issues that can be learnt from. The next parts feature articles about regional and market differences that managers will have to adjust to at present but may find that they become more broadly applicable later.

MARKET SPECIFICS

In January 1999, eleven European Union member countries introduced a common currency. Every dimension of business will be significantly changed as a result of the euro. Markets will be pushed closer together, competition is going to increase, and price transparency will force managers to coordinate prices more closely across borders. These implications are discussed in detail by Ahlberg, Garemo, and Nauclée in the opening article of this part.

Despite an increasing opening of markets, impediments will continue to challenge businesses globally. While governmental controls may be decreasing, cultural barriers such as business practices will still remain. Czinkota and Kotabe discuss one of the most challenging markets in this regard, Japan, where the interlocking relationships among suppliers and manufacturers make market entry and development a daunting task to outsiders.

As market forces are changing the situation in Japan towards a more liberalized one, the same phenomenon is occurring in Central and Eastern Europe, where the task is to make economies competitive in the new global marketplace as shown by Springer and Czinkota.

In the early twenty-first century, the top ten emerging markets (such as China, India, and Brazil) already approach in size and character of the developed markets of North America, the European Union, and Japan. This growth does not mean that strategies can be necessarily extended to those markets without adjustment. James Gingrich, in the final article of this part, stresses the importance of making products affordable and investing in distribution capabilities as preconditions of success.

THE FUTURE

Many managers will face the increasing globalization of markets and competition. In many industries, the major players have decided to compete in all of the major markets of the world. The challenges in this process are considerable. Managers will have to assess their core businesses, formulate global strategy in terms of market choice and competitive strategy, develop appropriate programs to match the opportunities present, and make sure that their organizations are ready to leverage all possible resources across borders. The challenges the managers perceive in this endeavor are highlighted by Czinkota and Ronkainen in the closing article of this text.

References

Global Business Policy Council, *Globalization Ledger* (Washington, D.C.: A.T. Kearney, 2000), Introduction.

Regina Fazio Maruca, "The Right Way to Go Global," *The Harvard Business Review* 72 (March–April 1994): 134–145.

C.K. Prahalad and Gary Hamel, "The Core Competence of the Corporation," *The Harvard Business Review* 68 (May–June 1990): 79–91.

PART ONE

New Realities of the Global Marketplace

WHAT'S NEW ABOUT GLOBALIZATION?

Jane Fraser and Jeremy Oppenheim

A "superconductor" of knowledge and capital is about to reach the right temperature

A $21 trillion market will emerge—with no natural owners

The challenge will be to leverage brands, ideas, and people

The biggest opportunities will be the ones that look most local

Cynics ask, "What's so important about globalization? It's been under way for decades." In some respects, they are right. The underlying processes have indeed been evident for some time, though without making much more than a modest impact on the world's economy. Apart from the relatively small international trade in goods and services and a few industries that globalized early, national economies have remained predominantly local.

But all this is changing. Suddenly, the pace of globalization has quickened. The gradual process that gave companies ample time to adjust has gone for good. In just a couple of decades, our economy will become substantially global.

In the past, globalization amounted to little more than evolutionary change in a few scale-driven industries. In the future, its impact will be ubiquitous, affecting services as well as manufacturing, and emerging market economies as well as the developed world. As a result, corporations in almost every sector will face the huge challenge of learning to play in a globalizing economy where many of the old rules no longer apply, and where the new rules are still being created. The global prize has never been more golden; the gales of destruction never more fierce.

Jane Fraser is a consultant in McKinsey's New York office and Jeremy Oppenheim is a consultant in the London office. Copyright © 1997 McKinsey & Company. All rights reserved.

Definition of Terms

International	A world economy composed of markets that are largely contained within national boundaries
Multinational	A company that operates in a number of countries and competes primarily within national markets
Globalization	The process by which the world's economy is transformed from a set of national and regional markets into a set of markets that operate without regard to national boundaries
Global company	A company that is able to operate across national boundaries in pursuing both international and global opportunities

A FUNDAMENTAL TRANSFORMATION

The transformation now taking place in the world economy is unlike anything we have experienced before. The increasing availability of global capital, coupled with advances in computing and communications technology, is serving to accelerate the processes of globalization. Economies are becoming superconductors of vast flows of capital and transplants of production techniques. The barriers to globalization are coming down wherever you look: not just in Western Europe, North America, and Japan, but in the emerging giants of China, India, Brazil, Russia, and Indonesia.

Underpinning these changes are three mutually reinforcing factors:

- The growing scale, mobility, and integration of the world's capital markets
- The increasing irrelevance of national borders as regulation is liberalized and other economic barriers fall
- The expanding ability to leverage knowledge and talent worldwide through technology.

GLOBAL CAPITAL MARKETS

The growth and integration of the world's capital markets are the engine of globalization. As foreign exchange and bonds become more integrated, the law of one price begins to apply throughout the world. As equity markets start to integrate in their turn, capital becomes more mobile.*

---

*For a more detailed account of this topic, *see* Lowell L. Bryan and Diana Farrell, *Market Unbound: Unleashing global capitalism.* John Wiley, New York, 1996, and "Buy stocks, shun bonds," *The McKinsey Quarterly,* 1996 Number 2, pp. 166–77.

• EXHIBIT 1 •

Capital Market Trends

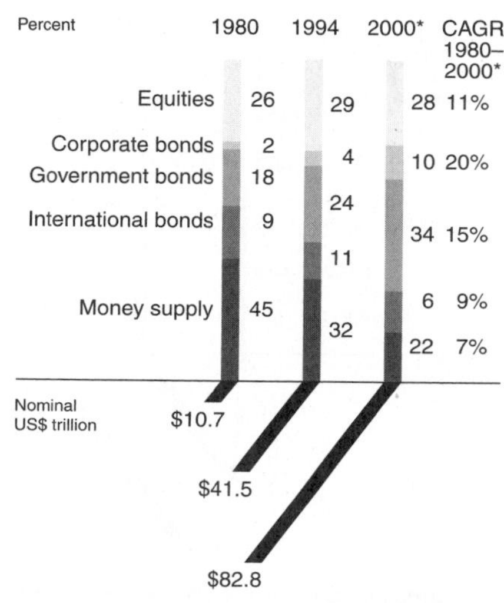

*Estimated

Crossborder capital flows rose from $536 billion in 1991 to $1,258 billion four years later. These totals exclude foreign direct investment, which itself soared from an average of $26.2 billion between 1986 and 1990 to over $250 billion by 1996. The world's stock of liquid financial assets grew from $10.7 trillion in 1980 to $41.5 trillion in 1994, and is expected to exceed $80 trillion by the year 2000 (Exhibit 1).

A rising proportion of these flows is going to the emerging markets that used to seek their finance primarily from official sources such as the World Bank and the IMF. Today, almost 50 percent of direct foreign investment and well over 10 percent of portfolio capital flows are directed toward these markets, even though they account for less than 25 percent of world dollar-denominated GDP. Moreover, these flows are increasingly oriented toward the long term: Endesa of Chile was able to issue a century bond for $200 million in early 1997. And even when there are crises, as in Mexico in 1995, private investors are usually willing to reinvest as soon as they see that underlying economic imbalances are being tackled.

The impact of these capital market developments is striking. First, they are driving a convergence of economic policy across more and more countries. Economies that the capital markets perceive as fiscally responsible and politically committed to market-based policies attract the international capital they need to finance growth and infrastructure development. This is as true for emerging markets as it is for more developed economies.

Second, a deepening pool of internationally mobile capital is pursuing profitable investments. No longer the ally of vested interests within a closed national economy,

• EXHIBIT 2 •

WORLD STOCK MARKET CAPITALIZATION

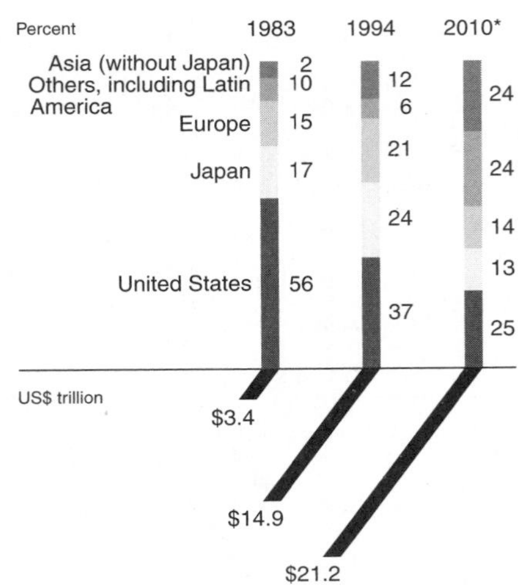

*Estimated
Source: BZE; Baring; *IFC: Guide to World Equity Markets;* McKinsey analysis

capital is increasingly available to anyone capable of generating high returns, wherever in the world they may be. Companies that used to face capital constraints can now obtain virtually limitless supplies of relatively inexpensive capital to fund their growth (Exhibit 2).

Third, the capital markets are enforcing shareholder value and market capitalization as the dominant metrics for measuring corporate performance. And as they become the arbiter of companies' destinies, the equity markets are discriminating more and more powerfully between weak and strong performers. Since 1986, the stakes needed to enter the S&P top 10 have risen from $18.4 billion to $70.7 billion. With so much capital seeking out high returns, those companies that do deliver exponential global growth are richly rewarded in their market capitalization.

As capital markets grow and mature, the financial instruments that can be used to unbundle and manage different classes of risk become more sophisticated. Ten years ago, infrastructure projects in emerging markets were almost always financed through public sector resources. Today, despite regulatory and exchange rate risk, more and more of these projects are funded by private sector sponsors. They are able to disaggregate the various components of the risk, allocate them to the players that are in the best position to bear them, and then securitize the project financing, spreading risk efficiently through the capital markets. Thanks to developments such as these, the world's capital markets now possess both the power and the instruments to globalize the world economy.

A GLOBAL ARENA

With the greater mobility of capital comes an expansion in the scale of the profit opportunity. We estimate that the value of the world economy that is "globally contestable"—that is, open to global competitors in product, service, or asset ownership markets—will rise from approximately $4 trillion in 1995 to well over $21 trillion by 2000, boosted by emerging markets and new sectors joining the fray (Exhibit 3). This trend to economic openness looks set to continue, fueled by communications technology and by the power of the idea that markets create freedom and expand individual choice.

In the past decade, the legitimacy of the state's role in running national economies has come under question: witness the demolition of the Berlin Wall, the wave of economic liberalization across Latin America, and the explosive dynamism of capitalism with a Chinese face. As regulation is relaxed and other barriers—such as foreign exchange controls, ownership restrictions, and access to capital, infrastructure, and information—are overcome, opportunities to globalize products and relationships and capture country differences are growing exponentially. In the financial, utility, and transportation sectors, among others, the creed of national interest and natural ownership

• EXHIBIT 3 •

EXPANSION OF THE GLOBAL ARENA

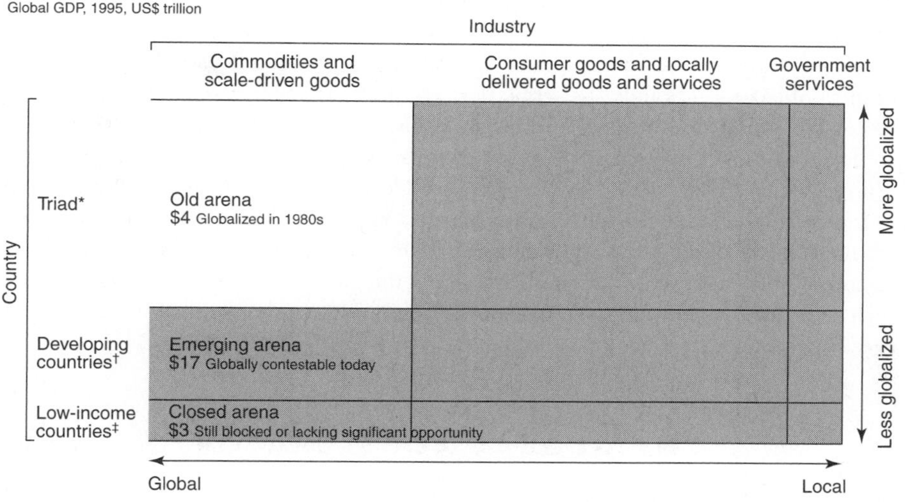

*19 OECD countries from North America, Western Europe, and Asia; Japan and Australia included
†68 countries with middle income per capita, plus China and India
‡Countries of small absolute size and low income per capita

that has kept international competition at bay is being swept away. The profit opportunities now there for the taking are worth hundreds of billions of dollars; moreover, unlike most such opportunities in national economies, they have no natural owner.

Consider personal financial services, which has an annual pretax profit opportunity worth roughly $300 billion, of which over 95 percent is currently captured by nationally based competitors. Within a decade, this opportunity is likely to double in value, quickly becoming accessible to global competitors via transplants or electronic distribution. Existing national players will see their profitability come under threat as they face hundreds if not thousands of new competitors, any one of which could, if it plays the game well, reap extraordinary rewards. In much the same way, almost all industries, from food to electronics, are becoming globally contestable.

GLOBAL KNOWLEDGE ECONOMICS

Three decades of constant progress in information and communication technologies have triggered a complex pattern of social and economic change. This technological revolution is shaping the process of globalization by providing new tools and infrastructures with which to capture global opportunities.

Evolving technologies and the worldwide deregulation of the telecommunication industry cut the marginal cost of computing and communications almost to zero. The upgrading of the world economy's computing and communications infrastructure is enabling a massive increase in the crossborder information flows that serve to reduce the risks associated with unfamiliarity, speed up the arbitrage of price anomalies, and stimulate consumer demand for world-class products, services, and brands. Soon, services that used to require a local physical presence will be opened up to electronic delivery, amplifying companies' ability to reach consumers across the globe.

More subtly, technological change is also driving up the relative value of all forms of intangible asset—brands and reputation, intellectual property, software, media content, talent—throughout the world. Many of these assets have huge scale effects when leveraged globally, giving intangible-rich companies strong incentives to shape their industries along global lines. The likes of Coca-Cola, Microsoft, Glaxo Wellcome, and Marriott Hotels are benefiting from a business approach that seeks to minimize investment in fixed assets and maximize the ability to leverage brands, standards, management skills, and intellectual property across the global arena. It is no accident that such companies are among the top performers for their shareholders over the past decade.

THE GLOBAL ACCELERATOR

The combination of capital market developments, broader market access, and knowledge intensification is driving an exponential change in the pace, scale, and scope of globalization. Pace is increasing because the globalization process is fueling itself—and because the infrastructure for diffusing technology and ideas globally has become much more powerful. Scale, because the share of world GDP that is effectively globalized is set to rise from around 20 percent today to well over 50 percent in the next 10 to 15 years. And scope, because as globalization's footprint expands, so do opportunities to combine resources and segment markets in new ways.

ABUNDANT OPPORTUNITIES

The globalization process, as we have seen, is driven by global capital seeking profits across national borders. As the barriers around national economies fall, an abundance of opportunities suddenly and simultaneously become accessible. And as companies capture these opportunities, they in turn spur the globalization of the world's markets.

Two types of opportunity arise from this process. The first derives from the specialization and scale effects that can be exploited by a player that successfully leads the globalization of a good or service such as package delivery, personal computers, or jet engines. The second originates in the variations in factor cost productivity and patterns of demand that exist because most of the world's economic activity still takes place in national markets. Crossborder participants are able to exploit these country differences in skill sets and productivity, and to arbitrage labor price differentials, taxes, and so on.

Only a decade ago, most OECD countries and almost all emerging markets held the telecom sector, power, a large chunk of banking, and the whole of education and healthcare in state ownership. What the state did not own, it regulated. Today, these sectors are fast becoming local private domains, and, little by little, global private domains. As more industries become globally contestable, it is paradoxically those that appear most local—those with natural barriers to foreign competition and limited physical scale effects—that will offer the richest pickings to the pioneering companies that seek to capture them. Such will be their size and growth that they represent a prize too big for major players to ignore.

GLOBAL TRAILBLAZERS

Trailblazing corporations have their foot on the global accelerator. These pioneers realize how large the profits can be for a player that captures arbitrage opportunities between countries or shapes a global industry. They understand the dynamics of globalization: first find a way around national barriers, and then turn them to your advantage. They know how to shape an industry to play to their own strengths.

They recognize that unplanned globalization can destroy value for all of an industry's participants, leading as it does to wars of attrition in which players contest away value in country after country, eventually commoditizing the entire industry. They need look no further than automobiles, semiconductors, interbank FX trading, and public telecom switching equipment to see that not all globalization is profitable. They know how to create opportunities through deep knowledge of local markets married with global reach—opportunities that others are unable to see until they are converted into real profit streams.

Pioneering corporations in search of global profits are driving the globalization of their industries. There is no structural reason why soft drinks should be global while beer and spirits remain much more local. The only difference is that Coca-Cola has redefined soft drinks as a global industry. Similarly, it was hardly inevitable that trainers should become the only global footwear product. But Nike and Reebok drove their business in a global direction, creating global brands, a global customer segment, a global supply chain, and a set of global imitators.

Much the same is true of fast food, aircraft production, construction equipment, and credit cards. One or two players shape an industry on a global basis, and we all discover with hindsight that there are global scale and skill effects in R&D, the supply chain, branding, knowledge management, talent development, and risk diversification, to name but a few.

A GRADUAL TRANSITION

Though the forces of globalization are strong, the world is not about to be converted overnight. The process will rather be one of gradual transition over several decades. Some sectors of the economy, particularly government services, will remain predominantly closed (Exhibit 4), though even these will feel some effects. EDS's recent multiyear outsourcing contract with the UK tax authorities is surely a sign of things to come in core government functions.

Nor does globalization erase the differences between countries or render local knowledge, local talent, and local relationships obsolete. Quite the opposite: privileged access to country-specific intangible assets of this kind will be critical to success. However, it will also be vital to understand what differs and what remains the same from one country to another, and to command assets that can be leveraged worldwide.

The greatest threat to this trend will come if local companies deny its existence and refuse to adapt. To do so will put millions of jobs at risk in advanced economies. Such companies will find that standing still is no answer in a global economy in which other players are racing ahead.

Since about two-thirds of the world's economy and almost all services are still in the early stages of globalizing, it seems likely that most of the great growth firms of the twenty-first century have yet to be born. These companies will start out with a vision of the world as their market; they will share few of the mental constraints that inhibit the incumbents; they will seek to recruit and develop the best talent from all nationalities; and they will aspire to a market capitalization that seems enormous today. Lacking all respect for the status quo and having nothing to gain by preserving it, they will be the architects of discontinuity in their industries. Many will be from outside America and Western Europe.

Firms with a national focus are not alone in having to adjust. Even large, successful multinationals in such global industries as automobiles and chemicals face tremendous upheavals. As they watched their industries mature into global structures with unfavorable economics, they lost the advantages they had traditionally derived from superior access to capital and local skills. They must now learn how to prosper in a

• EXHIBIT 4 •

THE STATE OF PLAY

Size of industry based on world GDP
1995 US$ trillion

	Category	Industries		
1	**Physical commodities** Petroleum, mineral ores, timber	2.0	23%	Globalized
2	**Scale-driven business goods and services** Aircraft engines, construction equipment, semiconductors, airframes, shipping, refineries, machine tools	1.0		
3	**Manufactured commodities** Refined petroleum products, aluminum, specialty steel, bulk pharmaceuticals, pulp, specialty chemicals	2.8		
4	**Labor skill-/productivity-driven consumer goods** Consumer electronics, personal computers, cameras, automobiles, televisions	0.9	15%	Accelerating globalization
5	**"Brandable," largely deregulated consumer goods** Soft drinks, shoes, luxury goods, pharmaceuticals, movie production	0.5*		
6	**Professional business services** Investment banking, legal services, accounting services, consulting services	2.5		
7	**"Hard to brand" globally, largely regulated consumer goods and services** Food, personal financial services, television production, retail distribution channels	6.3	50%	Early globalization, still
8	**Local (unbranded) goods and services** Construction materials, real estate, funeral homes, education, household services, medical care, utilities	6.4		
9	**Government services** Civil servants, national defense	3.0		
	Total	$25.3		

*Provisional

Source: World Development Report (World Bank www.worldbank.org), McGraw-Hill/DRI *World Economic Outlook* 1996; United Nations 1995 National Income Accounts; McKinsey analysis

world where most of the best new opportunities are in services, and where the key to profitability is to leverage intangible assets such as knowledge, talent, and people.

THE MANAGEMENT CHALLENGE

This new era presents a fundamental challenge to all but those very few companies that have already learned how to ride the globalization whirlwind.

CLOSING DOWN . . .

With greater freedom and choice come intensifying competition, diminishing control, accelerating product cycles, and deepening uncertainty. The new global economy is one in which most companies, unable to rely on patronage or position for protection, are permanently vulnerable. The scale of the global opportunities, the complexity of the competitive arena, and the relentless performance discipline imposed by the capital markets will force companies either to specialize and become world class and world scale in their chosen field, or exit. In industry after industry, globalization is raising the stakes and forcing national and regional players to double or quit. The next decade will see shakeouts and consolidation in new and old industries alike—even in such highly fragmented industries as machine tools, which had appeared relatively immune from globalization-driven restructuring until the recent transatlantic takeover activity.

In the face of these global opportunities and threats, many companies are finding that the very ways in which they develop strategies and organize themselves are becoming obsolete. And as the complexity of integrating information and formulating strategies grows, the time available for making decisions shrinks.

Many companies respond to these challenges by "closing down" the problem. That is, they choose to narrow the range of opportunities they pursue to fit the capacity of their existing processes for developing strategies and their existing organization for making decisions. They do this by closing their eyes and ears to what is going on, or by avoiding making commitments to anything other than cutting costs and selling harder. Instead of making informed strategic choices, they bury their heads in the sand. Then they lament that they have a growth problem in a world with an excess of global opportunities.

. . . OR OPENING UP

When you look behind the success stories of leading globalizers, you find companies that have learned how to think differently from the herd. They seek out different information, process it in a different way, come to different conclusions, and make different decisions. Where others see threats and complexity, they see opportunity. Where others see a barren landscape, they see a cornucopia of choices.

Freed from self-imposed constraints, they discover they have limitless scope. Rather than let others shape their future, they take steps to define the global industries in which

0015209

• EXHIBIT 5 •

OPEN VERSUS CLOSED STRATEGIC MODELS

Leading Globalizers	
Closed Model	Open Model
Sees globalization as a threat	Sees globalization as creating an overabundance of new opportunities
Familiar only with the home market; centralized decision making	Invests to become an insider everywhere; decentralized "eyes and ears"
Attractive primarily to local talent; exclusive culture	Able to attract the best talent worldwide; inclusive culture
Takes industry rules as a given	Shapes new industry rules
Prefers to own assets	Comfortable working through partnerships and webs
Seeks to maximize share of the pie	Seeks to maximize size of the pie

they operate. Open minded, they see the world as it is: in transition, moving toward a single market, but at the same time teeming with local diversity in industry dynamics, regulations, and customer requirements.

If changing one's mindset is half the battle, shifting to open strategic and organizational models is the other half (Exhibit 5). In the old world of national economies, companies had relatively little freedom in where and how to compete. Size was achieved through diversification or integrated business systems. The rules of the game within each national market were relatively stable, and most incumbents enjoyed massive advantages over new entrants. Even when players started to compete as multinationals, the business logic did not change; it was simply rolled out and tailored to a series of segmented national markets.

By contrast, companies operating in a global economy enjoy virtually infinite scope in strategy and organization. If anything, they face too many choices: how to define their industry, which customer segments to target, which countries to prioritize, how to manage the risks in uncertain geographies, how best to rationalize the business portfolio, what to own and what to influence, how to manage a complex network of external relationships, how to shape their organization's internal architecture, and which levers to pull to overcome the rigidities of the formal structure. Consider the oil and gas industry, for instance. Until recently, most major oil companies pursued the same vertically integrated strategy in the same few markets, but they are now entering a new era marked by a diversity of geographic and product strategies and by varying degrees of organizational openness. In a similar way, the landscape of the auto industry is becoming increasingly complex as the number of players, markets, and customer segments multiply to create a dazzling array of new opportunities and organizational models. The

challenge for companies is to avoid getting blinded by the possibilities and to open up their strategic posture and organizational model.

Choices are made easier when companies understand what is new about globalization. With this in mind, they can identify strategies that fit the processes under way, instead of conflicting with them. They can shape opportunities by concentrating on pieces of the business in which they have world-class skills and proprietary intangible assets. They can create open business ecologies that thrive on constant change, translate diversity into strength, attract top talent from all over the world, and leverage third-party capabilities.

We are on the brink of a major long-term transformation of the world economy from a series of local industries locked in closed national economies to a system of integrated global markets contested by global players. This is a world where capital is freely available to those with the necessary assets and skills, where intangible and not physical assets are the source of strategic differentiation, and where a glut of opportunities are up for grabs. Within a global arena that is expanding to four times its former size, standing still means falling behind in the race for position and opportunity. Creating a shared understanding of this reality is the principal leadership task for most corporations. Without a global mindset, companies risk being marginalized; with it, the opportunities they face will seem almost limitless.

LABOR'S NEW INTERNATIONALISM

Jay Mazur

THE SEATTLE MESSAGE

The fervent protests that accompanied the World Trade Organization (WTO) meeting in Seattle last November showed just how urgent the issues of globalization and trade are to working Americans. Joining with environmentalists, consumer advocates, and human rights activists, the labor movement's message from Seattle could not have been clearer: The era of trade negotiations conducted by sheltered elites balancing competing commercial interests behind closed doors is over. Globalization has reached a turning point. The future is a contested terrain of very public choices that will shape the world economy of the 21st century. The forces behind global economic change—which exalt deregulation, cater to corporations, undermine social structures, and ignore popular concerns—cannot be sustained. Globalization is leaving perilous instability and rising inequality in its wake. It is hurting too many and helping too few. As President Clinton himself has said, if the global market is to survive, it must work for working families. A first step toward that goal is building labor rights, environmental protection, and social standards into trade accords and the protocols of international financial institutions—and enforcing them with the same vigor now reserved for property rights.

These concerns of the labor movement are often caricatured as protectionist, parochial, and out of touch with the realities of the global economy. This is a dangerous misreading of the labor movement's position. Confusing labor's concerns over fairness with rising isolationism in America and abroad will only hinder the adoption of the reforms needed. Trade policies that ignore the rights and needs of workers move the

---

Jay Mazur is President of the Union of Needletrades, Industrial, and Textile Employees (UNITE) and Chair of the AFL-CIO International Affairs Committee.

world backward, not forward. The cacophonous voices in the streets of Seattle represented tomorrow's challenge, not yesterday's nostalgia. They imagined a world in which prosperity is shared by those who produce it, in which nations treat each other, the earth, and its people with dignity and respect. The protesters demanded accountability for the powerful and a voice for the voiceless. Such idealism has a practical effect. Shared prosperity increases the purchasing power of workers, creating new demand to absorb the excess capacity that now depresses global markets. The fragile institutions of the emerging global economy will therefore be braced by the democratic tonic that gives working people a place at the economic and political table. In the words of John Gray, former adviser to Margaret Thatcher, the global market and free trade are not natural phenomena but creatures of state power, "an end product of social engineering and unyielding political will." Inevitably, the effort to enforce such a system engenders a democratic response.

THE DARK SIDE OF GLOBALIZATION

Tragically, too many working people are losing out in the new world economic order. The most recent U.N. Development Report documents how globalization has dramatically increased inequality between and within nations, even as it connects people as never before. A world in which the assets of the 200 richest people are greater than the combined income of the more than 2 billion people at the other end of the economic ladder should give everyone pause. Such islands of concentrated wealth in a sea of misery have historically been a prelude to upheaval.

The benefits of the global economy are reaped disproportionately by the handful of countries and companies that set rules and shape markets. The vast majority of trade and investment takes place between industrial nations, dominated by global corporations that control a third of world exports. Of the 100 largest economies in the world, 51 are corporations. Private financial flows have long since surpassed public-development aid and remain remarkably concentrated; 80 percent of foreign direct investment in developing and transition economies in the 1990s went to just 20 countries, much of it to China.

Increased trade has not resulted in anything near uniform growth. Only 33 countries managed to sustain 3 percent annual GDP growth on a per capita basis between 1980 and 1996; in 59 countries, per capita GDP declined. Eighty countries have lower per capita incomes today than they did a decade or more ago. And contrary to conventional wisdom, those left behind are often the most integrated into global trade. For example, sub-Saharan Africa has a higher export-to-GDP ratio than Latin America, but its exports are mainly primary commodities, leaving those nations vulnerable to the volatility of those markets. The recent Africa trade bill—passed by Congress without debt relief provisions or enforcement of labor rights and environmental standards—merely offers old wine in new bottles.

Millions of workers are losing out in a global economy that disrupts traditional economies and weakens the ability of their governments to assist them. They are left to fend for themselves within failed states against destitution, famine, and plagues. They are forced to migrate, offer their labor at wages below subsistence, sacrifice their children, and cash in their natural environments and often their personal health—all in a desperate struggle to survive.

To be fair, globalization has brought dramatic benefits in some countries. Ironically, the greatest successes have been in East Asia—those very nations that did not play by the rules of the so-called Washington consensus of privatization, deregulation, fiscal austerity, and lower trade barriers. Many of those countries protected their markets, redistributed land, invested in education, targeted and subsidized their exports, and purposefully ran mercantilist trade surpluses, all of which Washington winked at during the Cold War. But in recent years, most of these countries succumbed to pressures to open their economies and deregulate their financial systems. As a result, they became the major victims of the recent global economic crisis that thrust literally millions of working people back into poverty. As Paul Krugman, the MIT economist, concluded in *The Return of Depression Economics*, these Asian economies were vulnerable not because of crony capitalism but because "they had opened up their financial markets, because they had, in fact, become better free market economies, not worse."

The last financial crisis was unusual only in its severity and scope. As the World Bank's former chief economist, Joseph Stiglitz, has noted, the deregulated global economy has produced a "boom in busts"—financial crises of increasing depth and regularity. Whereas speculators are often bailed out, workers are not. Education and health budgets are slashed to pay off debts. Children are taken from school. Millions lose their jobs. Real wages fall sharply. Families break up. Social unrest, crime, and violence increase. In short, macroeconomic data can tick upward, but working families suffer the effects for years. Poverty and desperation still haunt Thailand, Indonesia, and South Korea today even as foreign capital returns to those markets. Mexico's economy may have recovered from its 1996 crash, but many small business owners remain ruined. Mexican workers have lost 25 percent of their purchasing power since the 1994 North American Free Trade Agreement. The very remedies that the International Monetary Fund prescribes to nations in crisis—devaluation, austerity, cutbacks in social services to entice foreign speculators by increasing imports—ensure that workers, domestic producers, and peasants pay for a crisis they did not create.

One lasting effect of recurrent financial instability has been slower economic growth. The volatility of speculative capital flows encourages caution, leading governments to enforce stricter fiscal and monetary policies. As a result, as the economists John Eatwell and Lance Taylor have shown, the last 25 years of deregulation have been accompanied by slower rates of growth in both industrial and developing countries. For working people, slow growth translates into increased unemployment and underemployment, stagnant wages, and growing insecurity.

The results across the globe sharply contrast with the rosy picture painted by globalization's promoters. As millions of people move from countryside to cities, from peasant villages into informal sectors of urban economies, the standard of living has risen dramatically in a few countries. But the World Bank also reports that 200 million more people this year are living in absolute poverty (on less than $1 a day) than in 1987—a remarkable figure given the relative success of the Chinese economy. In much of Latin America, the lost decade of the 1980s has been followed by the stagnation of the 1990s. In much of Africa, debt, destitution, and disease continue to block development. Russia, once an industrial nation, has been reduced to bartering. China, the eternal next great market, has been caught in a deflationary spiral for two years.

Even in the industrial nations, which benefit the most from the global economy, the record is mixed. Japan is still struggling to emerge from a decade of stagnation. Europe suffers from slow growth, chronic unemployment, and downward pressure on wages and working conditions. In the United States, after the longest period of continued growth since the 1960s, relative wages still have not recovered the ground lost over the last decades. Wage inequality has hit levels not witnessed since the Gilded Age of the 1890s, with the average CEO now earning 416 times more than a worker. Fewer workers have adequate health insurance and pensions. People find themselves working longer hours, with less job security, and running harder to stand still.

In global terms, this mix of rising inequality, slow growth, and falling or stagnant wages increases excess capacity in industry after industry, across the globe. Workers are not making enough to buy the products that they produce. Even Federal Reserve Chair Alan Greenspan worried aloud about the threat of deflation as the Asian crisis threatened to spread around the world.

These problems stem from the top. As the World Bank's Stiglitz has noted, the Washington consensus on globalization does not concern itself with inequality or "externalities" like environmental damage, child labor abuses, or hazardous workplaces. The rules-based system developed in global trade rounds—developed largely by and for multinational corporations—requires countries to rewrite commercial codes, uproot traditional ways of farming, and protect copyrights. But the system takes no responsibility for the human costs of these policies.

Now enforced by the WTO, these rules not only avoid responsibility for the impact of these disruptive policies on workers and the environment, they also frustrate national and local efforts to legislate and live by deeply rooted social values. The citizens of Massachusetts are told they cannot prohibit their state government from contracting with companies that do business with Burma's brutal dictators. Workers watch helplessly as their well-paying jobs are given to other workers forced to live on wages that lock them in misery. Laws for cleaner gasoline are struck down as discriminatory. Regulations to protect endangered species are declared to be restraints on trade. In this democratic age, the legitimacy of any modern economic system should be measured by the quality of life afforded the many, not by the license provided the few. For working people everywhere, these realities have produced a growing reaction against the terms and conditions of the global order.

A WHOLE NEW WORLD

Not surprisingly, unions have found themselves at the forefront of the challenge posed by globalization. They have always operated across borders; their ideological roots—and much of their early membership—grew out of the internationalist perspective of the European labor movement of the last century. When American corporations were still huddling behind tariff barriers, workers were organizing international associations based on the principles of solidarity and social justice. These values have constantly drawn unions into the global arena over the great issues of war and peace, democracy and despotism. And this century's history has demonstrated that the correlation between strong, independent unions and authentic democracy is not accidental—a lesson with the utmost relevance for the unfolding debate over the rules of the new global economy.

Organized labor has perhaps been slow in reacting to globalization. After World War II, the social-democratic compromises struck in different industrial nations emphasized full employment and a social contract. For 25 years, companies and workers grew prosperous together. Trade had relatively little impact on economies—and when it did, exports provided a source of jobs. Only a few particularly vulnerable industries were disrupted by imports. Meanwhile, the international role of the labor movement was more geopolitical than industrial; during the Cold War, the AFL-CIO defined its international mission mainly through the prism of anticommunism. The principal structures of the international labor movement, the International Confederation of Free Trade Unions (ICFTU), and even the industrially based international trade secretariats were all seen as instruments in the bipolar struggle against communism, enjoying active government support. Strong, independent unions were seen as vital in strengthening democracy and distributing the benefits of prosperity to ensure that workers felt they had a stake in market economies.

The collapse of the Soviet Union changed government perspectives toward labor. Unions have been viewed as less politically relevant and obstacles to corporate interests. A broad ideological offensive by corporations has portrayed unions as outmoded relics of a bygone age. But as big business has gone global and wages an increasingly aggressive assault on unions, the labor movement has become more, not less, internationalist. Virtually every major industrial dispute in the United States now has an international dimension. Not only do companies use the threat of moving abroad to trump workers' wage and benefit demands, but companies themselves are often foreign firms. A third of the members of the million-member United Food and Commercial Workers union, for example, are employed by non-U.S. companies. As corporate mergers and alliances accelerate the global integration of capital, more unions find themselves in a similar situation.

In response, unions have to reach across borders to forge the same kind of strategic international links among workers and their allies that corporations have formed in shaping the new economy—and are increasingly linked by the same modern communications technologies that corporations have deployed so effectively to exploit their own mobility. A poll of AFL-CIO unions a few years ago found that two-thirds were engaged in international activity as a necessary extension of their normal organizing and bargaining; 87 percent said they needed to do even more on the global scene.

Not so long ago, a major union's international activity could be carried out by a single person who might even have had other organizational responsibilities. This is no longer possible. The most advanced unions now involve many of their departments—organizing, research, political action, public relations, education, legal, health and safety, and corporate affairs—in diverse strategies. In turn, these strategies forge effective links with overseas partners, coordinate industrial actions, lobby governments, take legal action, and simultaneously publicize all this activity in more than one country. International-trade secretariats, headquartered in Europe, link unions from different countries in the same industry and play a critical role.

THE POWER OF POSITIVE LINKING

In dealing with management, today's unions understand that they must have an accurate picture of the company's entire global structure to pressure effectively its vulnerable points and establish links with workers and unions around the world. One especially dramatic example of this strategy was the 1997 United Parcel Service (UPS) strike, involving 185,000 members of the International Brotherhood of Teamsters. The strike was settled after two weeks on terms considered favorable to the union; many saw it as a sign of labor's renewed vigor.

The strike succeeded through preparation by Teamsters members at UPS, who mobilized across America and effectively campaigned to gain public support. But international solidarity also played a critical role. As the dominant firm in the U.S. courier market, UPS could have endured a long national strike. But the Teamsters knew that UPS was fighting stiff competition in Europe and made breaking into that market a high priority. Europe was the vulnerable point in the company's global structure—and there they struck.

In mapping this strategy, the Teamsters relied on a broad international support network that they had built up over many months. A year before the strike, the Teamsters had formed a World Council of UPS unions with help from the International Transport Workers Federation. Communications were established between UPS unions, and a series of meetings was held with union representatives from the United Kingdom, France, the Netherlands, Belgium, Italy, Spain, Canada, Germany, Brazil, Ireland, and the United States. No two unions had exactly the same relationship with the company. Many represented UPS workers; others were trying to organize them; still others represented workers at competing firms who would suffer if UPS succeeded in undercutting industry standards. Some enjoyed a relatively good relationship with their employers, others not. The degrees of leverage and militancy varied from country to country. Activities restricted in some countries were allowed in others. Such are some of the extraordinary complications involved in organizing workers globally. But the unions identified enough common ground that the council could hammer out a set of demands for a UPS World Action Day in the spring of 1997, calling a meeting in Washington, D.C., that coincided with the final stages of the Teamsters' negotiations with UPS.

Representatives from UPS looking across the table at the Teamsters' "guests" from around the world realized that the damage from this strike could not be contained within the United States. On UPS World Action Day, the company was hit with more than 150 job actions or demonstrations worldwide, including work stoppages in Italy and Spain. Major European customers began questioning the company's reliability. The credible threat that this strike could spread and undermine a crucial element in the company's business strategy was reinforced by escalating solidarity actions. The day after the company learned that a French transport-workers union planned to close UPS operations at Paris' Orly Airport, the strike was settled—in no small part, according to union negotiators, due to this unprecedented international campaign.

The difficulty in organizing a campaign on this scale cannot be underestimated, but neither can the results. Most unions now understand that they must match the mobility and agility of employers in the global economy. And workers understand that conditions abroad clearly affect their prospects at home.

True, some industries—like time-sensitive transportation companies—are more susceptible than others to this type of campaign. But all corporate structures have points of vulnerability, and unions are becoming increasingly effective in identifying them. Linked by computer, phone, and fax, sharing research and planning, energized by periodic face-to-face contact, and working with an increasingly active and sophisticated base of more than 150 million organized workers worldwide, the labor movement is inexorably bringing its force to bear on the global economy.

Picket lines of major strikes now almost routinely radiate internationally. Teamsters in Atlanta, steelworkers in South Carolina, and hotel workers in California get help from unions in Europe, Japan, and South Africa. Requests for solidarity actions flow in all directions—if not with the velocity of currency transactions, then with equal urgency and perhaps more staying power. Corporations are also discovering that when they sit down to bargain with a union, they may look across the table at representatives of workers from more than one country. This now happens in many industries, from low-tech companies producing pickles in Mexico and Michigan to multinational communications giants in the United States, Canada, and the United Kingdom.

THE RACE TO THE BOTTOM

Globalization is most destructive in countries where independent unions do not exist and organizing is suppressed. Many developing countries market their export-processing zones as union-free to attract investment; the sweatshop *maquilla* factories in Central America are only one example. A recent International Labor Organization (ILO) study of 850 of these zones around the world, which employ 27 million workers, found that free trade unions and minimum labor standards are "extremely rare." This enormous mass of unorganized workers poses the central challenge to the international labor movement. Although many of these workers are concentrated in the so-called developing world, millions of others live and work in industrialized countries. They are the human beings quantified by the U.N. statistics cited earlier, victims of the growing inequality in the global economy. Without the ability to organize, bargain collectively, or strike, these workers are caught in what globalization looks like to an awful lot of people: a race to the bottom. It will not end until policymakers recognize that no nation is too poor to enforce the basic human rights of its workers.

Faced with masses of unorganized workers across the world, unions find themselves harking back to an old strategy in the apparel industry: "following the work."

After workers organized unions in New York City in the 1920s, manufacturers shifted work across the Hudson River to New Jersey, into the "foreign zones" (as any place outside of New York's garment district was then called) in search of cheaper and more compliant labor. The union responded by following the firms and organizing workers there. When the companies moved on to Philadelphia and the Midwest, the union followed again, but it also realized that basic national standards were needed to put a floor underneath workers. Many other unions soon reached the same conclusion, uniting to campaign hard for what became the Fair Labor Standards Act in 1938, setting hours, conditions, and a minimum wage for the new national economy. This combination of dynamic organizing and national legal standards created a powerful labor movement that raised the standard of living for millions of working families and bolstered the ideals of American democracy.

In recent years, as the corporate descendants of these employers have taken the next step and moved production halfway around the world, it first seemed that they had dropped off the face of the earth. But pitting American workers against their counterparts abroad, who are forced to live at the very margins of human existence, gradually made itself apparent in lowered wages and standards at home. The dismal working conditions in Asia and Central America set the standards for the notorious sweatshop discovered in El Monte, California, in 1995. Unions once more had to learn to follow the work—and to campaign for core labor rights and standards everywhere to ensure that the global rules were respected at home and abroad.

UNITE, for example, has worked closely with its trade secretariat, the International Textile, Garment, and Leather Workers Federation, over the past five years to help organize the half-million apparel workers in Central America and the Caribbean. Although political boundaries divide these workers from those in Mexico, the United States, and Canada, the trade agreements underpinning globalization in the region—as well as the outsourcing strategies of the large U.S. manufacturers and retailers—have in effect created a unitary and contiguous regional labor market in these industries of some two million workers.

Because workers in this market's southern tier are systematically denied the right to organize and bargain collectively, their wages are artificially suppressed to about one-tenth of those in the industry's organized sectors in the North. Not surprisingly, most of these workers live below the official poverty lines of their own countries. Abysmal standards are driving down wages and conditions of workers throughout the industry. So just as unions had to "follow the work" across the Hudson River in the 1930s, they have been forced to follow the work across the southern U.S. border in the 1990s, supporting the labor movement in neighboring countries, training organizers, coordinating campaigns, lobbying governments to enforce their laws, and appealing to the American people's sense of fairness and social justice.

Progress has been slow but real. Unions and human rights groups have exposed shameful working conditions for women and children. Thousands of workers throughout Latin America have built and joined unions that did not exist a few years ago. Multinational corporations are being forced to accept responsibility, at least verbally, for working conditions in their vast global production chains. Governments feel the heat from citizens demanding corrective action, and companies from consumers. Firms such as Nike and celebrities such as Kathie Lee Gifford have discovered this reality.

At least half the clothes purchased by Americans are still made in sweatshops at home and abroad. Companies like to say that consumers do not care about anything except a good bargain, but polls show that people are willing to pay more if they can be assured that their clothes were not made in sweatshops. Meanwhile, a new generation of student activists has joined the labor movement in the war against sweatshops. Churches have passed resolutions and distributed flyers to parishioners. City councils and state legislatures have prohibited the purchase of sweatshop goods. A social movement of potentially tremendous force has begun to gather that can affect the bottom line and the laws of the land.

A SEAT AT THE TABLE

For years governments ignored demands to include labor and environmental rights in trade agreements, confident that there was no political cost in doing so. This is now changing. Unions are forging new alliances with environmentalists, human rights groups, and religious and consumer activists. Perhaps the most stunning demonstration of this alliance's political force was Congress' rejection last year of "fast-track" trade authority for President Clinton—not once but three times over the last two years. This new alliance insists that any trade-negotiating authority include labor rights and environmental protections as conditions for opening trade. Most of the House of Representatives now supports that position. Certainly a majority of the public does, including most voters in both parties.[1] The blocking of "fast track" made it clear that representatives of this new popular movement must have a seat at the table.

The debate over "fast track" and trade in general can no longer be portrayed as an argument between free trade and protectionism. The demand for enforceable labor rights in global trading accords, built into conditions of the international financial institutions and enacted into U.S. trade agreements and laws, is not an effort to build walls against the global economy. It is an effort to build rules into it, and a floor under it, to lift wages and conditions up rather than drive them down.

Fortunately, there is much agreement already over the substance of core labor rights. Last year, business, labor, and government representatives from 173 nations reaffirmed core labor standards as fundamental human rights, including freedom of association and the right to organize and bargain collectively. They also called for the elimination of forced labor, child labor, and employment-related discrimination. Virtually every independent labor federation has endorsed the ICFTU'S call for building labor rights into

[1]A 1996 Wirthlin Worldwide poll found the American public favored workers' rights and environmental issues in trade agreements by an overwhelming 73 to 21 percent. In a 1997 Peter Hart poll for the AFL-CIO, 72 percent of respondents said that it was very important to include labor and environmental standards in trade agreements, as well as food-safety standards (97 percent), workplace health and safety standards (94 percent), laws against child labor (93 percent), the freedom to strike (92 percent), a minimum wage (81 percent), and the right to form unions (78 percent).

the global trading system. The divide is not between North and South; it is between workers everywhere and the great concentrations of capital and the governments they dominate.

Enforcing core labor rights does not guarantee working conditions. But it does empower workers to act collectively—a right they have theoretically enjoyed for at least 50 years. It is time to enforce that right. When workers can join independent unions, they vastly increase their chances of lifting themselves and their families out of poverty and making their concerns felt in legislatures too often dominated by private interests. In addition, wealth and income tend to be spread more widely and economic demand better sustained, while speculative booms and busts tend to be more limited.

After Seattle, the demand for labor rights and other social standards can no longer be ignored. If the WTO and other institutions cannot accommodate those demands, it is they who will be weakened, not the movement to fix the system. Attention will turn to national and local politics, opposition to trading accords will build, and support for protection and subsidy will increase. Companies will find themselves increasingly vulnerable to exposure and embarrassment, to consumer boycotts and worker protests. Citizens will insist that their food be protected, their air not be poisoned, their water not be fouled. Human rights activists will demand sanctions against barbarous regimes. Workers will demand recourse. The failure to heed them will feed the dangerous new strains of isolationism rising throughout the world.

The labor movement is deeply committed to this struggle for reform and the construction of a new internationalism. It is a struggle that takes place at the plant gate, in local and national legislatures, and in international negotiations. The stew of national and international laws and institutions that emerges will not be smooth or bland. But the recent transformation of the world economy has not been matched by changes in political institutions. Workers, social activists, and ordinary citizens are now beginning to demand and mobilize for those changes. Future generations will surely have difficulty comprehending why today's leaders were debating not how to implement these reforms but whether or not they were even worthy of consideration.

PART TWO

Environments

A NATIONAL EXPORT ASSISTANCE POLICY FOR NEW AND GROWING BUSINESSES

Michael R. Czinkota

Exporting is one of many market expansion activities of the firm. As such, exporting is similar to looking for new customers in the next town, the next state, or on the other coast; it differs only in that national borders are crossed, and international accounts and currencies are involved. Yet, these differences make exports special from a policy perspective.

From a macro perspective, exports are special because they can affect currency values and the fiscal and monetary policies of governments, shape public perception of competitiveness, and determine the level of imports a country can afford. Abroad, exports augment the availability and choice of goods and services for individuals, and improve the standard of living and quality of life. On the level of the firm, exports offer the opportunity for economies of scale. By broadening its market reach and serving customers abroad, a firm can produce more and do so more efficiently, which is particularly important if domestic sales are below break even levels. As a result, the firm may achieve lower costs and higher profits both at home and abroad. Through exporting the firm benefits from market diversification, taking advantage of different growth rates in different markets, and gaining stability by not being overly dependent on any particular market. Exporting also lets the firm learn from the competition, makes it sensitive to different demand structures and cultural dimensions, and proves its ability to survive in a less familiar environment in spite of higher transaction costs. All these lessons can make the firm a stronger competitor at home. Finally, since exporting is

---

Michael R. Czinkota is a faculty member at the School of Business, Georgetown University.

only one possible international marketing strategy, it may well lead to the employment of additional strategies such as direct foreign investment, joint ventures, franchising or licensing—all of which contribute to the growth and economic strength of the firm, and, on an aggregate level, to the economic security of a nation.

THE EXPORT COMPETITIVENESS OF NEW AND GROWING BUSINESSES

Many see the global market as the exclusive realm of large, multinational corporations. It is commonly explained that almost half of U.S. exports are made by the 100 largest corporations, and that 80 percent of U.S. exports are carried out by only 2,500 firms. Overlooked is the fact that thousands of smaller sized firms have been fueling a U.S. export boom, which has supported the economy in times of limited domestic growth. A large portion of export shipments from the United States are for less than $10,000 and there are more than 100,000 U.S. firms that export at least occasionally.

The reason for this export success of smaller firms lies in the new determinants of competitiveness, as framed by the wishes and needs of the foreign buyers. Other than in the distant past, where price alone was at the forefront, buyers today also expect an excellent product fit, high levels of corporate responsiveness, a substantial service orientation, and high corporate commitment. New and growing firms stack up well on all these dimensions compared to their larger brethren, and may even have a competitive advantage.

Take the issue of product fit. In today's era of niche marketing, where specialization rather than mass production is prized, the customization of operations is often crucial. In a large corporate system, changes are often subject to delays as various layers of management are consulted, costs recalculated, and multiple communication levels exercised. In a smaller operation, procedures can more easily be adopted to the special needs of the customer or to local requirements.

Smaller firms can offer clearer lines of accountability since the decision maker can be more visible and responsive to the customer. During negotiations, or later on, if something does not go according to plan, the customer knows who to contact to fix the problem. Smaller firms are better equipped to handle exceptions. Since international sales situations have high variability, either in terms of the timing or the nature of the sale, a smaller firm can provide a more flexible framework for the decision process. Exceptions can be handled when they occur rather than after waiting for concurrence from other levels of the organization. Smaller firms offer their customers better inward and outward communication linkages, which are direct between the provider of a service or product and its user. The result is a short response time. If a special situation should arise, response can be immediate, direct, and predictable to the customer, providing precisely those competitive ingredients that reduce risk and costs.

Smaller firms also have the most to gain from the experience curve effects of exporting. Research by the Boston Consulting Group has shown that each time cumulative output of a firm doubles, the costs on value added decrease between 20 to

30 percent. Due to the small original base, it is much easier for a new or growing business to double cumulative output and reap the resulting benefits than it is for a large established firm. Most importantly, once a small firm goes international, it usually does so with the full commitment of the owner and top management. The foreign customer therefore knows that this is an activity which has management's heart and soul behind it. In today's times where we are moving, on a global level, away from transaction marketing and toward relationship marketing, such a perception may be crucial in providing the winning edge.

COPING WITH OBSTACLES

All these advantages do not remove the existing obstacles to international market prosperity. Smaller firms in particular tend to encounter five types of export-related problem areas (Kotabe and Czinkota 1992). One of these concerns logistics—arranging transportation, determining transport rates, handling documentation, obtaining financial information, coordinating distribution, packaging, and obtaining insurance. Another one consists of legal procedures and typically covers government red tape, product liability, licensing, and customs/duty issues. The servicing of exports is a third area, where the firm needs to provide parts availability, repair service, and technical advice. Sales promotion is a fourth area; firms need to cope with advertising, sales effort, and the obtaining of marketing information. The fifth problem area concerns foreign market intelligence, which covers information on the location of markets, trade restrictions, and competition overseas.

These obstacles, both real and perceived, often prevent firms from exporting. Many managers often see only the risks involved in exporting rather than the opportunities that the international market can present. As a result, the United States still underexports when compared to other nations. U.S. merchandise exports comprise only 7.5 percent of GNP, compared to 24.1 percent for Germany and 23 percent for Canada. On a per capita basis, the United Kingdom exported in 1992 $3,250 for every man, woman, and child. The figure for Japan is $2,660; for the United States, it is only $1,750. Given the plenitude of benefits to be derived from exporting, it therefore seems worthwhile and necessary to increase the export activities of U.S. firms.

A PERSPECTIVE ON EXPORT PROMOTION

Even though exports are important, in times of tight budget constraints and competing public priorities, it is important to ask why firms should be enticed into exporting through the use of public funds. Given the motivation of business activity by profit, one could argue that the profit opportunities for exporters should be enough of an incentive to motivate firms to export.

THE EXPORT DEVELOPMENT PROCESS

To explore this issue, it is helpful to understand the export development process within the firm. Typically, firms evolve along different stages to become experienced exporters (Czinkota and Ronkainen 1993). These stages start out with a firm being uninterested in things international. Management frequently will not even fill an unsolicited export order. Should such orders or other international market stimuli continue over time, however, a firm may move to the stage of export awareness, or even export interest. Management will begin to accumulate information about foreign markets and may consider the feasibility of exporting. At the export trial stage, the firm is likely to fill selected export orders, serve few customers, and expand into countries that are geographically close or culturally similar to the home country. At the export evaluation stage, firms consider the impact of exporting on overall corporate activities. If expectations placed in exporting are not met, the firm is likely to discontinue its export efforts and either seek alternative international growth opportunities or restrict itself to the domestic market. If the evaluation is positive, the firm will, over time, move on to become an export adapter, make frequent shipments to many customers in more countries, and incorporate international considerations into its planning.

In each one of these stages, firms have different concerns. For example, at the awareness level, firms worry mainly about information on foreign markets and customers. At the interest stage, firms become concerned about the mechanics of exporting. During the export tryout, communication, logistics, and the sales effort become key problems. At evaluation time, government regulations and financing take on greater importance. In the adaptation stage, service delivery and control are major issues. Figure 1 describes this export development process and summarizes these stages and concerns.

• FIGURE 1 •

THE EXPORT DEVELOPMENT PROCESS

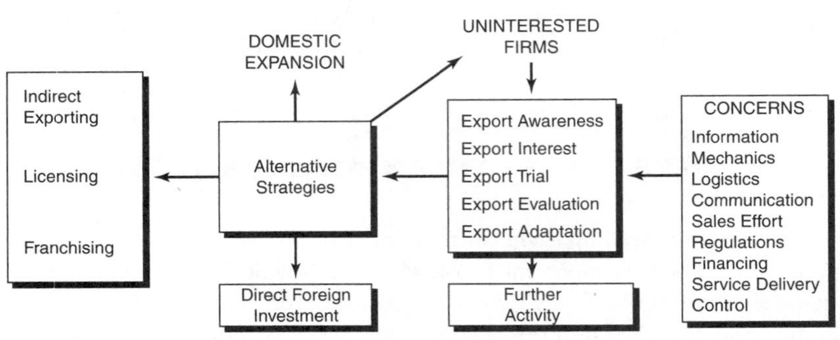

A DIVERGENCE OF PROFIT AND RISK

As a firm moves through these stages, unusual things can happen to both risk and profit. In light of the gradual development of expertise, the many concerns, and a firm's uncertainty with the new environment it is about to enter, management's perception of risk exposure grows. In its previous domestic expansion, the firm has gradually learned about the market, and therefore managed to have its risk decline. In the course of international expansion, the firm now encounters new factors such as currency exchange rates and their vagaries, greater distances, new modes of transportation, new government regulations, new legal and financial systems, new languages, and cultural diversity. As a result, the firm is exposed to increased risk. At the same time, due to the investment needs of the exporting effort, in areas such as information acquisition, market research, and trade financing, the immediate profit performance may deteriorate. Even though international market familiarity and diversification effects are likely to reduce the risk below the previous "domestic only" level, and increase profitability as well, in the short and medium term, managers may face an unusual and perhaps unacceptable situation—rising risk accompanied by decreasing profitability. In light of this reality, and not knowing whether there will be a pot of gold at the end of the rainbow, many executives either do not initiate export activities or discontinue them. A temporary gap in the working of market forces seems to exist. Government export assistance can help firms over this rough patch to the point where profits increase and risk heads downward. Bridging this short-term market gap may well be the key role of export assistance, and the major justification for the involvement of the public sector. Figure 2 illustrates this process.

• FIGURE 2 •

PROFIT AND RISK DURING EXPORT INITIATION

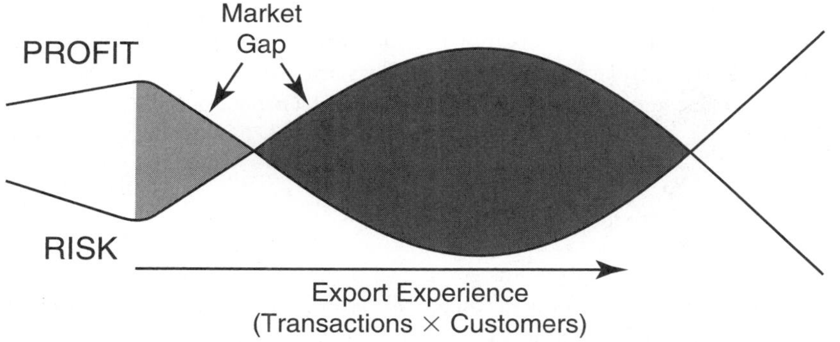

LINKAGES AMONG ASSISTANCE COMPONENTS

If export assistance and promotion are to be rendered, it becomes important to consider how budgets and efforts should be expended in order to be most effective. Figure 3 provides a structural perspective of the linkage between export assistance, the firm, the international market and, eventually, export performance. The firm is separated into its organizational and its managerial dimensions. Organizational key determinants of business and export success are size, human and financial resources, technology, service and quality orientation, information system, research capabilities, market insights and connections, and the firm's capabilities to manage regulations. The managerial characteristics that research has most closely linked to export success are education, international exposure, expertise, international orientation, and commitment. These two corporate dimensions, subject to the opportunities and constraints of the international market environment, determine the degree of the firm's export involvement. This involvement in turn will result in export performance, which can be measured in three different ways. Efficiency refers to the relationship between corporate input employed and the resulting outputs achieved. Typically, efficiency is measured through the proxy of export profitability. Effectiveness refers to relative business success when compared to other competitors in the market, and is often measured in terms of market share and export sales growth. Competitive position addresses the overall strength of a firm arising from its distinct competencies, management style, and resource deployment. Typical indicators here are the overall quality and competence of a firm's export activities.

Export assistance can aim at the organizational characteristics and capabilities of the firm and try to improve those. It can also work with the managerial characteristics and contribute to their positive change. All this is subject to continued involvement on the part of providers of export assistance with the international market environment, both in terms of learning from as well as shaping the environment. Export assistance will be most effective when it either reduces the risk to the firm or increases its profitability from export operations, particularly when the stage-specific concerns of firms are taken into account. For example, providing information on market potential abroad is likely to decrease the risk (both real and perceived) to the firm. Offering low-cost credit is likely to increase the profitability. Macro assistance in the foreign market environment can consist of international trade negotiations designed to break down foreign barriers to entry. Micro assistance consists of learning from the foreign market and its customers, and passing on that knowledge to enable domestic firms to adjust to that market.

AN INDUSTRY EXAMPLE

It is important to recognize the linkages between these efforts and the need for them to occur simultaneously. Otherwise there will be more results like the ones obtained from the U.S.–Japan wood products initiative. In that particular case, which the author researched with the U.S. General Accounting Office (U.S. GAO 1993), U.S. trade negotiations with Japan were conducted for more than a decade, so that more U.S.

• FIGURE 3 •

EXPORT ASSISTANCE AND PERFORMANCE—A STRUCTURAL MODEL

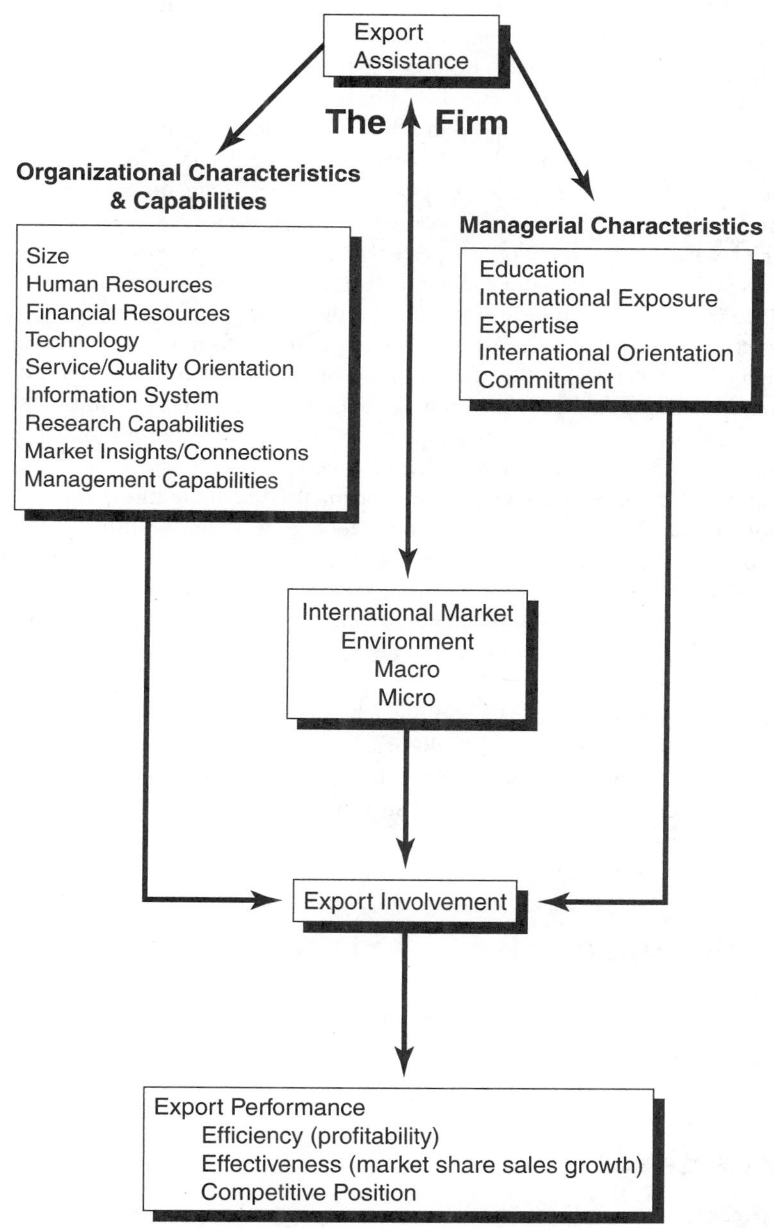

solid wood products could enter the Japanese market. High-level meetings, ongoing negotiations, government financial support, and industry demonstration projects were to achieve that goal. Japanese building codes and product certification procedures were changed and tariffs were lowered. The Foreign Agricultural Service spent more than $17 million to promote U.S. wood-product sales to Japan. The result? Canadian lumber companies are the leading wood exporters to the Japanese market. There were only marginal increases in U.S. exports and export-related jobs.

There are reasons for this outcome. U.S. products were not tailored to the Japanese market. Japanese builders prefer post-and-beam construction, which requires 4 × 4 inch lumber and 3 × 6 foot modules to match the standard tatami mats that cover floors. But U.S. companies were either unaware of those requirements or unwilling to meet them. Instead, the U.S. producers focused on the standard 2 × 4 products used in the United States, even though only 7 percent of new homes in Japan use that standard. In effect, U.S. negotiators and companies focused their energies on increasing the U.S. presence in the smallest part of the market, rather than pursuing the biggest market. This focus was the result of trying to sell what is produced, rather than producing what foreign customers want to buy. In addition, some of the U.S. firms that did enter the Japanese market did so with only limited enthusiasm and commitment. In contrast to the Canadian firms, many companies paid little attention to product quality and appearance and did not deliver after-sales service. Few firms translated their product information into Japanese or wrote manuals describing the new type of construction. Those U.S. companies that did try to vigorously pursue the new market encountered major problems in obtaining information about specific market requirements. They also had trouble adjusting their production processes to meet Japanese product specifications and obtaining financing to pay for new equipment and larger export inventories. Without these resources, their efforts were severely handicapped.

In sum, a well-intended approach did not achieve its deserved success since the focus rested on the wrong opportunities, the needs of customers were not sufficiently taken into account, firms were unable or unwilling to adjust to market requirements, and the linkages between all these components were not taken into account.

SOME POLICY IMPLICATIONS AND ISSUES

Here then are some conclusions about the dimensions that should guide export assistance efforts, in particular where new and growing businesses are concerned. There are only six of them, but each one is equally crucial.

CLARITY OF PURPOSE

Agreement needs to be reached on what export assistance is to achieve. Some of the objectives currently competing with each other are global fairness, the opening of world markets, and economic activity and jobs in the United States. Public funds are too scarce, as is our capacity to negotiate, and our capability to achieve negotiation success—to invest funds and government attention solely to right wrongs or for the sake of fairness. There needs to be explicit recognition of the fact that the times are over when the United States opened foreign markets simply for the well being of the world. Though it might be a delightful side effect to also see other nations' trade increase after the United States has broken down trade barriers, the key focus should rest on U.S. employment.

Clarification is also needed for the time frame involved. Given a short-term orientation, emphasis on a temporary increase in the export sales of multinational corporations will be most desirable. A more long-term orientation will concentrate efforts on introducing more and new firms to the global market.

TIGHTNESS OF FOCUS

Export assistance needs to achieve either a specific reduction of risk or an increase in profits for firms. It should be concentrated primarily in those areas where profit and risk inconsistencies produce market gaps, and be linked directly to identifiable organizational or managerial characteristics that need improvement. Otherwise, assistance supports only exports that would have taken place anyway. Such a focus, of course, requires the implementation of evaluation criteria and measurement mechanisms, which determine the effectiveness of export assistance (Cavusgil 1990; Seringhaus and Rosson 1990). I believe that for policy purposes, such measurement should not be based on the firm's export performance, which is mainly controlled by the corporation. Rather, the measurement should be based on the export involvement of the firm, focusing on the number of customers, transactions, and countries served.

COORDINATION OF APPROACHES

Coordination must occur both within and outside the government. Within government, it will be crucial to set overall effectiveness priorities and to trade off export assistance programs across agencies. Otherwise, an economic sector with relatively low employment effects could consume resources in an over proportionate fashion while priority industries would suffer from insufficient support. The fact that the agricultural sector spends about 74 percent of total federal export promotion outlays may serve as an example (U.S. GAO 1992). Externally, export assistance must be directly linked to domestic industries to ensure that the policy gains abroad can be taken advantage of by firms. Doing so must include collaboration for both product and process technologies, which now play a crucial role in attaining global competitiveness, similar to the much supported field of science. For example, the issue of quality performance can well become the focus of a cooperative effort throughout an entire industry, its suppliers and customers alike. Rather than concentrate only on the well entrenched industries, it is particularly important here to include a focus on sunrise industries.

EMPHASIS ON STRENGTHS

Within government, export assistance should emphasize those areas where government can bring a particular strength to bear—such as contacts, prowess in opening doors abroad, or information collection capabilities. Externally, programs should aim at the large opportunities abroad. As far as firms are concerned, attention should not just concentrate on assisting or bailing out industries in trouble, but also on helping successful firms do better.

TARGETING OF CRUCIAL FACTORS

Export assistance is likely to have the greatest impact when it serves the needs of companies. Programs therefore should start out by analyzing the current level of international involvement of the firm and then deliver assistance appropriate to the firm's needs. For example, help with after-sales service delivery is most appropriate for firms at the adaptation stage; firms at the awareness stage worry much more about information and mechanics. Assistance must also take foreign market conditions and foreign buyer preferences into account, and communicate the resulting constraints and opportunities to domestic firms. It is easier to sell what is in demand.

BOLDNESS OF VISION

In spite of the need to improve ongoing programs, there should be a spark of boldness which goes beyond ensuring that things are done right, but checks whether one can do more right things. One could, for example, think about domestic and international efforts to set standards for technology and quality. One could go beyond products in such an effort and also include services and agriculture. One could even include the grading of enzymes, meats, hormones, and other products developed by biotechnology firms. There could be efforts to develop the domestic mentoring services of a senior executive corps to provide much needed international experience to new and growing firms. Or one could think about the development of a national forfeiting institution to be of major assistance in handling the financial and documentation aspects of exporting.

In a world of rapidly changing global realities, the future is shrouded in much uncertainty. Yet the likelihood of continued and closer global linkages and interdependence is high. Our firms need to be prepared for the global marketplace. If we can help them to grow and successfully meet the competition on foreign shores as well as on ours, we will have strengthened them and the nation.

References

Cavusgil, S. Tamer. "Export Development Efforts in the United States: Experiences and Lessons Learned." In *International Perspectives on Trade Promotion and Assistance,* eds. S.T. Cavusgil and M.R. Czinkota, 173–83. New York: Quorum Books, 1990.

Czinkota, Michael R., and Ilkka A. Ronkainen. *International Marketing.* 6th ed. Fort Worth: Harcourt, 2001.

Kotabe, Masaaki, and Michael R. Czinkota. "State Government Promotion of Manufacturing Exports: A GAP Analysis." *Journal of International Business Studies* 4 (1992): 637–58.

Seringhaus, Rolf F.H., and Philip J. Rosson. *Government Export Promotion: A Global Perspective.* London: Routledge, 1990.

United States General Accounting Office. *Agricultural Marketing: Export Opportunities for Wood Products in Japan Call for Customer Focus.* Washington, D.C.: Government Printing Office, May 1993.

United States General Accounting Office. *Export Promotion: U.S. Programs Lack Coherence.* Washington, D.C.: Government Printing Office, March 1992.

EXPORT CONTROLS AND GLOBAL CHANGES

Michael R. Czinkota and Erwin Dichtl

REASONS FOR EXPORT CONTROLS

Since the 1950s West Germany and the United States have been forceful supporters of the principles of free trade. This approval was fundamental in building strong trade linkages and improving the level of economic welfare in the Western world. In spite of this emphasis on limited government interference with trade, however, there also emerged a consistent and growing need to control exports. There are a lot of good reasons why governments have to control their exports. Some goals are the prevention of exports of natural cultural assets, of animals and plants subject to the protection of species agreement, of scarce goods and of substandard food and agricultural products. Most important is the prevention of exports of nuclear, biological and chemical weapons, conventional armaments and facilities, instruments and knowledge which enable their production (Dichtl, 1994a, p. 1; 1994b, p. 1726). The latter matter is a central element of foreign policy and security regulations of most countries. Over the years, not all countries based their trade on similarly strict measures. Some nations such as Germany and the United States subject their export intentionally to stricter regulations than their competitors in the world market.

Nevertheless, a very extensive and sophisticated multilateral export control system had evolved in the Western world. Driven by the insight that export controls are likely to remain ineffective if not harmonized across nations, the Coordinating Committee on Multilateral Export Controls (COCOM) was founded in 1949. This multilateral organization held the ultimate authority over the decision of what could or could not be exported (Czinkota, 1984). Even though not all COCOM members always shared

Prof. Dr. Michael R. Czinkota, School of Business, Georgetown University, Washington, D.C., USA /Prof. Dr. Dr h.c. Erwin Dichtl, Institute of Marketing, University of Mannheim, Mannheim, Germany.

the same perspective with regards to the implementation of several specific export controls, there was a jointness of vision. Export controls were considered as an important element of national policy, since they permitted strategic action without the deployment of weapons or military force. The cohesive COCOM regime existed within the Western world until the spring of 1994. The talks concerning the successor organisation to COCOM named New Forum are still continuing.

In the post–World War II days the COCOM members initiated many collaborative activities in order to prevent that unauthorized exports could slip through the meshes of the export control net. But since the dissolution of COCOM the loopholes in the export control net have been widening rapidly. Conflict areas are increasing and are threatening to undermine the foundation and intention of export control enforcement.

The most important legal basis for export controls in the Federal Republic of Germany are the European Community Dual-use Ordinance, the German Foreign Trade Law (AWG), the German Foreign Trade and Payments Ordinance (AWV) and the German War Weapons Control Law (KWKG). In addition, there are a series of United Nations (UN) resolutions to which the German export control law is regularly adapted. Nevertheless, one must discuss the issue without sinking into legal minutiae since doing so would require a degree of precision in phraseology which would not be very conducive to the understanding of the real concerns which loom larger than legal codification.

GLOBAL CHANGES AND THE NEW GENERAL FRAMEWORK FOR EXPORT CONTROLS

A great number of changes have occurred, which have essentially altered the traditional conditions of export controls (Czinkota/ Ronkainen, 1995, p. 108; Dichtl, 1994a, p. 2; Panel on the Future Design and Implementation of U.S. National Security Export Controls, 1991, pp. 12–17). As a result, both the focus and the principal objective of export controls have been fundamentally influenced.

The most important changes have been the lifting of the Iron Curtain and the subsequent collapse and disappearance of the Soviet Union and the Eastern Bloc. At the same time there has been an enormous increase of crises points around the world. Furthermore, quite a number of countries from the Third World desire ABC-weapons and the technology to make use of them. For example, a country like Libya can do little with its poison gas shells without a suitable delivery system (Hucko, 1993, p. 15). In former times the key issue in the export control field was how to prevent the procuring of strategic technology through the members of the Warsaw Pact. Nowadays the principal export control activities must be concentrated on the Third World.

Inevitably export controls have moved from a "strategic balance" to a "tactical balance" approach. Nevertheless, even though the political hotspots addressed may be less broad in terms of their geographic expanse, the danger emanating from regional disintegration and local conflict may be just as severe to the world community as earlier strategic concerns with the Soviet Union. As a result, a new system of export controls had to be created which was to include especially Russia, the Ukraine, and other Eastern European nations.

Another change which has taken place derives directly from the first. There has been a loosening of mutual bonds between allied nations. In former times Western Europe, the United States and Japan together with emerging industrialized nations, held a generally similar strategic outlook. This outlook was driven by the common endeavour to reduce the influence of the Soviet Union. After the disappearance of the Eastern Bloc, however, individual national interests which heretofore had been subsumed under the overall strategic objective came to the fore. As a result, differences in perspectives, attitudes, and outlooks can lead to increasing conflicts between major players in the world trade field.

For example, during the time of the Cold War many nations have built up a huge armaments industry. With millions of jobs at stake, these industries are now gradually being reduced in size. In spite of gradual defense conversion, for many firms the road to immediate survival consists in an increase of exports. This fact collides with the desire for restraint in the export of weapons. In consequence the conflict between national goals can lead to major inequities in export control policy formulation and enforcement. Given the obligation of governments to preserve and to create jobs, there is an unavoidable tendency to look towards the loosening of trade restrictions as one reaction to such developments.

Furthermore, differences in the attitudes concerning export controls are exacerbated by the need of countries to safeguard their own divergent industrial or rather export interests. Due to industrial structures, these interests vary across nations. For example, Germany, with a strong world market position in motors, machine tools, and chemical raw materials, will think differently from a country like the United States, which sees computers as an area of its competitive advantage. It is therefore understandable that the United States strives to maintain certain restrictions, vis-à-vis the former Eastern Bloc states, for those products for which its firms are not highly competitive. Doing so, however, would affect the Federal Republic of Germany and its engagement in Eastern Europe to a much greater degree.

In a similar fashion, there was a dissent between the United States and Japan concerning Israel; the United States also disagreed with France concerning Iraq and with Italy because of Libya. With Japan and Germany, there were difficulties of opinion with regard to Iran. All of these divergent interests cause the multilateral negotiations to proceed only slowly.

The increased foreign availability of high technology products has also caused a major change. While in earlier decades, industrializing countries mainly participated in world trade, in the past decade, the number of participants in the international trade field has grown rapidly. In consequence, high technology products are available worldwide from many sources. The following example reveals what is at stake here: In the United States it is believed that an elimination of controls for products for which there is unrestrained foreign availability and a simplification of the licensing procedures would increase United States exports by more than $30 billion (Richardson, 1993). With each $1 billion of exports contributing, on average, to the creation of more than 20,000 jobs, such a change could materially affect domestic economic growth. As a result, any restrictions on the shipment of such products become more difficult to enforce.

In addition, the speed of technical progress and dissemination of information and innovation around the world has increased. An example illustrates the technical change achieved worldwide. The current life cycle of computers is only 18 months. More than seventy percent of the sales of the data processing industry was the result of the sale of devices which did not exist only two years ago. Experts estimate that this percentage will rise to eighty percent in 1995 (Freedenberg, 1994, p. 2).

In this context one must also question if the latest technology is required in order for a problematic country to engage in "dangerous" activity. For example, nuclear weapons and sophisticated delivery systems were developed by the United States and the Soviet Union well before supercomputers became available. Therefore, it is reasonable to assert that researchers in countries working with equipment which is less than state of the art or even obsolete may be able to achieve a threat capability which can result in major destruction and affect the world order.

From the control perspective, there is also the issue of equipment size to be considered. In former times, due to their size, high technology products used to be difficult to hide. Any movement of such high technology equipment was easily detectible. Nowadays, the components needed for state of the art technology have been miniaturized. Much leading edge technological equipment is so small that it has become nearly impossible to closely supervise the transfer of such products.

Besides, major problems have emanated from the changing structure of multilateral corporations. Most firms grow more independent and often maintain hundreds of establishments operating around the globe. Therefore, they are increasingly less likely to be affected by prohibitive export control laws which are only imposed by individual countries. Frequently, they are able to circumvent the unfavorable export controls and the resulting burden to their activities. Many firms are doing so already today in order to avoid restrictions on corporate activities such as genetic research or on tax rates (Dichtl, 1994a, p. 6).

Often, overly stringent local export impediments can simply be overcome by transferring activities to a country which offers a comparatively more advantageous export platform. For example, in the European Union every exporting corporation knows that it is comparatively easy to fulfil delivery obligations out of Greece or Portugal. Whoever chooses this detour does not, a priori, do something illegal. Many appreciate simply the speed and lack of complexity of the export control procedures offered by these countries. As long as the essential export control regulations are not totally harmonized worldwide, every person who wants to can, by founding a subsidiary, shift export activities into a country with less restrictive export rules.

Finally, there is the issue of changing support for export controls by politicians, business communities and by individual citizens. On account of the decrease in strategic threat, and the very real possibility of losing business to competing firms which are subject to less stringent export controls, the willingness of the communities to support the cost of export controls, be they lost sales or lost profits, is decreasing rapidly. Taken together with the increased trade dependence of nations and stagnating domestic economies, such unwillingness can well lead to the undermining of a "voluntary" export control regime.

All these changes have a major impact on the future existence and enforcement of export controls. They have already caused a lot of conflicts of nations and companies. In essence, they have led to the present situation in which uncertainty and inequality predominate.

THE DETERMINATION OF CONTROL CRITERIA

DETERMINING PROBLEMATIC COUNTRIES

The control net which has to be created can be focused on countries, goods or both. Capacity can be a further criterion in the sense that the export of a personal computer is no problem, but that of a super computer may be worrisome (Dichtl, 1994a, p. 2).

For three reasons it seems imperative that the categorization of countries and the list of products to be controlled should be harmonized. There must be equality in competition, which has to be guaranteed worldwide. In addition, one must consider that the expenditure for obtaining information and imposing coordination would rise to immeasurable levels if, with the import of every part of a complicated assembly project, one would need to examine whether the government of the country of origin would have misgivings about the export of the end-product to a particular country in the world. Furthermore, this would be the end of sensible international cooperation which is especially needed in research and development. If there were no advance agreement about the permissible export countries, cooperation would frequently be impossible. This would run counter not only to the national goals of employment and economic growth, but would also affect national security interests.

The fact that a country is treated as a pariah by another country or by the community of nations does not signify the end of all exports to that country. A potential seller who sees a chance of a rewarding business deal in a problematic part of the world might be tempted to interpret legal regulations in his favour, or to look for loopholes, in order to stand up against those foreign competitors who are legally less restricted. This is particularly the case when restrictive regulations can be circumvented with relative ease.

If a country imposes harsher restrictions on its enterprises than are imposed on their foreign competitors, it basically is asking for corporate circumvention. The Federal Republic of Germany tries to prevent such maneuvers through a series of precautionary measures specially designed for this purpose. For instance, under certain conditions an export enterprise is obligated to:

- appoint on the highest level of the enterprise a person to be responsible for exports,
- continuously examine buyers concerning their reliability,

- supervise the resale of merchandise by customers,
- provide an end user certificate for sold merchandise.

Violators of export control rules receive draconian punishment. There is, however, the question of how much criminalistic shrewdness a firm must apply to discover black sheep among its customers. After all, firms want to sell products, not hold them back.

DETERMINING GOODS TO BE CONTROLLED

Production, transporting and trading of objects, materials and organisms which are identified as armaments are extensively controlled all over the world. In the Federal Republic of Germany, the details of armaments are covered in the so-called War Weapons List which is a part of the War Weapons Control Law. This list distinguishes between atomic, biological and chemical weapons (Part A) and conventional weapons of war (Part B). The list is enumerative, but comprehensive. As such, it provides the legal security and clarity intended by German legislators (Epping, 1991, p. 278).

Apart from the War Weapons List, the Federal Republic of Germany has also another, much more expansive list: The Export List, in Part I, enumerates the following three sections:

- A: weapons, munitions, and armament material
- B: other goods
- C: dual-use goods (Joint List of the European Union).

Part II essentially contains agricultural goods subject to export controls either due to a quality norm or because of international obligations, for example, the coffee or cacao agreement. The entire list comprises about 200 pages.

The dual-use goods included in Part I, section C require special attention. Almost any good can be used for civilian as well as military purposes. The classic example is a pesticide factory, which can also be used to produce poison gas (Hucko, 1993, p. 15). But the classification of military use products, dual-use products and civilian use products, and the achievement of a multilateral agreement on such a classification, is very problematic. It is difficult enough to clearly define weapons. It is even more problematic to achieve consensus among nations regarding dual-use products. The problem becomes even greater when one attempts to classify and list subcomponents and regulate their export.

In consequence, the German War Weapons Control List and the German Export List deviate substantially from the control lists of other countries. The differences between the individual control lists lead to a distortion of competition. Even if governments were to be able to agree on lists and to continuously update those, the implementation of the resulting export controls would cause a lot of difficulties.

LIMITS TO THE CODIFICATION OF EXPORT CONTROLS: SOME EXAMPLES

THE LACK OF CONTROL OVER THE DIFFUSION OF INFORMATION RELEVANT TO WEAPONS PRODUCTION IN PROBLEMATIC COUNTRIES

In times of blueprint exports it would be insufficient to keep only the export of physical goods under surveillance. The transfer of knowledge and technology proves to be of equal importance. It is, therefore, hardly surprising that German Foreign Trade Law also covers construction drawings, other manufacturing documents, and the transfer of technology (Dichtl, 1994b, p. 1728). Here, however, the export control process encounters the dilemma between desire and capability.

Weapons-relevant information can easily be exported via books, periodicals and disks. Therefore, their content would have to be controlled as well. If this seems quite impossible, another issue would be to prevent foreigners from gaining access to such sources during visits or from making use of data networks across borders. It would mean the regulation of attendance of individuals at conferences and symposia. It also implies controlling the flow of data across national borders which, given today's communication systems and highways such as the Internet, would appear to be a difficult, if not an insurmountable task. In enterprises and university institutes one is often not aware that a coworker, who is from a country considered to be problematic, may gain access to security sensitive materials in the course of research and development. Yet, one may be subject to punishment under German law in such instances.

An example for the impossibility of controlling the flow of data across national borders are so-called virtual computers (Freedenberg, 1994, pp. 8 – 10). These are computers which are networked with software. The result is larger than the simple addition of the individual machines would be. In the United States, a widely distributed system of this kind is the Parallel Virtual Machine, which was developed at the Oak Ridge National Laboratory, and is accessible at no charge to authorized users via the Internet. This software, which is only one of many, is distributed in thousands of copies in the United States and other countries. In Europe a similar system called Paramacs has the largest market share. These systems are not supervised by any export authority, much less controlled.

THE INCREASING IRRELEVANCE OF THE CAPACITY CRITERION

In determining products which require an export authorization, their capacity and capability have so far played a certain role. However, this criterion is increasingly made obsolete by technical progress. This shall be illustrated by the following example. The enormous technical progress in the data processing industry was accompanied by a radical change in computer architecture (Freedenberg, 1994, p. 5). In former times, one used to have to replace a PC or a workstation with a new computer. Today, it is possible to simply exchange motherboards or microprocessors with more efficient new ones.

Instead of spending thousands of dollars or marks, upgrades can be achieved with much less investment.

But there is an additional decisive aspect: Today's machines can be connected to more than one microprocessor. Therefore, a user can basically customize and update configurations almost at will. Traditional criteria used to determine the capacity of data processing equipment can therefore no longer fulfil the function assigned to them for purposes of export controls. A user simply acquires additional chips, from whomever, and uses the expansion slots to enhance the capacity of his computer. The components needed for all this often are extremely miniaturized. Given these circumstances, the export of any computer technology can basically not be prevented.

PRINCIPLES OF GERMAN GOVERNMENTAL AUTHORIZATION PRACTICE

According to German law, in the cases which require an export authorization, a potential exporter is entitled to such authorization if his contract does not materially endanger the purposes of the Foreign Trade Law and the War Weapons Control Law. The operational meaning of this statement can be found in paragraph 7 of the Foreign Trade Law (Hucko, 1993, p. 31). It obliges the persons concerned to:

- ensure national security,
- prevent disturbing the peaceful coexistence of nations, and to
- avoid considerable disturbance of the foreign relations of the Federal Republic of Germany.

The granting of an authorization can furthermore be made subject to the fulfilment of certain factual and personal requirements. Some of these are: the observance of specific declarations and the integrity and reliability of the applicant. In paragraph 3 the Foreign Trade Law also states that within admissible and possible limits economic interests must be taken into account (Hucko, 1993, p. 27).

In a series of exploratory interviews with representatives of large enterprises it was ascertained that authorizations are granted by the Federal Export Office without problem, although the procedure usually requires a lot of time. Nobody reported that orders had been lost because of an export ban. Both results are not surprising. Important enterprises only go to the pertinent authorities if they are relatively sure of their cause. To have an export application rejected would be considered as a personal defeat by the responsible parties. It would also be an indication that the Intelligence Services, which at times assist in the decision, apparently know more than the applicant. As a result, the share of rejected export applications is low. Thus, it is not surprising that, according to calculations by the Federal Export Office, the 1993 ad valorem share of rejected export applications for goods of Part I of the Export List, measured as a portion of the Federal Republic of Germany's total export volume, amounted to only 0.09%. Of 42,023 applications made, only 369 were rejected.

The ability to report lost orders presupposes that sellers and buyers have held negotiations with each other. At any rate, one can only speculate about the number of instances in which German firms were not even considered as suppliers because of the strict German export control law. Obviously, it is common practice that competitors attempt to eliminate potential German exporters with the argument that if they were awarded the contract, they would not be allowed to deliver. Even if they were able to get an export permit, it is claimed that the restrictive legal regulations would not enable them to guarantee the supply of spare parts. No wonder that German exporters press politicians of all parties hard to work towards an international harmonization of export control laws.

A CALL FOR A NEW MULTILATERAL EXPORT CONTROL REGIME

The foundation of a new multilateral export control regime must mainly take three considerations into account. The first one is the acknowledgement of the fact that exports are useful and are to be encouraged. They contribute to economic welfare and enable companies to compete successfully. They offer choices to the world marketplace, and important cost opportunities to producers. It is through the existence of exports that the development of some products and technologies becomes possible at all. For example, many high technology products could not be developed and produced were it not for the burden sharing and fixed cost distribution effects achieved through exports.

The second consideration should be the recognition that export controls are necessary. Nevertheless, government interference in trade through export controls should be minimized. Even if enormous technical progress would make it possible to monitor all exports of all components, the costs added to business transactions due to such a control system would be extremely high. On the one hand such a control system would demand growing governmental expenditures which have to be covered by increases in governmental income. On the other hand the extensive reporting requirements would impose large costs on firms. Therefore, one is forced to the conclusion that there is an urgent necessity for an elimination of licensing procedures through the creation of license-free zones which encompass a great number of countries of the world.

The third consideration is that there must be an achievement of reasonable equality in competition. Leading politicians and managers have become conscious of the fact that the implementation of export control regimes will fundamentally influence the competitive position of countries and companies. Inequality in control regimes will unavoidably lead to the circumvention of export controls. The effectiveness of controls will be substantially diminished. Consequently, there is a growing need for equality in export controls. Only a commonly accepted multilateral export control regime can lead to fair conditions in competition.

Based on these three considerations, a new multilateral export control regime can be built up. Within such a regime, the main focus should be put on the export of nuclear, biological and chemical weapons, conventional armaments and highest technology. Such being the case, controls will only concern few products, few producers and few destinations. For those products and technologies, high fences will have to be built.

Nowadays export controls must especially be focused on regional security issues which may be subject to significant alterations in relatively short periods of time. For such controls, rapid planning as well as swift and sudden global implementation are required (Czinkota, 1995, p. 5). To prevent major disruption, damage, or delay, export controls will need to be designed decisively and immediately communicated to the business community. In addition, the controls must be accompanied by as much additional economic muscle as the controlling countries can muster. For example, it is conceivable that tough export controls are accompanied by simultaneous domestic market access restrictions through import controls. Furthermore, controls could be reinforced by including the financial dimensions of business. It is recommendable to include the domestic financial community and international ones such as the International Monetary Fund, the World Bank, or interregional banks.

Whenever export controls are necessary, their implementation must be effective. Nowadays it is no longer possible to control all exports from an industrial country. The undertaking proves to be simply too costly and too complicated. In addition, the criteria applied up to now to the licensing process are no longer based on reality. The potential of slipping through the meshes of the law is enormous. The solution to the problem cannot be the development of a higher degree of legal precision, even though this seems to be the currently preferred alternative. Already, at this time, the tasks imposed on corporations by the State appear to be exceedingly onerous, both professionally and financially.

It seems, therefore, worthwhile to consider the creation of a clear, simplified export control law which moves away from the approval of individual cases and limits itself to the prosecution of illegal conduct (Dichtl, 1994a, p. 15). Similarities will be found in Criminal Law. Here, too, no approval is required. Rather, issues are defined which are not conducive to the peaceful coexistence of people. Attacked are only offenses against the rules of the game. Transferred to the area of export controls, such an approach would mean a very broad spectrum of intervention possibilities on the one hand. On the other hand, they would only be triggered by suspicious facts or by random spot checks. Nevertheless, violations of export control law must lead to draconian punishment.

Furthermore, in a simplified law, export controls should not be exclusively product based. In the future, they have to be increasingly end-user based. Because products are easy to substitute or replicate, it is probable that better consensus can be achieved internationally in identifying those end users who should under no circumstances be able to procure sensitive products and technologies.

Besides, it will be important to make use of existing technology to accelerate the licensing process. In a decade in which databases can easily be accessed throughout the globe for business research purposes, it will become less and less acceptable to require lengthy delays for business licensing applications. It will be necessary to design a licensing process, which although thorough and precise, affects the ongoing conduct of global business as little as possible. Besides, such a licensing process will have to be capable of responding quickly to changing political realities by being responsive to crises around the world. The system must also be able to track and adjust to technical developments in order to relinquish controls on outdated technologies, but maintain them on products, technologies and services which are worth controlling (Czinkota, 1995, p. 5).

An export activity is in principle noticeable and documented at various points. The exporter must get an export authorization, give notice to the custom authorities and provide an export declaration. In addition, sales tax forms must be filled in, and usually forwarding agents, shippers or airlines get involved. The proceeds of the goods sold are received by the bank of the seller. Possibilities to become aware of suspect developments are abundant. Given the fact that an export transaction is typically noticeable and involves intermediaries and many participants, harsh punishment perhaps accompanied by rewards for whistleblowers would have a major dampening effect on the desire to circumvent export controls.

The increasingly global economy, with its manyfold trade linkages, requires that in the future governments and industry cooperate more closely in achieving export control goals. In addition, effective multinational export controls require international collaboration. In consequence, there is a renewed need for multilateral deliberations on a case-by-case basis when the invocation of export controls is necessary.

Export controls represent an important instrument to protect national and global security. As such, they are a reasonable deviation from the otherwise strong encouragement of free trade. However, the controls themselves must be reasonable, must be purposeful, and they must become the exception to the rule. A new multilateral export control regime must reduce the burden on enterprises while at the same time ensuring that the world will become a better and safer one (Czinkota, 1995, pp. 5–6).

References

Czinkota, M.R. (1995), A New Export Control Regime. Security in a Volatile Environment, World Business Policy Brief, Georgetown University Center for International Business Education and Research, Washington, D.C., January 1995.

Czinkota, M.R. (Ed.) (1984), Export Controls—Building Reasonable Commercial Ties with Political Adversaries, New York, 1984.

Czinkota, M.R./ Ronkainen, I. (1995), International Marketing, Fourth Edition, Fort Worth, Texas, 1995.

Dichtl, E. (1994a), Defacto Limits of Export Controls. The Need for International Harmonization, Paper presented at the Second Annual Consortium for International Marketing Research (CIMaR) Conference, Rio de Janeiro, 1994.

Dichtl, E. (1994b), Faktische Grenzen der Exportkontrolle. Die Notwendigkeit einer internationalen Harmonisierung der Ausfuhrüberwachung, in: BB—Betriebsberater, Volume 49, 1994, Number 25, pp. 1726–1730.

Epping, V. (1991), Exportfreiheit und Exportkontrolle, in: DWIR—Deutsche Zeitschrift für Wirtschaftsrecht, Volume 1, 1991, Number 7, pp. 276–285.

Freedenberg, P. (1994), Testimony before the Subcommittee on International Finance and Monetary Policy of the Committee on Banking, Housing, and Urban Affairs, United States Senate, Manuscript, Washington D.C., February 3, 1994.

Hucko, E.M. (1993), Außenwirtschaftsrecht-Kriegswaffenkontrollrecht, Textsammlung mit Einführung, Fourth Edition, Cologne, 1993.

Panel on the Future Design and Implementation of U.S. National Security Export Controls (1991), Finding Common Ground: U.S. Export Controls in a Changed Global Environment, Washington, D.C., 1991.

Richardson, D.J. (1993), Sizing up U.S. Export Disincentives, Washington, D.C., 1993.

THE ASIAN CRISIS: LESSONS FOR CRISIS MANAGEMENT AND PREVENTION

Richard Brealey

Woody Allen, in a graduation day speech, remarked, "More than any other time in history, mankind faces a crossroads. One path leads to despair and utter hopelessness. The other to total extinction. Let us pray we have the wisdom to choose correctly." The international financial institutions must have felt that they confronted a similar predicament when faced by the successive financial crises in Asia, Russia, and Brazil. These events have prompted renewed debate about crisis prevention and resolution. In particular, it has been argued that the IMF should serve as an international equivalent of the domestic lender of last resort that can assist countries hit by a creditor panic or currency flight. The difficulties for the IMF in fulfilling this role are its relative lack of resources and the problem of distinguishing between the illiquid and insolvent borrower. Moreover, as we show later, the behavior of asset prices on the announcement

---

Richard Brealey is Special Adviser to the Governor of the Bank of England and Visiting Professor of Finance at the London Business School.

This article was first published in *International Finance*, Vol. 2 No. 2 (1999), pp. 249–272, and is reprinted here with permission of the publisher. *International Finance* is a new journal published by Blackwell Publishers, Oxford, and edited by Benn Steil, Senior Fellow, and Linda J. Wachner, Chair in Foreign Economic Policy, at the Council on Foreign Relations in New York.

To obtain a sample copy or take out a subscription, see the Blackwell website: http://www.blackwellpublishers.co.uk, send an e-mail to jnlinfo@blackwellpublishers.co.uk, or contact either of the following: Blackwell Publisher Journals, P.O. Box 805, 108 Cowley Road, Oxford OX4 IFH. Tel: +44(0)1865 244083, fax +44(0)1865 381381; Journals Marketing (INFI), Blackwell Publishers, 350 Main Street, Malden, MA 02148, USA. Tel. +1(781)388 8200, fax +1(781)388 8210.

Earlier versions of this paper were presented at an IFA Donor seminar at the London Business School and at the 1998 Capital Markets Conference in Stockholm. I am grateful for comments from Xavier Freixas, Andrew Haldane, Costas Kaplanis, Mervyn King, and Oren Sussman. The views expressed in the paper are nevertheless personal views and they do not necessarily represent the policy of the Bank of England.

of IMF assistance provides little encouragement for the view that the IMF's intervention helps countries to resolve a problem of financial panics. An alternative role for the IMF is to use its leverage to enforce policy changes on affected countries. This role does not assume that a country's creditors are subject to contagious panics, and the form and quantity of assistance that is needed to impose conditions are not the same as those required to stem a creditor panic.

The fact that IMF support has been a response to the withdrawal of funds by international banks (and capital flight by domestic investors) has led to concern that the IMF is simply bailing out the banks and thus to calls for a redistribution of the burden. This view seems to be colored by the assumption that international banking is not a competitive activity, so that the banks are able to collect economic rents from the IMF's assistance. Proposals for burden-sharing further assume that the form of private sector lending would be unaffected by attempts to "bail in" the private sector. A related concern is that the prospect of IMF assistance to troubled countries leads to a moral hazard problem on the part of both lenders and borrowers. This moral hazard argument does not sit well with the huge losses that have been made by foreign investors in the affected countries, nor with the extreme reluctance on the part of borrowers to seek IMF assistance.

The strong limitations on the international community to resolve a major international financial crisis suggest that the focus of public policy should be on crisis prevention rather than resolution. It is foolish to look for a single panacea. Debate has focused *inter alia* on alternative exchange rate systems, the structure of banking and bank supervision in emerging markets, and on the systems of corporate governance and control ("crony capitalism"). Rather less attention has been given to the issues of capital structure. It is clear, however, that the capital structures of governments, financial institutions, and corporations contributed to the severity of the crises in the affected countries. In particular, the high levels of bank borrowing and the maturity and currency mismatches incurred by the banks endangered the solvency of the banks and limited the policy responses of governments.

The next section of this paper provides some brief background material on the Asian crisis and the events that led up to it. The third section discusses the role of the IMF and the related issues of burden-sharing and moral hazard. Section 4 turns to the topic of crisis prevention and discusses the role of capital structure in reallocating the real risks in emerging market economies. Section 5 reviews briefly some of the policy implications and Section 6 concludes.

THE ASIAN FINANCIAL CRISIS

The float of the Thai baht in July 1997 was the first step in a series of financial crises that first swept through Thailand, the Philippines, Malaysia, Indonesia, and Korea, and subsequently spread to Russia and on to Brazil. In each of the affected Asian countries, there was a substantial flight of capital by both domestic and international investors. Foreign exchange reserves, which had been growing rapidly, were depleted even more rapidly, with Korea losing $25 billion in usable reserves in just over a month. Throughout the region governments attempted with little success to stem this pressure on reserves by increasing short-term interest rates, which in the case of Indonesia rose to over 80 percent. The capital flight resulted in a remarkable period of turbulence in the foreign exchange markets. Volatility in the rupiah, which had been a fraction of 1% per day under the crawling peg, reached 12% per day,[1] roughly the annual volatility of most western equity markets. By its low point in 1998, the rupiah had lost 80% of its value in nominal terms and about 70% in real terms. Each of the other affected Asian currencies depreciated by more than 38%.

Many of the crisis countries found themselves in a debt trap, where the cost of rolling over loans forced them into spiralling debt levels and public sector deficits. In such cases the reduction in the wealth levels of the citizens needed to escape from such a trap was politically infeasible. Raising interest rates to protect the currency increased the burden of servicing domestic government debt and drove the government into yet larger deficits, while allowing the currency to depreciate increased the cost of foreign currency debt and threatened the solvency of the banking system through which much of the foreign currency debt was channelled.

Concerns over possible defaults caused the spread over U.S. Treasuries to widen to between 8 and 18% for the affected Asian countries. Each country also experienced a run on the banks. Since the second half of 1997, several hundred financial institutions have been closed down, suspended, or nationalized, and recapitalization needs are estimated to range between 18 and 34% of GDP for the crisis countries.

The consequences for all the affected countries have been severe. In Indonesia GDP fell by 14% in 1998 and by an average of over 7% in the five affected Asian countries, though that still leaves income per head substantially higher than it was at the start of the decade. In the region of $120 billion of capital has left these countries. Would-be borrowers in many developing countries have been effectively cut off from access to the capital markets, while liquidity has been severely affected, and spreads have increased. The losses to foreign creditors and equity investors in East Asia and Russia amount to an estimated $350 billion.[2]

The East Asian story has since been more or less repeated in the other crisis countries. In each case capital flight has put pressure on reserves, which the government has attempted to fight by very high domestic interest rates and fiscal restraint. In Russia the depth of the problem and the reluctance of the government to pass needed reforms has resulted in a debt moratorium and *de facto* default.

THE SEEDS OF THE CRISIS

What at the time seemed so surprising about these events was that many of the countries had seemed models of economic success. In the words of one commentator, "From 1945 to 1997 the Asian economic miracle fueled the greatest expansion of wealth, for the largest number of persons, in the history of mankind."[3] In the affected Asian countries, growth in real GDP had averaged 7% a year since 1990, with relatively little pressure on consumer prices. Brazilian real GDP grew at an annual rate of 4.5% between 1993 and 1996, while in five years inflation fell from 2500% to under 3%. Even Russia appeared to be making progress with its problems. Inflation in 1997 was below 15% compared with nearly 900% five years earlier. The ruble had stabilised and GDP in 1997 grew slightly after declining in each of the previous five years.

However, it is easy with hindsight to see that the seeds of the emerging market crisis of 1997/98 were sown earlier in the 1990s, when improvements in the access to financial markets and apparent high returns on investments caused a surge of capital inflows into many emerging markets. By 1996 the total net private capital inflow to the affected Asian countries had reached $73 billion, up from just $25 billion six years earlier.

The risks involved in this huge capital inflow to Asian emerging markets were exacerbated by the fact that most of it was in the form of bank debt. In 1996, the year preceding the Asian crisis, 61% of the capital flows to the affected countries consisted of bank lending.[4] Most of the external debt was contracted by the private sector and, except in Indonesia, the money was largely channeled through local banks that relent the money to local businesses. Net interbank borrowing by banks in the five most troubled Asian countries amounted to about $43 billion annually during 1995 and 1996. Most of this lending was denominated in dollars. Foreign bank debt amounted to 45% of GDP in Thailand, 35% in Indonesia, and 25% in Korea. This debt generally had a maturity of less than one year.[5] In contrast, the average maturity of the loans made to local companies by the banks was longer than a year and the loans were commonly denominated in the local currency. Thus banks assumed both a maturity mismatch and a currency mismatch. In Thailand, where there are restrictions on the open foreign exchange positions of banks, the banks limited their currency risk by relending in dollars. However, since their clients did not have the foreign currency earnings to repay these debts, the banks simply traded a currency risk for a credit risk.

During the 1990s bank credit in most Asian countries grew rapidly by between 12 and 18% per annum in real terms. In many countries this resulted in large exposures to particular sectors, notably property,[6] and to overconcentration to single borrowers. In Korea the average book debt-to-equity ratio of the corporate sector reached nearly 200% and the top 30 chaebols had a debt-equity ratio of more than 400%. This is despite the fact that even before the onset of the crisis these chaebols were barely profitable.[7] The weakness in the banking system was (as so often) hidden by the gap between the book and market value of the loans. In Indonesia Moody's has estimated that the proportion of loans that are nonperforming could be as high as 75%. In Korea nonperforming loans may amount to 150 trillion won.

Most currencies were pegged principally against the dollar, despite the fact that a high and increasing proportion of external trade was with countries in the Asian region. These currency pegs had the effect of disguising the risks involved in the foreign currency loans and offered apparently low-risk profits on investment in local fixed interest markets. Thus the capital inflow reflected in part "arbitrage" activity by banks and investors, who were able to borrow dollars and relend in the local currency at a profit as long as the peg to the dollar was maintained. The currency peg also meant that the risk was largely a jump risk, where the high probability of a small profit disguised the smaller chance of a substantial loss. Thus, when the currencies began to depreciate, there was little opportunity for banks to take corrective action by lifting their positions.

What made the currency pegs unsustainable was the sharp fall in the growth of exports from the region. This stemmed from a combination of an appreciation in the real exchange rates particularly relative to the yen, together with the weak Japanese economy, increasing competition in export markets from China and Mexico, and excess capacity in many exporting industries such as the semiconductor, petrochemical, and automobile industries. By 1996 the current account deficit in the five Asian countries had reached $55 billion.

THE INTERNATIONAL RESPONSE TO FINANCIAL CRISES

The events of 1997–98 have prompted increased debate about the international response to such financial crises. This section considers the role of international institutions in crisis prevention and management. Specifically, it seeks to answer the following questions:

1. What is the role of the IMF?
2. Who benefits from IMF assistance?
3. How should the burden be shared?
4. How serious is the problem of moral hazard?
5. How can the IMF help with crisis prevention?

WHAT IS THE ROLE OF THE IMF?

The IMF was established in 1947 to buttress the Bretton Woods's system of fixed exchange rates and was intended to provide temporary assistance in the event of destabilizing speculation and consequent balance of payments difficulties. But its role has changed to one of engineering major structural reforms and providing assistance in the face of possible default on international loans.

Much of the debate on the effectiveness of the IMF in the recent international crises has centered on the appropriateness of its programs. But there have also been more fundamental questions about its role in crisis management and prevention. Why would the private sector not be prepared to lend to affected countries at "fair market rates"? Is there an imperfection in the private capital markets that justifies the existence of an international lender of last resort? Are there multiple equilibria in financial markets, so that a simple nudge from an international financial institution could transport us safely from a bad equilibrium to a good one? Unless these questions can be answered, we do not know whether an IMF is needed at all or in what circumstances and in what form it should provide assistance.

The following quotations may illustrate the sharp divergence of opinion over these issues:

> *"The crises have brought home the absolute indispensability of the IMF as the core provider of emergency, conditioned international support to countries in financial difficulty. . . . Without the IMF, even those countries that are committed to reform might face default . . . which could have devastating effects on their own economies and significantly raise the risks of contagion in other markets."*
>
> LAWRENCE SUMMERS (1998)

> *". . . the question is whether there is a need for an agency that will act as lender of last resort for countries facing a crisis. There is such a need: it arises both because international capital flows are not only extremely volatile but also contagious, exhibiting the classic signs of financial panics, and because an international lender of last resort can help mitigate the effects of this instability, and perhaps the instability itself. . . I will argue not only that the international system needs a lender of last resort, but also that the IMF is increasingly playing that role and that changes in the international system now under consideration will make it possible for it to exercise that function more effectively."*
>
> STANLEY FISCHER (1999)

> *"IMF resources have been used to 'bail out insolvent emerging market banks and international bank lenders.' The costs have been (1) undesirable redistributions of wealth from taxpayers to politically influential oligarchs in developing economies; (2) the promotion of excessive risk taking and inefficient investment; (3) the undermining of the natural process of deregulation and economic and political reform which global competition would otherwise promote."*
>
> CHARLES CALOMIRIS (1998)

> *"The role of a lender of last resort is not to bail out failed banks. Its job is to assure that solvent financial institutions do not fail because of lack of liquidity. . . . Since 1971, the IMF has been looking for new things to do. It has now solved its problem by creating moral hazard, allowing international banks to avoid the risks they undertake by imprudent lending. The IMF encourages the behavior that creates the problems."*
>
> ALAN MELTZER (1998)

In common with most advocates of active IMF involvement, both Summers and Fischer emphasize the danger of "panics" in financial markets and of consequent "contagion." By contrast, Calomiris and Meltzer place more weight on the dangers of moral hazard that results from the prospect of an IMF "bail-out."

One of the roles envisaged for the IMF, and suggested in Stanley Fischer's 1999 paper, is as an international equivalent of the domestic lender of last resort.[8] The function of the domestic lender of last resort is to prevent destabilising runs on the banking system. One way that this could arise is from a liquidity mismatch. For example, a bank may be solvent as long as all depositors agree to maintain their investment, but subject to a run if each depositor is concerned that others are about to withdraw their cash. This possibility stems from the fact that depositors cannot coordinate their actions. The solution is to establish a benevolent lender of last resort that can prevent such runs simply by standing ready to provide whatever liquidity is needed.[9]

In practice, pure liquidity panics are rare and bank runs are more often motivated by insolvency worries. Here also problems may arise because depositors are unable to coordinate their actions or pool their information. For example, each depositor may rationally draw inferences about the bank's solvency from the actions of the other depositors. So a small initial loss of deposits can lead to a cascade of withdrawals.[10] If a lender of last resort has superior information or can pool the information available to individual depositors, it may be able to distinguish a bad cascade from a good cascade and nudge the market towards the appropriate outcome.[11]

The liberalization of the world's capital markets in the past 20 years has led to large capital flows into and out of emerging markets. While this is not necessarily a cause for concern, it may leave countries exposed to the type of liquidity or information-motivated panics that are used to justify a domestic lender of last resort. An international lender of last resort is clearly not necessary to protect a country's banking system against runs on its domestic book, but may, for example, be needed where banks have large foreign currency books.

This view that there is an important role for an international lender of last resort relies heavily on the view that financial markets are prone to bubbles, panics, and contagion. However, while models of rational multiple equilibria that produce bubbles and panics are fun to construct, it is not clear that they work better than simpler models. For example, surveys of bank runs suggest that these runs generally reflect shared and justified worries about the bank's solvency and that well-capitalized banks are not subject to runs.[12] If financial markets do function well most of the time and aggregate information efficiently, then the capital withdrawals that have been experienced in a number of emerging markets are more likely to indicate basic structural weaknesses in the country's banking and exchange rate system than a failure of coordination between lenders. Thus, the case for an international lender of last resort depends heavily on the lender's access to superior information about the solvency of the country's banking system.

Unlike a domestic lender of last resort, the IMF's ability to respond to a liquidity run is limited by its lack of resources. For example, between 1992 and 1996 the *net* amount disbursed by the IMF under the Standby Arrangements and Extended Fund Facilities was about $18 billion. During the same period the total net private capital flows to emerging markets was over $1 trillion. The events of 1997–98 led to an increase of two-thirds in the IMF's net lending. Nevertheless, at the end of January 1999 the total amount owing to the IMF under Standby Arrangements and Extended Fund Facilities was still only $41 billion, far smaller than the amount of private capital that has been withdrawn from emerging markets.

This lack of resources may be less crucial in the case of a solvency run. If the IMF does have superior information that allows it to distinguish between solvent and insolvent countries, then its willingness to put its money where its mouth is could serve as an important signal to the private sector. Such a signal could bring large welfare gains to the country in the form of reduced costs of further private sector credit (and an unrecoverable windfall gain to the value of existing loans by private sector banks).

Unfortunately, the signals provided by the IMF's involvement are likely to be mixed. Recourse to the IMF generally occurs only when the patient is in need of intensive care. As Radelet and Sachs (1998) suggest, the "arrival of the IMF gives all the confidence of seeing an ambulance outside one's door." Thus news that the IMF is willing to provide assistance may be overshadowed by the news that the country needs it. Moreover, even if the IMF is particularly well qualified to assess country prospects, it is often under strong political pressure to extend assistance to borrowers, such as Russia, where there are clear doubts about the country's ability to service its debts. This muddies the signal provided by IMF assistance.

An alternative rationale for the IMF is that while private sector lenders may wish to impose conditions on the local government, they find it difficult to do so. Thus the IMF may be able to attach conditions that would be impossible for the private sector.[13] If this is the case, there could be an overall welfare gain. Of course, this raises the question as to why the government could not voluntarily bind itself to the same courses of action at the time that the loan is needed. The answer may lie partly in the difficulty of specifying these actions *ex ante* (hence the use of staged IMF lending) or in the fact that a populist government may find it easier to justify to its citizens conditions that have been imposed by an external body. The fact that the required reforms are packaged with IMF lending both allows the IMF to exert leverage and provides an incentive for it to monitor the implementation of the reforms. However, the gains in this case may be linked only weakly to the extent of the support.

These two models of the IMF's role do not sit happily together and have different implications for the form of its assistance. For example, there is little place for staged lending or conditionality for a lender of last resort, whose function is to stem a panic resulting from liquidity or solvency concerns. On the other hand, staged lending is an essential tool for enforcing policy changes.

WHO BENEFITS FROM IMF ASSISTANCE?

It is not easy to measure the effect of IMF programs and more often than not the debate is liable to get mired in speculation about what might have happened in the absence of support. An alternative approach is to focus on changes in asset values at the time of the announcement of IMF assistance. In some ongoing research with Evi Kaplanis of LBS, I have been looking at the relative performance of equities, bonds, and currencies in the weeks surrounding the announcement of IMF support.[14] The results are preliminary, but they suggest three things:

1. During the two years preceding the announcement of support, there is a sharp relative fall in equity prices in the affected countries. Bond prices and exchange rates also decline sharply, though this fall is over a shorter period.
2. In the days immediately following the announcement of IMF support, there is no statistically significant change in the value of each asset class.
3. In the months following the announcement of IMF support, asset prices show

> little abnormal movement. This is exactly what any believer in efficient markets would predict, but it does not support those who believe that markets are seized by irrational panics that cause them to overshoot.

If these results stand up to further analysis, then it is difficult to argue that the IMF decision to provide assistance is an important signal as to the health of the beneficiary or that it provides information to the markets about the recipient's willingness to accept desirable reforms. However, the tests are insufficiently powerful to determine whether there is a gain in asset values that exceeds the very limited degree of subsidy in the IMF assistance.

HOW SHOULD THE BURDEN BE SHARED?

IMF assistance is typically a response to a flight of private capital from the affected country. Often the cash helps the country to repay maturing debts. This has prompted concern that the IMF is simply bailing out the international lending banks and that there should be some form of burden-sharing.

It seems unlikely that IMF aid simply goes into the pockets of the international lending banks. International banking is a highly competitive activity and therefore the prospect that IMF support may be available in the event of difficulties is likely to be reflected in the interest rates that banks charge. Of course, in this case IMF assistance would be simply a form of Third World aid, the benefits of which are shared between the fortunate countries that do not subsequently require assistance and the unfortunate ones that do.

If IMF assistance enables countries to repay maturing bank debts, any unanticipated announcement of assistance would result in an increase in the value of the equity of lending banks. In practice, there do not appear to be any abnormal returns in equity prices of international banks, which may suggest either that the IMF assistance is regarded as an automatic response to a balance of payments crisis and is therefore fully anticipated, or (more likely) that the news of IMF assistance percolates slowly and the amount of the subsidy is too small to observe.

If IMF support does result in increases in the value of private sector debt, the IMF could try to recapture some of these value enhancements by arranging, for example, a moratorium on private sector debt. Certainly, the IMF may have a coordinating role between private lenders in cases where they have a common interest in renewing their lines. This is the crisis manager role that has been described by Stanley Fischer (1999). However, the suggestion of compulsion would not sit well with the arguments that have been made for an international lender of last resort. If private sector lenders are reluctant to continue to lend even when the IMF has offered assistance, there is a message that one would do well to heed.

If some form of enforced "burden-sharing" was anticipated, it would be reflected in higher interest rates on developing country debt. It is also dangerous to assume that the structure of private-sector lending would be independent of attempts to recapture any value enhancement. In particular, lenders would have an incentive to structure the debt to make it easier to exit before the imposition of a moratorium. This is exactly the opposite of the financial structures that one would like to see in developing countries.

HOW SEVERE IS THE PROBLEM OF MORAL HAZARD?

Critics of the IMF's role commonly contend that the prospect of IMF assistance leads to a moral hazard problem. International banks, it is suggested, are tempted to lend recklessly to emerging markets, and the governments and banks in these countries are tempted to borrow excessively. The first point to make is that this does not *necessarily* reduce social welfare, for it is arguable that, given the underdeveloped equity markets in developing economies, these countries have suffered from a shortage of risk capital rather than an excess. While this suggests the need to encourage the supply of equity capital, the existence of an international financial institution that partially underwrites the risk of the lending banks may serve as a second-best solution to the shortage of risk capital.

There is little doubt that the prospect of IMF assistance creates a potential moral hazard; but while it is difficult to provide convincing evidence, it seems likely that the danger is often overstated. The subsidy in IMF loans is negligible compared with the losses that have been suffered by investors in East Asia, Russia, and Brazil. Neither the promised yields or volatility of emerging market debt are consistent with the notion that investors regarded these loans as low risk. Nor does the rapid capital outflow at the onset of a crisis suggest that investors were confident of being bailed out if they maintained their positions. Given the heavy losses that investors have taken on their emerging market books, their caution was right.[15]

Nor is it clear that the debtors take much comfort in the prospect of IMF assistance. Not only are governments generally reluctant to call on IMF help, but the financial crises in these markets typically impose considerable costs on all the country's citizens. In almost all cases the appeal for IMF assistance has led to considerable domestic unrest, a fall in the government, and a change in the governor of the central bank. It is difficult therefore to believe that politicians and business people are tempted to pursue reckless policies in the belief that they will not suffer the consequences.

THE ROLE OF THE IMF IN CRISIS PREVENTION

Financial crises have resulted in large wealth losses, but there is relatively little that the IMF can do to replace this lost wealth. Despite the popular image of huge bailouts, the subsidy provided by the IMF (or "burden" in the eyes of its critics) is negligible compared with the wealth losses that the borrowing countries have experienced. This suggests that prevention of international crises should take precedence over cure.

An interesting issue is how far the IMF can play a role here beyond that of an experienced consultant. One problem for the IMF has been that countries are reluctant to seek assistance and do so only as a last resort. This shows up in the preceding asset returns. For example, over the two years before a country seeks IMF support, equity prices on average experience a relative decline of 35%. In the case of bank stocks the relative decline is about 40%. It is possible, therefore, that the need for IMF assistance would be reduced if countries could be encouraged to make earlier policy changes. This seems to be the motive behind President Clinton's proposal for contingent credit lines.

Unfortunately, it has proved difficult to devise a scheme that both maximizes the Fund's ability to influence economic policies without at the same time risking excessive strain on the Fund's resources. Suppose, for example, that the IMF offered a committed line of credit that would be rolled over as long as the country continues to follow IMF-approved policies. A country that entered into such an arrangement would be induced to follow the agreed policies because it wished both to maintain the insurance of the line of credit and to avoid the negative signal associated with a refusal to renew the line. However, such a scheme would also leave the IMF with a potentially large open liability. It is probably for this reason that the agreed facility does not involve a firm commitment on the part of the Fund. Instead, loans under the facility will depend on the health of the IMF's resources,[16] evidence that the country is the victim of "contagion" that is largely outside its control, and the country's willingness to pursue a further agreed set of policies. By seeking to retain leverage at the time that the funds are released, the IMF is giving up most of the leverage at the time that the facility is entered into and is reducing the incentives for any country to apply for the facility. Thus, in the trade-off between exerting leverage and retaining flexibility, the Fund has placed almost exclusive emphasis on flexibility.

CRISIS PREVENTION AND THE LESSONS FROM THE ASIAN CRISIS

We argued above that there are strong limitations to the ability of any international financial institution to resolve a major financial crisis and that the focus of public policy should be on prevention rather than cure.

Debate about possible policy responses has focused on a number of issues. First, part of the blame for recent financial crises has been laid at the door of pegged exchange rates and this has led to the view that countries need to choose between freely floating currencies on the one hand and currency boards or enlarged currency areas on the other.[17] Second, the substantial capital flows to and from the affected countries have prompted concern about excessive speculation and raised the question whether governments should throw sand into the speculative works in the form of a Tobin tax or capital controls.[18] A third set of issues centers on corporate ownership and governance in the affected countries, for it has been argued that discipline has been weakened by the degree of conglomeration in corporate structures and the close relationships between non-financial corporations and banks.[19]

This paper bypasses these issues and focuses instead on the role of capital structure in the recent financial crises.

CAPITAL STRUCTURE AND THE DISTRIBUTION OF RISK

One of the principal lessons from recent events centers on the distribution of risk. The Asian crisis occurred first in the real economy, where huge overcapacity and increasing costs led to a sharp fall in profitability. The crisis in the real economy showed up in the financial sector in the form of large capital outflows, falling asset prices, and insolvencies in financial institutions. There are always likely to be shocks in the real economy, but countries and their institutions can adopt financial structures that ensure that the consequences of these shocks are distributed efficiently. Two features of the financial structure in the affected Asian countries were a particular source of difficulty:

- Many of the banks borrowed dollars and reinvested in domestic currency loans. Their willingness to do so was enhanced by their belief that the governments were committed to maintaining the currency pegs. Some banks believed that they had hedged the currency risk by also making dollar loans to local companies. But, since the borrowers had no dollar income with which to repay these loans, the banks found that they had merely substituted credit risk for currency risk.
- The currency mismatch was also accompanied by a maturity mismatch, with banks funding in the short-term interbank market and then relending at longer maturities. Thus banks faced a problem of rolling over existing loans as they matured and could do so only on very unfavourable terms. Governments also funded themselves with very short-term debt, so that they too were faced with the problem of rolling over maturing loans at very high rates. This created a conflict between the need to reduce the government deficit and the need to raise interest rates to protect the currency and thus the cost of foreign currency debt, much of which was incurred by the banking system.

The choice of financial structure is largely a problem in risk distribution. Capital can be provided in the form of either equity or debt. The heavy reliance on debt finance by many East Asian companies meant that only a small reduction in profitability was needed to produce financial distress and default, the costs of which were borne largely by local banks. This points first to the need to improve the supply of equity in these countries. This is particularly important in the case of capital inflows. Since developing economies are often relatively undiversified, foreign equity ownership has the advantage of spreading that risk widely.

Foreign equity investment can be either in the form of portfolio investment or direct investment. Portfolio investment is more easily reversed than direct investment. Thus heavy net purchases of East Asian equities by foreign investors were replaced by modest net sales in 1997.[20] Although these sales were necessarily taken up by domestic investors, many of the foreigners who sold their stock converted the proceeds to dollars and this contributed to the pressure on exchange rates. In contrast to portfolio investment in equities, foreign direct investment in the affected Asian countries declined only modestly, while for Asia as a whole it actually increased.[21]

Unlike equity, debt brings with it the risk of default, but debt instruments may differ on a number of dimensions that affect the allocation of risk:

- *Currency:* The recent financial crises have highlighted the risks for governments, banks, and industrial companies of unmatched foreign currency borrowing. Clearly, loans between different currency zones must always involve a currency risk for some party, but it is undesirable that these risks should be concentrated in the developing country and particularly in its banking system.
- *Maturity:* Borrowers that finance with a succession of short-term loans must roll over their loans at rates that reflect their changing credit risk. As the debt maturity is lengthened, more of that default risk is passed to the lender. Thus long-term debt effectively provides the borrower with insurance against a rise in the default premium. Of course, such insurance does not come free, for the lenders will charge a higher rate of interest on long-term risky loans.[22]
- *Guaranteed Lines of Credit:* A related mechanism for risk-shifting involves guaranteed lines of credit. For example, a group of foreign banks have entered into a firm commitment (i.e., without a "material adverse change" clause) to lend Argentina up to $7 billion against collateral at 200 basis points above LIBOR. Similarly, Mexico has arranged a simple overdraft facility for about $3 billion. In both cases the governments paid a commitment fee and in exchange the banks took on the risk of movements in the default premium.
- *Interest Rate:* Long-term *variable-rate* debt shifts the risk of changes in the default premium from the borrower to the lender. With long-term *fixed-rate* debt, both the default premium and the risk-free interest rate are fixed. In the case of corporate debt, the impact on risk depends on the effect of interest rate changes on the value of the firm's assets. However, since major financial crises typically involve both a sharp rise in real interest rates and a fall in the nominal value of corporate assets, the issue of fixed rate debt avoids the prospect of an increase in debt-servicing costs at the time of declining profits.

  Since increases in the domestic short-term interest rate are a common response to a financial crisis, long-term fixed-rate government debt frees the government from the conflict between raising interest rates to protect the currency and holding down its borrowing costs. Governments have a further reason to prefer the issue of fixed-rate, long-term debt, since it plays a role for governments which is similar to that of equity. Governments have uncertain income. If there is an unanticipated fall in the real value of this income stream, then the government can seek to recover the deficit from its citizens in the form of higher taxes or poorer services. However, particularly in developing countries, it may be infeasible to require the citizens to bear all the risk of the government's activities, so that the bondholders may need to take on part of that risk. The adjustment to interest rates that is needed to enforce real wealth losses on the bondholders is much smaller if the government is financed largely by long-term nominal debt denominated in its domestic currency.

- *Call Provisions:* Call provisions on bonds may have both a signalling and an incentive effect, since a borrower that is prepared to pay a premium for the right to repay early has an incentive to maintain the value of its debt and credibly signals its confidence that it can do so.
- *Structured Debt:* Structured debt makes it possible to tailor debt service more closely to the borrower's ability to pay. This may be particularly important for sovereign governments that cannot issue equity directly. One possible response, suggested by the insurance industry, is to issue catastrophe or "forgiveness" bonds, the payments on which are reduced in the event of a defined catastrophe. An alternative is to index the debt service to some measure of economic output. Thus Mexico has issued oil-linked bonds, while Bulgaria has issued GDP-indexed bonds. A somewhat simpler solution is to combine an issue of straight debt with simultaneous commodity or equity swaps. For example, a government could gain considerable protection against the effects of an economic crisis by entering into an equity swap whose payments are linked to the level of its domestic equity index.[23]
- *Debt Conversion:* Debt brings with it the risk of default and, in countries where the bankruptcy code is undeveloped or its application unpredictable, this may raise the cost of debt. A somewhat unconventional solution might be to develop debt that converts automatically to equity as the value of the borrower's assets declines. Since the role of bankruptcy codes is to ensure the orderly transfer of ownership to the debtholders in the event of default, such a security would build the bankruptcy mechanism directly into the debt contract and would therefore substitute for local bankruptcy law.
- *Securitization:* The Asian crisis highlighted the problems caused by domestic banks that acted as intermediaries between international lending banks and local corporate borrowers. The cost of financial distress in the corporate sector therefore fell first on the local banking system. This could be avoided if the debt was securitized or was raised directly from the overseas banks.

We have argued that the financial crisis in Asia was exacerbated by the financial structure of the countries, notably the high degree of corporate leverage, the dominance of local bank financing, and the currency and maturity mismatch of this bank lending. The result was that risk was poorly diversified and unduly concentrated on the country's banking system. There is no single optimal capital structure for either corporations or governments. We cannot say, for example, that local currency debt is always less risky than foreign currency debt or that fixed rate debt is preferable to variable rate debt. Our discussion, however, illustrates the importance of both the level and design of debt in allocating risk.

Notice that changes in capital structure redistribute risk and can therefore mitigate the consequences of future wealth losses. But the time to redistribute risk is before you lose all your wealth. The bankrupt gains little by resolving never to go to the casino again. Once the losses have occurred, they cannot be recovered by voluntary debt restructuring. Voluntary restructuring can shift the time pattern of cash flows and their risk; it cannot affect value. It is part of crisis prevention; it has little role to play in crisis resolution.

POLICY IMPLICATIONS

In this section we sketch some of the policy implications for developing countries, most of which flow fairly directly from our analysis of the issues. We begin with the role of foreign capital.

Since a high proportion of foreign investment in developing countries has been in the form of short-term debt, it has provided little risk pooling and led to substantial capital outflows with an associated pressure on reserves. Policy, therefore, needs to be aimed at increasing the proportion of foreign capital that is in the form of foreign direct investment or equity portfolio investment. In particular, liberalization of foreign direct investment or inward equity portfolio investment needs to be undertaken in parallel with that of short-term banking flows.

There are some encouraging indications that an increasing proportion of foreign capital in emerging markets is of a long-term nature. For example, foreign direct investment in emerging markets has increased by 30% a year since 1990 and by 1997 had reached nearly 50% of private capital inflows to emerging markets (though it remained relatively unimportant in Southeast Asia).[24] Foreign direct investment depends in part on the absence of government constraints that are often designed to protect particular local industries, but it is also heavily dependent on a benign political, legal, and institutional infrastructure.

Since 1980 an increasing fraction of the indirect investment in emerging markets has been securitized, with the result that both equity and bond investment have grown at the expense of bank lending. This has had two advantages. While these portfolio flows have been more volatile than direct investment, they are at least more stable than short-term banking flows. Also proportionately more of the risk has been borne by foreigners and thereby pooled. In some countries the growth in foreign equity investment has been hampered by direct restrictions on ownership. For example, before May 1997 foreign equity investment in Korea was inhibited by the fact that investors as a group were not permitted to hold more than 20% of the shares of any Korean firm.[25] But, even where there have been no such formal constraints on foreign equity holdings, investment has been restricted by the costs of accessing overseas markets. There are various actions that may help to cut these access costs. For example, trading costs could be reduced by making it easier for firms to list on overseas exchanges and by deregulating the domestic exchanges. Other (and potentially much larger) costs arise from the difficulties of acquiring information about an overseas market and therefore depend on, among other things, the quality of accounting data and the regulation of trading activity. The growth of specialist country funds suggests that investing through such funds may have helped to economize on the costs of collecting information.[26]

We have stressed the role of short-term bank loans in the Asian crisis. Such short-term loans shift risk from the lender to the borrower, who must take on the uncertainty about the default premium when the loans are rolled over. Therefore, contrary to some recent suggestions, the regulatory authorities who are responsible for the solvency of the *lending* banks have no reason to encourage them to increase the maturity of their interbank loans. However, the regulators for the *borrowing* banks do need to be concerned about both the maturity and currency mismatch of the bank portfolios. Moreover, the heavy sectoral concentration of these loan portfolios and the very high leverage of many corporate borrowers emphasize the need for much stronger supervision of the lending practices of the local banks and of the valuation of their loans.

While there are dangers in abrupt increases in competition, there is a strong case in many developing economies for reducing barriers to entry by foreign banks, which would facilitate direct loans from these banks to corporates rather than by way of the interbank market. Such competition is also likely to be the best antidote to uncommercial lending practices by domestic banks.

Corporations in the crisis countries had not only expanded productive capacity with little regard for prospective returns, but they financed this expansion largely by borrowing. Thus, a relatively small decline in economic activity led to widespread defaults, the cost of which was borne by the banking system. This suggests three further policy aims. The first is to promote greater use of equity finance. Deregulation of the underwriting market can help to reduce the costs of issuing equity, while the supply of equity finance can be enhanced by encouraging foreign equity ownership and by increasing domestic institutional ownership.[27] The second policy aim should be to reduce the *cost* of default by improved bankruptcy procedures. The third is to reduce the *probability* of default by encouraging more efficient hedging. In some cases there already exist efficient hedging instruments. For example, the development of the swap market has provided borrowers with a low-cost way to separate the currency of the loan from their exposure to that currency. The problem therefore was not that the means for hedging were absent, but that Asian corporations and banks were confident that the currency pegs would be maintained and were content to take on the risks of foreign currency borrowing. But currency fluctuations are not the only macro risks that threaten corporations and governments in developing countries. Particularly for governments, which are unable to issue equity explicitly, there is a clear need for them to design debt structures that hedge against the principal risks. There is much talk about involving the private sector in crisis prevention.[28] The greatest potential contribution of commercial and investment banks to crisis prevention would be to devise and market efficient hedging instruments to corporations and governments.

CONCLUSION

Underlying public policy towards international crises is the view that markets are subject to a succession of contagious bubbles and panics, which the authorities can, and should, attempt to ameliorate through intervention. However, significant progress in developing policy will be made only when it is recognized that financial markets generally function well and that international financial institutions have neither the resources nor the superior information to stem the wealth losses that these crises cause. Thus the principal function of the IMF should not be to counteract supposed failures of financial markets by acting as a lender of last resort, but rather to use its ability to impose conditions that would be difficult for private institutions to require.

There has been considerable concern that the primary beneficiaries of IMF assistance are the major international banks, which have been able to avoid the consequences of their imprudent lending and have therefore little reason to be any more prudent in the future. These concerns are almost certainly misplaced. International banking is a competitive activity and there is no reason to suppose that the banks have been able to appropriate to themselves the (very small) subsidy in IMF loans. Nor does the yield and volatility of developing country debt suggest that lenders regard that debt as underwritten by the IMF. Moves to "bail in" private lenders by (say) a moratorium on debt service are likely to be counterproductive, since they are likely to increase the cost of private sector debt and induce banks to exit even more rapidly.

The emphasis of public policy should be on crisis prevention rather than resolution. The Asian crisis was prompted by huge industrial overcapacity and increasing costs, which led to a sharp fall in profitability. This crisis in the real economy showed up in the financial sector in the form of large capital outflows and considerable strains on the domestic banking system. This suggests the need to develop financial structures that can more efficiently distribute risks in the real economy.

A large proportion of foreign capital was in the form of short-term, foreign currency interbank loans. This capital inflow was not only easily reversed but the risks were concentrated in the developing countries' banking system. Where capital consisted of foreign direct investment or equity portfolio investment, capital flows were much more stable and the risk was efficiently pooled with foreign investors.

Unlike equity, debt brings with it the risk of default. This risk, however, is influenced by the structure of the debt. For example, we noted how the risk of changes in the default premium can be reduced by an extension in debt maturities and we showed how structured debt can be used to reduce the risk of default. It is also undesirable that default risk should be borne solely by domestic banks. The pool of lenders can be widened both by encouraging the entry of foreign banks and by securitization of corporate debt.

There are some encouraging signs that some of these changes in financial structure have already been taking place. For example, an increasing proportion of capital inflows into emerging markets has been in the form of foreign direct investment and more of the indirect investment has consisted of bond and equity investment rather than bank loans. Nevertheless there are a number of possible institutional reforms that could help to accelerate these processes.

Notes

1. International Monetary Fund (September 1998).www.imf.org
2. Quoted in *Institute of International Finance* press release April 13, 1999.
3. Jackson (1999).

4. Institute of International Finance (April 1999a).
5. In a profit analysis of financial crises in emerging markets, Radelet and Sachs (1998) find that the ratio of short-term debt to reserves is strongly associated with the onset of a crisis.
6. In 1996 property lending as a percentage of total lending was 25 percent in Malaysia, 20 percent in Indonesia, and 18 percent in Thailand (International Monetary Fund, October 1998).
7. For example, in early 1997 six chaebols filed for bankruptcy (International Monetary Fund, October 1998).
8. See also Sachs (1995).
9. The role of a lender of last resort in preventing liquidity runs was first suggested by Thornton (1802) and developed by Bagehot (1873). A formal model of bank runs is provided by Diamond and Dybvig (1983).
10. For early models of rational cascades see Banerjee (1992) and Welch (1992).
11. It is also sometimes argued that an international lender of last resort is needed to counter attempts at market manipulation or irrational speculation that leads to excess volatility in asset prices.
12. See, for example, Kaufman (1994).
13. The IMF's experience in dealing with crisis situations may also give it an important consultancy role in determining the appropriate policy response.
14. Returns are measured relative to returns on similar assets in a sample of emerging markets. The results of the exercise are similar regardless of whether the announcement date is defined either by a news or press release by the IMF or by press comment that may precede such a release.
15. Share prices of banks with large exposures to emerging markets have also reflected investor concern about potential losses.
16. The agreed contingent credit line scheme envisages that a country will normally have access to between 300% and 500% of its Fund quota.
17. If financial crises are a consequence of fixed exchange rates, then it is arguable that the IMF should abandon its traditional role of providing funds to countries to defend a currency peg. This view was expressed forcefully by Robert Rubin (1999).
18. For a discussion of the role of capital controls see, for example, Dooley (1996) and Eichengreen, Mussa, et al. (1998).
19. For relevant discussions on these issues, see Myers (1998) and Rajan and Zingales (1998).
20. Institute of International Finance (April 1999).
21. While foreign direct investment accounted for about half of private capital inflows into all emerging Asian markets before the crisis, it accounted for only about one-sixth of the private flows to the affected countries. This difference between the liquidity of direct and portfolio investment may go some way towards explaining why some countries were relatively insulated from the shocks that affected other parts of the region. For example, while China shared the problems of a chronically weak banking system, an over-levered corporate sector, excess capacity in many industries, and a sharp expansion of domestic credit, the ratio of foreign direct investment to financial investment in China was substantially higher than in the most affected countries (Lardy 1999). As a result China did not experience the capital outflows of its neighbors.
22. See Merton (1974). Note that this does *not* imply that longer-term debt raises the cost of capital for emerging markets. Capital structure irrelevance propositions are not violated simply by changes in debt maturity.

23. An alternative which would largely eliminate the possibility of moral hazard would be to link payments to a regional equity index.
24. As a result of the capital outflow in 1998 from crisis countries, direct investment rose in that year to 84 percent of net private flows to emerging markets (Institute of International Finance, April 1999).
25. This proportion was increased progressively to 50 percent in December 1997. Restrictions on foreign investment in long-term Korean corporate bonds have been even more severe.
26. Between 1990 and 1995 the number of U.S. country funds increased about fivefold and the assets under management increased from $13 billion to $109 billion (Serra (1999)). For evidence that country funds economize on information costs, see J.A. Frankel and S.L. Schmukler, (1997), "Country Funds and Asymmetric Information," Working paper, Center for International and Development Economics, University of California, Berkeley, May 1997.
27. This is frequently associated with the development of private pension schemes.
28. See, for example, International Monetary Fund (March 1999) and Institute of International Finance (April 12 1999b).

GLOBALISM VS. NATIONALISM VS. E-BUSINESS: THE WORLD DEBATES

Martin Vander Weyer, Mark Landler, and Doug Garr

EUROPE: DESPITE UNIFICATION, LOCAL LAWS MIGHT TAKE THE "E" OUT OF "EU"

In May 1999, Victor Chandler International, Britain's leading independent bookmaker, announced that it was shifting its betting operation from London, England to Gibraltar. British-based horseracing fans would henceforth be able to place their bets by telephone, and in due course via the Internet, without the necessity of paying the 9 percent betting tax that earns Her Majesty's Treasury some £7 billion (about $11 billion) per year. The Ladbrokes division of Hilton P.L.C. and other major British bookmakers rapidly followed with similar online–offshore schemes.

This sudden revolution in the betting business highlights some of the challenges now facing European lawmakers as a result of the rapid advance of e-commerce. Internet trade may suck business toward Europe's low-tax centers, of which Gibraltar is one, but is the best response to be found in tax harmonization across the European

Martin Vander Weyer is associate editor of The Week magazine in London, and a regular commentator on business and economic issues for several British newspapers and magazines. He is author of "Falling Eagle: the Decline of Barclays Bank" to be published by Weidenfeld & Nicolson, London in February 2000. Before becoming a journalist, Mr. Vander Weyer spent 15 years as an international investment banker. Additional research for this article was provided by Simon Nixon.

Union, or in competitive tax cuts and incentives in individual member states? What consumer protection rules, if any, ought to apply to a transaction in which, for example, a French resident bets in Gibraltar on an Irish race through a bookmaker whose ultimate corporate owner is British? What moral issues are raised by a sudden upsurge in low-cost e-gambling? Is it in the public interest for Internet betting traffic to be monitored by regulators—on the watch for money-laundering activity, for example—or would that be an unwarranted invasion of privacy?

The non-European student of such questions might imagine that the European Union—a highly sophisticated "single market" embracing 370 million citizens in 15 countries—is ideal ground for a fertile and orderly multinational marketplace in e-commerce. But most Europeans would greet that assumption with a cynical shrug. New car prices (fixed by manufacturers) vary by more than 40 percent between Britain and the rest of the E.U.; Britain and France have recently engaged in a ferocious fight over France's refusal to allow the import of British beef, and a dozen uncoordinated national air traffic control systems cause daily havoc for airline passengers. In the field of technology, Europe cannot even agree on a common design for a domestic electrical plug.

The E.U.'s worst-kept secret is that it is a continent of thinly disguised (and sometimes wholly undisguised) national protectionism; of no common language; of widely differing legal and consumer cultures and attitudes toward privacy, and of elaborate trade legislation arrived at by grindingly slow negotiation and imposed with varying degrees of vigor in different member states.

But there have been many points of progress as well, most significantly in the January 1999 launch of the euro, and the growth in cross-border mergers—in oil, steel, aerospace, telecommunications and other sectors. At the most practical level, Europe now has well-developed, competitively priced distribution services—run by the likes of D.H.L., T.N.T. and the Dutch Post Office—which ease the logistics of long-distance shopping. So it would be wrong to imply that there is no hope for a coordinated European e-commerce regime. In fact there is everything to play for, and the game has barely begun.

Even the most cursory survey of legislative proposals and market patterns reveals two things. First, how far Europe still is from being a true single market; second, how different the European and United States markets are in every respect other than their massive size. And to take full advantage of the potential of e-commerce, European governments must also learn to embrace some foreign concepts: legislative minimalism and self-regulation. Each new technical advance does not require a new law. European consumers need to accept the concept of shopping across distant borders. And to do so, they need to be persuaded that their rights as consumers are internationally protected in a way that can be easily and inexpensively tested in court.

Until recently, Europe trailed far behind the United States in its use of, and enthusiasm for, the Internet. Britons may cross the English Channel in large numbers to buy cheap booze in France, but European consumers in general have barely begun to appreciate the possibilities of cross-border cyber-shopping, or the power of the new medium to drive prices downward.

Awareness of the Internet's possibilities has increased markedly in the past year, however. Europe's stock-market analysts, business columnists and even gossip columnists talk of little else: British I.P.O.'s such as Freeserve and QXL have been many times oversubscribed, and Frankfurt's Neuer Markt has become the fashionable continental bourse for smaller high-tech stocks. New e-millionaires abound, particularly in Britain, with the likes of 26-year-old Martha Lane Fox (whose £6 million, or $9.5 million, business, lastminute.com, has been valued at £400 million, or $640 million) becoming instant celebrities. (Ironically, one of Britain's most successful e-pioneers, Planet Online founder Paul Sykes, is also one of its most vociferous anti-European political campaigners—proof that the idea of the Internet as a force for European integration has yet to catch on.)

The excitement generated by such names has everything to do with the phenomenal rates of growth anticipated for e-commerce businesses. Only 10 percent of European citizens use the Web today (according to British government figures) and total European e-commerce is estimated (by Andersen Consulting) at $19 billion, around 20 percent of the United States figure; by 2003, European e-commerce could reach $430 billion, or 60 percent of United States levels; 50 percent of Europeans will be Web users by 2006.

Across Europe, the pattern of e-commerce development has varied a great deal country by country. Scandinavians, for example, are early adopters, driven partly by the excellence of indigenous manufacturers such as Ericsson of Sweden and the Nokia Corporation of Finland, and already rival Americans in terms of Internet usage per capita. France, on the other hand, has been slow to take to the Web, partly because of linguistic resistance and partly because 70 percent of French households are already equipped with the less-sophisticated Minitel information terminals, and are reluctant to switch. Germany leads the European field in its share of global Internet use, with 15.5 percent of non-United States Internet traffic, compared to 6.6 percent in Britain and only 3.8 percent in France. Despite Germany's lead, it is severely held back by the restrictiveness of its consumer protection laws.

Legislators across the E.U. know that action is required to keep up with developments. But can they cope with the speed of changes in technology and devise a system that facilitates growth in trade rather than driving it toward less restrictive regimes? One of the vital differences, highlighted by Richard O'Neill of the British Department of Trade & Industry's e-commerce unit, is between those governments that see e-commerce as an economic opportunity to be developed, and those that see it merely as a legislative challenge to be brought under control. Britain and Ireland are firmly in the first category; Germany and France are, so far, firmly in the second.

The E.U.'s first attempt to resolve these questions was not encouraging: The draft E-Commerce directive first published in May 1998 provoked outrage because it proposed that e-businesses should comply with the protection laws of each country they sell to, and that each consumer should have the right to sue those businesses in the consumer's home country. This overturned the rule-of-origin convention at the heart of the single-market structure, which allows a business that complies with its home-country consumer-protection laws to trade anywhere in the E.U. It also interferes with Brussels Convention rules on jurisdiction in commercial disputes.

Consumer groups welcomed the proposals, which they argued agreed with a little-used section of the rule-of-origin convention, according to which consumers are allowed to sue in their own home country if sales were targeted there. But industry lobbyists (including the European employers' federation, U.N.I.C.E.) were horrified by the proposition, which would require mail-order businesses to cope with 15 different jurisdictions—a minefield for suppliers. In Germany, for example, heavy discounting is illegal except at specified times of year (in rules designed to protect neighborhood stores), and two-for-one offers and lifetime guarantees are banned. The American Express Corporation is currently locked in a tussle about its ability to offer the same customer loyalty deals to German cardholders that it offers to consumers in the rest of the world.

Hearings (involving no fewer than 400 parties) were convened in November 1999 to re-examine the issues exposed by the draft E.U. directive. But there are still deep concerns about the underlying approach. "These changes could nullify the whole spirit of the Internet," Brussels-based lawyer Michael Pullen told the Financial Times. The thinking behind them is "10 years out of date," according to a British Conservative member of the European parliament, Michael Harbour. "We're in an entirely new era and we're asking all the wrong questions. Speed and openness are the keys to e-commerce legislation. The only practical solution is through self-regulation."

That message has perhaps its best chance of being taken to heart in Britain, where Tony Blair's Labour government is eager to advertise its business-friendly credentials. "Information is the key to the modern age," Mr. Blair declared recently. "The prize of this new age is to engage our country fully in the ambition and opportunity which the digital revolution offers." In keeping with Labour's rebranding of Britain as a modern, creative economy, the target is to become "the world's best environment for electronic commerce" by 2002. Mr. Blair has appointed an e-ambassador, Alex Allan, and an e-minister, Patricia Hewitt, who speaks of "our desire to build the knowledge economy." Britain's advantages include the English language; the most competitive, liberalized telecommunications market in Europe, and the free-flowing capital markets of the City of London. In the past, the City has not always been good at providing seed capital for high-tech startups, but Europe's venture capital industry is now firmly centered in London and increasingly focused on Internet opportunities. British recipients accounted for almost half of all funds invested by members of the European Venture Capital Association in 1998.

Britain hopes to attract e-commerce by providing advanced skills and infrastructure. Policies such as a computer loan scheme for low-income families, and computer training for all age groups, are designed to familiarize the entire British population with the Internet. But a legislative framework is urgently required, and the Blair administration's first tentative steps at one ran into fierce criticism—this time from civil libertarians rather than trade bodies. At the core of the forthcoming electronic communications bill, promoted by Ms. Hewitt, are provisions to recognize electronic signatures and digital certificates, which verify that signatures and users match. Earlier drafts, however, included controversial police powers (all the more provocative for having been proposed by Labour politicians who would traditionally have opposed such intrusions) to unscramble encoded e-mail or demand the handing over of private encryption keys.

This is not a simple debate. As has been extensively argued in the United States, unmonitored encryption protects pornographers, terrorists and money-launderers. But state interference in private communication smacked too much of Big Brother for the vociferous defenders of British civil liberties, who argued that it contravenes, among other things, the right to silence and the right against self-incrimination. Caspar Bowden of the Foundation for Information Policy Research said that the government is being "bludgeoned back from the preposterous position" it first adopted on these issues. But the measures are in fact due to reappear in the slightly different form of a Home Office bill on investigatory powers, which will reignite the row.

So the British and European legislative framework for e-commerce is still in its infancy, and there are large areas yet to be tackled. These include the full gamut of data protection and privacy issues. Under the European Convention on Human Rights, for example, employees are entitled to e-mail privacy; yet employers are regarded in law as the publishers of their employees' e-mails, and—as test cases against companies such as Norwich Union P.L.C. and British Gas have established—can be held legally responsible for their content.

The liabilities of Internet service providers for the content they transmit have also yet to be determined, although again there have been test cases in both Britain and France of holding I.S.P.'s responsible for material passing through their systems. Copyright presents peculiar difficulties, because in some European countries it is automatic, while in others it is established only by registration; the development of MP3 technology, enabling high-quality music recordings to be downloaded from the Internet, brings new urgency to the question of copyright protection. The issue of censorship raises its head not only in relation to different national standards on sexual pornography, but also in the case of books like Hitler's "Mein Kampf," which has been banned in Germany since World War II, yet is now selling briskly to German buyers through Amazon.com in the United States.

Which European countries achieve leadership in e-commerce depends not only on the intelligent resolution of these esoteric matters, but also on taxes. There is broad agreement that sales taxes should apply at local rates at the point of supply, but (as the Gibraltar bookmaking example demonstrates) there are many other wrinkles to be exploited. Capturing taxes on the profits of e-commerce entrepreneurs whose servers can be located anywhere in the world is an altogether bigger challenge. E-commerce patterns across Europe may well be driven in this early phase by differences in tax treatment, and Ireland has already grabbed the advantage by instituting a 12 percent tax rate for Internet businesses (compared to a standard rate of 28 percent for other Irish businesses, and rates of 30 percent-plus across most of Europe). The British government has ruled out such specific incentives, but has hedged its bets by introducing capital gains tax cuts and R&D allowances that are designed to appeal directly to Web entrepreneurs.

As ever, it will be the entrepreneurs and consumers who set the pace in European e-commerce development, and the governments that trail behind. E.U. official Paul Timmers spoke recently of "the clock ticking away" as European governments decided whether "to enter the Digital Economy with conviction." The existing structure of Europe's single market ought to provide an ideal framework for borderless e-commerce. But in the real world, the expectation must be that Brussels will belabor the task, loading the e-commerce sector with unworkable rules that, in due course, will have to be taken apart and reconstructed in a more rational way. In the meantime, one consultant warned, legislative obstacles and failures of coordination could reduce E.U. e-commerce potential by as much as one-third.

The biggest risk is not that business will be lost to European tax havens, but that it will be lost to the E.U. altogether. The spoils will go only to those European nations with the most enlightened combination of business incentives and the lightest touch in legislation.

ASIA-PACIFIC: IN CHINA, MALAYSIA AND SINGAPORE, FREEDOM AND CONTROL DANCE A DIGITAL MINUET

On a recent cloudless morning in Hong Kong, ABN Amro Bank N.V. gathered several hundred of its Asian customers together to present a new range of e-commerce services for conglomerates, multinationals, manufacturers and trading companies. The mood in the hotel ballroom was as sunny as the skies outside.

The bank's executives noted that the global market for e-commerce was projected to grow from $43 billion in 1998 to $1.3 trillion in 2003. Much of that growth would be generated in Asia, the world's most populous continent, which is projected to comprise an e-commerce market worth $32 billion by 2003.

Politics scarcely intruded. Francis Kong, a senior vice president and e-commerce expert at ABN Amro, dismissed worries about state interference in the development of e-commerce. "A lot of Asian countries talk about controlling the Internet, but I think it's impossible," he said.

But Mr. Kong's remark pointed out one of the biggest perils of Asian electronic commerce. With geographically vast, untapped markets like China and Indonesia, Asia is potentially a Valhalla for Internet-based business. But its growth might easily be hobbled by governments that are deeply ambivalent about the prospect of opening their economies and political systems to the free flow of goods and information.

In order to develop and thrive, e-commerce must jump several hurdles, which, while not unique to the region, are nonetheless more pronounced there. One of the most formidable hurdles is the difficulty in setting transactions, since relatively few Asians use credit cards. Another potential obstacle is the prevalence of piracy in computer software and CD's—products that are often sold through the Internet. And, given the region's vast geographical expanse, e-commerce entrepreneurs must find a way of distributing their products across Asia.

Mark Landler has been the Hong Kong bureau chief of The New York Times since March 1998. He covers economics and politics in Greater China and Southeast Asia, ranging from Beijing, China to Jakarta, Indonesia. Before that, Mr. Landler was a business reporter for The Times in New York, covering media and telecommunications, and media editor of Business Week magazine. Mr. Landler is a 1987 graduate of Georgetown University and was a Reuter Fellow at Oxford University.

On paper, at least, Asia will attract e-merchants for the same reason it attracts sellers of cameras, cars and laundry detergent. It is home to half the world's population—2.7 billion people, many of whom are young and have rising incomes. Internet usage, while still behind that of the United States and Europe, is growing at an amazing rate. By 2003, Asia will have 63 million Internet users—a compound annual growth rate of 40 percent since 1997, according to the International Data Corporation.

Asia's combination of infant industries and enormous population has led to eye-popping e-commerce growth projections: According to I.D.C., China's e-commerce will generate $3.8 billion in revenue by 2003, up from $8 million in 1998. South Korea will generate $4.9 billion, compared to $57 million in 1998. And Taiwan's market will be worth $2.8 billion, up from $45 million in 1998.

In the wake of the recent Asian economic crisis, many of the region's leaders view the Internet—and e-commerce—as the road that will take them back from the brink of economic ruin. In order to develop reputations as technology-friendly countries, they are scrambling to build technology parks, attract foreign investors and wire their cities for electronic communication. As always in Asia, grand projects and aggressive state involvement are the order of the day.

In Malaysia, for instance, Prime Minister Mahathir Mohamad recently inaugurated the Multimedia Supercorridor, a 750-square-kilometer swath of land south of Kuala Lumpur, which is meant to be an instant Silicon Valley. In Hong Kong, a local property tycoon is building a more intimate technology park on 64 acres overlooking the harbor. Singapore plans to construct a $2.9 billion Science Hub that will host local and foreign technology companies, as well as a university.

Several Asian countries, notably Singapore, have also pledged to create fully wired societies—giving all their citizens access to broadband communications, including wide access to e-commerce opportunities. Hong Kong recently went so far as to make information technology the centerpiece of its economic recovery strategy.

Despite these ambitious future plans, at present the Asia–Pacific region trails the Western world in Internet usage, and is even farther behind when it comes to e-commerce. I.D.C. estimated that the region's entire market for e-commerce was only $700 million in 1998. More than 60 percent of that came from Australia, which has a well-developed e-commerce market, primarily in consumer services like travel and subscriptions to magazines and online news services.

Furthermore, Asia is not a homogeneous market. It varies widely by language, culture, literacy and wealth. Singapore's wired society has little in common with the Sumatran villages of neighboring Indonesia. Hong Kong's nascent cyberport is worlds away from the rusting industrial ports of mainland China. Although China and India are far and away the largest markets in Asia by population, I.D.C. forecasts that they will trail Australia and South Korea in e-commerce revenue even in 2003.

How Asian governments regulate the Internet will also differ from country to country. Many regimes—including historically suspicious ones like the Chinese Communist Party—profess to welcome the Internet. And while no Asian country has prohibited online services so far, the leaders' public positions are notoriously unreliable; what sounds fine in principle may prove nettlesome in practice. As the Internet begins to have a political impact in Asian countries, the policies of the various regimes will shift—and in some cases harden.

The advent of e-commerce has revived an old debate in Asia: globalism versus nationalism. While Asian governments are eager for global markets—and the accompanying foreign capital, technology and trade—they remain loath to accept the necessary byproducts of openness, transparency and accountability. Indeed, during the Asian financial crisis, the countries that maintained or erected barriers to the global economy, like China and Malaysia, fared better than those that, like Thailand and Indonesia, left their markets open. These successes may fuel isolationists in the regime who hope to reap the Internet's benefits without opening up their economies to a freer flow of goods, labor, content and information.

Perhaps no country better illustrates the subtle balance between globalism and nationalism than China, where President Jiang Zemin has declared the Internet one of the nation's most powerful growth engines. Beijing has watched as dozens of American Internet companies have rushed into the country to invest in Web startups. E-commerce companies are beginning to overcome Chinese consumers' fears about buying online.

China's largest e-commerce company, 8848.net, recently announced that its revenue had nearly quadrupled to 8.2 million renminbi (about $1 million) during the latest three-month period. The company—which sells personal computers, scanners, books and office equipment—won a $30 million investment from the International Data Group, the parent of market research company I.D.C. Its name, 8848.net, refers to the height (in meters) of Mount Everest, and the company indeed seems headed for the pinnacle of China's cyber-world.

And 8848.net is only one of a thousand cyber-flowers blooming in today's China. American Internet heavyweights like America Online, Yahoo and Intel are lining up to underwrite Internet service providers, portals and e-commerce companies with names like Sohu.com and Sina.com. China.com, a Hong Kong–based I.S.P., recently joined NASDAQ in one of the year's most successful initial public offerings.

But China's bright prospects may be dampened by political realities. Just as China's Internet business was heating up this year, Wu Jichuan, the powerful Minister of Information Industries, reminded outsiders that foreign investment in China's Internet business was, strictly speaking, illegal. Although Beijing had turned a blind eye to foreign investments, Mr. Wu threatened to enforce the law. His new guidelines on foreign investment will be issued by the end of 1999.

Prospective Internet investors were cheered by the landmark 1999 trade agreement between China and the United States, which seems likely to force Mr. Wu into a more open stance. China currently bars foreign companies from distributing products in its domestic market. The United States—China trade deal may prove to be a breakthrough in distribution as well. As part of the agreement, China has agreed to allow American companies to gain distribution rights over a three-year period. As it seeks a seat in the World Trade Organization, China will no doubt extend those rights to other nations. But until these major legal impediments are worked out, the cyber-speculators are staying on the sidelines.

Entrepreneurs and venture capitalists contend that China cannot afford to slam the door on foreign involvement in the Internet. The promise is too great, the development too rapid and the spread of the Net too insidious for the authorities in Beijing to control it, they say. Other China-watchers, however, note that it is precisely the anarchic nature of the Internet that is unsettling to the regime.

If there was any doubt about the Internet's potency as a tool of political protest in China, it was demolished during the crackdown on the Falun Gong, a spiritual and exercise movement outlawed by the government. Despite a vitriolic propaganda campaign against the movement, Beijing was unable to prevent it from using the Internet to spread news about the repression throughout the country and the world.

Even strict business uses of the Internet may meet difficulties in Asia. In China, e-commerce companies must apply for licenses to sell products, and in the current political atmosphere, it is difficult to imagine the government making it easier for foreign companies to participate in the e-commerce business. And with the regime concerned about internal uses of the Net, even home-grown players may find themselves stifled.

The picture is brighter, however, in other Asian countries. Singapore, Thailand, Malaysia and the Philippines have all drafted laws to accelerate the development of e-commerce. For instance, each has passed legislation that gives legal standing to electronic contracts and digital signatures—both of which are crucial for reliable business-to-business online transactions.

Hong Kong has followed suit. There, the government has sought to jump-start e-commerce through a program called Electronic Service Delivery, which will eventually deliver government documents, such as permit applications and income tax forms, over the Internet. Though Hong Kong reverted to Chinese sovereignty in 1997, the former British colony retains control over most of its regulations and remains one of Asia's freest economies.

There are a number of Nationalist tendencies in Asian countries that might create inhospitable conditions for e-commerce. In Singapore, for example, the government strictly prohibits pornography on the Internet. Although it has relaxed its regulations on businesses over the last two years, its repressive political climate could affect the distribution of Internet content of all kinds.

As part of the Malaysian government's effort to attract foreign technology companies to the Multimedia Supercorridor, it has pledged to allow the unfettered flow of information on the Internet. Still, the government has been alarmed by the ability of its opponents to use the Internet to bypass the country's compliant, pro-government news media. Anwar Ibrahim, the deputy prime minister who was ousted by Dr. Mahathir in September 1998, and later convicted of corruption and sex-related charges, became a political martyr in large part because his supporters circulated news about his plight on the Internet. According to government critics, their online activism is now monitored.

But Malaysia's economic policies may trouble prospective Internet investors even more than its political policies. Last fall, the government imposed sweeping controls over its currency and capital markets. Dr. Mahathir claimed that the move was necessary to thwart foreign currency speculators from attacking Malaysia's currency. Be that as it may, these controls also locked foreign investment capital in the country. Malaysia now claims the unorthodox policy was a success with the economy recovering and investors returning. But Malaysia's readiness to throw up barriers to the outside world is unsettling for those who want to sell products through the global marketplace of the Internet.

UNITED STATES: A PRESIDENTIAL CAMPAIGN TESTS THE E-BUSINESS INFLUENCE OF SILICON VALLEY AND BIG LABOR

For the moment, most Internet transactions begin in the United States. Whether the United States can maintain its formidable lead in the virtual space race will depend on whether a Republican or Democrat enters the White House in January 2001. Even more, it depends on which Republican or Democrat is elected. When it comes to such front-line issues as taxation and trade (and such secondary economic areas as immigration quotas and tort reform), the subtle differences between the various Presidential candidates' positions will have starkly different implications for the future of electronic commerce.

Economists of every political stripe generally agree that e-business is good for the United States economy, and that this is an opportunity that we can't afford to botch by too much—or too little—government intervention. But politically, e-business could foment the kind of passionate debate that both NAFTA and GATT did during President Bill Clinton's first administration. As with those international trade agreements, regulation of the Digital Economy raises several important questions: Will a laissez-faire government policy further expand the growth of e-business beyond the country's borders? At what expense to the American economy and its workers will this growth take place?

The 1998 Tax Freedom Act, which legislated a national moratorium on taxing Internet goods and services, is scheduled to expire in 2001. With $31 billion in domestic e-business revenues projected for that year, a lot is riding on who will be in the White House shaping the successor policy. Will the Internet become a world-transforming engine, or will it sputter because bureaucrats are eager to tap a new revenue stream? Beyond questions of taxation, other Internet issues will arise in this election, such as immigration policies that will determine whether or not labor-starved Web enterprises will be allowed to hire necessary workers from abroad.

The early front-runners, Democrat Vice President Al Gore and Republican George W. Bush, governor of Texas, have been courted aggressively by Information Age business interests. In return, the candidates have sought support within the nation's high-tech corridors. By advocating an aggressive free-market position, Bush has received considerable backing from groups that have traditionally supported the Democrats.

Doug Garr is author of "IBM Redux: Lou Gerstner and the Business Turnaround of the Decade" (HarperCollins Publishers, 1999). Previously, he was an aide to New York Governor Mario Cuomo.

Gore also has an open-trade philosophy, although he is slightly more sympathetic than the Republicans to government intervention and regulation. Although Gore dazzled the digerati with his ease with the technological culture—he was the first vice president to use a laptop—some economists believe Gore is less predictable than Bush when it comes to e-business issues. For instance, the Clinton Administration faltered when it initially resisted legislation in two areas high-tech industrialists considered crucial: limiting Y2K liability and expanding the number of high-tech immigration visas. Although the Administration eventually capitulated on both, its hesitation gave some high-tech power brokers reason to wonder just how friendly Gore would be.

Former Senator Bill Bradley is even more of an unknown quantity. After leaving the Senate in 1996, he spent a year at Stanford University making the rounds of Silicon Valley high-tech luminaries. John Roos, a Silicon Valley attorney and a longtime Bradley supporter and fundraiser, is convinced Bradley understands the culture. "He'll do what's best for the Valley economy," said Mr. Roos. Some economists, however, wonder whether his liberal reputation on social and labor issues might make him less sympathetic to business interest than Gore.

Republicans who are heavily vested in the Information Age will likely favor Senator John McCain, who is even more supportive of open markets than Bush. Some multinational corporations, including the Motorola Corporation and the Boeing Company, applauded his fight against the use of unilateral trade sanctions to achieve foreign policy goals. As chairman of the Senate Commerce Committee, McCain led the fight to regulate the telecommunications industry when he crafted the ambitious Telecommunications Act of 1996. Later, he said the bill hadn't gone far enough in deregulating the telecommunications marketplace and opening up the competition. As cable, telephony and the Internet become more interdependent, Senator McCain's knowledge of the federal regulatory bureaucracy in these areas would benefit him and the industries enormously.

On the opposite end of the spectrum from McCain is Reform Party candidate Pat Buchanan, who is skeptical of the benefits of e-business. Robert Crandall, a economist at The Brookings Institution, worries that Buchanan would "want to tax the New Economy to keep the old economy alive."

Although Buchanan has not stated his e-business views in a any position papers, his spoken remarks offer a few clues. In a 1998 speech entitled "Free Trade Is Not Free," Buchanan compared the global economy to the unicorn, characterizing both as mythical beasts who exist only in the imagination. "Free trade does not explain our prosperity; free trade explains the economic insecurity that is the worm in the apple of our prosperity," he said.

Stephan Moore, director of fiscal policy studies at the Cato Institute, believes Buchanan "would be a disaster" for the New Economy. Others agree. Alan Reynolds, director of economic research at the Hudson Institute, labeled Buchanan the "ultimate trade warrior," a pure isolationist who would not want goods coming across the nation's borders—a position sure to displease e-business leaders.

In sum, although Bush and Gore both tend toward moderate views, high-tech entrepreneurs are slightly more comfortable with Bush. They'd prefer McCain over either front runner, however, because they believe he understands their industry best. Bradley has built a small core of loyal support in Silicon Valley because he sounds appropriately libertarian on business issues while maintaining a liberal, Democratic view on social issues. Buchanan, on the other hand, is anathema. And Republican upstart Steve Forbes is an enigma: scion of a business-magazine company that has historically favored open trade, but openly courting the right-wing, isolationist constituency that might otherwise back Buchanan.

At this point in the campaign, most candidates want to keep their options open and are reluctant to specify their e-business policies. Still, some real differences have already emerged when they have been pressed about the most significant domestic issues: taxation, trade restriction, immigration, labor law, tort reform and antitrust (especially the fate of the government's suit against the Microsoft Corporation).

TAXATION

The most visible e-business issue is whether to tax goods and services sold on the Internet. Every candidate except Buchanan currently endorses the 1998 Tax Freedom Act, which placed a three-year moratorium on state and local taxes on Internet transactions. These positions reflect political expediency, which may fade after Election Day. "There's a reason why this moratorium expires after election—because nobody wanted to deal with it," said Aaron Lukas, trade policy analyst at the Cato Institute. Indeed, there is a good chance we will see such a tax imposed during the next administration, no matter who wins the Presidency. A recent study by Ernst & Young showed that state and local governments are losing $170 million in potential tax revenues each year because of the Internet. The National Governors Association favors a tax on Internet goods and services that would be determined by the product's point of origin (the same way catalogue sales are taxed).

In a speech to the Washington Council on International Trade, Gore argued that "we must fight to keep the Internet a global free-trading zone, and establish a permanent moratorium on tariffs in cyberspace." Bradley currently opposes a Net tax, but has left his options open. "I think that it's too early to make a judgment about what the Internet is actually going to become, and you don't want to stifle it at this stage," he said. Bush also favors the e-tax moratorium, a position that puts him at odds with his fellow governors. McCain is the most vociferous opponent of any Internet tax. In fact, he believes the moratorium should be extended to include "all the ramifications of taxing sales of goods across state and international boundaries," he said in a recent Senate speech.

LABOR AND IMMIGRATION

Most high-tech jobs cannot be filled with untrained American workers. There are now approximately 346,000 American job vacancies for computer programmers, systems analysts, computer scientists and engineers. Yet every year, many thousands of foreign students earn advanced degrees from American universities in fields related to these occupations, and then return home because their student visas run out. This shortage of high-tech labor will become a major political issue in the next few years.

High-tech entrepreneurs are disappointed that Clinton has been reluctant to relax visa restrictions. Most Silicon Valley immigrants fall into a visa category known as H-1B. The New Democratic Caucus has pushed hard to raise the 65,000-worker limit of H-1B foreigners to 105,000, and Congressional Democrats have proposed legislation to issue special "T" visas for the technology industry job openings paying $60,000 a year or more. In 1998, the Clinton Administration initially opposed the H-1B visa bill because it feared it would cost Americans jobs. "That really alienated a lot of the people in the high-tech industry, even though Clinton ultimately signed the bill," according to Rob Atkinson, the director of technology and the New Economy project at the liberal Progressive Policy Institute. Gore still has not distanced himself from this position on visas.

Bush and Gore both are willing to increase immigrant labor to relieve immediate shortages, but neither encourages it as much as McCain, who has vowed to double the number of H-1B visas to more than 200,000. Only Buchanan wants to close American borders to foreign workers. Bradley has not yet weighed in, although some economists feel he would be sympathetic to high-tech employers despite his pro-labor overtures.

TRADE

While all the candidates support free trade, they each have different approaches to achieving it. Bush is not quite as evangelical as McCain when it comes to easing export sanctions, but he understands that software, backbone equipment and other technology related to e-business growth has to be exported and imported with as few restrictions as possible. A Bush position paper states that "there has been too little opportunity for America's high-tech exporters to make their case about what should be restricted and what should not. As president, Governor Bush will fix the . . . system by developing a tough-minded, common sense export control policy that significantly narrows the scope of restrictions on commercial products, while building walls around technologies of the highest sensitivity." If Bush were elected, one would expect the international doors to commerce to be opened wide, unless there were a compelling foreign-policy crisis. Presumably, the Bush Administration would be as horrified as Clinton's was by the International Business Machine Corporation's illegal sales of supercomputers that ended up in Russian nuclear labs. (I.B.M. was fined by the federal government in 1998 and paid the maximum penalty for violating export laws.)

Either Democratic candidate—Gore or Bradley—would probably be tougher than any Republican on Internet trade restrictions. High-tech executives were relieved last September when they finally won the battle to get the Clinton Administration to advocate relaxing export controls on encryption products.

The capital gains tax is also a hot-button issue. Although many established information-based companies rely on federal funding for research and development, the venture capitalists who fund high-tech startups rely on the benefits of the capital gains tax rate. According to the National Venture Capital Association, individual investors typically provide more than 90 percent of startup capital for small companies. Congress lowered the capital gains tax rate from 50 percent to 28 percent in 1978, and to 20 percent in 1980. Many in the wired world want it reduced further. The Cato Institute's Stephan Moore predicts that Gore would favor the status quo regarding capital gains, while Bradley might increase the rate. The Republicans, he said, particularly Bush, would likely lower the rate, perhaps to 15 percent.

On research and development, the Republicans probably will shy away from federal support. Federal R&D spending has suffered cuts over the past decade; the trend could continue. "I predict a significant cut in federal support for R&D if Bush gets elected," said the Progressive Policy Institute's Rob Atkinson.

TORT REFORM

Litigation, especially tort reform legislation, is one issue where Bush and Gore have clear differences. "Gore's in a ticklish spot," said Mr. Crandall of The Brookings Institution. "On the one hand, he wants to court high-tech companies, and on the other, he doesn't want to alienate the plaintiff's bar, which is a huge contributor to his party. Whereas Bush doesn't have that conflict; there's no way the plaintiff's bar is ever going to support him." Indeed, as governor, Bush signed a well-publicized tort reform bill, limiting corporate liability for Texas businesses—which include Dell, Texas Instruments, Compaq and CompUSA. Bradley has not stated a position here, and Buchanan has been silent as well.

While the Clinton Administration signed a bill limiting corporate liability on Y2K mishaps, it did so reluctantly. "Now, there's the sense that with Bush, you don't have to worry about that stuff," said the Progressive Policy Institute's Mr. Atkinson. McCain pushed hard for passage of the Y2K act, which gives big business yet another reason to support him.

Another potentially litigious issue is privacy protection. Electronic networks ease the sharing of sensitive personal medical and financial data. Although every candidate respects the right to privacy, the balance between personal privacy and new technology has yet to be struck. For the most part, the Presidential candidates have remained silent on the question. "Gore is eager to tinker with the system, while Bush is more inclined to rely on market forces," said Gregg Sidak, an economist with the American Enterprise Institute for Public Policy Research.

ANTITRUST

Unless the Microsoft Corporation and the United States Justice Department reach a settlement during the next few months, the new president will have to confront the issue of monopolistic business practices. In this case, he (all the leading candidates are male) will be repeating history: Nixon was consumed with the I.T.T. antitrust case in 1968, and Reagan was faced with the protracted I.B.M. suit in 1982. (Both presidents pressured their Justice Department to withdraw the cases.)

There is little doubt that the Microsoft case will influence the debate over whether government intervention stifles high-tech creativity. Speculation that Bush would withdraw the Justice Department suit against Microsoft was fueled when he addressed a group of high-tech executives in October and promised them less interference from Washington. He would "always take the side of innovation over litigation," he said in a not-so-oblique reference to key language used during the suit's proceedings.

Given his position as vice president, Gore is, understandably, supporting the status quo. Just weeks after the Justice Department ruled in favor of the government, Gore visited the Microsoft campus in Redmond, Washington to campaign among employees and did not fare well during a spirited Q&A session. Yet despite hostility in Redmond, Gore's position in Silicon Valley is solid, especially among the many companies that agree that Microsoft has been a predatory monopolist that needs to be reined in.

PENDING LEGISLATION

Whoever does become the next president will have to shape a national e-commerce policy on a domestic as well as a global scale. At home, he will have to decide whether to sign the flurry of Internet bills that were hammered out during the waning days of the Clinton Administration. Already legislation has been written to restrict Internet gambling, authorize digital signatures, outlaw Internet sales of guns and alcohol, and regulate consumer privacy and the spread of junk e-mail. Since most of this legislation was created piecemeal, the next Administration will have to shape a consistent e-business policy.

Internationally, the next president will have to manage the ongoing negotiations that began at the recent, tumultuous World Trade Organization meeting in Seattle. American negotiators are hoping to achieve four e-commerce related goals during this round of trade talks: a moratorium on Internet tariffs, a basic set of rules regulating e-commerce trade, an agreement to refrain from excessive e-commerce regulation, and an agreement to treat products in the electronic world in the same way they are treated in the real world. With the largest investment in Internet-related businesses, no country—or president—will have a greater stake in influencing the future of e-commerce.

BUSINESS ETHICS ACROSS CULTURES: A SOCIAL COGNITIVE MODEL

Alexander D. Stajkovic and Fred Luthans

As globalization becomes a reality, today's multinational corporations (MNCs) face a growing challenge of adapting effectively to different cultures. Emerging with global competitiveness are new alliances and management practices that require increased interaction from employees working in different cultures. Paying attention to cultural variations is important because the potential for costly misconceptions and errors substantially increases when international managers interact with foreign partners whose values, beliefs, and behavioral patterns are different from their own. However, if these are well understood and properly managed, cultural diversity can lead to more flexible adaptations and more successful global business practices. Paralleling the interest in comparative international management in general has been the quest for the better understanding of business ethics across cultures.

Although there is general agreement that ethical business conduct enhances chances of organizational success, MNCs still face the challenge of how to determine what constitutes ethical conduct in different countries simply because what is ethically "right" and "wrong" is culturally determined (Adler, 1997). If MNCs are to develop ethical business practices contingent and sensitive to cultural differences, a better understanding of the factors contributing to ethical standards and the impact that ethical behaviors have on subsequent standards and conduct becomes critical. To date, little effort has been given to the development of a conceptual framework for the identification and analysis of such factors and their relationships. The purpose of this article is to fill

Alexander D. Stajkovic, Department of Management and Systems, Washington State University, Pullman, WA 99164-4736 <alexs@wsu.edu>. Fred Luthans, Department of Management, University of Nebraska, Lincoln, NE 68588-0491 <fluthans@unlinfo.unl.edu>.

this void by proposing a social cognitive model of business ethics that can begin to help international managers better understand how business ethics is perceived and conducted across cultures.

BACKGROUND

Although business ethics has been given considerable attention in the last two decades, the field is still lacking agreement in terms of both theoretical background (Trevino & Weaver, 1993; Werhane, 1994) or research methods used to explore ethics and ethical decision making (Randall & Gibson, 1990). Traditionally, the field of business ethics has been dominated by a philosophical perspective which has depended greatly upon normative concepts and qualitative methods (Donaldson, 1982; Gauthier, 1986). Although most business ethics scholars would agree that a philosophical approach has contributed to the theoretical foundation, the problem is that the philosophical normative concepts have largely not been grounded in nor related to existing business practices.

The philosophical approach to business ethics has recently been extended by the development of several specific models suggesting relationships between key variables and ethical behaviors. These models have been based either on the general assumptions of ethical theories such as utilitarianism, rights of justice, and differential association (Ferrell & Gresham, 1985), or on broad concepts from humanistic psychology such as moral development (Jones, 1991; Trevino, 1986), and even theological foundations (Hunt & Vitell, 1986). In the meantime, researchers from management and marketing have been struggling to interpret how the proposed ethical constructs from disciplines in the humanities relate and transfer to more specific organizational and more recently cultural environments in different countries (Akaah & Riordan, 1989; Becker & Fritzsche, 1987).

Our model shown in Figure 1 goes beyond the philosophically based ethics models and offers an alternative. Based on social cognitive theory (Bandura, 1986; Wood & Bandura, 1989), the model shows the interacting relationships believed to uniquely influence business ethical standards and conduct across cultures. The intent of this model is to provide a conceptual framework that identifies and relates comprehensive key factors with explanatory properties leading to propositions.

The major premise of Bandura's social cognitive theory is that human action is determined by the triadic interaction among the specific environment (e.g, institutional factors), person (e.g, personal factors), and behavior itself (e.g., organizational actions) all within a particular social context (e.g., national culture). Besides Bandura's perspective of the triadic interaction of antecedent variables, the consequence side of our model draws from Skinner's operant behaviorism, Thorndike's classic law of effect (for a summary of this behavioral approach see Luthans & Kreitner, 1985; Stajkovic & Luthans, in press), and the recent research concerning feedback-standard discrepancy reduction (Carver & Scheier, 1981; Kluger & DeNisi, 1996; Locke & Latham, 1990). In defining the specific content of the institutional, personal, and organizational

• FIGURE 1 •

MODEL OF FACTORS AFFECTING BUSINESS ETHICS ACROSS CULTURES

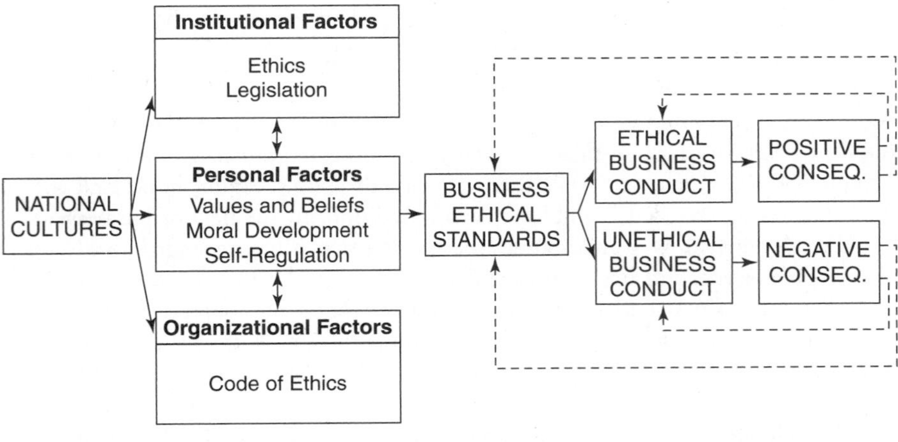

factors relevant to international management, we also draw from the related theory and research on culture clustering (Hofstede, 1980, 1991; Trompenaars, 1994) and work to date on perceptions of business ethics across cultures (Ciulla, 1991; Becker & Fritszche, 1987).

Although there are many definitions of business ethics (DeGeorge, 1984; Gatewood & Carroll, 1991), our model defines business ethics as a set of established rules, standards, or principles for morally "right" behavioral conduct in specific situations (Lewis, 1985), and in specific cultures when applied internationally (Ciulla, 1991; DeGeorge, 1994). Our model operationalizes business ethics in specific cultures as:

1. perceptions of ethical standards,
2. ethical behavioral conduct, and
3. unethical behavioral conduct.

The remainder of the article first gives detailed attention to the cultural context and then specifically examines the antecedents (institutional, organizational, and personal) and consequences of ethical behaviors across cultures.

CULTURE AS THE CONTEXT FOR BUSINESS ETHICS

As shown in Figure 1, the model indicates that analysis of business ethical standards and resulting ethical behavioral conduct is grounded in the unique characteristics of each national culture. This is because culture represents the broad specter of accumulated knowledge that people use to interpret their experiences and generate social behaviors (Spradley, 1979); it provides the foundation from which human thought and action originally develop. Business ethics cannot be adequately examined in an acultural context since culture shapes the meaning of all the concepts brought to bear on ethical inquiry. A simple example of cultural context is provided by the word "contraband," which has a negative ethical connotation in the U.S., but in Spanish speaking cultures the same word is "contrabando," which means literally "against the bandits," a positive ethical connotation.

Analysis of business ethics within a cultural context also encourages reaching a balance between the assumption that ethics is universal and timeless on the one hand, and the practical need to interpret business ethics according to particular situations and times. Based on these arguments, we next review two widely recognized approaches to cross-cultural analysis and draw connections between particular cultural attributes and the factors in the model (institutional, organizational, personal) that influence the formation of ethical standards.

GENERALLY RECOGNIZED CULTURAL ATTRIBUTES

Most of the empirical evidence indicating that different countries could be compared according to specific cultural dimensions has been generated by the research on culture clustering (Hofstede, 1980, 1991; Trompenaars, 1994). In particular, in the biggest organizationally based study ever conducted (116,000 IBM respondents in 70 countries), Hofstede demonstrated that different countries could be clustered into four specific cultural dimensions: (1) power distance, (2) uncertainty avoidance, (3) individualism vs. collectivism, and (4) masculinity vs. femininity.

Power distance refers to the extent to which members of a certain culture accept that power in institutions and organizations is distributed unequally. Uncertainty avoidance represents people's general tolerance of ambiguous situations; the higher the tolerance for ambiguity, the greater the willingness to take and accept risks inherent in ambiguity. The cultural dimension of individualism exemplifies people's tendency to primarily care about themselves and their immediate families, and collectivism depicts people's need to belong to and function within groups, organizations, or collectives. Finally, Hofstede defines masculinity as "a situation in which the dominant values in society are success, money, and things" and femininity as "a situation in which the dominant values in society are caring for others and the quality of life" (1980, p. 420).

The work of another Dutch researcher, Fons Trompenaars, has emerged as perhaps the most recently recognized attempt to cluster countries according to cultural dimensions. In another huge study (15,000 managers in 28 countries), Trompenaars (1994) developed a theoretical framework consisting of five cultural dimensions: (1) universalism vs. particularism, (2) individualism vs. collectivism, (3) neutral vs. affective, (4) specific vs. diffuse, and (5) achievement vs. ascription, and two specific orientations: (1) orientation towards time, and (2) orientation towards the environment.

Universalism vs. particularism has to do with orientation towards rules and objective truths. Whether people regard themselves primarily as individuals or as part of a group is referred to as individualism vs. collectivism. The nature of affective expression in interpersonal interactions falls along a neutral versus affective continuum. The specific versus diffuse dimension deals with the range of interpersonal involvement across the private and public domains. Finally, the dimension of personal status was termed achievement vs. ascription. Regarding the two cultural orientations, Trompenaars classified time orientation as sequential or synchronic. Orientation toward the environment reflects the source of motivation and values stemming either from the individual or the external environment.

CULTURAL ATTRIBUTES AND INSTITUTIONAL, ORGANIZATIONAL, AND PERSONAL FACTORS

These widely recognized approaches to culture clustering have empirically demonstrated that different *combinations* of the cultural dimensions can determine the relative differences between various societies. There is no one-to-one relationship between any cultural dimension and the factors presumed to in turn determine ethical standards. Rather, culture clustering can be used as the foundation to systematically interpret cultural differences, while at the same time recognizing that different cultural dimensions may have a different impact on either institutional, organizational, or personal factors. For example, Hofstede (1980, p. 154) proposed that uncertainty avoidance has a strong relationship with institutional factors by arguing that "ways of coping with uncertainty belong to the cultural heritage of societies, transferred and reinforced through basic institutions." Further on, Hofstede and Bond (1984) revealed that power distance tends to be more related to organizational factors by finding that the higher the power distance, the greater the obedience to authority at all managerial levels. As another example, Trompenaars (1994) indicated that there is a strong relationship between the achievement cultural dimension and individual striving towards performance excellence. In other words, the antecedent factors of ethical standards are greatly influenced by the general cultural context as well as specific cultural dimensions.

THE TRIADIC IMPACT OF INSTITUTIONAL, ORGANIZATIONAL, AND PERSONAL FACTORS

In the creation of business ethical standards, a social cognitive perspective suggests that people are neither instinctive self-producers of ethical standards, nor spontaneous transmitters of institutional, organizational, or personal ethical norms. Rather, the theory would explain creation of ethical standards and subsequent ethical behavior in terms of a triadic reciprocal interaction among the key variables. Institutional and organizational factors are defined as macro-level forces that are cognitively processed by individuals, that in turn give rise to ethical standards. The social cognitive approach examines ethical standards at the individual level of analysis where people cognitively process the relevant information generated by macro-level forces. The focus is on the creation of an individual's perceptions of business ethical standards and resulting ethical behavior in social (cultural) settings.

Considering the nature of the interaction, the three factors impacting ethical standards affect each other bidirectionally rather than unidirectionally. Because of this bidirectionality of influences, people's ethical standards and subsequent ethical conduct could, for example, be determined by the varying impact of their legal institutions, the respective policies of their organizations, and their personal values and beliefs. Based on this line of reasoning from social cognitive theory, we propose that:

> **P1:** *The perceptions of business ethical standards are formed at the individual level through cognitive assessment, using self-regulative processes, of combined triadic influences of institutional constrains (e.g., ethics legislation), organizational circumstances (e.g., policies and codes of ethics), and personal variables (e.g., values and beliefs) that are all shaped by the specific cultural context.*

The following sections provide specific examples of each of the key factors contributing to business ethics across cultures.

INSTITUTIONAL FACTORS

Perhaps the best example of an institutional factor would be ethics legislation. A broader sociological network of institutional environment may include many factors related to business ethics, such as political policies (Ciulla, 1991), dominance of particular norms of societal morality (DeGeorge, 1984), or the impact of cultural diversity on the coherence of moral values within a society (Larkey, 1996). Although our model recognizes the wider importance of these institutional factors, for the purpose of tangible analysis, we focus on the formal legislation. A set of legal regulations enforceable in the courts of law is particularly relevant to business ethics either at home or in a host country. The model also recognizes that the presence of ethical legislation, or the lack thereof, can have a different impact in different cultures. Ethics legislation in the U.S., France and Germany, and Japan provide examples.

1. *The Impact of Ethics Legislation in the United States.* The United States Congress expressed concerns for bribery involving U.S. businesses overseas by passing major ethical legislation in the form of the Foreign Corrupt Practices Act (FCPA) of 1977. Since this legislation explicitly prohibits bribery of foreign officials by U.S. businesses, a complaint raised was that high ethical standards embodied in the FCPA could result in a major loss of business. Critics argued that the FCPA, which makes it illegal to influence foreign officials through personal payment or political contributions, could result in competitive problems for U.S. MNCs. The logic was that if managers of U.S. MNCs could not offer bribes or "gifts" in their international dealings, they would not be able to compete against those who did. Research has not supported such a claim. For example, in the first five years since the passage of the FCPA, Graham (1983) found that U.S. exports to traditionally "bribe prone" countries such as those in the Middle East have actually increased. Subsequent investigations revealed that once bribes were removed as a competitive tool, more U.S. MNCs were

willing to do business in those countries. For example, IBM, which has been very successful in international markets over the years, refuses to pay even small "lubrication" payments permitted under the FCPA.

2. *Business Ethics Legislation in France and Germany.* Business ethical conduct in European countries, such as France and Germany, is also shaped by legislation or the lack thereof. However, it is important to recognize that the institutional legal forces in these European countries may result in a much different set of actual ethical behavior than is found in the U.S. For example, a study by Becker and Fritzsche (1987), who surveyed 124 U.S., 72 French, and 70 German managers, asked each manager to respond to a series of five vignettes that examined ethical situations related to coercion and control, conflict of interest, the physical environment, paternalism, and personal integrity. In most cases, the U.S. managers' responses were quite different from those of their European counterparts. In particular, when managers were asked how they would respond to the request for a bribe to obtain a contract, the U.S. managers surveyed were opposed to paying the money; 39% of them said that a bribe was illegal under the Foreign Corrupt Practices Act and thus unethical. However, only 12% of the French felt that way, and none of the Germans agreed. Moreover, 55% of the French and 29% of the Germans said that paying the money was not unethical but merely the price to be paid for doing business. In other words, the legal impact does not seem to be as great in these European countries as it is in the U.S. However, it must also be recognized that there are cultural differences within Europe. For example, France's Renault a few years ago stopped negotiations with Italy's Fiat after discovering that a number of the Italian automaker's top executives had been implicated in bribes.

3. *Legislative Fine Lines in Japan.* Business ethical standards and conduct in Japan also appear to be shaped by the institutional factor of legislation, but perhaps even less directly than in Europe. Japanese legislation on ethical issues tends to draw a very fine line between legal and illegal conduct. An illustration is the widely publicized bribery scandal involving the Recruit Company. This Japanese company was originally founded as a publisher of help-wanted magazines. It soon expanded into a multibillion dollar firm involved in job training, condominium selling, and computer networks. In an effort to curry favor with important people, the company began giving influential businesspeople and politicians an opportunity to buy cut-rate stock in the company-owned real estate subsidiary. When the company's shares were eventually listed on the Neike exchange, the early shareholders all made large returns on their investment. In contrast to the U.S., these actions by the Recruit Company per se are not illegal in Japan. However, in return for their largesse, the company was given special favors by some of these influential stockholders. This was illegal in Japan and those found guilty were convicted. The implication of this example is that legislation might not be as directly influential in affecting ethical business standards and conduct in Japan, especially for foreign MNCs, because it may be difficult to distinguish between legal and illegal activities.

This different impact of legislation on ethics is probably true in other Asian countries as well, especially in China. Although China has legislation prohibiting pirating of intellectual property, enforcement has to date been at best inconsistent and at worst nonexistent. Not only is it estimated that 90% of computer software in China has been pirated from U.S. firms, but today there are highly visible fake cans of Coca-Cola, fake McDonald's hamburger restaurants, and even fake versions of the Jeeps that Chrysler manufactures with a joint-venture partner in Beijing.

ORGANIZATIONAL FACTORS

The organizational factors influencing perceptions of ethical business standards and subsequent conduct are usually more direct than the institutional factors. An organization's code of ethics is an example. These codes are largely influenced by the degree to which organizational policies and practices emphasize the importance of ethics in doing business (Langlois & Schlegelmilch, 1990). Ten years ago in the U.S., three-fourths of Fortune 500 companies had drafted some form of a code of ethics (Ciulla, 1991), and the trend continues (Whetten & Cameron, 1995). Although the purpose of most ethical codes is to spell out ethical guidelines, the content of ethical codes has been found to be significantly different across different organizations and cultures (Cohen, Pant & Sharp, 1992).

1. *Codes of Ethics in U.S. Companies.* U.S. companies developed codes of ethics primarily as instructions on how to react in situations when faced with a moral dilemma in the course of doing business. These are also the first line of defense against illegal activities and protection against legal suits (Ciulla, 1991). In terms of their content, over 80% of the ethical codes in U.S. companies mention customers, 86% discuss relations with suppliers, and a vast majority of the codes are concerned about the government's legal impact, while 55% address employee conduct (Langlois & Schlegelmilch, 1990). Directly relevant to the model is the fact that most ethical codes in U.S. companies specifically indicate what kind of business conduct is perceived as unethical.

   Ethical codes in U.S. firms may spell out examples of unethical conduct, such as bribery, the use of insider information, treatment of customers in terms of fraud or overcharging, low product safety, and unacceptable business practices in terms of social and environmental responsibilities (Schlegelmilch, 1989). For example, as a result of company-promoted ethical standards, Dow Corning has ceased its foreign sales of silicone-filled breast implants citing its obligation to apply the same ethical standards of business conduct internationally as it does domestically. Also, as the result of their corporate codes of conduct, Nike, Reebok, and Levi Strauss have all instituted rigorous procedures for auditing for human rights violations their imports from certain factories around the world. For example, Levi's managers are following the code that: "We should not initiate or renew contractual relationships in countries where there are pervasive violations of basic human rights."

2. *Codes of Ethics in European Companies.* Ethical codes in European organizations are a relatively new, but growing phenomena. The proportion of European businesses with developed codes of ethics significantly increased from 14% in 1984, to 41% in 1988, to almost complete adoption (Langlois & Schlegelmilch, 1990). Although the idea of ethical codes was largely borrowed from the U.S., there are interesting differences in the content of these codes between the U.S. and European companies (Cohen et al., 1992). European codes of ethics mostly emphasize codetermination and a sense of belonging and responsibility to overall society (Langlois & Schlegelmilch, 1990), and, in contrast to the codes in the U.S., focus less on the specific issues of procedural and distributive justice. The emphasis on the more macro ethical issues of European codes may help explain why it took Swiss-based Nestle seven years to change its marketing strategy for Similac baby formula, which is attributed to a number of infant deaths around the world because of the lack of proper instructions for preparing it.

3. *Japanese Codes of Ethics.* The Japanese use of codes of ethics is quite unique. Japanese MNCs tend to have dual codes of ethics: one for domestic operations, and one for international ones (Hatchoji, Nishikawa, Ohinata, Ichihari & Takahashi, 1988). The codes for Japanese domestic operations typically define business ethics through traditional proxy variables of job security, seniority-based promotions, collectivism, and price stability, and, more philosophically oriented, spiritual noblesse oblige, the expression of unconventional thinking, and transcendentalism (Taka & Foglia, 1994). However, for Japanese firms' international operations, the codes generally recommend "enlightened self-interest" (Hatchoji et al., 1988). This enlightened self-interest entails creating codes of ethics in accordance with other cultures' ethical concerns, values, and expectations. In other words, it appears that Japanese codes of ethics for international operations are pragmatically developed to comply with the ethical concerns of other cultures, primarily to avoid conflict, but also to be competitive in the global economy. As Hatchoji and colleagues suggest, to be competitive, while at the same time trying to reduce conflict, Japanese firms must develop ethical business standards "at a level no lower than that of the United States and European enterprises, the first comers" (1988, p. 1).

   Some prominent Japanese firms have learned the hard way that they must adapt to the ethics of the host country. For example, several years ago Honda of America Manufacturing, Inc. agreed to $6 million in back pay to resolve a discrimination complaint and Sumitomo Bank's U.S. operation was handed a $2.6 million sex discrimination verdict. More recently, Mitsubishi Motor Manufacturing of America has been hit with a lawsuit seeking millions in compensatory and punitive damages for allegedly allowing sexual harassment in one of its U.S. plants. However, it should also be noted that the Japanese concern for the safety and health of workers may be unmatched anywhere in the world (Wokutch, 1990). In other words, Japanese MNCs, like others around the world, may have to have more cultural sensitivity and concern in some areas of their ethical codes, but not in others.

PERSONAL FACTORS

The personal factors that affect perceptions of ethical business standards could involve many psychological constructs. However, we feel that conceptually the most relevant would be interactive influences of individual values and beliefs, stage of moral development, and, especially from the social cognitive perspective, self-regulated mechanisms.

1. *Values and Beliefs.* Although they have been conceptualized in a variety of ways, personal values can be defined as the most enduring personal characteristics of individuals that represent the foundation for moral judgment, personal standards, critical decisions, and life directions (Whetten & Cameron, 1995). While definitions of personal values may differ, there seems to be general agreement that values influence subsequent behaviors by either providing: (a) the basis for the development of individual attitudes which lead to specific behaviors, (b) the criteria for judgment, preference, and choice that determine standards of performance, or, according to social adaptation theory, (c) individual cognition that facilitates adaptation to the social environment. Since every individual brings his/her values and related beliefs into the organization, values seem to be an important part of the personal antecedents of business ethics.
2. *Moral Development.* Kohlberg (1976) argues that the way in which values and beliefs are translated into ethical standards and conduct depends on the stage of an individual's moral development. People at a low level of moral development tend to make decisions primarily based on a type of hedonistic framework (seeking pragmatic ways of getting ahead and avoiding getting into trouble). At an intermediate level, individuals focus on upholding the legal requirements and conforming to expectations by either peers, supervisors, or society at large. At the highest stage of moral development (principled level), however, individuals develop an internal set of ethical principles that are more important to the individual per se, rather than either legal or social expectations. In fact, following these ethical standards at the highest level may even involve breaking the law if necessary (civil disobedience) to sustain high moral standards (e.g., Greenpeace actions on protecting the environment).

SELF-REGULATION

A social cognitive perspective would suggest that people use self-regulated mechanisms to influence themselves in order to determine, regulate; and sustain their ethical standards and subsequent ethical behaviors (Bandura, 1986; Wood & Bandura, 1989). The basic human capabilities through which people exercise self-influence in regulating their behaviors would include: (1) symbolizing and forethought; (2) vicarious learning; and (3) self-reflection.

1. *Symbolizing and Forethought Capability.* Bandura suggests that humans have extraordinary symbolizing and forethought capability that allows them to successfully change and adapt to their respective environments (i.e., different cultures).

By using symbols, people process and transform visual experiences into internal cognitive models that in turn serve as guides for future actions. Through symbolizing activity, people also ascribe meaning and form to their past experiences. Rather than learning proper behavioral responses only by enacting behaviors, and possibly suffering painful costs of missteps, people usually test possible solutions symbolically first, and then eliminate or accept them on the basis of perceived outcomes before engaging into action.

In the creation of perceptions of ethical business standards and resulting conduct, under this capability of self-regulation, international managers would first ascribe meaning to their experiences regarding previous ethical conduct. These experiences would serve as a basis for new perceptions of what should be the current ethical standard. The newly created ethical perceptions would again be modified by the perceptions of plausible outcomes that the new ethical standards and subsequent behaviors are likely to produce. In other words, using symbolizing capability, international managers would first cognitively evaluate their previous ethical experience which in turn would result in a broader concept of ethical standards for the near future. Then, using forethought capability, they would anticipate the likely consequences of those ethical standards, modify them if needed, and set final ethical standards. Thus, through the symbolizing and forethought capabilities, international managers guide the creation of ethical standards in anticipatory fashion; the future acquires causal properties by being represented cognitively by symbols and forethought exercised in the present.

2. *Vicarious Learning Capability.* Bandura proposes that almost all forms of learning can occur vicariously by observing the behavior of others and the subsequent consequences of these behaviors. This capacity to learn by observation enables international managers to obtain and accumulate rules for initiating and controlling different behavioral patterns without having to acquire them gradually or incrementally by risky trial and error. The type of business ethical standards that international managers create for themselves may be strongly influenced by the opportunities to vicariously observe ethical business behavior of others, and importantly, the consequences these others experience for their behaviors. For example, at Procter & Gamble everyone knows the story about the outstanding brand manager who was fired for overstating the features of a product. Although this incident happened a number of years ago, P & G managers have learned a lasting lesson that ethics are more important than an undeserved increase in sales.

   The acquisition of ethical business standards vicariously seems critical for learning culturally appropriate ethical behaviors in international business. This is because if international managers were to base their ethical conduct only on trial and error in a given cultural context, this could (and often does) result in costly consequences, especially in the complex global arena. In fact, the more complex the environment (e.g., across cultures), and the more costly the possible mistakes of unethical conduct (e.g., important international business dealings), the stronger must be the reliance on vicarious learning. Very simply, the existence of vicarious learning supports the importance of the common adages for serving as an appropriate model for ethics across cultures that multinational business leaders must "walk the talk" and recognize that "actions speak so loudly that the words cannot be heard."

3. *Self-Reflective Capability.* Bandura emphasizes the importance of a self-reflective capability which enables people to think and analyze their experiences and thought processes. By reflecting on their different personal experiences, international managers can generate specific knowledge about their environment and about themselves. Among the types of knowledge that managers doing business across cultures can derive from self-reflection, none is more central to human functioning than their judgment of their capabilities to deal effectively with different environmental realities. These types of perceptions are known as self-efficacy beliefs. Thus, the ethical business standards international managers set for themselves will also be determined by the belief about their personal capability to successfully execute those standards through their actual behavioral conduct.

THE IMPACT OF PERSONAL FACTORS ON BUSINESS ETHICS ACROSS CULTURES

The differences in the extent to which personal factors impact perceptions of ethical business standards across cultures can be found in examples comparing the ethical decision making in the U.S. with European countries.

1. *The Impact of Personal Factors in the U.S.* Business practices in the United States tend to treat ethics as the responsibility of individual managers who make the final decisions about proper ethical standards and subsequent ethical conduct (Taka & Foglia, 1994). In determining ethical standards, U.S. managers tend to apply individual moral norms and take full personal responsibility for the ethical decisions made. Being largely at the intermediate stage of moral development, most U.S. managers also strongly focus on upholding the legal requirements of their jobs relevant to ethical conduct (Whetten & Cameron, 1995).

   Considering the emphasis given to individual moral norms, adherence to legal conditions, and the importance of personal responsibility, a social cognitive perspective would suggest that ethical standards of U.S. managers would mostly be determined by symbolic and forethought self-regulative influences. In particular, by using symbolic capabilities, U.S. managers would first ascribe meaning to their personal experiences regarding previous ethical conduct, and then, by using forethought self-regulation, they would anticipate the likely consequences (mostly legal) before they set the final ethical standards. Whether the ethical standards will be enacted into actual ethical conduct will depend on the strength of the personal belief that those standards will result in proper ethical behaviors.

2. *The Impact of Personal Factors in Europe.* Events in European history have created the social circumstances in which moral and ethical values of individual managers must combine and interact with those of other stakeholders (e.g., trade unions) in defining the meaning of business ethics. This pattern of determining the ethical business standards is reflected in giving the central role to "communicative ethics." This is an ethics of consensus which emphasizes the sense of common understanding based on the socio-economic exchanges of good reasons (Steinmann & Löhr, 1989). As a result, the level of analysis for European business ethics is placed at the intersection between stakeholders from different social entities (e.g., corporations, unions, business associations) that tend to transcend the level of individual moralism. Thus, in determining ethical standards, European managers tend to emphasize social conformity where legitimate business interests are defended while recognizing interests of other stakeholders who, in fact, may be only remotely connected to a particular ethical decision (Mahoney & Vallance, 1992).

   Considering the emphasis on the "trans-individual" level of analysis and the importance of social conformity in most European countries, a social cognitive approach would suggest that European managers may focus more on vicarious self-regulation rather than U.S. managers. By observing the enactment of ethical standards of important others who also have a stake in the decision making process, European managers can accumulate the additional information on relevant ethical norms that can in turn help them modify and align their personal moral and ethical preferences. In fact, the greater the emphasis on social conformity, as for example in France, the stronger would be the reliance on vicarious learning of ethical standards from relevant stakeholders whose socio-economic interests are to be taken into account. Finally, whether these trans-individual types of ethical standards would be enacted depends on the extent to which individual managers believe that they sufficiently meet the ethical expectations of relevant others.

THE IMPACT OF CONSEQUENCES OF ETHICAL CONDUCT

Our discussion so far has mainly been concerned with the antecedent factors of ethical standards and conduct. The model in Figure 1 also shows that the ethical or unethical business conduct of international managers will produce positive or negative consequences. The model suggests that these consequences would feed back to and then modify or change the perceptions of business ethical standards which will in turn impact subsequent ethical conduct. After presenting the assumptions and dynamics of the role that consequences play, the propositions stemming from feedback-standard discrepancy reduction conclude the discussion of the social cognitive model.

THE ASSUMPTIONS AND DYNAMICS OF CONSEQUENCES

To begin with, several important assumptions about the consequence side of the model should be noted. Like the antecedent factors, this part of the model focuses at the individual level of analysis. Regarding environmental consequences, the focus is on the contingent consequences experienced by the individual international manager, and not on organizational consequences that do not affect this person. Thus, the feedback process will alter perceptions of ethical standards and subsequent behaviors only when the manager personally experiences the consequences of his/her actions. As noted before, this line of reasoning is based on the classic law of effect and operant principles of behavioral psychology. Specifically, this behavioral approach simply states that contingent environmental consequences determine subsequent behaviors.

A possible limitation of the behavior-consequence part of the model is the possibility of unethical behavior producing positive consequences (e.g., a bribe lands a contract) and vice versa (e.g., refusing to give a bribe loses a contract). If the occurrence of unethical behavior produces positive consequences or ethical behavior produces negative consequences, these are idiosyncratic. Yet, if such contradictions persist over time in a given culture, then the model would predict that the ethical standards and conduct would change accordingly (e.g., bribes become an accepted practice in certain cultures).

The situation in which business conduct was perceived as ethical by relevant others (e.g., business partners, customers, suppliers, local governments, consumer groups), and for which the consequences were positive (e.g., an increased volume of sales, a lucrative contract, or large commission or bonus), does not pose practical nor conceptual problems since these consequences will tend to positively reinforce the existing ethical standards. However, the situation in which business conduct was perceived as unethical and for which consequences were negative and punishing would lead to corrective actions. Thus, following a behavioral approach to the consequence dimension of the model, we propose that:

> **P2a:** *Positive environmental contingent consequences will reinforce and enhance existing ethical standards and accelerate ethical behaviors. However, negative or punishing environmental contingent consequences will change or modify ethical standards and decelerate existing behavior.*

FEEDBACK-STANDARD DISCREPANCY REDUCTION

Besides the law of effect and operant principles, feedback-standard discrepancy reduction can also be used to explain what and how corrective actions in business ethics across cultures may occur. Considering the various cognitive mechanisms which operate on perceived ethical standards, there is general agreement that feedback information regulates human action by initiating the evaluation of and stimulating the corrective reaction to the feedback-standard discrepancy (Bandura, 1986; Carver & Scheier, 1981; Locke & Latham, 1990). Although the cognitive conceptualizations generally agree on how people evaluate this discrepancy, they differ in their explanations of the reactions to it. For example, according to control theory, when a negative discrepancy is perceived (based on the comparison of the ethical standard with the negative feedback) people tend to reduce the gap by either changing the (unethical) behaviors, the perceived (ethical) standard, or by "leaving the scene" (delegating the decision or quitting). However, according to goal-setting theory, if feedback-standard discrepancy is perceived (consequences indicate that ethical performance was below the perceived standard), people are motivated to accomplish the (ethical) standard, typically by increasing the subsequent effort (Locke & Latham, 1990).

According to social cognitive theory, much of human behavior is initiated and regulated by internal self-set standards and self-evaluative reactions to exerted behaviors (Bandura, 1986; Wood & Bandura, 1989). After personal (ethical) standards have been set, incongruity between (unethical) behavior and the standard against which it is measured activates self-evaluative reactions, which, in turn, serve to further influence subsequent action. Thus, for feedback-standard discrepancy reduction, the social cognitive approach is in contrast with both the negative feedback control models and the goal-setting approach. In particular, according to control theory and the goal-setting approach, if there is no discrepancy between standards and the results of behavioral action, the motivational process stops since effort tends to be reduced or, at best, maintained. According to social cognitive theory, even if there is no incongruity between (ethical) self-standards and present (ethical) performance, international managers would tend to set higher ethical standards for themselves and activate future ethical behaviors to satisfy the new standards. Thus, taking a social cognitive approach to the consequence dimension of the model, we propose that:

> **P2b:** *The extent to which business ethical standards will be actually changed will largely depend on the self-assessment of the personal ethical standard in relation to the emitted behavior; the more central the ethical standard is to the international manager's belief system, the less likely the change.*

> **P2c:** *The change of behavior will depend on the complexity of the required change; the more simple the requirement (e.g., increase in effort), the more likely the change. However, the more complex the behavioral requirement (e.g., changing the old practice of giving bribes), the more likely the delegation.*

SUMMARY AND CONCLUSIONS

The major purpose of this article was to provide a comprehensive social-cognitive model that identifies and relates the factors and processes that affect business ethics across cultures. Within the cultural context, the key antecedent factors that triadically interact to influence ethical standards were broadly identified as institutional, organizational, and personal. The model also outlined how the perceptions of standards of business ethics can be developed, how they affect subsequent ethical conduct, and how both ethical standards and behaviors could be changed due to the impact of environmental consequences.

The next step would be to conduct empirical research to verify the direct links proposed between specific cultural dimensions such as Hofstede's uncertainty avoidance, power distance, and individualism, and the institutional, organizational, and personal factors. Research would also be needed on the formation of business ethical standards. The model does identify some of the broad antecedent factors and the role of consequences contributing to business ethical standards and conduct, but empirical validation of these variables, relationships, and processes remains to be demonstrated.

Although the intent of the model is to identify the critical variables and understand the process and relationships that go into business ethical standards and conduct across cultures, there are clear implications for the practice of international management. For example, the model points out that practicing international managers must first recognize the all important cultural context for ethical standards and conduct. Although lip service is given to the recognition of cultural differences, the model emphasizes that ethics is in fact grounded in the culture. The model also points out the importance of institutional, organizational, and personal factors. In particular, practicing international managers should recognize that they are influenced, and can actively influence ethics across cultures, by: institutional legislation; organizational codes of conduct; and personal values and beliefs, moral development, and self-regulation.

The social cognitively based self-regulation can be operationalized through a training approach utilizing modeling and/or role playing techniques. For example, as part of negotiator or expatriate orientation and training, the trainees could watch tapes and then role play culturally appropriate ethical behavior that is then reinforced. Finally, practicing international managers must set up reward systems (both formally and informally) for ethical behaviors of others responsible to them and for themselves. The consequence side of the model very simply says that you get what you reward, and that includes ethical behaviors across cultures.

In conclusion, although the comprehensive model presented here can provide a new conceptual framework, or at least a point of departure for the better understanding, research, and application of business ethics across cultures, we do recognize the important contributions of previous approaches. However, a social cognitive approach to the study of business ethics across cultures seems to provide an important and needed additive contribution for both theory development and actual practice.

References

Adler, N.J. (1997). *International dimensions of organizational behavior*, 3rd ed. Cincinnati, OH: South-Western College Publishing.

Akaah, I.P., & Riordan, E.A. (1989). Judgments of marketing professionals about ethical issues in marketing research: A replication and extension. *Journal of Marketing Research*, 26: 112–120.

Bandura, A. (1986). *Social foundations of thought and action.* Englewood Cliffs, NJ: Prentice Hall.

Becker, H., & Fritzsche, D. (1987). A comparison of the ethical behavior of American, French, and German managers. *Columbia Journal of World Business*, 22: 87–95.

Carver, C.S., & Scheier, M.F. (1981). *Attention and self-regulation: A control theory of human behavior.* New York: Springer-Verlag.

Ciulla, J.B. (1991). Why is business talking about ethics: Reflections on foreign conversations. *California Management Review*, (Fall): 67–86.

Cohen, J.R., Pant, W.L., & Sharp, J.D. (1992). Cultural and socioeconomic constraints on international codes of ethics: Lessons from accounting. *Journal of Business Ethics*, 11: 687–700.

DeGeorge, R.T. (1984). *Business ethics*. New York: Macmillan.

DeGeorge, R.T. (1994). International business ethics. *Business Ethics Quarterly*, 4: 1–9.

Donaldson, T. 1982. *Corporations and morality*. Englewood Cliffs, NJ: Prentice Hall.

Ferrell, O.C., & Gresham, L.G. (1985). A contingency framework for understanding ethical decision making in marketing. *Journal of Marketing*, 49: 87–96.

Gatewood, R.D., & Carroll, A.B. (1991). Assessment of ethical performance of organizational members: A conceptual framework. *Academy of Management Review*, 16: 667–690.

Gauthier, D. (1986). *Morals by agreement*. Oxford, England: University Press.

Graham, J.L. (1983). Foreign corrupt practices: A manager's guide. *Columbia Journal of World Business*, (Fall): 89–94.

Hatchoji, T., Nishikawa, Y., Ohinata, Y., Ichihari, G., & Takahashi, S. (1988). *Future stage of corporate social responsibility in the era of overseas production*. Tokyo: Hitachi Research Institute.

Hofstede, G. (1980). *Culture's consequences: International differences in work-related values*. Beverly Hills, CA: Sage.

Hofstede, G. (1991). *Culture and organizations: Software of the mind*. New York: McGraw Hill.

Hofstede, G., & Bond, M. (1984). The need for synergy among cross-cultural studies. *Journal of Cross-Cultural Psychology*, 15: 417–433.

Hunt, S.D., & Vitell, S. (1986). A general theory of marketing ethics. *Journal of Macromarketing*, 6: 5–16.

Jones, T.M. (1991). Ethical decision making by individuals in organizations: An issue-contingent model. *Academy of Management Review*, 16: 366–395.

Kahn, W.A. (1990). Toward an agenda for business ethics research. *Academy of Management Review*, 15: 311–328.

Kluger, A.N., & DeNisi, A. (1996). The effects of feedback interventions on performance: A historical review, a meta-analysis, and a preliminary feedback intervention theory. *Psychological Bulletin*, 119: 254–284.

Kohlberg, L. (1976). Moral stages and moralization: The cognitive-development approach. Pp. 31–53 in T. Lickona (Ed.), *Moral development and behavior: Theory, research and social issues*. New York: Holt, Rinehart & Winston.

Langlois, C.C., & Schlegemilch, B.B. (1990). Do corporate codes of ethics reflect national character? Evidence from Europe and the United States. *Journal of International Business Studies*, 21: 519–539.

Larkey, L.K. (1996). Toward a theory of communicative interactions in culturally diverse workgroups. *Academy of Management Review*, 21: 463–491.

Lewis, P.V. (1985). Defining business ethics: Like nailing jello to the wall. *Journal of Business Ethics*, 4: 377–383.

Locke, E.A., & Latham, G.P. (1990). *A theory of goal-setting and task performance*. Englewood Cliffs, NJ: Prentice Hall.

Luthans, F., & Kreitner, R. (1985). *Organizational behavior modification and beyond*. Glenview, IL: Scott, Foresman.

Mahoney, J., & Vallance, E. (1992). *Business ethics in a new Europe*. Boston, MA: Kluwer.

Randall, D.M., & Gibson, A.M. (1990). Methodology in business ethics research. A review and critical assessment. *Journal of Business Ethics*, 9: 457–471.

Schlegelmilch, B.B. (1989). The ethics gap between Britain and the United States: A comparison of the state of business ethics in both countries. *European Management Journal*, 7: 57–64.

Spradley, J.P. (1979). *The ethnographic interview.* New York: Rinehart & Winston.

Stajkovic, A.D., & Luthans, F. (in press). A meta-analysis of the effects of organizational behavior modification on task performance: 1975–1995. *Academy of Management Journal.*

Steinmann, H., & Löhr, A. (1989). *Unternehmensethik.* Stuttgart, Germany: Poeschel.

Taka, I., & Foglia, W.D. (1994). Ethical aspects of Japanese leadership style. *Journal of Business Ethics,* 13: 135–148.

Trevino, L.K. (1986). Ethical decision making in organizations: A person-situation interactionist model. *Academy of Management Review,* 11: 601–617.

Trevino, L.K., & Weaver, G.R. (1993). Business ethics/business ethics: One field or two. *Business Ethics Quarterly,* 4: 113–128.

Trompenaars, F. (1994). *Riding the waves of culture: Understanding diversity in global business.* Burr Ridge, IL: Irwin.

Werhane, P.H. (1994). The normative/descriptive distinction in methodologies of business ethics. *Business Ethics Quarterly,* 4: 175–180.

Whetten, D.A., & Cameron, K.S. (1995). *Developing management skills.* New York: Harper Collins College Publishers.

Wokutch, R.E. (1990). Corporate social responsibility Japanese style. *Academy of Management Executive,* 4(2): 56–74.

Wood, R., & Bandura, A. (1989). Social cognitive theory of organizational management. *Academy of Management Review,* 14: 361–384.

AN EMERGING GREEN MARKET IN CHINA: MYTH OR REALITY?

Ricky Y.K. Chan

An awareness of environmental degradation has been a long time coming in China. Since declaring its open-door policy in late 1978, China has been paying a high ecological price for its rapid economic growth in terms of worsening pollution and an accelerating depletion of many critical resources. Compared to other ecologically advanced countries, China's apathy toward the environment is evident. On average, the country spends less than 1 percent of its GDP on environmental protection, whereas the corresponding spending ratios for the U.S. and Australia are 2.5 percent and 5 percent, respectively. Indeed, China's spending ratio is even lower than Hong Kong's 1.5 percent—a territory, say Martinsons, So, Tin, and Wong (1997), that is notoriously known as "the most ecologically unsound place in the world."

As the environment continues to worsen, the Chinese government has begun to reckon the severity of the problem. Measures such as the recent enactment of various antipollution laws and the preparation of new criminal codes for environmental offenses have shown the country's determination to tackle the problems. On the consumer side, incidental commentaries also suggest that increasingly affluent and educated Chinese citizens are more inclined to purchase eco-friendly products than before. This development gives both international and domestic marketers a promising opportunity to cultivate a lucrative green market in the world's most populous country (1.2 billion people).

Nevertheless, as systematic empirical investigation of green consumers in China is virtually nonexistent, how far the anecdotal evidence really reflects reality is yet to be

---

Ricky Y.K. Chan is an associate professor of business studies at the Hong Kong Polytechnic University. The work described in this article was supported by a research grant from the Hong Kong Polytechnic University.

verified. As such, marketers who plan to invest aggressively in China's green market based solely on this limited information may do so at great peril.

How "green" are Chinese consumers? To attempt to provide businesses with more information on assessing the potential of China's environmental market, a survey was conducted in two of the most developed yet polluted cities of China—Beijing and Guangzhou. It is hoped that the findings can also help the Chinese government fine-tune its nationwide environmental strategies.

THE SURVEY

With the assistance of a research agency, 300 households from each of the two cities were randomly selected based on a self-compiled sampling frame. Within each selected household, an adult member (aged 18 or above) was interviewed, answering questions about his or her general environmental attitudes, green consumption behaviors, and demographic backgrounds. Researchers collected 549 usable questionnaires for the survey: 279 from Beijing and 270 from Guangzhou. Overall, the major demographic characteristics (gender, marital status, age, education, and income) of the respondents were comparable to those of the entire Chinese population.

GENERAL ENVIRONMENTAL ATTITUDES

The respondents were asked to answer 12 seven-point attitude statements (1 = strongly disagree; 7 = strongly agree) adopted and modified from Berberoglu and Tosunoglu's (1995) environmental attitude scale, which was specifically developed to study inhabitants of a developing country on its way to industrialization. Responses were then factor-analyzed and five meaningful factors emerged (see Table 1): (1) environmental apathy, (2) general environmental concerns, (3) perceived inefficacy over environmental problems, (4) attitudes toward population control, and (5) attitudes toward the use of nuclear power.

Further light can be shed on the Chinese people's environmental consciousness by examining the composite scores of the five factors. As shown by Factor 1 (2.97 out of 7), the respondents are far from environmentally apathetic; Factor 2 shows a considerably high level of general environmental concerns (5.18 out of 7). Nevertheless, the respondents tentatively agree that there is not much they can do about environmental deterioration. As for their attitudes toward specific environmental issues, they tend to agree that there is a need to control the ever-growing population and, curiously, they are somewhat optimistic about the use of nuclear power.

In short, the foregoing empirical findings effectively portray the eco-friendliness of today's Chinese and corroborate the anecdotal evidence that they are, in general, environmentally concerned rather than apathetic. Despite their general concerns about environmental issues, today's Chinese may feel somewhat incapable of rectifying the problems solely through their own efforts. Such feelings are probably attributed to their

• TABLE 1 •

Factor Analysis Results of the 12 Environmental Attitude Statements

Extracted Factor and Constituent Attitude Statements	% of Variance Explained	Composite Score
Factor 1: Environmental apathy	20.72	2.97
I am not interested in the population growth of the world.		
I don't mind living near a nuclear power plant.		
I don't bother cutting down on my use of electricity.		
Factor 2: General environmental concerns	14.25	5.18
It is annoying to see people do nothing for the environment.		
To see gray clouds above the city makes me feel down.		
Environmental problems should be given top priority.		
Factor 3: Perceived inefficacy over environmental problems	9.73	4.08
Cutting down on the amount of water used will not help solve the problem of water shortages.		
I don't think turning the lights off when leaving a room will save much energy.		
Factor 4: Attitudes toward population control	8.53	5.44
The population growth rate of China should be decreased.		
There are more people on the Earth than it can feed.		
Factor 5: Attitudes toward the use of nuclear power	7.90	4.76
Nuclear power is a reliable and clean source of energy.		
China is in need of nuclear power plants.		

Note: The total percentage of variance explained by the five factors combined is 61.13%. The composite score is equal to the average summated mean score of the constituent attitude statements, ranging from 1 = strongly disagree to 7 = strongly agree.

inadequate environmental knowledge and the lack of facilitating support (such as insufficient collection points for recyclable waste) from the government. With regard to the issue of population explosion, Chinese support the notion of population control. Indeed, it is not surprising to find such views among the inhabitants of the world's most populous country.

In contrast, Chinese attitudes toward the use of nuclear power differ considerably from those generally exhibited by citizens of developed countries. These attitudes echo the country's recent determination to vigorously develop its nuclear power industry to fuel future economic growth. In addition to its existing three nuclear reactors, China has plans to build at least eight more to pursue a tenfold increase in its nuclear generating capacity by 2010. Apparently, the country's well-proclaimed energy policy, together with its corresponding aggressive propaganda, has significantly influenced the public's perception about the use of this economical but potentially disastrous source of energy.

SEGMENTATION BY ENVIRONMENTAL ATTITUDES

Given that attitudes are often regarded as an important antecedent of behaviors, it is logical to infer that people holding different environmental attitudes are likely to have varying degrees of actual commitment to eco-friendly activities, such as green purchases. This inference warrants classifying customer segments according to environmental attitudes to provide marketers with useful insights into assessing the potential of a country's green market.

In this study, such segmentation was achieved through cluster analysis of the composite scores of the five factors generated earlier. Four valid customer segments were derived from the analysis, as seen in Table 2: (1) Basic Greens, (2) Sprouts, (3) Eco-bystanders, and (4) Basic Browns.

On the whole, Basic Greens appear to be the most environmentally conscious Chinese consumers; they are far from being apathetic to the problem, and their score on general environmental concerns is the highest among the four segments. In general, they disagree that they are ineffective in addressing ecological problems. They strongly support the notion of population control and exhibit negative attitudes toward the use of nuclear power. As revealed by the survey, Basic Greens represent 18 percent of all the respondents.

Sprouts are similar to Basic Greens except that they exhibit completely different attitudes toward the use of nuclear power—the most positive among the four segments. This difference may well reflect an underlying controversy among environmentalists about the use of nuclear power. For many, the concern is with the difficulties inherent

• TABLE 2 •

CLUSTER ANALYSIS OF THE FIVE ENVIRONMENTAL ATTITUDE FACTORS

FACTOR/NUMBER (%) of RESPONDENTS	SEGMENT 1 BASIC GREENS 99 (18%)	SEGMENT 2 SPROUTS 126 (23%)	SEGMENT 3 ECO-BYSTANDERS 187 (34%)	SEGMENT 4 BASIC BROWNS 137 (25%)
Environmental apathy	2.09	2.01	3.18	4.25
General environmental concerns	5.79	5.52	5.70	3.69
Perceived inefficacy over environmental problems	3.22	2.34	5.53	4.37
Attitudes toward population control	6.01	6.00	5.37	4.61
Attitudes toward the use of nuclear power	3.07	5.85	5.41	4.06

Note: Numbers refer to composite scores of the factors and range from 1 = strongly disagree to 7 = strongly agree.

in managing the various "low-probability, high-consequence" risks in the industry. Nevertheless, a handful of environmentalists seem to think otherwise and urge the revitalization of nuclear power as a safe and dependable source of energy. Indeed, they are even more worried about the emissions of carbon dioxide from fossil fuels and the consumption of enormous amounts of land from bio-fuels. These divergent views on nuclear power will probably continue for some time before a consensus can be reached.

Although their level of general environmental concerns is not as high as that of Basic Greens or Eco-bystanders, Sprouts have the potential to emerge as the most promising green consumers in China. When compared to the other segments, they express the strongest disagreement over their perceived inefficacy over environmental problems. Given their strong faith in their own ability to rectify the problems, they are probably highly inclined to translate their pro-environmental attitudes to corresponding consumption behaviors. On the premise that this survey sample is reasonably representative, the foregoing analysis will be highly encouraging for green marketers, because close to one-quarter of the Chinese respondents belong to this segment.

Unlike the other segments, Eco-bystanders agree most about their inefficacy over environmental problems. In addition to inadequate environmental knowledge and infrastructural support, this strong agreement may, in turn, reflect their strong adherence to the traditional Chinese concept of *yuan*, the belief in the predetermined and unalterable relationships among things and individuals of the universe. Given their low perceived efficacy over environmental problems, Eco-bystanders are by no means loyal followers of the doctrines of sustainable living and consumption, even though they do express concerns about environmental issues.

However, because Eco-bystanders account for a large proportion (34 percent) of the present sample, and probably the entire Chinese population, it is worthwhile for green marketers and policy-makers to earnestly work out plans to stimulate the desired behavioral responses from these onlookers. To help Eco-bystanders develop more confidence in their own ability to combat environmental problems, the message that "things can be changed" should be well spelled out. In this context, those responsible for environmental promotion perhaps need to publicize not only the perils suffered by the planet, but also the improvements that active, concerned groups have brought and can continue to bring about.

Basic Browns are the most environmentally unconscious Chinese citizens. Owing to their lack of concern about environmental problems, they seldom take part in any eco-friendly activities. One-quarter of the survey respondents belong to this category. Should the survey be representative, the presence of a considerable proportion of Basic Browns may pose a major obstacle for China in advancing its nationwide environmental movement.

POSSIBLE DEMOGRAPHIC DIFFERENCES

To aid in understanding the four segments of survey respondents, their demographic characteristics are shown in Table 3. More than half of the Basic Greens (57 percent), Sprouts (63 percent), and Eco-bystanders (54 percent) are male, compared to only 41

• TABLE 3 •

DEMOGRAPHIC CHARACTERISTICS OF THE FIVE SEGMENTS

CHARACTERISTICS	BASIC GREENS	SPROUTS	ECO-BYSTANDERS	BASIC BROWNS
Male	57%	63%	54%	41%
Female	43%	37%	46%	59%
Single	27%	30%	25%	28%
Married	73%	70%	75%	72%
18–29 years old	37%	41%	35%	37%
30–39 years old	26%	32%	27%	26%
40–49 years old	22%	17%	20%	16%
Over 49	15%	10%	18%	21%
Below high school education	9%	14%	11%	43%
High school education	20%	34%	34%	24%
University education or above	71%	52%	55%	33%
Earns below Rmb1,000* per mo.	47%	49%	49%	50%
Earns Rmb1,000–1,399 per mo.	22%	14%	19%	20%
Earns over Rmb1,399 per mo.	31%	37%	32%	30%

*US$1 = Rmb8.4

Note: Chi-Square test for gender and education is significant at $p<0.05$.

percent of the Basic Browns. Taken together, these differences seem to indicate that men are more environmentally concerned than women. As suggested by previous environmental studies, men's traditionally greater involvement in political and community issues probably contributes significantly to these more positive attitudes.

In terms of educational background, 71 percent of the Basic Greens are university graduates. This proportion is significantly higher than that of the Sprouts (52 percent), Eco-bystanders (55 percent), and Basic Browns (33 percent). Such a finding suggests a positive association between environmental consciousness and education, and echoes previous environmental studies. In those studies, education has consistently been demonstrated as the only demographic variable that correlates positively with environmental consciousness.

In sum, most of the demographic variables under investigation are not as effective as attitudes in segmenting the Chinese green market. Nevertheless, the discriminatory power of gender and education identified above can still provide green marketers with some additional clues to better locate their target customers.

GREEN CONSUMPTION BEHAVIORS

As mentioned earlier, the survey comprises a few questions covering respondents' green consumption behaviors. Specifically, these questions concern: (1) the additional amount respondents are willing to pay for a green version of a product, and (2) whether they have bought any eco-friendly batteries or detergent within the last six months. Batteries and detergent were chosen because they had been identified as the best-known green goods among Mainland Chinese consumers during previous focus group sessions. The results are summarized in Table 4.

As expected, Basic Browns were the most uninvolved green consumers; only one-third of this group had bought either eco-friendly batteries or detergent within the previous six months. Moreover, they were willing to spend only 2.5 percent more for a green version of a product. This percentage is significantly lower than that of any other customer segments (Basic Greens = 6.0 percent, Sprouts = 5.8 percent, Eco-bystanders = 4.3 percent) or the entire sample (4.5 percent).

In terms of the additional amount they are willing to pay for green products, and judging from their purchase of eco-friendly batteries, Eco-bystanders are seen as more environmentally involved than Basic Browns. However, as far as the purchase of eco-friendly detergent is concerned, only 22.5 percent of Eco-bystanders had bought this item within the previous six months. This percentage is even lower than that of Basic Browns (33.3 percent). One plausible explanation for this peculiar finding is that Eco-bystanders do not believe the use of eco-friendly detergent can really help combat environmental problems, such as water pollution. The underlying factors accounting for such perceived inefficacy undoubtedly warrant further exploration in future studies.

Consistent with the general view, Basic Greens are seen as the most environmentally involved consumers. Among the four segments, they are willing to spend the most to acquire a green version of a product. Their purchasing rates for eco-friendly batteries and detergent are also the highest among the four segments. Sprouts are also actively involved in green purchases. In terms of the additional amount they are willing to pay for green products, as well as their purchase of eco-friendly batteries and detergent, they rank only after Basic Greens. Undoubtedly, Sprouts' strong faith in their ability to tackle environmental problems contributes significantly to their strong commitment to green consumption.

• TABLE 4 •

SUMMARIZED RESULTS CONCERNING RESPONDENTS' GREEN PURCHASES

	Basic Greens	Sprouts	Eco-bystanders	Basic Browns	Overall
How much respondents will pay over the original price for a green version of a product	6.0%	5.8%	4.3%	2.5%	4.5%
Percent of customers who have bought eco-friendly batteries in the last 6 months	46.9%	42.0%	35.2%	33.3%	38.4%
Percent of customers who have bought eco-friendly detergent in the last six months	40.8%	36.4%	22.5%	33.3%	31.7%

IMPLICATIONS

Although it is still classified as a developing country, China has been rapidly industrializing and urbanizing throughout the past two decades. With increasing affluence derived from rapid economic development, certain sections of the country have begun to realize the hazardous impact of environmental deterioration on their well-being. This realization certainly creates new challenges and opportunities for both businessmen and policy-makers.

However, only 18 percent of the surveyed respondents in this study are identified as Basic Greens. When this percentage is judged against similar findings from environmental studies of developed countries, it appears that China's green movement is still lagging behind. For instance, Roberts (1996) reports that 79 percent of U.S. citizens considered themselves environmentalists and 82 percent indicated they had changed their shopping habits to help protect the environment. Moreover, although U.S. consumers, on average, are willing to pay 6.6 percent more for a green version of a product, according to Hume (1991), the 549 Chinese customers in this study are only willing to pay an average of 4.5 percent more. Indeed, even when compared with the corresponding proportion (6.0 percent) of Basic Greens, U.S. consumers are still considerably more generous in their green spending.

Nevertheless, when taking into account the presence of a sizable proportion of Sprouts (23 percent) in our sample, the development of China's green movement is not as pessimistic as it first appears. Except for their peculiar preference for the use of nuclear power, Sprouts generally hold strong pro-environmental attitudes. As seen in Table 4, their commitment to green consumption is far from apathetic.

Thus, it seems that whether China's green market can be developed further depends a great deal on how effectively companies can translate Sprouts' pro-environmental attitudes to more proactive green consumption behaviors. Companies may need to pay more attention to the credibility of their environmental claims. They should realize that even the most environmentally concerned consumers are unwilling to pay extra for products whose environmental claims appear doubtful or unsubstantiated. Moreover, it may also be worthwhile for companies to invest more in "environmentalizing" their manufacturing processes and improving the quality of their green prouducts. Such investments will not only enhance their images as socially responsible, but will also boost the confidence of those already environmentally concerned customers in trying out the green products.

At the national level, these findings also shed light on how the Chinese government may fine-tune its environmental publicity strategies in advancing citizens' environmental involvement. For instance, Eco-bystanders will likely be more inclined to act on their environmental concerns if they believe their efforts can really help combat environmental problems. So the Chinese government should focus on convincing these people that they have the necessary capabilities to find effective solutions to ecological problems. Environmental education that can help citizens raise their knowledge about *how* to contribute to ecological well-being is imperative. It calls for the incorporation of more environmental elements into various levels of the Chinese educational system.

In addition, such "green" education should be supplemented by related civic education targeting the general public via various propaganda vehicles, such as TV and radio broadcasts and exhibitions.

The Chinese government can also raise citizens' perceived efficacy over environmental problems. One way to do this is through such infrastructural support as building more recycling and waste-disposal facilities for the public. Moreover, it should establish a comprehensive eco-certification scheme and clear environmental advertising guidelines to properly monitor green marketers' practices. These regulatory measures can help boost consumers' confidence in various available green products and assure them that what they buy will, in effect, contribute to environmental improvement.

The Chinese government is by no means a dropout in the recent worldwide ecological movement. Particularly within the last decade, it has formulated a series of laws and regulations to protect the environment. These measures have contributed to the gradual increase in environmental consciousness and green purchases among Chinese citizens. Although China's green market is yet to be lucrative, the empirical evidence from this study has clearly demonstrated its potential for further development. To fully realize this potential, joint efforts among the government, businesses, and citizens are indispensable. In view of China's dilemma of pursuing economic growth while protecting the environment, these joint efforts seem to be the only way to achieve a nationwide sustainable development and lead to a "win-win" solution for all the stakeholders in the long run.

More than 2,500 years ago, Lao Tzu, a great Chinese philosopher, already suggested to mankind to respect the way or *tao* of nature and work together toward ecological harmony. Apparently, this traditional wisdom shows no sign of obsolescence even in the run into the next millennium.

References

J. Arbuthnot and S. Lingg, "A Comparison of French and American Environmental Behaviors, Knowledge, and Attitudes," *International Journal of Psychology*, 10 (1975): 275–281.

G. Berberoglu and C. Tosunoglu, "Exploratory and Confirmatory Factor Analyses of an Environmental Attitude Scale (EAS) for Turkish University Students," *Journal of Environmental Education*, Spring 1995, pp. 40–43.

R.Y.K. Chan, "Environmental Attitudes and Behavior of Consumers in China: Survey Findings and Implications," *Journal of International Consumer Marketing*, 11, 4 (1999): 25–52.

R.Y.K. Chan and E. Yam, "Green Movement in a Newly Industrializing Area: A Survey on the Attitudes and Behavior of Hong Kong Citizens," *Journal of Community and Applied Social Psychology*, 5 (1995): 273–284.

Q. Chen, "Environmental Protection in Action," *Beijing Review*, September 7–13, 1998, pp. 8–12.

Fanny M.C. Cheung, "Psychopathology Among Chinese People," in M.H. Bond (ed.), *The Psychology of the Chinese People* (New York: Oxford University Press, 1993): 171–211.

James P. Dorian, *Energy in China: Poised for the 21st Century* (London: Financial Times Energy, 1998).

J.W. Head, "Using Criminal Sanctions to Fight Environmental Damage in the PRC," *East Asian Executive Reports*, September 15, 1995, p. 9.

J.W. Head, "China: Environmental Legislation: Report on Recent Developments," *East Asian Executive Reports*, January 15, 1996, pp. 13–14.

Chiang Ho, Wen-yung Ching, and I-ting Wang, *Introduction to Ecology* [in Chinese] (Beijing: Ching Hua University Press, 1994).

P.M. Homer and L.R. Kahle, "A Structural Equation Test of the Value-Attitude-Behavior Hierarchy," *Journal of Personality and Social Psychology*, 54, 4 (1988): 638–646.

Scott Hume, "Consumer Double-Talk Makes Companies Wary," *Advertising Age*, October 28, 1991, p. GR4.

Ling-yee Li, "Effect of Collectivist Orientation and Ecological Attitudes on Actual Environmental Commitment: The Moderating Role of Consumer Demographics and Product Involvement," *Journal of International Consumer Marketing*, 9, 4 (1997): 31–53.

Y.W. Liu, "Green Marketing: A New Marketing Era for China in the Coming Century," paper presented at the 10th Annual Academic Conference of the Chinese Marketing Association of Colleges and Universities, Shanghai, China, July 1994 [in Chinese].

M.G. Martinsons, S.K.K. So, C. Tin, and D. Wong, "Hong Kong and China: Emerging Markets for Environmental Products and Technologies," *Long Range Planning*, 30, 2 (1997): 277–290.

J. McEvoy, "The American Concern with the Environment," in W.R. Burch, N.H. Cheek, Jr., and L. Taylor (eds.), *Social Behavior, Natural Resources and the Environment* (New York: Harper & Row, 1972): 214–236.

Thomas H. Miles, *Tao Te Ching: About the Way of Nature and Its Powers/Lao Tzu: A Translation with Commentary* (New York: Avery Publishing Group, Inc., 1992).

M.G. Morgan, "What Would It Take to Revitalize Nuclear Power in the U.S.?" *Environment*, 35, 2 (1993): 6–9, 30–32.

T.M. Parris, "Nukes on the Net," *Environment*, January–February 1997, p. 45.

J.A. Roberts, "Will the Real Socially Responsible Consumer Please Step Forward?" *Business Horizons*, January–February 1996, pp. 79–93.

PART THREE

Strategies of Entry and Operations

MANAGING GLOBAL EXPANSION: A CONCEPTUAL FRAMEWORK

Anil K. Gupta and Vijay Govindarajan

There are at least five reasons why the need to become global has ceased to be a discretionary option and become a strategic imperative for virtually any medium-sized to large corporation.

1. *The Growth Imperative.* Companies have no choice but to persist in a never-ending quest for growth if they wish to garner rewards from the capital markets and attract and retain top talent. For many industries, developed country markets are quite mature. Thus, the growth imperative generally requires companies to look to emerging markets for fresh opportunities.

   Consider a supposedly mature industry such as paper. Per capita paper consumption in such developed markets as North America and Western Europe is around 600 pounds. In contrast, per capita consumption of paper in China and India is around 30 pounds. If you are a dominant European paper manufacturer such as UPM-Kymmene, can you really afford not to build market presence in places like China or India? If per capita paper consumption in both countries increased by just one pound over the next five years, demand would increase by 2.2 billion pounds, an amount that can keep five state-of-the-art paper mills running at peak capacity.
2. *The Efficiency Imperative.* Whenever the value chain sustains one or more activities in which the minimum efficient scale (of research facilities, production

Anil K. Gupta is a professor of strategy and international business at the University of Maryland, College Park, Maryland. Vijay Govindarajan is the Earl C. Daum 1924 Professor of International Business at Dartmouth College, Hanover, New Hampshire.

centers, and so on) exceeds the sales volume feasible within one country, a company with global presence will have the potential to create a cost advantage relative to a domestic player within that industry. The case of Mercedes-Benz, now a unit of DaimlerChrysler, illustrates this principle. Historically, Mercedes-Benz has concentrated its research and manufacturing operations in Germany and has derived around 20 percent of its revenues from the North American market. Given the highly scale-sensitive nature of the auto industry, it is easy to see that Mercedes-Benz's ability to compete in Europe, or even Germany, hinges on its market position and revenues from the North American market.

3. *The Knowledge Imperative.* No two countries, even close neighbors such as Canada and the United States, are completely alike. So when a company expands its presence to more than one country, it must adapt at least some features of its products and/or processes to the local environment. This adaptation requires creating local know-how, some of which may be too idiosyncratic to be relevant outside the particular local market. However, in many cases, local product and/or process innovations are cutting-edge and have the potential to generate global advantage. GE India's innovations in making CT scanners simpler, transportable, and cheaper would appear to enjoy wide-ranging applicability, as would P&G Indonesia's innovations in reducing the cost structure for cough syrup.
4. *Globalization of Customers.* The term "globalization of customers" refers to customers that are worldwide corporations (such as the soft-drink companies served by advertising agencies) as well as those who are internationally mobile (such as the executives served by American Express or the globe-trotters serviced by Sheraton Hotels). When the customers of a domestic company start to globalize, the company must keep pace with them. Three reasons dictate such an alignment. First, the customer may strongly prefer worldwide consistency and coordination in the sourcing of products and services. Second, it may prefer to deal with a small number of supply partners on a long-term basis. Third, allowing a customer to deal with different supplier(s) in other countries poses a serious risk that the customer may replace your firm with one of these suppliers even in the domestic market. Motivations such as these are driving GE Plastics to globalize. Historically, it supplied plastic pellets to largely U.S.-based telephone companies such as AT&T and GTE. As these firms globalized and set up manufacturing plants outside the U.S., GE Plastics had no choice but to follow them abroad.
5. *Globalization of Competitors.* If your competitors start to globalize and you do not, they can use their global stronghold to attack you in at least two ways. First, they can develop a first-mover advantage in capturing market growth, pursuing global scale efficiencies, profiting from knowledge arbitrage, and providing a coordinated source of supply to global customers. Second, they can use multi-market presence to cross-subsidize and wage a more intense attack in your own home markets. It is dangerous to underestimate the rate at which competition can accelerate the pace of globalization. Look at Fuji's inroads into

the U.S. market, historically dominated by Kodak. The trend is happening in other industries as well, such as in white goods, personal computers, and financial services.

In the emerging era, every industry must be considered a global industry. Today, globalization is no longer an option but a strategic imperative for all but the smallest firms. The following framework and set of conceptual ideas can guide firms in approaching the strategic challenge of casting their business lines overseas and building global presence:

- *How should a multiproduct firm choose the product line to launch it into the global market?*
- *What factors make some markets more strategic than others?*
- *What should companies consider in determining the right mode of entry?*
- *How should the enterprise transplant the corporate DNA as it enters new markets?*
- *What approaches should the company use to win the local battle?*
- *How rapidly should a company expand globally?*

CHOICE OF PRODUCTS

When any multiproduct firm chooses to go abroad, it must ask itself whether it should globalize the entire portfolio simultaneously or use a subset of product lines. Firms can make this choice randomly and opportunistically or in a well thought out and systematic manner.

Consider the case of Marriott Corporation, which was essentially a domestic company in the late 1980s. It had two principal lines of business: lodging and contract services. Besides other activities, the lodging sector included four distinct product lines: full-service hotels and resorts ("Marriott" brand), midprice hotels ("Courtyard" brand), budget hotels ("Fairfield Inn" brand), and long-term stay hotels ("Residence Inn" brand). On the other hand, contract services included the following three product lines: Marriott Management Services, Host/Travel Plazas, and Marriott Senior Living Services (retirement communities). As the company embarked on globalization, it had to confront the question of which one or more of these product lines should serve as the starting point for its globalization efforts.

Global expansion forces companies to develop at least three types of capabilities: learning about foreign markets, learning how to manage people in foreign locations, and learning how to manage foreign subsidiaries. Until firms develop these capabilities, they cannot avoid remaining strangers in a strange land, with global expansion posing a high risk. Engaging in simultaneous globalization across the entire portfolio of products compounds these risks dramatically. So it is often wiser to choose one or a small number of product lines as the initial launch vehicles for globalization. The choice should adhere to the twin goals of maximizing the returns while minimizing the risks associated with early moves abroad. These initial moves represent experiments with high learning potential. It is important that these experiments succeed for the firm because success creates psychological confidence, political credibility, and cash flow to fuel further rapid globalization.

Figure 1 presents a conceptual framework to identify those products, business units, or lines of business that might be preferred candidates for early globalization. Underlying this framework are two essential dimensions by which to evaluate each line of business in the company's portfolio—one pertaining to potential returns (expected payoffs) and the other to potential risks (required degree of local adaptation).

The first dimension focuses on the magnitude of globalization's payoffs, which tend to be higher when the five imperatives (listed at the beginning of the article) are stronger. Looking at the case of Marriott, it is clear that such imperatives are much stronger for full-service lodging than they are for the retirement community business. The primary customers of full-service lodging are globe-trotting corporate executives. In such a business, worldwide presence can create significant value by using a centralized reservation system, developing and diffusing globally consistent service concepts, and leveraging a well-known brand name that assures customers of high quality and service. In contrast, none of these factors is of high salience in the retirement community business, thereby rendering the imperatives for globalization much less urgent.

The second dimension of our framework concerns the extent to which different lines of business require local adaptation to succeed in foreign markets. The greater the extent of such adaptation, the greater the degree to which new product and/or service

• FIGURE 1 •

A FRAMEWORK FOR CHOICE OF PRODUCTS: ATTRACTIVENESS OF PRODUCT LINES AS LAUNCH VEHICLES FOR INITIAL GLOBALIZATION

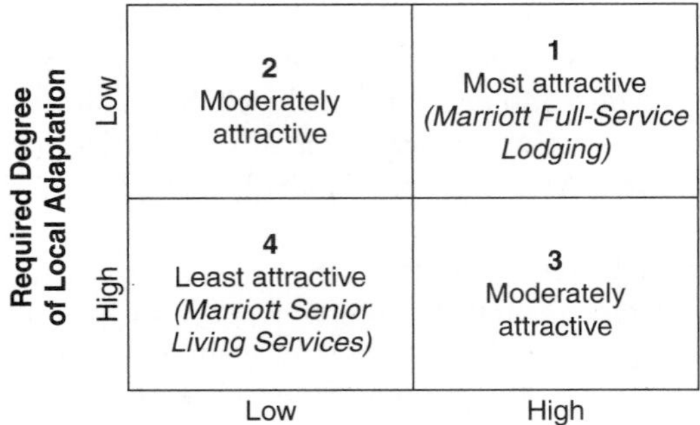

features would need to be developed locally rather than cloned from proven and pre-existing concepts and capabilities. Because any new development involves risk, the greater the degree of required local adaptation, the greater the risks of failure—particularly when such development entails the already significant "liability of foreignness." Marriott exemplifies these principles. Compared with full-service lodging, the retirement community business is a very local business and thus requires more local adaptation.

Combining both dimensions, as indicated in Figure 1, full-service lodging emerges as a particularly attractive candidate for early globalization. As the spearhead for globalization moves, it provides Marriott with a high return/low risk laboratory for developing the knowledge and skills needed for foreign market entry and managing foreign subsidiaries. Having thus overcome the "liability of foreignness," Marriott would be better positioned to exploit the globalization potential of its other lines of business.

To reiterate, hardly any line of business today is devoid of the potential for exploitation on a global scale. However, any multiproduct firm that is starting to globalize must remember that a logically sequenced rather than random approach is likely to serve as a higher-return, lower-risk path toward full-scale globalization.

CHOICE OF STRATEGIC MARKETS

Not all markets are of equal strategic importance. This is a central tenet of the conceptual framework presented in Figure 2. The following two dimensions determine the strategic importance of a market: (1) *market potential*, and (2) *learning potential*.

• FIGURE 2 •

DRIVERS OF A MARKET'S STRATEGIC IMPORTANCE

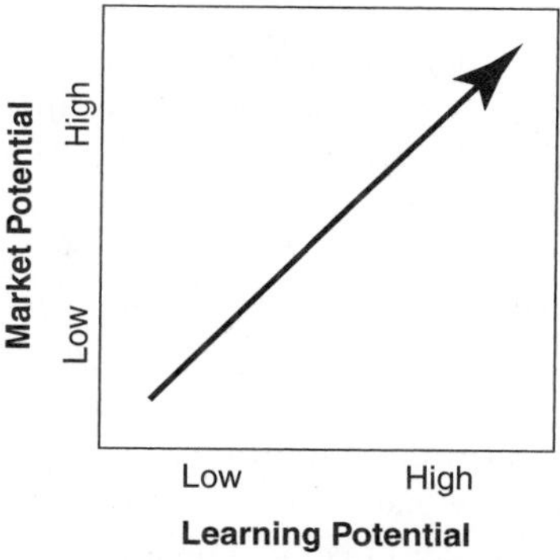

The concept of market potential encompasses both current market size and growth expectations for a particular line of business. For instance, one of the critical markets for AOL is Japan because 45 percent of the PCs sold in Asia are there. It is important to remember that, notwithstanding the importance of the size of a country's economy, market potential does not always go hand in hand with the country's GDP. A blindness to this reality has led some authors to conclude that companies are not global unless they are present in the triad of Europe, Japan, and North America. Such simplistic conclusions can often be dramatically fallacious. If you are managing ABB's power plant business, the bulk of your market for new power plants lies outside the triad.

There are two drivers of the learning potential of any market. The first is the presence of sophisticated and demanding customers for the particular product or service. Such customers (1) force a company to meet very tough standards for product and service quality, cost, cycle time, and a host of other attributes, (2) accelerate its learning regarding tomorrow's customer needs, and (3) force it to innovate constantly and continuously. France and Italy are leading-edge customer markets for the high fashion clothing industry—a fact of considerable importance to a company such as Du Pont, the manufacturer of Lycra and other textile fibers.

The second driver of a market's learning potential is the pace at which relevant technologies are evolving there. This technology evolution can emerge from one or more of several sources: leading-edge customers, innovative competitors, universities and other local research centers, and firms in related industries.

As indicated in Figure 2, the strategic importance of a market is a joint function of both market potential and learning potential. No firm is truly global unless it is present in all strategic markets. Nevertheless, despite their obvious importance, the timing of a firm's decision to enter strategic markets must also depend on its "ability to exploit" these markets. Going after a strategic market without such an ability is generally a fast track to disaster.

The ability to exploit a market is a function of two factors: (1) the height of entry barriers, and (2) the intensity of competition in the market. Entry barriers are likely to be lowest when there are no regulatory constraints on trade and investment (as in the case of regional economic blocks) and when new markets are geographically, culturally, and linguistically proximate to the domestic market. Even when there are low entry barriers, the intensity of competition can hinder a company's potential for exploiting a market. For example, the large U.S. market in the retailing industry has historically proven to be a graveyard for foreign entrants such as Marks & Spencer, precisely because of the intensity of local competition.

Figure 3 presents a conceptual framework that combines the two key dimensions—"strategic importance of market" and "ability to exploit"—to offer guidelines on how a firm can engage in directed opportunism in its choice of markets. The firm's stance toward markets that have high strategic importance and high ability to exploit ought to be to enter rapidly. By comparison, the firm can afford to be much more opportunistic and ad hoc with respect to markets that have low strategic importance but are easier to exploit. In the case of markets that have high strategic importance but are also very difficult to exploit, we recommend an incremental phased approach in which the development of needed capabilities precedes market entry. One attractive way for a

• FIGURE 3 •

A FRAMEWORK FOR CHOICE OF MARKETS

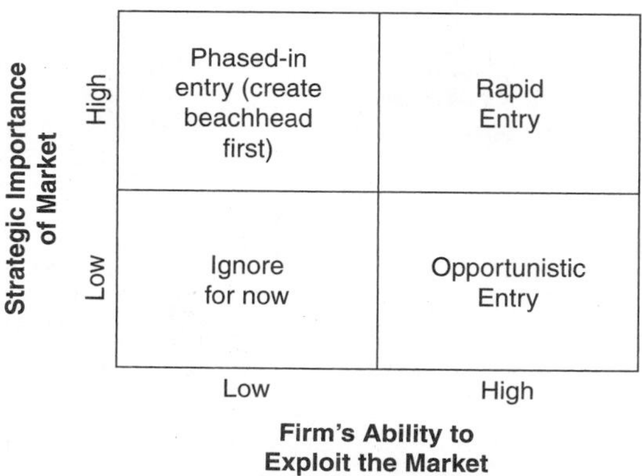

company to develop such capabilities is to first enter a *beachhead market:* one that closely resembles the targeted strategic market but provides a safer opportunity to learn how to enter and succeed there. Some commonly used examples of beachhead markets are Switzerland and/or Austria for Germany, Canada for the U.S., and Hong Kong or Taiwan for China. Finally, the firm should stay away from those markets that are neither strategic nor easy to exploit.

MODE OF ENTRY

Once a company has selected the country or countries to enter and designated the product line(s) that will serve as the launch vehicles, it must determine the appropriate mode of entry. The entry mode issue rests on two fundamental questions. The first concerns the extent to which the firm will export or produce locally. Here, the firm has several choices. It can rely on 100 percent export of finished goods, export of components but localized assembly, 100 percent local production, and so on.

The second question deals with the extent of ownership control over activities that will be performed locally in the target market. Here also, the firm faces several choices: 0 percent ownership modes (licensing, franchising, and so on), partial ownership modes (joint ventures or affiliates), and 100 percent ownership modes (fully-owned greenfield operations or acquisitions). Figure 4 uses these two dimensions to depict the array of choices regarding mode of entry that are open to any firm, and includes examples illustrating the variety of available options.

• FIGURE 4 •

ALTERNATIVE MODES OF ENTRY

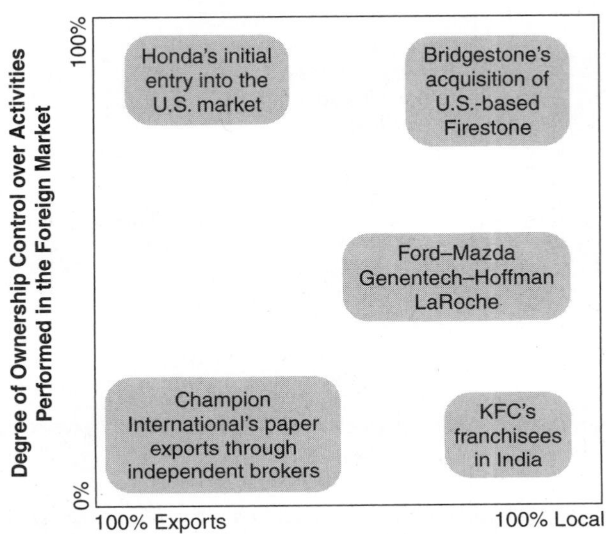

Choosing the right mode of entry is critical because the choice, once made, is often difficult and costly to alter. Inappropriate decisions can impose unwanted, unnecessary, and undesirable constraints on future development options.

Turning to the first question, greater reliance on local production would be appropriate under the following four conditions:

- *Size of local market is larger than minimum efficient scale of production.* The larger the size of the local market, the more completely local production will translate into scale economies for the firm while holding down tariff and transportation costs. One illustration of this argument is Bridgestone's entry into the U.S. market by acquiring the local production base of Firestone instead of exporting tires from Japan.
- *Shipping and tariff costs associated with exporting to the target market are so high* that they neutralize any cost advantages associated with producing in any country other than that market. This is why cement companies such as Cemex and Lafarge Coppee engage heavily in local production in every country they enter.
- *Need for local customization of product design is high.* Product customization requires two capabilities: a deep understanding of local market needs, and an ability to incorporate this understanding in the company's design and production

decisions. Localizing production in the target market significantly enhances the firm's ability to respond to local market needs accurately and efficiently.

- *Local content requirements are strong.* This is one of the major reasons why foreign auto companies rely heavily on local production in markets such as the EU, China, and India.

Turning to the second question, given the differing costs and benefits of local market activities, neither alliances nor complete ownership are universally desirable in all situations. Unlike the complete ownership mode, alliance-based entry modes have the advantages of permitting the firm to share the costs and risks associated with market entry, allowing rapid access to local know-how, and giving managers the flexibility to respond more entrepreneurially and much more quickly to dynamic global competition than the conquer-the-world-by-yourself approach. However, a major downside of alliances is their potential for various types of conflict stemming from differences in corporate goals and cultures.

Taking into account the pros and cons, then, alliance-based entry modes are often more appropriate under the following conditions:

- *Physical, linguistic, and cultural distance between the home and host countries is high.* The more dissimilar and unfamiliar the target market, the greater the need for the firm to rely on a local partner to provide know-how and networks. Conceivably, the firm could obtain the requisite local knowledge and competencies through acquisition. However, in highly dissimilar and unfamiliar markets, its ability to manage an acquired subsidiary is often very limited. Ford's decision to enter the Indian market through the joint venture (JV) mode rested partly on the company's need to rely on an experienced and respected local partner, Mahindra & Mahindra.
- *The subsidiary would have low operational integration with the rest of the multinational operations.* By definition, tighter integration between a subsidiary and the rest of the global network increases the degree of mutual interdependence between the subsidiary and the network. In this context of high interdependence, it becomes crucial for the subsidiary and the network to pursue shared goals, and for the firm to be able to reshape the subsidiary according to the changing needs of the rest of the network. Shared ownership of the subsidiary puts major constraints on the firm's ability to achieve such congruence in goals and have the requisite freedom to reshape subsidiary operations as needed.
- *The risk of asymmetric learning by the partner is (or can be kept) low.* In a typical JV, two partners pool different but complementary know-how into an alliance. Ongoing interaction between their core operations and the alliance gives each an opportunity to learn from the other and appropriate the other's complementary know-how. In effect, this dynamic implies that the alliance often is not just a cooperative relationship but also a learning race. If Firm A has the ability to learn at a faster rate than Firm B, the outcome is likely to be asymmetric learning in favor of Firm A. Thus, over time, Firm A may seek to dissolve the

alliance in favor of going it alone in competition with a still-disadvantaged Firm B.

- *The company is short of capital.* Lack of capital underlay Xerox's decision in the 1950s to enter the European market through an alliance with the Rank Organization of the U.K.
- *Government regulations require local equity participation.* Historically, many countries with formidable market potentials, such as China and Brazil, have successfully imposed the JV option on foreign entrants, even when all other considerations might have favored the choice of a complete ownership mode.

A company that decides to enter the foreign market through local production rather than through exports faces a secondary decision. It must decide whether to set up greenfield operations or use an existing production base through a cross-border acquisition. A greenfield operation gives the company tremendous freedom to impose its own unique management policies, culture, and mode of operations on the new subsidiary. In contrast, a cross-border acquisition poses the much tougher challenge of cultural transformation and post-merger integration. However, setting up greenfield operations also has two potential liabilities: lower speed of entry, and more intense local competition caused by the addition of new production capacity as well as one more competitor. Taking into account both the pros and the cons, Figure 5 provides a conceptual framework to determine when greenfield operations and/or cross-border acquisitions are likely to be the more appropriate entry modes.

This conceptual framework has two dimensions. The first pertains to the uniqueness of the globalizing company's culture. Nucor is a good example of a newly globalizing

• FIGURE 5 •

GREENFIELD VS. CROSS-BORDER ACQUISITION

Market Growth Rate	Low (Uniqueness of Corporate Culture)	High (Uniqueness of Corporate Culture)
High	Greenfield operations or cross-border acquisitions	Greenfield operations *(Nucor's entry into Brazil)*
Low	Cross-border acquisitions *(Int'l Paper's entry into Europe)*	Greenfield operations or cross-border acquisitions

Uniqueness of Corporate Culture

firm with a very strong and unique culture. It is significantly different from other steel producers in its human resource policies, egalitarian work environment, performance-based incentives, teamwork, decentralization, and business processes. The more committed a company is to preserving its unique culture, the more necessary it becomes to set up greenfield operations when entering foreign markets. This is because building and nurturing a unique culture from scratch (as would be feasible in the case of greenfield operations) is almost always much easier than transforming an entrenched culture (as would be necessary in the case of a cross-border acquisition).

Aside from corporate culture considerations, the impact of entry mode on the resulting intensity of local competition must also carry considerable weight in a firm's decisions. If the local market is in the emerging or high growth phase (such as the auto industry in China and India), new capacity additions would have little downside effect on the intensity of competition. In contrast, when the local market is mature (such as the tire industry in the U.S.), new capacity additions will only intensify an already high degree of local competition. Within the forest products industry, Indonesia-based Asia Pulp & Paper has used the greenfield mode for expanding into other high-growth Asian markets. In the same industry, the U.S.-based International Paper has pursued a different path and relied on the acquisition mode for its expansion into the mature European market.

TRANSPLANTING THE CORPORATE DNA

Having decided on a mode of entry for a particular product line into a particular target market, the challenge of building global presence moves on to implementing actual entry. Among the first issues the globalizing company must address is how to transplant the core elements of its business model, its core practices, and its core beliefs—in short, its DNA—to the new subsidiary. The following example illustrates the challenge of transplanting the corporate DNA.

After acquiring 2,000 employees from Yamaichi Securities, Merrill Lynch & Co. counted on an American-style investment advisor approach to build a high-trust image in the securities brokerage industry in Japan. Historically, says Sugawara (1999), the industry has been

> tainted by unsavory practices. . . . One well-known abuse . . . "churning"—in which sales people persuade naïve investors to buy and sell a lot of securities so the sales people can boost their commissions. Merrill Lynch promised that there would be no churning. Instead, its sales people were instructed to try to get an overall picture of customers' finances, ascertain their needs and then suggest investments. Something got lost in the translation, however. Japanese customers have complained that Merrill Lynch sales people are too nosy, asking questions about their investments instead of just telling them what stocks to buy.

As this example illustrates, obstacles to transplanting the corporate DNA can emerge from any of several sources: local employees, local customers, local regulations, and so forth. Given such obstacles, every company needs to develop clarity regarding what exactly its "core" (as distinct from "peripheral") beliefs and practices are. Such clarity is essential for knowing where the company should stay committed to its own beliefs and practices and where it should be willing to adapt. Having achieved this clarity, the company needs to build mechanisms to transfer core beliefs and practices to the new subsidiary. Finally, and most important, it needs to embed these beliefs and practices in the new subsidiary.

CLARIFYING AND DEFINING THE CORE BELIEFS AND PRACTICES

Core beliefs and practices can be defined at any of varying levels of abstraction. Take Wal-Mart's practice of promoting "Made in America" goods in its U.S. stores. Assuming that promoting the origin-of-manufacture is a core practice for Wal-Mart, the company can define the practice in more or less abstract terms. A more abstract definition would be, "Wherever we operate, we believe in promoting locally manufactured products." On the other hand, a less abstract definition would be, "We promote products that are made in America." As this example points out, defining core beliefs and practices in more abstract terms permits a higher degree of local adaptation. At the same time, if the core beliefs and practices become too abstract, they could lose much of their meaning and value.

Notwithstanding its criticality, the definition of what constitutes a company's core beliefs and practices is and must always be the result of learning and experimentation over time. This is because the answers will almost certainly vary across industries, across firms within an industry, and, for the same firm, across time. As observed astutely by a senior executive of a major global retailer, "Cut your chains and you become free. Cut your roots and you die. Note, however, that differentiating between the two requires good judgment, something that you acquire only through experience and over time."

TRANSPLANTING CORE BELIEFS AND PRACTICES TO THE NEW SUBSIDIARY

Transplanting core beliefs and practices to a new subsidiary, whether a greenfield operation or an acquisition, is always a transformational event—the challenge of transformation being greater in the case of an acquisition. The likelihood is very high that the transplanted beliefs and practices are likely to be at best partially understood and, in the case of an acquisition, will often be seen as alien and questionable. As such, transferring core beliefs and practices to a new subsidiary almost always requires transferring a select group of committed believers ("the DNA carriers") to the new operation. The size of this group would depend largely on the scale of the desired transformation effort. If the goal is to engage in a wholesale replacement of an entire set of preexisting beliefs and practices (as in the case of ABB's acquisitions in Eastern Europe), then it may be necessary to send in a virtual army of DNA carriers. On the other hand, if the goal is to create a new business model (as in the case of Mercedes-Benz's Alabama plant), then the transplants would need to be much fewer in number and would need to be very carefully selected.

Obloj and Thomas (1998) describe rather vividly how the invasion process worked in the case of ABB Poland:

> The transformation began with an influx and invasion of external and internal ABB consultants that signaled clearly the introductory stage of organizational change. Their behavior was guided by their perception of the stereotypical behavior of an inefficient state-owned firm typically managed by a cadre of administrators who do not understand how to manage a firm in a market economy. They did not initially perform any sophisticated diagnosis or analysis of local conditions or develop a strategic vision for the transformation process. Rather, they forcefully implemented market enterprise discipline in the acquired former state-owned firms by a series of high-speed actions. They implemented massive training efforts aimed at exposing employees and managers of acquired firms to the principles of the market economy, modern management principles, and the ABB management system. This was adopted in all acquired firms following Percy Barnevik's dictum that the key to competitiveness is education and reeducation.

EMBEDDING THE CORE BELIEFS AND PRACTICES

While the process of transplanting the corporate DNA starts with transferring a select group of DNA carriers to the new subsidiary, it can be regarded as successful only when the new beliefs and practices have become internalized in the mindsets and routines of employees at the new subsidiary. Achieving such internalization requires (1) visibly explicit and credible commitment by the parent company to its core beliefs and practices, (2) deepening the process of education and reeducation within the new organization right down to middle managers and the local work force, and (3) concrete demonstration that the new beliefs and practices yield individual as well as corporate success.

The approach taken by the Ritz-Carlton chain at its new hotel in Shanghai, China illustrates how a company can go about successfully embedding its core beliefs and practices in a new subsidiary. Ritz-Carlton acquired the rights to manage this hotel, with a staff of about 1,000 people, under its own name as of January 1, 1998. The company believed that, consistent with its image and its corporate DNA, the entire operation required significant upgrading. As one would expect, the company brought in a sizable contingent of about 40 expatriates from other Ritz-Carlton units in Asia and around the world to transform and manage the new property. What is especially noteworthy, however, is the approach the managers took to embed the company's own standards of quality and service in the hearts, minds, and behavior of their local associates. Among its first actions in the very first week of operations under its own control, the company decided to start the renovation process from the employee's entrance and changing and wash rooms rather than from other starting points, such as the main lobby. As one executive explained, the logic was that, through this approach, every employee would see two radical changes in the very first week: one, that the new standards of quality and service would be dramatically higher, and two, that they, the employees, were among the most valued stakeholders in the company. This approach served as a very successful start to embedding the company's basic beliefs in every associate's mind: "We Are Ladies and Gentlemen Serving Ladies and Gentlemen."

WINNING THE LOCAL BATTLE

Winning the local battle requires the global enterprise to anticipate, shape, and respond to the needs and/or actions of three sets of host-country players: customers, competitors, and government.

WINNING HOST COUNTRY CUSTOMERS

One of the ingredients in establishing local presence is to understand the uniqueness of the local market and decide which aspects of the firm's business model require little change, which require local adaptation, and which need to be reinvented. The global firm faces little need to adapt its business design if it targets a customer segment in a foreign market similar to the one it serves in its home market. However, if the firm wants to expand the customer base it serves in a foreign market, then adapting the business model to the unique demands of the local customers becomes mandatory.

Consider the case of FedEx when it entered China. As an element of its entry strategy, FedEx had to choose who its target customers should be: local Chinese companies or multinational corporations. The company chose to target multinational companies—a customer segment identical to the one it has historically served. Given the choice, FedEx was able to pretty much export the U.S. business model into China, including the use of its own aircraft, building a huge network of trucks and distribution centers, and adopting U.S.-style aggressive marketing and advertising. On the other hand, had FedEx selected local Chinese firms as its targeted customer segment, winning host country customers would have required a significantly greater degree of local adaptation of the business model.

Domino's Pizza is a good example of a company that has benefited from adapting its business model when it entered India. Unlike KFC, Domino's was successful in its initial entry into India, primarily because it tailored its approach to the Indian culture and lifestyle. Even though pepperoni pizza is one of the most popular items for Domino's in other markets, the company dropped it from the menu to show respect for the value Hindus place on the cow. Domino's also tailored other toppings, such as chicken, ginger, and lamb, to suit Indian taste buds.

WINNING AGAINST HOST COUNTRY COMPETITORS

Whenever a company enters a new country, it can expect retaliation from local competitors as well as from other multinationals already operating there. Successfully establishing local presence requires anticipating and responding to these competitive threats. Established local competitors enjoy several advantages: knowledge of the local market; working relationships with local customers; understanding of local distribution channels; and so on. In contrast, the new firm suffers from the "liability of newness." When a global firm enters a market, local competitors will feel threatened and will have a strong reason to retaliate and defend their positions. Such response constitutes entry barriers. In such a context, four possible options are available to the new invader.

1. Enter by acquiring a dominant local competitor.
2. Enter by acquiring a weak local competitor who can be quickly transformed and scaled up.
3. Enter a poorly defended niche.
4. Engage in a frontal attack on the dominant and entrenched incumbents.

- *Acquire a dominant local competitor.* Acquiring a dominant local firm will prove to be successful if the following three conditions are met: (1) there is significant potential for synergies between the acquisition target and the global firm; (2) the global firm has the capability to create and capture such synergies; and (3) the global firm does not give away the synergies from a huge acquisition premium up-front.

  A case of successful entry through acquisition of a dominant local competitor is Accor, the French hospitality company, which entered the U.S. market by acquiring Motel 6—the best managed market leader in the budget lodging category. On the other hand, Sony paid a huge premium to acquire Columbia Pictures; to date, however, it has had great difficulty in justifying this premium—despite the significant potential synergies between Sony's hardware competencies and the "content" expertise of Columbia Pictures.
- *Acquire a weak player.* Acquiring a weak player in the foreign market is an attractive option under the following conditions:

1. The global firm possesses the capabilities that are required to transform the weak player into a dominant player; and
2. The global firm has the ability to transplant the corporate DNA in the acquired firm very quickly.

The sheer act of acquiring a weak player signals to other local competitors that they will soon be under attack. It is therefore to be expected that local competitors will retaliate. If the global firm is unable to transform the weak player within a very short time, the player could become even weaker under attack from local competitors.

Consider Whirlpool's entry into Europe in 1989 by acquiring the problem-ridden appliance division of Philips. Unfortunately, Whirlpool could not quickly embed the capabilities to turn around Philips's struggling appliance business. In the meantime, two European rivals—Sweden's Electrolux and Germany's

Bosch-Siemens—got a wake-up call from Whirlpool's European entry. Quite naturally, the two invested very heavily in modernization, process improvements, new product introductions, and restructuring—all with a view to improving their competitiveness. The net result was a disappointment for Whirlpool in terms of its ambition to consolidate the white goods industry in Europe. By 1998, Whirlpool had 12 percent market share in Europe (half of its expected position) and was also underachieving in profitability. To quote Jeff Fettig, Whirlpool's head of European operations: "We underestimated the competition."

- *Enter a poorly defended niche.* If acquisition candidates are either unavailable or too expensive, the global firm has no choice but to enter on its own. Under such circumstances, it should find a poorly defended niche for market entry under the following conditions:

  1. Such a niche exists.
  2. The global firm can use that niche as a platform for subsequent expansion into the mainstream segments of the local market. That is, the mobility barriers to move from the niche market to the mainstream segments are relatively low.

     In the early 1970s, the Japanese car makers entered the U.S. market at the low end, a segment that was being ignored by the U.S. car companies and was thus a "loose brick" in their fortress. The Japanese companies used their dominance of the lower end segment to migrate to the middle and upper ends very effectively.

- *Frontal attack.* The global company can choose a head-on attack on the dominant and entrenched incumbents provided it has a massive competitive advantage that can be leveraged outside its domestic market. If this were not true, taking on an 800-pound gorilla with all the liability of "newness" could prove suicidal. Lexus succeeded in its frontal attack on Mercedes and BMW in the U.S. market mainly because of a dominating competitive advantage in such areas as product quality and cost structure. For instance, Lexus enjoyed a 30 percent cost advantage. For Mercedes, given the high labor costs in Germany where it manufactured its automobiles, such a cost advantage could not be neutralized quickly.

MANAGING RELATIONSHIPS WITH THE HOST-COUNTRY GOVERNMENT

Local government can often be a key external stakeholder, particularly in emerging markets. Two points are worth noting in this context.

1. The global firm can ill afford to ignore non-market stakeholders such as the local government. For instance, the Chinese government recently banned direct selling. This action has an important bearing on such firms as Mary Kay Cosmetics and Avon, which depend on a highly personalized direct marketing approach.

2. Managing the non-market stakeholders should be seen as a dynamic process. Instead of simplistically reacting to existing government regulations, the firm should also anticipate likely future changes in the regulatory framework and even explore the possibility of helping shape the emerging framework. Instead of appeasement or confrontation, persistence and constructive dialogue with the local government are often critical elements of winning the local battle.

Enron's entry into India is a telling example of an active approach to transforming the entering firm's relationship with host governments. In 1995, mostly due to ideological and political reasons, the Maharashtra government put a sudden halt to Enron's partly built, $2.5 billion power plant. Yet by 1999, not only had Enron won back the original contract for the 826-megawatt unit, it even succeeded in getting a go-ahead to triple the capacity to 2,450 megawatts, representing India's largest foreign investment and Enron's biggest non-U.S. project. Instead of giving up, Enron persisted and helped shape evolving public policy. In the process, the company learned a lesson, but so did the Indian government.

SPEED OF GLOBAL EXPANSION

Having commenced the journey of globalization, a company must still address one major issue in building global presence: How fast should it expand globally? Microsoft's worldwide launch of Windows 95 *on the same day* epitomizes using globalization for aggressive growth. By moving quickly, a company can solidify its market position very rapidly.

However, rapid global expansion can also spread managerial, organizational, and financial resources too thin. The consequence can be to jeopardize the company's ability to defend and profit from the global presence thus created. Witness PepsiCo's helter-skelter rapid expansion in Latin America during the first part of the 1990s. In most cases, Pepsi's ambitious agenda resulted in market positions that have proven to be both indefensible and unprofitable.

Taking into account the pros and cons, an accelerated speed of global expansion is more appropriate under the following conditions:

- *It is easy for competitors to replicate your recipe for success.* This possibility is obvious for fast food and retailing companies such as KFC and Starbuck's, where it is easy for competitors to take a proven concept from one market and replicate it in another unoccupied market with a relatively small investment. However, this phenomenon is observable in other, very different types of industries as well, such as personal computers and software. The rapid globalization of companies like Compaq, Dell, and Microsoft reflects their determination to prevent replication and/or pirating of their product concepts in markets all around the world.

- *Scale economies are extremely important.* Very high economies of scale give the early and rapid globalizer massive first mover advantages and handicap the slower ones for long periods of time. This is precisely why rapid globalizers in the tire industry, such as Goodyear, Michelin, and Bridgestone, now hold considerable advantage over slower ones, such as Pirelli and Continental.
- *Management's capacity to manage (or learn how to manage) global operations is high.* Consider experienced global players like Coca-Cola, Citicorp, Unilever, and ABB. Should such a company successfully introduce a new product line in one country, it would be relatively easy and logical to globalize it rapidly to all potential markets around the world. Aside from the ability to manage global operations, the speed of globalization also depends on the company's ability to leverage its experience from one market to another. The faster the speed with which a firm can recycle its learning about market entry and market defense from one country to another, the lower the risk of spreading managerial and organizational capacity too thinly.

Becoming global is never exclusively the result of a grand design. At the same time, it would be naïve to view it as little more than a sequence of incremental, ad-hoc, opportunistic, and random moves. The wisest approach would be one of *directed opportunism*—an approach that maintains opportunism and flexibility within a broad direction set by a systematic framework. Our goal here has been to provide such a framework.

References

D.A. Blackmon and D. Brady, "Just How Hard Should a U.S. Company Woo a Big Foreign Market?" *Wall Street Journal*, April 6, 1998, p. A1.

S. Ghoshal, "Global Strategy: An Organizing Framework," *Strategic Management Journal*, September–October 1987, pp. 425–440.

V. Govindarajan, "Note on the Global Paper Industry," case study, Dartmouth College, 1999.

G. Hamel and C.K. Prahalad, "Do You Really Have a Global Strategy?" *Harvard Business Review*, July–August 1985, pp. 139–148.

K. Iverson and T. Varian, *Plain Talk: Lessons from a Business Maverick* (New York: Wiley, 1997).

J.P. Jeannet and H.D. Hennessy, *Global Marketing Strategies* (Boston: Houghton Mifflin, 1998).

Jonathan Karp and Kathryn Kranhold, "Enron's Plant in India was Dead: This Month, It Will Go on Stream," *Wall Street Journal*, February 5, 1999, p. A1.

T. Khanna, R. Gulati, and N. Nohria, "Alliances as Learning Races," *Proceedings of the Academy of Management Annual Meetings*, 1994, pp. 42–46.

K. Obloj and H. Thomas, "Transforming Former State-owned Companies into Market Competitors in Poland: The ABB Experience," *European Management Journal*, August 1998, pp. 390–399.

G. Steinmetz and C.J. Chipello, "Local Presence Is Key to European Deals," *Wall Street Journal*, June 30, 1998, p. A15.

G. Steinmetz and C. Quintanilla, "Whirlpool Expected Easy Going in Europe, and It Got a Big Shock," *Wall Street Journal*, April 10, 1998, p. A1.

S. Sugawara, "Japanese Shaken by Business U.S.-Style," *Washington Post*, February 9, 1999, p. E1.

R. Tomkins, "Battered PepsiCo Licks Its Wounds," *Financial Times*, May 30, 1997, p. 26.

"Xerox and Fuji Xerox," Case No. 9-391-156, Harvard Business School.

EMERGING MARKET ALLIANCES: MUST THEY BE WIN-LOSE?

Ashwin Adarkar, Asif Adil, David Ernst, and Paresh Vaish

Global companies are looking to emerging markets for growth. Companies in emerging markets are looking for ways into the burgeoning global economy. Alliances can seem the obvious solution for both sides.

For global companies, limitations on foreign ownership make an alliance the only route into some markets. In other markets, alliances provide an appealing way to accelerate entry and reduce the risks and costs of going it alone. The US company Aetna Insurance, for example, recently announced a joint venture with Sul América Seguros, Brazil's largest insurance company. Aetna is reportedly investing $300 million, with a possible $90 million more to follow, for a 49 percent stake in the joint venture. The aim of the Brazilian-based alliance is to accelerate growth and introduce new products in health, life, and personal insurance and pensions. Aetna contributes expertise in products, information technology, and servicing, while Sul América brings local knowledge, an extensive distribution network and sales system, and its leading market position.

Companies in emerging markets can find the idea of an alliance equally attractive. For those in a position of strength, it can be a powerful vehicle for growth, or a way to leverage low-cost manufacturing or a unique distribution network. Samsung of Korea

---

Ashwin Adarkar is a consultant and Asif Adil and Paresh Vaish are principals in McKinsey's Mumbai office; David Ernst is a principal in the Washington, DC office. Copyright © 1997 McKinsey & Company. All rights reserved.

Author note: We would like to thank our colleagues Guido Conterno, Pedro Cordeiro, Heinz-Peter Elstrodt, Olivier Kayser, Thilo Mannhardt, Stefan Matzinger, Tony Perkins, Alejandro Plaz, Tino Puri, Dominique Turcq, and Jonathan Woetzel for their contributions to this article.

• EXHIBIT 1 •

ALLYING FOR TECHNOLOGY AND SKILLS

SELECTED SAMSUNG ALLIANCES

1970s CONSUMER ELECTRONICS	1980s SEMICONDUCTORS	1990s MULTIMEDIA
Joint ventures with Sanyo,* NEC, Corning (>$700 million sales)	Joint ventures with Texas Instruments, DNS, Towa	Joint ventures with Hewlett-Packard, GTE*
More than 50 technology licensing agreements, including RCA, JVC, Kelvinator, Matsushita, Toshiba, Philips, Casio	More than 90 technology and cross-licensing agreements, including Micron Technology, Sharp, Intel, Texas Instruments, NEC, Toshiba, General Instrument, Oki	Equity investment in AST, Array, IGT, CAI
	R&D consortium with LG, Hyundai for next generation DRAM	More than 30 technology licensing agreements, including Sega, Microsoft, Philips, Motorola, Mindscape
		R&D consortium with LG and ETRI for next generation TDX

Sales: $21 billion
25 out of 96 new businesses started via joint ventures

*Joint venture terminated
SOURCE: *History of Samsung Electronics*; KIS; press reports

has used several hundred technology licensing arrangements and joint ventures as vehicles to build a world-class electronics company (Exhibit 1). Of almost 100 new businesses it set up between 1953 and 1995, a quarter were initiated via joint ventures. For other local companies in emerging markets, alliances may appear to be the only way—short of selling the company outright—to survive once the home market has opened to new entrants bringing global brands or technology.

Given this pattern of mutual benefit, it is not surprising that alliances account for at least half of market entries into Latin America, Asia, and Eastern Europe (Exhibit 2). Some are successful. Nintendo and JVC both have alliances with Gradiente, Brazil's leading electronics company, to manufacture and/or market products under their own brand names as well as under the Gradiente brand. The alliances have helped Nintendo and JVC build volume rapidly in an important market, while Gradiente has become a profitable company with revenues of over $1 billion and its own skills, market position, and manufacturing capacity.

Yet the popularity of alliances between emerging market and global companies, and their apparent "win-win" character, can mask their difficulty. They are hard to pull

• EXHIBIT 2 •

Importance of Alliances in Emerging Markets

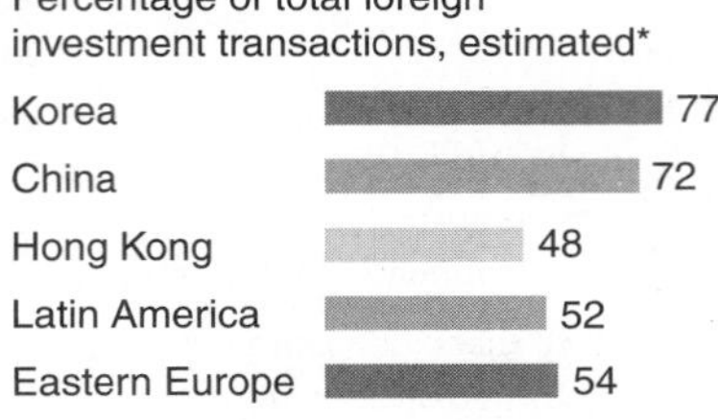

*Cumulative through January 1996 for Korea; 1994–95 for China; 1995 for Latin America, Eastern Europe; 1994 for Hong Kong

SOURCE: *China Statistical Yearbook*; Business Korea; Korean Ministry of Finance and Economy; Ernst & Young; America Economia; McKinsey analysis

off and often highly unstable—much more so than alliances between companies from similar economic and cultural backgrounds. Many have failed to meet expectations or have required extensive restructuring. Indeed, in recent years, numerous high-profile joint ventures in Asia and Latin America have been dissolved, restructured, or bought out by one of the partners.

Why are joint ventures in emerging markets proving so difficult? The answer lies in the fact that multinationals and companies in emerging markets must overcome formidable differences if they are to develop successful alliances.

First, most global companies are considerably larger than their emerging market partners, and possess deeper pockets and, often, broader capabilities. This makes it hard to find equal, complementary pairings—a balance that is the hallmark of successful and enduring alliances. Our research indicates that among alliances undertaken in India, the global company typically has 30 times the revenue of its local partner. One case makes the implications clear. A multibillion-dollar worldwide leader in the consumer non-durables industry and a $70 million Indian company enjoyed a successful joint venture that trebled its market share in four years and became the third-largest competitor in its industry. But the global partner then wanted to add capacity and make India a regional supply source for Asia and Africa. The local partner's share of the necessary investment, about $17 million, represented almost a quarter of its annual turnover. When it declined to invest, the global partner ended up buying out the venture.

Other differences result from ownership structure, objectives, culture, and management styles. State-owned enterprises can make frustrating negotiating partners for multinationals because they have no single decision maker; instead, they have to seek approval from a range of political constituencies. But a multinational can be an equally frustrating partner for a family-owned business if its country manager has to seek approval for decisions from other senior managers, while the patriarch or matriarch of the family business can make decisions unilaterally. Different types of companies also have different agendas. The family-run business may be more interested in ensuring a steady stream of dividends for shareholders than in maximizing growth or short-term shareholder value.

These challenges do not mean that emerging market alliances should be avoided. But they do raise the stakes. Before entering these deals, therefore, prospective partners should ask three questions. Is an alliance really necessary, or would an outright acquisition, direct investment, or contractual relationship suffice? How sustainable will an alliance be, given the partners' ambitions and strengths? And how should the strategy and tactics they adopt reflect the distinct challenges of alliances between global and emerging market companies?

Factors Driving Alliance Restructuring

A wave of alliance restructuring is just beginning to ripple through emerging markets, and is likely to persist. It is driven by five principal factors.

First, the expansion of free trade zones such as Mercosur and the Andean Pact promotes a regional approach to business, undermining national joint ventures. One alliance producing auto parts in Latin America, for example, has been restructured to cover a broader geographic region, with the aim of achieving scale economies.

Meanwhile, a consumer products company in China has rationalized several regional joint ventures in order to implement a national distribution strategy. This type of restructuring will be most pronounced where multinationals have invested in subscale manufacturing after being lured by hopes of privileged treatment and tariff protection.

Second, consolidation between local companies can lead to a situation in which two multinationals find themselves in partnership with the same local company, or *vice versa.* After a series of mergers within China, one local company is now in joint ventures with no fewer than five head-to-head global competitors. Similarly, mergers and global alliances between multinationals can expose joint ventures with two competing local partners in an emerging market.

Third, many multinationals have overestimated their partners' strength and now want to increase control. Fourth, as emerging markets become more important, global concerns are reevaluating their historic licensing and distribution alliances and considering how to expand (or break) these relationships. And finally, many family-owned businesses are reviewing their portfolios and seeking to restructure alliances in order to divest or to improve performance.

IS AN ALLIANCE REALLY NECESSARY?

Given the differences between partners and the complexities of managing a relationship, a reasonable (but rarely asked) question is: "Why are we forming an alliance in the first place?" If the main benefit of an alliance would be inside knowledge of customers, government, and suppliers, for example, the global company should ask whether it might be possible instead to hire five or ten key people who would bring those relationships.

In China and India, acquisitions and direct investments by overseas companies have increased, although alliances are still the main vehicle foreign companies use to enter the market. The proportion of wholly foreign-owned enterprises in China rose from less than 10 percent of incoming investment in 1991 to more than 30 percent in 1995.[1] In India, the figure grew from 5 percent in 1992 to 25 percent in 1995. Many global companies have operated as wholly owned entities in Latin America for decades.

Acquisitions can be equally effective for emerging market companies. Many companies have responded to globalization by looking to joint ventures or broad-based technology licensing arrangements with international partners, particularly when they needed to bridge a technology gap. But India's Piramal group, for example, has expanded its pharmaceuticals business at a compound annual growth rate of almost 60 percent since 1988, largely by acquiring other local pharma companies that already have non-equity licensing arrangements with global concerns.

Other emerging market companies are experimenting with "virtual" alliances—piecing together the technology or abilities they seek without forming an alliance. One large Indian textile manufacturer aspired to enter the clothing business, but lacked manufacturing technology and marketing expertise. Rather than form an alliance, it cobbled together what it needed by hiring experienced people, persuading the equipment manufacturers to serve as technical consultants, and licensing certain technologies. Since embarking on the program four years ago, the company has grown by 150 percent. Such a strategy would not suit all companies, however; the learning and coordination of relationships it involves call for highly developed skills and consume a great deal of management time.

These alternative approaches are especially relevant when technology is readily available and global brands are not needed. Cheap, double-edged razor blades based on a common technology continue to take 83 percent of the Indian market, for example, despite the introduction of high-quality blades by Gillette in 1993.

WILL THE ALLIANCE LAST?

When an alliance *is* deemed necessary, both companies should assess at the outset how the partnership will evolve—whether it is a marriage of equals that will endure, or something else. Achieving an equal balance in an emerging market is particularly challenging because of the differences in size, culture, skills, and objectives that we have mentioned. Such alliances are also vulnerable to rapid regulatory change (*see* text panel, "How alliances evolve").

Two factors influence the sustainability and likely direction of an alliance: each partner's aspirations—that is, the will to control the venture—and relative contributions. Aspirations can tip the balance. Does the global partner desire full control in the

How Alliances Evolve

Alliances tend to follow the pattern set by the deregulation of an industry and the opening of national markets. As regulations change, so do the options available to multinationals and local companies, with the result that alliance structures established under one set of rules can quickly become obsolete under another. Pressure to restructure or dissolve partnerships may ensue.

Emerging markets typically go through four evolutionary stages: nascent, frenzied, turbulent, and mature (*see* exhibit). In the **nascent** phase, strict regulation and lack of market transparency limit alliance activity to non-equity technology licensing and distribution arrangements. When the deregulation of an industry or a country gets under way, it can trigger an alliance **frenzy** as global companies seek to gain access to a new market, influence government policy, or build a portfolio of options, and local players attempt to acquire world-class skills. Many alliances formed in this stage are created to comply with local ownership provisions.

Further deregulation, and multinationals' growing familiarity with the local environment, lead next to a period of **turbulence.** This is characterized by the restructuring and dissolution of alliances as alternatives become available. Foreign partners can now decide to go it alone or increase their ownership stakes. As the market for corporate control develops, merger and acquisition activity commences.

When regulations unravel, those alliance structures driven by regulation rather than business economics become especially fragile. Until 1992, for example, India's Foreign Exchange Relations Act prohibited non-Indians from holding a stake greater than 40 percent in any Indian company. Since liberalization, this limit has been eliminated or raised to 51 percent in most industries. The result is that existing shareholder agreements are coming under strain as foreign partners attempt to increase their holdings.

The risk of conflict deepens if a multinational launches a wholly owned subsidiary that competes with its partly owned subsidiary. Questions then arise over where the parent company will want to launch its new products and focus its investment. The potential for trouble is obvious.

Eventually, as the market stabilizes, the **mature** stage is reached. At this point, the environment starts to resemble that of developed markets, in which alliance structures are driven primarily by business logic.

Four Stages of Market Evolution

Nascent → Frenzied → Turbulent → Mature

	Nascent	Frenzied	Turbulent	Mature
Market structure				
Regulations	Minimal regulatory freedom • Strict controls on ownership/capital repatriation • Strict regulatory oversight	Regulations relaxed • Near majority or majority foreign stake allowed • Operating restrictions still exist (e.g., bureaucratic approvals)	Regulations liberalized • Fully-owned subsidiaries allowed • Operating controls eased • Market for corporate control emerges	Market deregulated • Free equity and capital flows • Operating freedom • Active market for corporate control • Shareholder orientation
Transparency	Unfamiliar to outsiders "Outpost" mentality	Many global players present Few can replicate locals' market knowledge and government relationships	Many global players present Many global players have "insider" knowledge	Market integrated with global markets
Alliance focus				
Global players	Market skimming • Limited involvement • Technology licensing/distribution agreements	Market access • Build options • Understand local market • Influence government	Market growth • Prune options • Invest in winners	Market integration • Optimize global business system (e.g., by outsourcing) • Improve performance • New opportunities
Local players	Local game, local players	Upgrade capabilities • Products • Technology • Capital Provide "escort" service	Survival of fittest • Restructuring • Players without long-term advantage forced to exit • Strong locals go it alone	Genuine alliances • New markets • New products
Characteristics of alliance environment	Low-profile, non-equity-based collaborations	Rapid formation of many joint ventures	Dissolution of joint ventures; emergence of cross-border M&A, fully-owned subsidiaries	Full set of vehicles exist
Examples	Brazil (telecom)	China	India	Brazil (retail banking)

long run? (If it does, the alliance is likely to wind up in acquisition or dissolution.) Or does it want a permanent alliance in which the local partner provides specific elements of the business system, as with Caterpillar's long-standing relationships with its local distribution and service partners? Is the emerging market player's focus on the home market, or does it harbor global ambitions? If it does, and it wants to compete on its own against the multinational, conflict will be inevitable.

Ultimately, though, the evolution of an alliance will be driven by each partner's strengths and weaknesses, and by the relative importance of its contribution. Examples of valuable contributions might include privileged assets (ownership of mining rights or oilfield reserves, for example); advantaged relationships such as access to regulators, operating licences, and exclusive distributor relationships; or intangible assets such as brands, marketing, manufacturing, technology, management expertise, and patents.

Usually, the global company contributes intangibles, such as technology, brands, and skills, that grow in importance over time. The local partner's contributions, on the other hand, are more likely to be local market knowledge, relationships with regulators, distribution, and possibly manufacturing—assets that may fade in importance as its partner becomes more knowledgeable about the market, or as deregulation undermines (sometimes overnight) the value of privileged relationships or licences.

Manufacturing cost leadership can also be fleeting in a globalizing economy. If the local partner essentially provides an "escort" service, it will almost certainly become less important. A survey of Chinese joint ventures indicated that Chinese partners systematically deliver less value than expected in terms of sales, distribution, and local relationships.[2]

To assess whether an alliance will be a marriage for life and how it will evolve, partners in emerging markets should catalog the current contributions of each partner, plot how they are likely to shift (Exhibit 3), and negotiate to ensure that the venture will be sustainable or to protect shareholders against a likely shift in power.

FOUR PATHS

Emerging market alliances tend to evolve along one of four paths (Exhibit 4). The first is that trod by **successful long-term alliances** such as Samsung-Corning, established in 1973 as a 50–50 joint venture to make CRT (cathode-ray tube) glass for the Korean electronics market. Samsung needed a technology partner to pursue its strategy of integrating vertically into electronics components and materials; Corning wanted to expand in Asia. The joint venture had about 20 percent of the global market, revenue of $695 million, and net income of $49 million in 1996, with investments in Malaysia, India, China, and eastern Germany. Heineken and Anheuser-Busch also have a number of successful alliances with brewers in emerging markets, in which the local partner continues to produce and sell its local brand for the mass market, while producing or importing and selling the global partner's brew as a premium brand.

The second path involves a **power shift toward the global partner, often followed by a buyout.** Take the case of two consumer goods companies that formed an alliance to target the Indian toiletries market. At the outset, their contributions were balanced. The global company brought international marketing experience, world-class

• EXHIBIT 3 •

Assessing Bargaining Power

Determining factors	Importance of factor		Balance of power Now		Balance of power Future	
	High	Low	Us	Partner	Us	Partner
Product or process technology	☐	☐	☐	☐	☐	☐
Brand ownership	☐	☐	☐	☐	☐	☐
Channel control	☐	☐	☐	☐	☐	☐
Manufacturing capacity	☐	☐	☐	☐	☐	☐
Ability to invest in the business	☐	☐	☐	☐	☐	☐
Local relationships (e.g., regulators)	☐	☐	☐	☐	☐	☐
Global relationships (e.g., global suppliers; global customers)	☐	☐	☐	☐	☐	☐
Management control	☐	☐	☐	☐	☐	☐

• EXHIBIT 4 •

Four Possible Outcomes

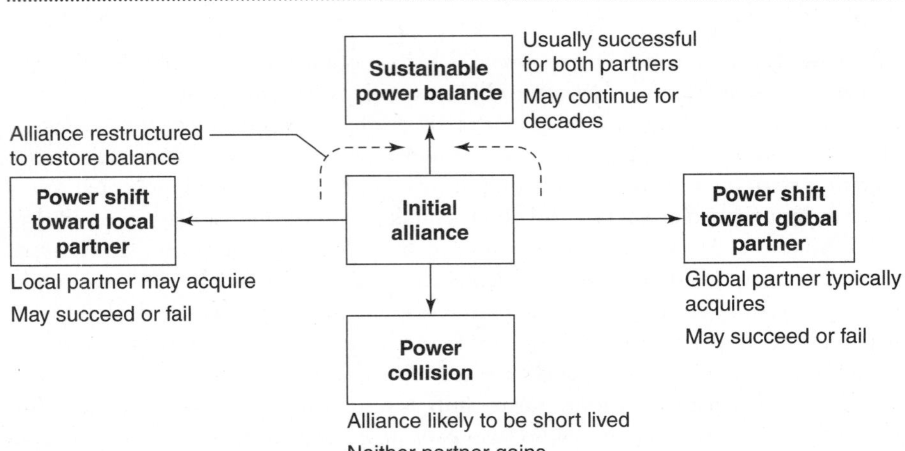

management systems, and additional volume to fill local manufacturing capacity. The local company brought the technology to make soap from vegetable fat (the use of animal tallow is banned in India), low-cost manufacturing, local market knowledge, and established products and brands. The global company wanted access to an enormous and potentially lucrative market; the Indian company aimed to increase its capacity utilization and enhance management and marketing skills and systems.

Gradually, however, the balance of power shifted. The global partner succeeded in getting an organization up and running and gained local acceptance for its product, whereas the Indian company was prevented from filling its capacity by slower than expected sales. Moreover, the expected transfer of skills and systems to the Indian partner never materialized, while its own brands, which had been transferred to the joint venture, suffered. The alliance was dissolved by mutual consent in 1996.

The way an alliance is structured and managed can determine its outcome. In one 50–50 joint venture, an emerging market company brought important relationships, brands, and distribution skills that might have led to a sustainable alliance had the venture been structured differently. But the global partner enhanced its own bargaining position by placing its people in key positions in marketing, manufacturing, and finance; introduced its own products and brands; built the manufacturing plant; and imposed its systems and culture on day-to-day operations. The venture reportedly lost money for several years until it was bought out by the global partner, whereupon performance improved. Notwithstanding this outcome, the emerging market partner may have rated the exercise a success, since it sold its 50 percent stake at a premium.

The third path sees a **shift of power toward the emerging market partner.** Local partners do sometimes build their bargaining muscle, increase their ownership stake, buy out their global partners, or exit the alliance to form other partnerships. Sindo-Ricoh illustrates how a power shift toward a local partner can lead to the restructuring and continued success of an alliance. Sindo has been Ricoh's exclusive distributor in Korea since 1962. It built low-cost manufacturing capability, expanded the relationship to a 50–50 joint venture, then took majority ownership with a 75 percent stake. In 1996, it boasted sales of $309 million and net income of $38 million.

The fourth path is **competition between partners, followed by dissolution or acquisition of the venture by one of them.** A 50–50 joint venture between GM and Daewoo to manufacture cars in Korea lost money until Daewoo acquired it outright. The partners had incompatible strategies: GM wanted a low-cost source for a limited range of small cars; Daewoo aspired to become a broad-line global auto manufacturer. Conflict and collision often result when the partners fail to agree on whether the joint venture or the parent companies will compete in related product areas or in other countries.

Finally, although alliances are often likened to marriage, a successful alliance does not *have* to last. Success is measured not by duration, but by whether objectives have been met. Take the joint venture between GE and Apar to make light bulbs for the Indian market. The arrangement was dissolved after only three years, yet GE emerged from it a leader in the Indian lighting industry, and Apar was handsomely remunerated.

Recognizing what path an alliance is following and how its balance of power is shifting is critical to ensuring that both partners have the opportunity to satisfy their objectives. Our research in Asia and Latin America—and a growing body of experience—identifies some practical steps that companies can take to address the challenges of emerging market alliances.

ALLIANCE STRATEGIES AND TACTICS FOR EMERGING MARKET COMPANIES

Companies in emerging markets must recognize that they may be vulnerable over the long term because of inherent power imbalances. Indeed, our research suggests that global partners are more likely to wind up with control when the balance of power shifts. On the other hand, emerging market partners may possess sources of value that cannot easily be replicated in the short term, such as customers, channel control, local brands, control over key supply sources, manufacturing capacity, and relationships with government officials and regulators. They should make the most of these bargaining assets. Above all, they should invest to ensure that they last.

Before a company can develop a strategy to build power, it must set objectives for the alliance that reflect its aspirations and a hard-nosed assessment of its own strengths. Is its goal to become a world-class operator able to compete in some areas with global companies on their own turf? Is it to develop a sustainable home-market alliance based on an enduring source of strength? Or is the alliance a defensive measure to protect the business against threats from global brands or technology? And is it acceptable—or even inevitable—that the alliance will evolve toward a sale?

When the aim is to develop a genuine alliance or build a platform for growth, strategies to maximize power include:

Invest Today to Build Power for Tomorrow

The most critical issue for local companies is how to establish a sustainable source of value and thus maintain the balance of power. There are a number of ways to do this:

Develop Your Own Brands Recent experience suggests that local brands can be more powerful than their owners tend to believe. In Brazil, electronics producer Gradiente has laid the foundation for more balanced partnerships by building name recognition and sales volume that match those of global brands. A Venezuelan building products manufacturer entering a joint venture with a global partner retained its own brands in several segments in which global technology was not required, and where craftsmen trusted the local product.

Control Distribution Distribution is an area in which emerging market companies typically have initial advantages that can be extended to enhance their bargaining power. One industrial equipment manufacturer in Latin America increased its influence over distributors—and its clout with its global partner—by offering inventory management systems, financing, and extensive technical support. Investing to keep the advantage is crucial. Rallis, an Indian agrichemicals company, owns the country's leading nationwide agricultural inputs distribution system and has distribution agreements with several global chemical companies. But though it may command the dominant dealer relationships today, new market entrants are beginning to go directly to the farmer. If direct distribution should take hold, what will happen to Rallis's power? Perhaps anticipating this, the company is itself experimenting with direct distribution.

Secure Proprietary Assets Most industry value chains in emerging economies have "chokehold" points—privileged assets in short supply. Locking these in can establish a continuing source of value. Indian Hotels owns the best properties near all the country's main tourist destinations, for example. And one metals company in Brazil entered a long-term arrangement with a key supplier for a crucial input that was in short supply.

Preemptively Acquire Local Competitors Provided that these acquisitions make sense in their own right, they can strengthen a local company's negotiating hand by limiting the entry options for would-be players.

Become a Regional Hub for Your Partner Many multinationals have their hands full exploring the larger emerging markets such as China and Brazil. Few have the time and management capacity to concentrate on smaller but still important economies such as Chile or Peru. Local partners can improve their market position and their long-term stature in a partnership by becoming a regional hub. One Indian engineering consumables company expanded its joint venture with a European manufacturer to distribute products throughout Asia. Similarly, a Colombian industrial concern acquired its counterpart in Peru and is expanding in Venezuela, thereby not only increasing the contribution it makes to its alliance with a European company but also strengthening its own position by attaining economies of scale in regional distribution.

Think Twice Before Allying with a Global Leader

Global market leaders are often the most obvious partners because of their products, skills, capital, and prestige. But they usually have global aspirations too, and may well seek to tighten their control over any alliance they undertake in order to optimize purchasing, pricing, product development, manufacturing, and brand strategy. Autonomous ventures—or, worse still, ventures in which a local partner calls the shots—can be anathema to truly global players. In the words of one chemical industry executive, "How can we serve our global customers in the same way across 20 or more countries when our partner operates the business? We can't even assure our customers that they can buy the same products with the same specifications from one country to the next."

Emerging market companies should ascertain whether a prospective partner is pursuing a "global" strategy—same brands, centralized decision making, global purchasing, unified R&D, consistent product portfolio and pricing—or a "global/local" strategy with, for instance, local and global brands, strong country or regional managers, and regional product development.

Considering alternative partners is especially important if the leading global players in an industry are inclined to swallow up local partners' stakes. A pattern has emerged in the behavior of one global consumer goods company in key emerging economies in Latin America and Asia. It enters a market by allying with a leading local consumer goods company; introduces its own brands, systems, and managers; becomes embroiled in conflict with its partner; and finally buys out the venture. An analysis of joint ventures in India indicates that majority control in 60 percent of Indo-American alliances lies with the US partner, while Asian partners have control in only 10 percent of their ventures with Indian companies. Europeans fall between these two extremes in their hunger for control.

Consider Less Obvious Partners

A smaller, non-global company may present less of a long-term threat to a company from an emerging market. One Latin American metals producer decided to form an alliance with a medium-sized German firm rather than a world leader. The alliance has prospered for 20 years, with neither partner aspiring to take full control. YPF, Argentina's privatized petroleum company, and Petrobras, Brazil's state-owned energy company, have proposed a $750 million project for the joint development and operation of a network of 1,500 gas stations, principally in southern Brazil, over five years.

An alliance with a global leader from a different industry is another possibility. Telecom companies from emerging markets could consider allying with information technology providers to build their capabilities, instead of entering more predictable arrangements with global telecom service companies.

Emerging market companies seldom consider taking a "financial" partner, yet this may make sense if they can build the internal capabilities to compete over the long term. Companies with attractive business propositions can win funding from sources as diverse as private equity funds, offshore Chinese holdings, and industrial investors.

Protect Your Future by Securing Access to Key Intangible Assets

Emerging market companies should consider locking in key assets such as brands, technology, or distribution rights for 10 to 20 years if possible, rather than risk losing them within a short period or being forced to renegotiate the venture. They should also think how they would survive termination of the alliance. This risk is highest when the local partner contributes physical assets and capital that rely on the intangible assets controlled by its global partner. One Andean Pact manufacturer of transport equipment would have faced the loss of a $200 million business had its partner rescinded the licence agreement on which their joint venture was based. It therefore insisted on a clause stipulating three years' notice of termination. A less canny Latin American industrial company had to consider a shotgun wedding with a new partner when its original partner quit before it had internalized the skills to operate the business alone.

Create World-Class Alliance Capabilities

For multibusiness companies that may form as many as 20 alliances across unrelated industries, it is better to employ a few experts with well-honed negotiating skills than

20 gifted amateurs. Mahindra & Mahindra, a leading Indian business house, has designated a single senior executive to work with the leaders of each business unit as they develop and manage their alliances to ensure that the lessons each one learns are transferred to the rest of the company.

We have assumed so far that emerging market partners do not wish to sell their share of the business. In actuality, they frequently do. The problem is that potential buyers can be unwilling to acquire joint ventures outright because of the importance of local operating know-how and relationships, or because of capital constraints. In this situation, a joint venture can be an effective step toward a sale, but the negotiations should look more like an auction than a typical alliance discussion. The local company should pursue simultaneous discussions with several potential partners or buyers, each of which should be asked to develop a proposal that includes an initial valuation for a controlling shareholding, proposed dividend flow, and terms for ultimate sale.

ALLIANCE STRATEGIES AND TACTICS FOR GLOBAL COMPANIES

Global companies, like locals, need to adapt their alliance approaches to succeed in emerging market alliances.

Position Early

Alcatel, VW, and AIG are leading operators in China today partly because they were early entrants into the telecommunications, automotive, and insurance industries, respectively. Procter & Gamble leads the Chinese detergents market because it secured access to production assets through majority ventures, then moved quickly to establish local sales and distribution. Early entrants frequently have more opportunities to lock up the most promising distribution channels, gain access to attractive production assets, and invest to build the business before competition intensifies.

In many product categories in emerging markets, the desirable assets, brands, and distribution systems are controlled by a handful of attractive partners. Once they are spoken for, competitors may be locked out, especially if the cost of setting up alternative distribution is prohibitive (as it is for many consumer goods), and where adding capacity (in chemicals, for example) would create overcapacity. India's health insurance market, which is about to be deregulated, is a case in point. In effect, India has a single government insurer, one hospital group with locations in various metropolitan areas, and no provider groups. The partner options are limited, even for early birds.

Shape the Market

The "toe in the water" approach of seeding dozens of growth options at low cost in many markets may seem appealing. In reality, however, joint ventures established in this way often perish from a lack of time or commitment. The global companies that do best in emerging market joint ventures invest heavily and act to shape the market by introducing new business approaches or products.

Think Broadly about your Partner's Capabilities and Consider the Overall Set of Relationships That it can Bring, not Just the Immediate Joint Venture or Licensing Proposition

The flow of opportunities that local partners, especially conglomerates, can contribute may exceed the value of the initial deal. When a multinational wants access to local relationships, it may be wise to consider companies outside its industry that could play an advisory or ambassadorial—rather than operating—role. It is in this light that Camargo Correa, one of Brazil's largest family-owned conglomerates, views its role in its long-standing alliance with Alcoa. Camargo encompasses one of the country's leading construction companies, and has widespread relationships with industry and government at all levels. It is also involved in related industries such as the development of power projects and infrastructure. Alcoa has the clear leading role in their aluminum smelting joint venture, while Camargo has, over time, assisted in negotiations with government authorities, built manufacturing facilities, and provided capital.

As most emerging economies are still at the nascent stage, industry experience may not be of lasting value in an alliance. Consider the case of a multinational seeking to join forces with a local company to enter India's non-durable consumer goods market. The key asset to acquire is distribution, but India's distribution system is archaic and will probably change dramatically over the next decade. The multinational could select the local market leader (and perhaps thereby educate a future competitor), but a more interesting choice might be a tobacco company, which is likely to have extensive retail distribution systems in India.

Identify the Key Decision Makers and Involve Them Early

This is especially critical when dealing with a state enterprise. In China particularly, proposals to establish joint ventures must often be approved by a dozen or more government or quasi-government entities.

Bring all your Global Capabilities to the Table

Global companies have a strong suite of technical skills, geographic presence, business units, and systems, but rarely bring their full power to the negotiating table. The losers in several recent joint venture negotiations in the Chinese automotive and machine tool industries offered a solid but narrow manufacturing partnership; the winners offered technology, local parts sourcing, and substantial capability building. One Latin American state enterprise selected its partner because it could provide technical expertise on the ground to improve the business. Another Latin American company places as much weight on how potential partners might help it secure growth opportunities as on the immediate business they could do together.

Recognize that a "51 Percent or Nothing" Mindset will close off Opportunities

Having 51 percent ownership does not guarantee control. Effective control has more to do with management structure, ownership of key intangibles such as technology and relationships, and knowledge. In fact, a 49 or 50 percent stake can provide an opportunity to gain full control later, with less risk and more flexibility.

In one emerging market joint venture, the global partner owns the brand, controls the patented process technology, and is rapidly building its knowledge of the local market—yet it has only a 50 percent stake because its local partner, while recognizing that it needs an alliance in order to introduce new products, is unwilling to sell the "family silver" by giving up 51 percent. The 50–50 venture has none the less proved attractive for the global partner, given that its other options were to sink $200 million into a greenfield operation, form a partnership with a second-tier player, or forget about entering the market. It will, after all, have effective control over the most important business levers, and be positioned as the logical buyer of the business should the partners fall out or the family owners decide to sell.

It is often worth asking, "What do we really need to make sure we can protect our interests in a 50–50 deal?" The notion of control can be broken down into rights to determine specific issues—capital expenditures, dividend policies, production volumes, and human resources, for instance. Some multinationals have found creative ways to address particular issues. One leading international oil company signed a 50–50 joint venture in the Indian market after concluding that a casting vote on capital expenditures was enough to protect its interests. Another global company agreed to a 50–50 joint venture with the proviso that it would have the right to build additional capacity if its partner vetoed expansion by the joint venture.

Beware of Entering Long-Term Licensing Arrangements without Performance Contracts

Many global companies have granted licences because they had no other way to enter a market, or because at the time the market was negligible. In so doing, some have tied up the value of their intangible assets without any exit mechanism or promise of fair value in return. One US manufacturer granted a 20-year exclusive licence covering several large emerging markets to a single company in the region, with royalty fees set as a percentage of revenues. When its partner underperformed and competitors proliferated, it had little leverage to renegotiate the arrangement.

Recognize that the Aims of Family Owners may Differ from those of Public Companies

For one family owner of a profitable business, assuring an annual dividend of $20 million was one of the key terms of its alliance agreement—far more important than maximizing the value of each partner's contribution. Other family owners may be concerned that their name will stay with the business and that the deal should not be seen as a sale, even when they want to transfer control. And there is usually some sensitivity about preserving operating roles for qualified family members. Acknowledging these wishes may cost little, but can be worth millions. It can make the difference between being the chosen partner or one of the runners-up.

Emerging market alliances can create sustainable growth platforms for both local and global companies. But they pose different challenges from those faced by alliances in mature markets, and are often less stable. Before getting caught up in the heat of negotiations, companies should ensure they have a clear strategy and endgame in mind. They should also determine not only how many chips prospective partners bring to the deal, but how the value of those chips will evolve.

Notes

1. "Multinationals in China: Going it alone," *The Economist*, April 19, 1997.
2. *See* Stephen M. Shaw and Johannes Meier, "'Second generation' MNCs in China," *The McKinsey Quarterly*, 1993 Number 4, pp. 3–16.

LOCALIZING IN THE GLOBAL VILLAGE: LOCAL FIRMS COMPETING IN GLOBAL MARKETS

Güliz Ger

A tourist seeking the authentic Moscow laments that Arbat street is no longer recognizable with its new architecture of Pizza Hut, McDonald's, Benetton, and French Perfumerie storefronts. Cities around the world have traffic-congested streets packed with Toyotas and BMWs, whole sides of buildings painted with Marlboro and Coca-Cola advertisements, and look-alike American-style shopping malls filled with Sony, Swatch, and Levi's. Advertising, cinema, and television project these images to the most remote parts of the globe. The world political economy of capitalism, global transport, communication, marketing, advertising, and transnational cosmopolitanism dissolve the boundaries across national cultures and national economies. The major agents of this global arena are transnational corporations (TNCs) that operate wherever opportunities arise within the global market. This article examines how local corporations (LCs) can compete with TNCs, in both home and foreign markets.

In the increasingly interdependent capitalist world system, firms based in affluent core countries—especially the European, American, and Japanese TNCs—have the greatest influence in determining what is produced and consumed. In 1990, there were 60 countries in the world that had Gross National Products of less than US$10 billion, while there were more than 135 transnational corporations with revenues in excess of that amount.[1] TNCs have proliferated widely and are now more powerful than ever. With global marketization and the spread of capitalism, many less affluent and transitional countries are regarded as new or unpenetrated markets for TNCs. Accordingly, discussions of competitive strategies for global marketing usually take the perspective of the TNCs or other firms from affluent countries.[2] Such discussions tend to focus on how TNCs and other Western firms can access foreign markets and, by so doing, further expand their operations. From this perspective, those whose competitiveness is to be further enhanced are the already more powerful and successful European, American, and Japanese firms.

However, the global business arena also includes the less powerful local firms for whom global competitiveness is even more crucial if they are to have a chance of survival. Local firms are constantly confronted and threatened with competition from TNCs in both home and foreign markets. To be globally competitive in this contemporary world of diversity, a more innovative, critical, and proactive approach than most LCs typically undertake is necessary. Unlike the traditional local firms whose tendency is to operate under the supposition that the market is beyond their control[3] or those firms who find reassurance and security (and local success) in following the lead of foreign firms, local firms that aim to be global must develop according to different criteria. The standard propositions concerned with improving marketing systems, product, price, promotion, and distribution are necessary but not sufficient. A consumer-orientation also does not suffice to make a local firm a global contender, especially if the accepted market definition is derived from global firms themselves, as is often the case. LCs cannot catch up with TNCs who are far ahead in the road and going very strong. However, they can take a different road.

There is an opportunity for LCs, inherent to their context, that allows them to select and develop alternative strategies fundamentally different from the ones followed by TNCs. Rather than operating in the already highly competitive markets shared and dominated by the TNCs, local firms can better take advantage of their potential by operating in alternative domains and "out-localizing" the TNCs, in both global and local markets. The intrinsic advantage retained by LCs is their "local" identity and culture. This can then be further developed to enable these firms to compete with "local" strategies aimed at defining the "authentic" in selected non-standard domains, such as in cultural goods and products for local conditions.

CONCEPTUAL FRAMEWORK FOR DEVELOPING STRATEGIES FOR LCs

The global context of production/competition and consumption sets the stage and provides opportunities for LCs. Within the global context, there are three key components of competitive success for LCs—unique perceived value, cultural capital, and alternative targeting and positioning based on the precept of localness. Use of resources and targeting/positioning work together to create a unique perceived value for any firm. In the case of LCs, cultural resources and positioning/representation of "localness" to alternative target markets can create a unique perceived value. Local firms can turn the opportunities provided by their context into competitive advantages through a process of empowerment. Competitive strategies for LCs are induced by and grounded in the interplay of the three components.

Conceptual Framework for Competitiveness of Local Corporations in Global Markets

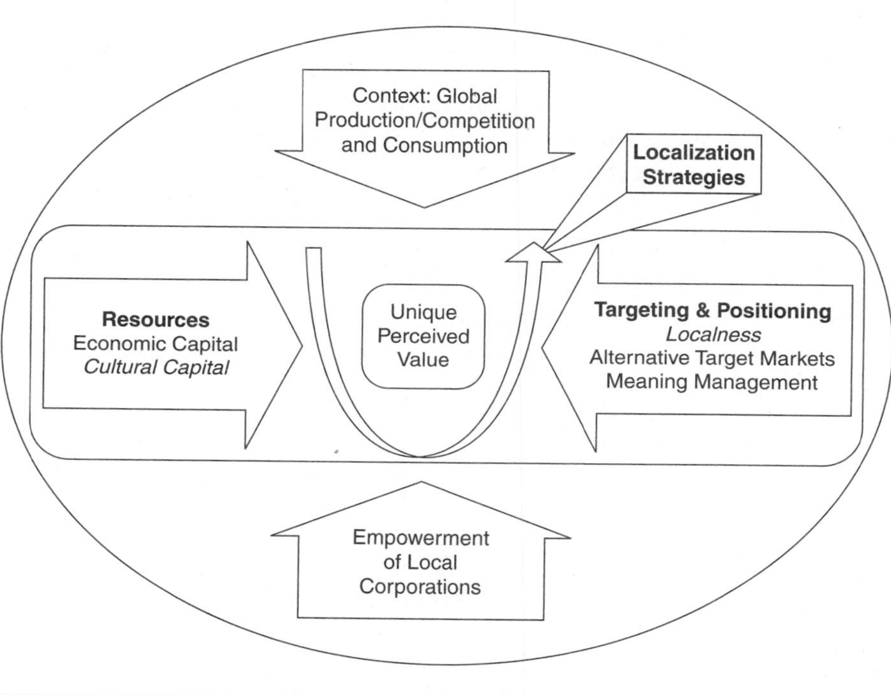

THE CONTEXT: GLOBAL PRODUCTION AND CONSUMPTION

Globalization consists of an ever-increasing number of worldwide chains of economic, social, cultural, and political activity as well as the intensification of levels of interaction between societies.[4] Global flows of people, money, technology and information, media images, and ideologies are diverse and complex.[5] Although these flows are dominated by TNCs, they are not unidirectional: in this nexus of multiple and asymmetric interdependencies, there is interplay and reciprocity. The development of taste and demand for such items as Vietnamese restaurants, Reggae music, Egyptian novels, Chinese films, Indian clothes, and Afghan jewelry in the U.S. and Europe are examples of peripheries talking back. Both the center and the periphery have become more visibly diverse and differentiated. This differentiating impact of globalization strengthens or reactivates national, ethnic, and communal identities and the pattern of interrelationships fuels a hybridization of social life. In fact, the new global cultural system actively promotes difference instead of suppressing it. Yet in the contemporary world of non-monolithic capitalism, the multiple centers—whose most important agents are the TNCs—define the reality, the "normal," and the "authentic" for production and consumption.

These diverse global marketplaces fuel and are fed by an increasingly widespread consumption.[6] However, although consumption orientation is spreading globally, consumer cultures are not homogeneous. Historical and current local conditions, interacting with global forces, shape the specific consumption patterns and meanings in each locality. Consumers use and experience consumption in their own unique context in dealing with the contradictions, changes, and uncertainties of their lives and worlds. Consumers draw from all available sources—global and local, new and old—as they use products to construct and communicate their identity, to relate to people, to mark social differences, to seek comparative status, and to pursue emotional and aesthetic pleasures.[7]

The global products of the "good life" are desirable in all societies. The type of product manufactured by European, American, or Japanese TNCs is generally regarded to be state-of-the-art, modern, original, high-quality, and therefore, highly desirable, in global markets. In contrast, products of LCs are generally regarded to be low-quality items, cheap imitations, old and outdated products, or, at best, traditional ethnic curiosities. What has been termed "country-of-origin" or "product-country image" affects product beliefs and the evaluations of consumers, importers, investors, distributors, and retailers.[8] In general, consumers' perceptions of quality for products made in developing countries are negative. In less affluent societies, the abrupt exposure to global products and communications brings a naive trust and veneration for the novel and the foreign. Consumers from as diverse societies as Vietnam, Turkey, and Trinidad prefer foreign goods and have low confidence in domestic products.[9] This fascination with global goods breeds an inability to respect domestic products or to notice their potential, and it results in a cultural dependency on foreign products and images. Even the Chinese, arguably the most self-respecting people of any of the developing countries, say "Heaven is abroad."[10]

However, consumers are increasingly interested in more than the standard, homogenized products of TNCs. They are actively seeking diversity in local products. In affluent societies, consumers are increasingly exposed to and are becoming more curious about foreign cultures, cuisines, clothes, music, art, spirituality, and travel. They are becoming more exploratory, playful, and active, thirsting after new experiences and meanings, and wanting to discover something exciting and, most importantly, unexpected.[11] In this search, consumers pursue difference: "a need is not a need for a particular object as much as it is a 'need' for difference (the *desire for social meaning*)."[12] Also, some consumers prefer green, simple, ethical, or responsible consumption. In less affluent societies, there is a revival of localism in consumption: consumers are expressing a return to their roots, reconfiguring global goods and their meanings to better fit local culture and, especially, mixing the old and the new from disparate sources.[13] Thus, the diversity of demand and interest in the local is increasing in both affluent and less affluent societies.

Both production and consumption are diverse, pluralistic, and interrelated in dynamic global markets. Local firms can identify opportunities provided by the heterogenizing global forces, the multiplicity of consumer cultures, the increasing exploratory behavior of consumers, the importance and prominence of images/symbols, and information technology.[14] With a clear and balanced understanding of their local strengths within the frame of global power relations, LCs can construct global images of authenticity and desirability for their "local" products in consumers' minds.

THREE COMPONENTS OF COMPETITIVE SUCCESS

UNIQUE PERCEIVED VALUE

Firms compete by delivering either greater value or comparable value at a lower cost. Competitive strategy is about being unique.[15] The fundamental challenge for an LC, aiming to outperform its global rivals, is in choosing a different set of activities in order to deliver a unique mix of value—that is, finding a new position and establishing a point of difference that it can preserve.

A point of difference becomes unique symbolically as well as functionally. Products are not merely useful, they are also meaningful. For example, Coke, a prototypical TNC product, is unique with its taste and bottle (both of which are patented) as well as its image. Coke is not only a beverage, it also embodies the characteristics of being young, modern, active, and American. Image and product become one: the perceived quality and value of the product rests in the meaning the consumer gives to the product. That meaning is constructed in the experience of shopping and consumption. Moreover, the symbolic meaning is now more important than ever in the global arena. Both the number and variety of products are increasing at a tremendous rate, and this trend is based less and less on technological differences and increasingly on symbolic ones.

Thus, the challenge for competitive strategy is not only with regard to the more obvious issues (technology, innovation, quality, know-how, and R&D), but also with regard to the symbolism associated with uniqueness, and with the symbolism of global versus local products. It is one thing for LCs to improve the technical quality of their products. It requires quite different strategies and thinking in order to be innovative in ways that can overcome the negative stereotypes and images—at home and in foreign markets—associated with products from underdeveloped countries. It is not only goods, but also symbols that are being produced in the process of production, pricing, distribution, and promotion. Thus, the management of a code of meanings is critical in delivering a unique perceived value.

CULTURAL RESOURCES

Global business is an arena in which firms compete for capital, and superior resources are critical sources of advantage.[16] Compared to the TNCs, LCs are clearly at a disadvantage with respect to economic resources. However, there are alternatives. LCs can focus on and develop other types of capital, such as cultural capital, as a resource that can lead to competitive advantage. An adaptation of Bourdieu's sociological analysis of capital provides a conceptual basis for the potential resources of firms and his notion of cultural capital for individuals can be extended to that of firms.[17]

Bourdieu argues that capital is a basis for domination and that types of capital can be exchanged for other types of capital. Social life consists of a struggle for position or domination: individuals seek to circumnavigate the constraints social structure sets against them. The objective is to accrue capital, which refers to the attributes, possessions, or qualities of a person that is exchangeable for goods, services, or esteem. Capital takes time to accumulate and has the potential to produce profits and to reproduce itself in identical or expanded form.

Capital exists in many forms. Bourdieu identifies three types of capital: economic capital (material things); symbolic capital (prestige, status, legitimate authority); and cultural capital (culturally valued taste and consumption patterns—including art, education, skills, sensibilities, and creativity). Capital acts as a social relation within a system of exchange and refers to all goods, material and symbolic, that seem to be rare and valuable. The structure of the distribution of different types of capital at a given point in time represents the structure of the social world—i.e., the set of constraints that govern its functioning.

Cultural capital is a special form of resource, a proficiency in the consumption of and the discourse about prestigious cultural goods. Cultural capital exists in three forms. In its *embodied state,* it is a cultural competence that derives a scarcity value from its position in the distribution of cultural capital and yields profits of distinction. In its *objectified state,* cultural capital is the product of historical action in the form of cultural goods—material objects and media such as writings, paintings, monuments, and instruments. As the cultural capital incorporated into the means of production increases, the collective strength of the holders of cultural capital also tends to increase. However, the collective strength of the holders of cultural capital will only increase if the holders of the dominant type of capital (economic) do not set the holders of cultural capital in competition with each other. In its *institutionalized state,* cultural capital is a certificate of cultural competence—an officially recognized and guaranteed competence. A cultural resource has the potential to be converted into capital when an institution sanctions a particular resource as capital. Official recognition makes it possible to establish conversion rates between cultural capital and economic capital by guaranteeing the monetary value of the former. Di Maggio suggests that cultural entrepreneurship involves the purposeful restructuring of symbolic elements to shape and portray them as resources and, potentially, as capital.

These notions imply that when cultural resources and goods are made prestigious, they are potentially convertible into economic capital. Such a conversion will be most likely when cultural resources are symbolically reshaped and institutionally validated. Extending these notions of cultural capital and applying them to firms within the current global context, greater chances exist for local firms with respect to their cultural resources rather than their economic resources. LCs can build upon their cultural competencies and resources and use them to improve their position. LCs can rely on cultural capital to construct a sustainable, unique value and offer the symbolism of authenticity and prestige.

The three main challenges for ventures that attempt to capitalize on cultural capital are to avoid being appropriated or taken over by TNCs, to avoid ending up as a temporarily popular trend, and to avoid the trivialization of local cultures. These challenges necessitate a means to make authenticity globally acknowledged. Cultural productions involve invention and representation. For example, Ulin argues that the reputation of Bordeaux wines, believed to follow from superior techniques of vinification and ideal climate and soil, involves a reinvented wine growing tradition and a representation as cultural capital.[18] The *Appellation Controlée* system in France provides regional endorsement of the original and the unique, such as Bordeaux wines, Cognac and Calvados brandies, and Brie and Camembert cheeses. Analogously, LCs can develop, reinvent, restore, express, and display local cultural capital. The objects and experiences that are commodified and marketed as cultural difference are dependent on concepts of cultural and aesthetic authenticity. However, just as regions in France—and not the European Union—define quality, so can organized LCs provide local definition and expression of authenticity. By defining and expressing authenticity themselves and not leaving it to the global market, LCs can establish quality and originality symbolism for their products. By exercising such control over the production and presentation of their culture, LCs can also avoid trivialization. Authentication involves copyrighting and patenting cultural productions as well as other institutional means of recognition and certification. Official sanctioning by an organization will supply the object with the necessary accreditation of its authenticity and quality, and consequently it will enable conversion from cultural to economic capital. The challenges of being appropriated, trivialized, or turned into a passing fad also necessitate both forming alliances with other organizations and strategic use of global media. As the cultural goods of LCs proliferate, the collective strength of these LCs will tend to increase. Marketing cultural productions globally, with the symbolism of authenticity and quality, will make the country image and image of local products in domestic and foreign markets more positive and increase the appeal of products of other LCs from that country.

For example, it is conceivable that *hamams* (Turkish baths) can be reinvented and represented as an authentic cultural product. Elegant and luxurious *hamams,* built according to ancient designs and with domes decorated with small stained glass windows that create a reflected array of colorful light through the vapor rising from the marble hot water pools, could be popularized throughout Turkey and the world. Brochures or web sites can link *hamams* to the current global health trends and also inform global consumers about the sociocultural role of *hamams* in historical civilization. As an alternative to spas and saunas, *hamams* could appeal to discriminating consumers seeking diversity in relaxing leisure experiences. The key issue would be finding an institutional means of authentication, recognition, and certification for *hamams* and obtaining cultural property rights or cultural patenting.

Locating and mobilizing resources to transform them into a unique value requires an innovative approach and creative thinking. Creativity and innovative thinking in the conception of strategies are founded not only on analysis, but on insight and intuition as well. There is a much greater potential for innovation and creativity if entrepreneurs build upon the locally existing strengths, roots, culturally embedded memories, and tacit knowledge. Extrapolating from lifelong practices and indigenous pools of knowledge will foster self-confidence—which, in turn, is critical for activating and enabling insight and intuition. Relying solely on external, imported know-how usually reduces self-confidence and has the potential to repress local creativity. Moving toward internal strengths and cultural competencies can foster opportunities for innovation. The major challenge for entrepreneurs is to restructure cultural and symbolic elements so that they are shaped as cultural capital that can eventually be converted to economic capital.

TARGETING AND POSITIONING: LOCALNESS

Shaping cultural and symbolic elements into capital involves positioning and representing offerings as being of a unique perceived value for target consumers. Local culture is the most accessible yet least utilized resource for local firms. Local entrepreneurs can find or create niches based upon their unique local properties and can transpose local strengths and potentials into profitable national or transnational businesses.

Consumers: Alternative Target Markets

Finding and targeting segments likely to respond positively to the possible offerings are key success factors in any competitive strategy. The issue for LCs becomes that of targeting alternative segments whose preferences and desires match the cultural resources of the firm and/or who are not the conventional target markets of or are underserved by TNCs. The context of global production and consumption suggests three alternative target markets: global consumers seeking alternative goods and experiences; local consumers seeking nostalgia and a return to roots; and global underprivileged consumers.

Firm's Positioning Strategy: Managing the Meaning of "Local"

Because image is critical to the unique value, the challenge for the firms trying to improve the perceived quality and value of a product is the management of symbols and meanings as well as of the production process. Meaning is created and managed by invention, construction, signification, and representation (symbolism) of a product. The predominant image of local products is either exotic souvenirs or low-quality objects. Positive symbolism has to be constructed to counteract the market resistance posed by a negative product-country image. In both home and foreign markets, LCs must position and manage the constructed meaning (image) of their products, based on existing conceptions but with a positive twist. For example, the meaning of a *hamam* can be managed to represent it as a unique, distinctive, exotic, cultural, healthy, and relaxing leisure experience. In order to manage meanings and processes effectively, managers must have an understanding both of the meanings of products and brands in particular sociocultural contexts and of the processes of communication in a world engulfed by images.

EMPOWERMENT OF LOCAL FIRMS FOR GLOBAL COMPETITIVENESS

A process of empowerment can enable LCs to successfully compete with the more dominant TNCs in local and/or global markets. This process requires a creative and innovative mentality, a global/local vision, self-crafted marketing strategies and practices, alliances and partnerships, and the development of a supportive political environment.

MENTALITY AND ATTITUDE: INNOVATIVE RATHER THAN IMITATIVE

An LC needs to be dynamic and innovative to exploit its cultural resources and to build and manage a unique value. LCs must avoid directly transplanting the marketing practices and research methods of other countries.[19] They must not simply copy foreign firms. Locally rooted creative products will reduce feelings of deficiency, increase self-worth and self-respect, and foster pride in the local, leading to an empowering and confidence-building cycle. Self-defined authenticity and self-expressed cultural capital will also empower the LCs. Learning-by-doing will make innovative tendencies and practices more potent in time.

GLOBAL/LOCAL VISION

Innovative local firms need to be sensitive to the new global reality that consists of forces of both globalization and localization as well as rapid change. These enterprises must develop a profound understanding of inter- and intra-cultural dynamics. The greater availability and accessibility of global media, the Internet, tourism, and other means of intercultural interaction make it possible for more people to develop this understanding than ever before. LCs need much more than marginal forms of integration into the world economy. They must interact with TNCs and LCs from other countries in order to have the opportunity to learn from them, to learn about themselves, and to form alliances with them. They must go beyond exports and establish deeper connections and integrated relationships in international markets with the emphasis being on the specificity of the local. They must realize that the best markets may lie beyond the neighboring countries or other habitual export markets. Local firms need to be present in many global markets, developed and developing, in order to compete with the TNCs.

STRATEGY, SKILLS, AND KNOW-HOW

Conventional wisdom mistakenly states that in order to modernize marketing to be more effective and efficient, firms in developing or transitional countries must transfer marketing know-how, education, and practices from the West. However, good marketing is not a set of skills and practices to be adopted wholesale from developed countries. Instead, LCs must develop, mold, and employ their emergent, locally specific marketing skills and practices. Marketing practices must be appropriate for the particular local context and, hence, they must be crafted locally.

In shaping their own practices, LCs seeking a unique differential advantage must move with a strategic long-term perspective.[20] They must focus on customer care, while improving productivity and quality, and must aim for value-added improvements and brand equity. They should build skills in financing, accounting, database formation and analysis, and diagnosis. Furthermore, they should develop and use information technologies based on an understanding of the interplay between technology and culture. They should focus on diagnosis rather than optimization and should regard strategy as essentially dynamic, requiring continual adjustments and change.[21] They must understand the symbolic competitive frame within which they and their products are perceived and must manage the meaning they communicate to their consumers, employees, and other stakeholders.

LCs should not blindly transfer marketing research methods from developed countries as these have a biased focus on middle-class consumers and on marketing problems that typically arise in developed societies. Instead, they must be creative in designing and using low-cost marketing research, consumer research, and environmental scanning. If the task is to create and communicate meaning, researching attitudes toward products and purchase intentions is no longer sufficient. Since standard market research methods imported from the West do not attempt to uncover the desires and experiences of the poor, LCs must rely on qualitative research and ethnographic understanding of rural and underprivileged consumers, of ethnic and religious subcultures, and of consumers undergoing transition (such as migration to the cities or an abrupt encounter with global media, marketing, and tourists).

ALLIANCES AND PARTNERSHIPS

Faced with the threat of marginalization, strategic alliances are more critical for LCs than for TNCs. Dholakia uses the term "interorganizational marketing" to refer to organizations linked on a long-term basis by joint ventures, contracts, franchises, projects, and other methods.[22] Such linkages create globe-spanning networks that "are able to mobilize resources and pursue opportunities more effectively than even giant firms unaffiliated with such networks.[23] Various forms of cooperation, networking, and partnerships can empower LCs. Such relationships can be formed with other LCs (at home and in other countries) to reap the benefits of mutual competitive advantage (e.g., raw materials, human resources), to join forces against the TNCs, and to learn from each other. Relationships can even be formed with TNCs themselves. LCs can also network with and obtain assistance from local and global governments, non-governmental organizations, or civil associations.[24] Such networking and collaboration—through pooling resources, competencies, and skills—enables creative projects and increases the local capability and power against TNCs.

Recent critiques suggest that globalization tends to solidify "a new set of class divisions—between those who prosper in the globalized economy and those who do not."[25] As transitional countries attempt to integrate into the world economy, there is the threat of social disintegration. The Lyon summit of the Group of Seven, held in

June 1996, gave a communiqué titled "Making a Success of Globalization for the Benefit of All." The leaders recognized that globalization raises difficulties for certain groups, and they wrote:

> In an increasingly interdependent world we must all recognize that we have an interest in spreading the benefits of economic growth as widely as possible and in diminishing the risk either of excluding individuals or groups in our own economies or of excluding certain countries or regions from the benefits of globalization.[26]

Proponents of cultural diversity (e.g., UNESCO), organizations interested in reducing the negative consequences of globalization (e.g., WHO, UNDP, immigration institutions), and some educational institutions could well be interested in helping LCs to help themselves and be proactive in spreading the benefits of globalization.

One example is the case of the extractive products in the Amazon region.[27] This case illustrates how an alliance that employed the forces of capitalism while still valuing local knowledge and ecosystems was able to reap financial benefits. Rubber-tappers and forest peoples (supported by Cultural Survival, a people-oriented organization) formed a partnership with progressive international entrepreneurs to market Brazil nuts and other tropical forest products to Northern consumers interested in environmentalism. This provided lucrative markets for both sides. Other specialty products, such as fashionable health or ethnic goods or botanical medicine, can be sold in world niche markets using this model of global cooperation.

Another form of cooperation that can be advantageous to LCs is the "information partnership," where information, research, and other data are shared with other local firms. Local firms can share investments in hardware and software and reduce risks in "cutting-edge" technology investments.

> Through an information partnership, diverse companies can offer novel incentives and services or participate in joint marketing programs. They can take advantage of new channels of distribution or introduce operational efficiencies and revenue enhancements. Partnerships create opportunities for scale and cross-selling. They can make small companies look, feel, and act big, reaching for customers once beyond their grasp. Partnerships can make big companies look small and close, targeting and servicing custom markets. Partnerships, in short, provide a new basis for differentiation.[28]

ACTING UPON THE POLITICAL ENVIRONMENT

The viable strategies for any firm are irrevocably intertwined with local conditions such as political stability issues, state policies or other initiatives, relations with foreign and local capital, regional economic blocs, and cultural and educational factors that influence consumers, stakeholders, and human resources.[29] Public policy clearly contributes to how conducive the environment is for the strategies recommended to foster globally competitive local firms. However, local firms are also able to shape their environment and they can help initiate governmental or civil action to establish an enabling context.

LOCALIZATION STRATEGIES FOR LCs TO COMPETE WITH TNCs

While LCs cannot "out-globalize" TNCs, they can "out-localize" them in both global and local markets. Even if the TNCs "think globally, and act locally" and undertake product, package, promotion and advertising modifications, the LCs are still going to have the unquestionable advantage in the local domain. The local firm, thinking and acting both globally and locally, can successfully compete with the TNCs in its own local arena as well as in certain segments of the global turf—segments that seek localness either for variety or as a symbol of resistance, or parts that have local conditions and desires (similar to the home turf) to which the TNCs do not pay attention and to which LCs' products can cater. LCs can compete by creating their own niche either in the local home market or as a global player in alliance with transnational institutions or other local firms in multiple similar markets across the world.

The role of symbolism in constructing a unique value implies that LCs have to be successful globally or at least have some global presence before the image of local products can be improved at home. Hence, LCs must not aim to start locally and grow slowly to be global. Rather, they must aim either to start in a foreign market or to have a simultaneous presence in both foreign and local markets. That is, they must go fully global to the extent that capital and knowledge constraints can be overcome. In fact, the existence of "Born Globals," whose management viewed the world as its marketplace right from the birth of the firm, has been observed in many countries.[30]

This can be done in domains where the TNCs are not as strong, but not in the typical or "modern" industries such as cars, electronics, and hamburgers. This does not rule out the possibility that some local firms can compete with foreign brands head-on. If they make long-term investments and prune their product lines, LCs can make the few brands they focus on world class, even in "modern" sectors such as durables and clothes. However, global competitiveness is more likely if LCs provide alternatives to standard mass products and services.

LOCAL AS AN ALTERNATIVE TO THE MODERN "NORMAL" GLOBAL

Local firms can reinvent, reconstruct, and repackage local products, services, and places. LCs can take advantage of consumer tendencies in the new world of hyperreality, cyberreality, and exploratory consumption. They can produce a variety of "toys" for the global consumer seeking diversity (the affluent cosmopolitans in modernizing domestic markets as well as in foreign markets). LCs can offer alternative products for the non-conformist or ethically concerned consumers. LCs can offer prestige by providing the unique, the exotic, the unusual.

For instance, in Turkey, there is a trend in up-market restaurants to bring back forgotten regional cuisines to compete with the Western-style restaurants serving a mix of quasi-European dishes. Similarly, localized eateries can successfully compete with the multinational fast-food chains, such as McDonald's. A successful Turkish example of this type of entrepreneurship is that of Ibrahim Tatlises (a Turkish pop music and television star) who is now planning to expand his *lahmacun* (thin, pizza-like dough with meat and spices) fast-food chain to New York. In such a way, local enterprises can take local tastes into the global arena in many lines of business and be successful.

Local firms can discover unnoticed national or export potential in what are considered to be regional or local peculiarities. They can then build them into rare, unique specialty products by mingling local culture with modern business. In Turkey, for example, traditional products such as raki (a distilled alcoholic drink), lokum (Turkish delight), embroideries, carpets and kilims, ceramic and copper wares, and herbal teas can be recreated to connote uniqueness and distinction in just the same way as French Bordeaux wines. Shopping malls, fashioned after traditional covered bazaars, can offer alternative shopping spaces and experiences both in Turkey and throughout the world. They can appeal to those bored with the look-alike American malls.

LCs can serve national or global markets by reviving local cultures through a revitalizing of local crafts, making them youthful and fashionable. By collaborating with small-scale producers in villages, as in the successful silk business in Thailand,[31] LCs can increase marketability of their goods and enable such a repositioning strategy. Beymen, an upscale Turkish store, organizes villages to weave top-quality sheets, curtains, bedspreads, and tablecloths using traditional materials and designs and then presents these textiles as fashionable goods. Local peculiarities can also be rebuilt, positioned, and communicated as environmentally friendly, natural products. Examples that appeal to global consumers are health foods, botanical medicine, natural soaps, herbal teas, and natural olive oil. Many products—from natural local drinks to expensive jewelry—await entrepreneurs to recognize their potential and build them into world products.

Similarly, unspoiled nature sites, nomadic or rural life, and special spaces can provide sustainable eco-tourism. Hotels restored from old houses or old Kervansarays and accommodations provided in nomadic tents would be more welcome to the alternative tourist than the standard Hiltons and Sheratons. With such an approach, Hungarian Danubius Hotels & Spas modernized natural thermal sites and are marketing them to Western European tourists.[32]

Associating the usually negative notion of "underdeveloped" with the positive "natural," "unspoiled," "exotic," and "rare" provides a way to circumvent negative country images. Relating other negative associations to positive concepts or emphasizing existing positive beliefs and symbols will also reinforce favorable imagery.[33] This strategy of local-as-an-alternative does not have to be restricted to traditional or ethnic products. High-tech goods can also be based on local strengths and history. For instance, the start-up firm Sebit is in the process of producing state-of-the-art educational multimedia CD-ROMs, involving an Ottoman mapmaker, for home sales in Turkey and sales to the New York state school system. The CD-ROMs, titled *Piri the Explorer Ship: A Multicultural Exploration via Piri Reis's Map of 1513,* involve an edutainment game. Sebit, a spin-off of a Turkish National Science Foundation project, is working with historians, artists, educators, and a Turkish film director living in New York.

For this strategy to generate more than souvenirs, LCs should emphasize cultural goods and experiences that add to the cultural capital of the individual. The concept of cultural goods originally referred to artistic/cultural resources and heritage, but now includes natural resources and mass-distributed cultural merchandise such as films, records, and software.[34] Exploring consumers, tourists, and collectors prize cultural goods for their emotional, sentimental, symbolic, intellectual or scientific value. Demand for cultural capital has increased in the context of volatile global markets and technological innovations. Export of a variety of cultural products will enable the local firms to make a larger global impact.

INFORMATION GOODS

In addition to and consistent with the products grounded in local culture, LCs should emphasize experiences and goods related to these experiences. They need to focus on services and production of images and ideas—film, music, books, plays, virtual activities, nature activities, culturally enriching travel and education, artworks, art events, and media (print, broadcast, electronic). There is an increasing interest in experiences in the arts and entertainment, education, leisure, health care, and travel. Accordingly, related service industries have been increasing. There are many more opportunities now than ever before to export films, animation, design, and music through the global media.

Furthermore, such products also require little in terms of economic capital investment. In their model of international trade, Douglas and Isherwood define consumption of three sets of goods: a staples set (natural resources), a technology set (intensive use of both skill and economic capital), and an information or services set (special skills and specialized information).[35] Douglas and Isherwood argue that

> [the service] sector, though it uses highly specialized skills . . . also gives employment to quite unskilled workers. . . . [T]his gives the services sector a capacity to absorb and pay better an unskilled rural population made surplus to a more capital intensive agriculture. Similarly, many who gain employment in producing information services do not need long training or specialized skills.[36] It is a feature of the tertiary, or services sector, that it calls for relatively little support from capital investment. It also has scope for employing a relatively untrained labor force. This means that a strongly developed tertiary sector is a potential source of innovation, since there is no heavy investment tied up in capital equipment which would have to be discounted if a radical change were contemplated.[37]

Thus, to take advantage of this opportunity for innovation without intensive economic investment, LCs should go into the information set of goods, such as services and information technology, rather than staples or manufactured technology goods. For example, the development of software may be particularly lucrative in some underdeveloped countries where there is an engineering emphasis in education and skilled manpower is available. The Czech firm Bonton in entertainment and the Hungarian firms Graphisoft in architecture software and Recognita in character-recognition software are examples of Central European entrepreneurial firms "making a splash beyond their borders."[38] Information goods, including images and ideas, overlap with and nurture cultural goods and help build quality and originality symbolism around local products.

GOODS FOR THE LESS AFFLUENT WORLD

Local firms can identify market segments to which TNCs are not sensitive enough and where LCs have a competitive advantage, such as in basic consumer benefits, distribution, or after-sale networks. User-centered,[39] environmentally friendly, low- or high-tech, and low-price products and services can appeal to the underprivileged consumers in both domestic and global markets.

One approach involves designing and producing low-cost appropriate technology alternatives suitable to local conditions. In Turkey, for example, where there was a widespread need for low-price telephone switchboards in small offices and rural areas, two electrical engineers designed fully automatic electronic telephone exchanges. The firm they set up in 1986, Karel, now sells these innovative PBXs, PBX add-ons, and other complementary products locally as well as in 22 countries such as Poland, Hungary, Romania, Jordan, Tunisia, Saudi Arabia, Lebanon, Egypt, Iran, Nigeria, Central Asian Republics, Greece, Spain, Portugal, and even in the USA. In some countries, the price differential of Karel with the closest price competitor runs up to fivefold.

Common factors in the global peasant and slum markets can make it worthwhile to target the poor and design products and services for their conditions and desires. Not only are peasant and slum lifestyles around the world amazingly similar, but these markets are also unexpectedly receptive to new products. Sewage treatment, waste disposal systems, potable water supply, health services, community infrastructure schemes, communication, retailing (e.g., innovative mobile stores that reach the slums and rural areas), and transportation (e.g., planes for short and unpaved runways, vehicles for local climates and road conditions) are some areas that provide global opportunities. For example, a Chinese firm supplies tube wells (to obtain clean water where underground water levels are close to the surface), pipes, fittings, and pumps to Bangladesh. Thai firms penetrated peasant markets in China with an appropriate technological innovation—walking tractors. Although ignored due to an urban-middle-class and high-tech mindset among managers, rural residents and the slum poor may well be lucrative markets.[40] There are opportunities to be taken advantage of by fulfilling the desires of this immense market. Yet, Western firms generally do not pay attention to the poor, and, following their lead, local firms do not either.

User-centered, socially desirable, and culturally appropriate products, such as small efficient gas stoves, solar cookers, wood-conserving cable drums, and electronic voting machines can be commercially successful. LCs, either on their own or in cooperation with institutes such as India's National Institute of Design, can employ responsible and culturally appropriate product design and distribution.

CONCLUDING THOUGHTS

By moving with an in-depth understanding of global production and consumption dynamics and grounding their actions in the local culture and strengths, local firms can be global contenders and out-localize TNCs in the global village. With diverse consumer meanings and product-country images in the multiple consumer cultures of the world, where consumers negotiate sameness and difference, LCs can offer difference—local alternatives to compete with the standard TNCs. Three domains described which could be developed to outlocalize the TNCs are the local-as-an-alternative (especially cultural goods), information goods, and products designed to accommodate similar local conditions and the desires of the poor and alternative consumers of the world. To be a global player in these alternative domains, the local firm must develop an innovative perspective; global and local vision; self-designed strategies, skills, and know-how; alliances; and a supportive political environment.

Conventional imitation of TNCs has been considered the only way for an LC to be a successful global player. Local culture has been ignored and devalued in attempts to progress and modernize. In attempting to compete globally, most LCs are blind to the fact that local culture is a valuable resource to be capitalized on.

Global interconnectivity is inevitable. To meet this challenge, LCs must negotiate globalization. Local firms can best achieve this by drawing upon local culture and diversity and offering something different from what TNCs are able to offer. They must investigate areas that TNCs are ignoring—the local context, the urban and rural poor, and small local markets with similar conditions all over the world. They must shape their own product and consumption meanings in consumers' minds. While local firms cannot undermine TNCs' domination of global markets, they can avoid being excluded or marginalized.

LCs need to be both sophisticated in the ways of global business *and* intuitive. They also need to be more diagnostic than optimizing, and more insightful and interpretive than analytical. To increase their long-term effectiveness, LCs must out-localize the TNCs. By developing and using cultural resources and taking advantage of various forms of global media and electronic commerce, LCs can succeed in having a non-marginal presence in the global village. This involves not only taking part in the global flows of products and money, but also contributing to global flows of information, media, images, and ideas. This contribution is stronger if expressed as self-authentication of the local. Construction, expression, and management of meanings of quality and authenticity can provide a sustainable positive global image for local goods and firms. This, in turn, will increase respect for domestic products and reduce the domestic cultural dependency on foreign products and images in local markets, hence fostering and sustaining the competitiveness of local firms in the long term. By playing the alternative game of out-localizing the TNCs, LCs can become successful global players.

Notes

1. Leslie Sklair, "Competing Models of Globalization: Theoretical Frameworks and Research Agendas," working paper, London School of Economics and Political Science, 1993. Related discussions include Marc T. Jones and Alladi Venkatesh, "The Role of the Transnational Corporation in the Global Marketplace: A Critical Perspective," in Russell W. Belk, Nikhilesh Dholakia, and Alladi Venkatesh, eds., *Consumption and Marketing: Macro Dimensions* (Cincinnati, OH: Southwestern, 1996), pp. 282–310; Barbara Stallings, ed., *Global Change, Regional Response: The New International Context of Development* (Cambridge: Cambridge University Press, 1995).

2. See, for example, S. Tamer Cavusgil and John R. Nevin, "State-of-the-Art in International Marketing: An Assessment," in Ben M. Enis and Kenneth J. Roering, eds., *Review of Marketing* (Chicago, IL: American Marketing Association, 1981), pp. 195–216; Susan P. Douglas and C. Samuel Craig, "Evolution of Global Marketing Strategy: Scale, Scope, and Synergy," *Columbia Journal of World Business,* 24/3 (Fall 1989): 47–59; Nigel M. Healey, "The Transition Economies of Central and Eastern Europe: A Political, Economic, Social and Technological Analysis," *Columbia Journal of World Business,* 29/1 (Spring 1994): 62–70; Erdener Kaynak, ed., *Sociopolitical Aspects of International Marketing* (Binghamton, NY: Haworth Press, 1991).
3. Erdener Kaynak, *Marketing in the Third World* (New York, NY: Praeger, 1982).
4. This paragraph draws from Ash Amin, "Placing Globalization," *Theory, Culture and Society,* 14/2 (1997): 123–137; Benjamin R. Barber, "Jihad vs. McWorld," *The Atlantic Monthly,* 269/3 (1992): 53–63; Mike Featherstone, ed., *Global Culture: Nationalism, Globalization and Modernity* (London: Sage, 1990); Jonathan Friedman, "Being in the World: Globalization and Localization," *Theory, Culture and Society,* 7 (1990): 311–328; Ulf Hannerz, "Notes on the Global Ecumene," *Public Culture,* 1 (Spring 1989): 66–75; A. King, "Architecture, Capital and the Globalization of Culture," *Theory, Culture and Society,* 7 (1990): 397–411; Edward W. Said, *Culture and Imperialism* (London: Chatto & Windus, 1993); Richard Wilk, "Learning to be Local in Belize: Global Systems of Common Difference," in Daniel Miller, ed., *Worlds Apart: Modernity Through the Prism of the Local* (London: Routledge, 1995), pp. 110–133.
5. Arjun Appadurai, "Disjuncture and Difference in the Global Cultural Economy," *Theory, Culture and Society,* 7 (1990): 295–310.
6. See Mike Featherstone, *Consumer Culture and Postmodernism* (London: Sage, 1991); Güliz Ger and Russell W. Belk, "I'd Like to Buy the World a Coke: Consumptionscapes of the 'Less Affluent World'," *Journal of Consumer Policy,* 19/3 (1996): 74–104; Annamma Joy and Melanie Wallendorf, "Development of Consumer Culture in the Third World: Theories of Globalism and Localism," in Russell W. Belk, Nikhilesh Dholakia and Alladi Venkatesh, eds., *Consumption and Marketing: Macro Dimensions* (Cincinnati, OH: Southwestern, 1996), pp. 104–142; Clifford J. Shultz II, Russell W. Belk and Güliz Ger, eds., *Consumption in Marketizing Economies* (Greenwich, CT: JAI Press, 1994); Alladi Venkatesh, "Ethnoconsumerism: A New Paradigm to Study Cultural and Cross-Cultural Consumer Behavior," in Janeen Arnold Costa and Gary Bamossy, eds., *Marketing in a Multicultural World: Ethnicity, Nationalism, and Cultural Identity* (Thousand Oaks, CA: Sage, 1995), pp. 26–67.
7. Colin Campbell, *The Romantic Ethic and the Spirit of Modern Consumerism* (Oxford: Basil Blackwell, 1987); Mary Douglas and Baron Isherwood, *The World of Goods: Towards an Anthropology of Consumption* (New York, NY: Basic Books, 1979); Grant McCracken, *Culture and Consumption: New Approaches to the Symbolic Character of Consumer Goods and Activities* (Bloomington, IN: Indiana University Press, 1988).
8. "Product-country image" refers to the socially constructed symbolic and stereotypic image or the representations related to products from a country and its competitors in the minds of consumers, importers, investors, retailers, and tourists. See Søren Askegaard and Güliz Ger, "Product-Country Images as Stereotypes: A Comparative Study," *Proceedings of the International Association for Research in Economic Psychology,* 21st Annual Colloquium, Paris, 1996, 13–28; Sri Ram Khanna, "Asian Companies and the Country Stereotype Paradox: An Empirical Study," *Columbia Journal of World Business,* 21 (Summer 1986): 29–38; Nicolas Papadopoulos and Louise Heslop, eds., *Product-Country-Images: Impact and Role in International Marketing* (New York, NY: International Business Press, 1993).

9. Güliz Ger, "The Positive and Negative Effects of Marketing on Socioeconomic Development: The Turkish Case," *Journal of Consumer Policy,* 15/3 (1992): 229–254; Güliz Ger, "Human Development and Humane Consumption: Well-Being Beyond the 'Good Life'," *Journal of Public Policy and Marketing,* 16/1 (Spring 1997): 110–125; Miller (1997), op. cit.; Clifford J. Shultz II, "Balancing Policy, Consumer Desire and Corporate Interests: Considerations for Market Entry in Vietnam," *Columbia Journal of World Business,* 29/4 (Winter 1994): 42–52; Sklair (1991), op. cit.
10. Elisabeth Croll, *From Heaven to Earth: Images and Experiences of Development in China* (London: Routledge, 1994), p. 222.
11. A. Fuat Firat and Alladi Venkatesh, "Liberatory Postmodernism and the Reenchantment of Consumption," *Journal of Consumer Research,* 22/3 (1995): 239–267; Yiannis Gabriel and Tim Lang, *The Unmanageable Consumer: Contemporary Consumption and Its Fragmentation* (London: Sage, 1995).
12. Jean Baudrillard, "Consumer Society," in Mark Poster, ed., *Jean Baudrillard: Selected Writings* (Cambridge: Polity Press, 1970/1988), p. 45.
13. For the identity-expressive consumption in less affluent countries, see Ger and Belk (1996), op. cit.
14. For forces of information technology, see Arthur G. Armstrong and John Hagel III, *Net Gain: Expanding Markets Through Virtual Communities* (Boston, MA: Harvard Business School Press, 1997); Regis McKenna, *Real-Time: Preparing for the Eventuality of Everything* (Boston, MA: Harvard Business School Press, 1997).
15. See, for example, Michael E. Porter, "What is Strategy?," *Harvard Business Review,* 74/6 (November/December 1996): 61–78.
16. George S. Day and Robin Wensley, "Assessing Advantage: A Framework for Diagnosing Competitive Superiority," *Journal of Marketing,* 52 (April 1988): 1–20.
17. See Pierre Bourdieu, *Distinction: A Social Critique of the Judgment of Taste* (Cambridge, MA: Harvard University Press, 1984); Pierre Bourdieu, "Forms of Capital," in J.G. Richardson, ed., *Handbook of Theory and Research for the Sociology of Education* (New York, NY: Greenwood Press, 1986), pp. 241–258; Paul DiMaggio, "Review Essay: On Pierre Bourdieu," *American Journal of Sociology,* 84/6 (May 1979): 1460–1474.
18. R.C. Ulin, "Invention and Representation as Cultural Capital—Southwest French Winegrowing History," *American Anthropologist,* 97/3 (1995): 519–527.
19. Kenneth Simmonds ["Transition Marketing," *Society and Economy,* Quarterly Journal of Budapest University of Economic Sciences, 3 (1994): 9–22] also argues for the inappropriateness of direct technology or know-how transfers. See Joy and Ross [(1989), op. cit.] for a theoretical discussion of the futility of direct technology or know-how transfers in places with different development or modernization trajectories since development is not linear and progress not unidirectional. Ger [(1997), op. cit.] provides an elaborate discussion of alternative cultures (love and aesthetics) that enable local agents to avoid a catch-up-and-imitate culture.
20. See, for example, David A. Aaker, *Strategic Market Management* (New York, NY: John Wiley, 1995); David A. Aaker, *Managing Brand Equity* (New York, NY: Free Press, 1991); Armstrong and Hagel III (1997), op. cit.; George S. Day, "Continuous Learning About Markets," *California Management Review,* 36/4 (Summer 1994): 9–31; Nikhilesh Dholakia and Ruby Roy Dholakia, "The Changing Information Business: Toward Content-Based and Service-Based Competition," *Columbia Journal of World Business,* 30/2 (Summer 1995): 94–104; Orville C. Walker, Harper W. Boyd, Jr., and Jean-Claude Larréché, *Marketing Strategy* (Chicago, IL: Irwin, 1996).

21. For the importance of diagnosis, see Simmonds (1994), op. cit.
22. Nikhilesh Dholakia, "Industrial Policy, Competitiveness, and the Restructuring of World Markets," in Paul Bloom, ed., *Advances in Marketing and Public Policy,* 1 (Greenwich, CT: JAI Press, 1987): 187–216.
23. Ibid., p. 195.
24. For a discussion of the political and economic linkages that underlie Southeast Asian success stories, see Clifford J. Shultz II and Anthony Pecotich, "Marketing and Development in the Transition Economies of Southeast Asia: Policy Explication, Assessment and Implications," *Journal of Public Policy and Marketing,* 16/1 (Spring 1996): 55–68.
25. Dani Rodrik, "Has Globalization Gone Too Far?" *California Management Review,* 39/3 (Spring 1997): 29–53, 34. See also John Sherry, "Cultural Propriety in the Global Marketplace," in A. Fuat Firat, Nikhilesh Dholakia, and Richard P. Bagozzi, eds., *Philosophical and Radical Thought in Marketing* (Lexington, MA: Lexington Books, 1987), pp. 179–192.
26. Rodrik (1997), op. cit., p. 30.
27. Peter H. May, "Savage Capitalism: International Market Alliances to Conserve Neotropical Forests," in Frank J. Dietz, Udo E. Simonis and Jan van der Straaten, eds., *Sustainability and Environmental Policy: Restraints and Advances* (Berlin: Edition Sigma, 1992), pp. 226–236.
28. Benn R. Konsynski and F. Warren McFarlan, "Information Partnerships—Shared Data, Shared Scale," *Harvard Business Review,* 68/5 (September/October 1990): 114–120, 115.
29. Policy issues and recommendations are beyond the scope here. For more detailed treatments, see Linda F. Alwitt, "Marketing and the Poor," *American Behavioral Scientist,* 38/4 (1995): 564–577; Rudolf Buitelaar, "Changing Production Patterns, Poverty, and the Role of Consumer Unions: Some Conceptual Notes With Reference to Latin America," *Journal of Consumer Policy,* 14 (1991): 195–206; Ger (1997), op. cit.; Gary Gereffi, "Global Production Systems and Third World Development," In Barbara Stallings, ed., *Global Change, Regional Response: The New International Context of Development* (Cambridge: Cambridge University Press, 1995), pp. 100–142; D. Paul Schafer, "Cultures and Economies: Irresistible Forces Encounter Immovable Objects," *Futures,* 26/8 (1994): 830–845.
30. Tage Koed Madsen and Per Servais, "The Internationalization of Born Globals: An Evolutionary Process?" *International Business Review,* 6/6 (1997): 561–583.
31. For the successful silk business in Thailand, see Jeffrey A. Fadiman, "Tapping Third World Peasant Markets," in Hendrick Serrie and S. Brian Burkhalter, eds., *What Can Multinationals Do for Peasants? Studies in Third World Societies,* Publication No. 49 (Williamsburg, VA: William and Mary College, 1994): 53–84.
32. Reported in *Business Week,* June 30, 1997, pp. 20–27.
33. See Alice M. Tybout, Bobby J. Calder, and Brian Sternthal, "Using Information Processing Theory to Design Effective Marketing Strategies," *Journal of Marketing Research,* 18 (1981): 73–79.
34. Françoise Codron-Anty, "The Concept of 'Cultural Property' Applied to Health," *Proceedings of the International Association for Research in Economic Psychology,* 21st Annual Colloquium, Paris, 1996, pp. 847–859.
35. Douglas and Isherwood (1979), op. cit.
36. Ibid., p. 183.
37. Ibid., p. 197.
38. *Business Week* (June 30, 1997), op. cit., p. 25.

39. The notion of "user-centered" design has been discussed by Donald A. Norman, *The Design of Everyday Things* (New York, NY: Doubleday, 1988); Victor Papanek, *Design for the Real World* (Toronto: Bantam Books, 1973); Nigel Whiteley, *Design for Society* (London: Reaktion Books, 1993).
40. For an excellent discussion of peasant markets, see Hendrick Serrie and S. Brian Burkhalter, eds., *What Can Multinationals do for Peasants? Studies in Third World Societies,* Publication No. 49 (Williamsburg, VA: William and Mary College, 1994). What Serrie and Burkhalter discuss for peasants applies, to a great extent, to the urban slum consumers in the developing world. Simmonds [(1994), op. cit.] and Fadiman [(1994), op. cit.] provide discussions of the urban middle-class mindsets and blindness of managers.

PART FOUR

Functional Areas

DYNAMICS OF CORE COMPETENCIES IN LEADING MULTINATIONAL COMPANIES

Briance Mascarenhas, Alok Baveja
and Mamnoon Jamil

A "core competence," as articulated by Prahalad and Hamel,[1] has three traits: it makes a contribution to perceived customer benefits; it is difficult for competitors to imitate; and it can be leveraged to a wide variety of markets. Knowing a firm's core competence is important for developing strategy. By concentrating on their core competence and outsourcing other activities, managers can leverage their company's resources in four ways: they maximize returns by focusing on what they do best; they provide formidable barriers against the entry of competitors; they fully utilize external suppliers' strengths and investments that they would not be able to duplicate; and they reduce investment and risk, shorten cycle times, and increase customer responsiveness.[2]

Several studies have emerged on core competencies, and they have typically examined the conditions that make a competence valuable[3] or have sought to identify actual core competencies in firms.[4] Consequently, while we know more about how to evaluate and identify core competencies, the dynamics of competencies are still not clear. Little is known about how core competencies arise in the first place and how managers can develop them. Furthermore, if a firm's core competencies change over time, a static view can be misleading and can encourage the building of inappropriate types of competencies.

The authors would like to thank the executives who participated in the study from Boeing, Campbell Soup, Citicorp, Crown Cork and Seal, HCL, Inductotherm, Lockheed Martin, Melitta, Merck, National Starch and Chemicals, Okidata, and Siemens. The study benefited from the comments of R. Sambharya. The study was supported by a CIBER research grant from the United States Department of Education.

METHODOLOGY

To analyze the dynamics of core competencies, the authors conducted case studies of 12 multinational companies. The companies selected are leaders in global market position and are characterized by their longevity, high levels of profitability, or low top management turnover. They are based in four countries—United States, Germany, India, and Japan—and represent firms from diverse industries ranging from service to manufacturing sectors and from consumer to industrial products. The companies are detailed in Table 1.

Top executives familiar with their firm's way of competing and its industrial context were interviewed. The executives were given the general definition of a core competence and were asked to elaborate on industry developments, their firm's competencies, how they were created, how their competencies changed over time, and the competencies they were planning for the future. The information provided by executives was cross-checked with documentary sources, such as company annual reports, sales catalogs, newsletters, business press reports, academic case studies, videos, book histories, and company web sites on the Internet.

The analysis was conducted in three stages. In the first stage, the researchers performed detailed case write-ups for each company, including transcripts of team meetings with company executives. In the second stage, cross-company comparisons were made. The third stage mapped out the sequence in which firm competencies were developed over time. These sequences are compared across firms to develop a dynamic model of how competencies are strengthened, leveraged, and developed.

Finally, the executives were contacted again to check the accuracy of reporting and to make any desired changes. Table 2 reports the competencies uncovered across the 12 companies.[5]

TYPES OF COMPETENCE

The identified competencies fall into three basic groups: superior technological know-how; reliable processes; and close relationships with external parties. These three types of competencies are consistent with competencies found in prior studies.[6]

SUPERIOR TECHNOLOGICAL KNOW-HOW

A technological competence involves a deep understanding of a subject area. This deep understanding arises from an early, substantial, and continuous involvement in that area. It includes knowledge of the scientific properties, inter-relationships, and latest developments in a subject area. This knowledge is valuable if competitors do not have a similar knowledge base and if the knowledge can be converted into superior products for customers.

• TABLE 1 •

Characteristics of Firms Studied

Firm	Primary Industry	Country of Origin	Outstanding Characteristics
Siemens	Capital Goods	Germany	Second largest German industrial firm. Founded over 150 years ago, operates in 120 countries and has over 380,000 employees.
Merck	Pharmaceuticals	United States	Rated 'the most admired corporation in America' five years running. Second largest global drug firm.
Boeing	Aircraft Manufacturing	United States	Global market share leader. Founded in 1916. Has had six CEOs during this period.
Citicorp	Financial Services	United States	Largest U.S. bank and a pioneer in international markets.
Melitta	Food Processing	Germany	Privately held firm that operates in over 100 countries. Melitta coffee is ranked second in market share in Europe.
Campbell Soup Company	Food Processing	United States	Founded over 125 years ago. Operates in over 120 countries, has 43,000 employees. Most consistently profitable firm in food processing industry in the 1990s.
Okidata	Computer Office Machines	Japan	Founded over 110 years ago. Pioneered the dot-matrix printer technology.
Lockheed Martin	Defense Aerospace	United States	Largest global defense company
Crown, Cork, and Seal	Packaging	United States	Largest global packaging company, with $10 billion in sales and 312 plants worldwide. Founded in 1892. Has had five CEOs since its inception 104 years ago.
HCL	Software	India	Largest computer company from India that is rapidly expanding internationally.
National Starch and Chemicals	Specialty Chemicals	United States	Founded in 1895. $2.5 billion in sales, 168 million in net income, 8,500 employees in 125 facilities in 36 countries in 6 continents. Has had 6 CEOs in its 100 year history.
Inductotherm	Induction-Driven Furnaces for Melting and Welding	United States	Global market share leader with 85% of the U.S. market and 50% of the global market. Founded 40 years ago.

• TABLE 2 •

Companies Competencies by Type

Firm	Technological Know-How	Reliable Process	Close Relationship with External Parties
Siemens	Semiconductor know-how that cuts across its 14 divisions.	Reliable high-quality, low-cost manufacturing achieved through master/apprenticeship program. Innovation productivity fostered by a long tradition of managing innovation process.	Close ties to German banks provide access to capital to finance customer purchases.
Merck	Excellent functional specialists in research and manu-facturing help to achieve superior performance.	High ethical standards and controls reduce risk of drug failures. Strong record of obtaining drug approvals from policy-makers.	Strong relationship with the profession helps to attract new talent. Credibility with the demanding Food and Drug Administration in the U.S. helps to obtain approvals internationally.
Boeing	Flexible design and assembly of aircraft.	Large scale international system integration for millions of parts that go into a plane.	Close relationship with suppliers helps to make rapid design changes.
Citicorp	Has sophisticated financial product and market trading know-how in the United States.	Ability to provide its 100 million customers any financial service, anywhere, in any currency over its own global network at a low cost without failures.	Leverages its local customer contacts from early international entries over its global network of affiliates to develop their international business.
Melitta		Ability to provide customers a consistent, high-quality 'coffee enjoyment' experience by being the only player that offers an integrated package of coffee makers, coffee filters, and coffee blend.	Uses its 'relationship marketing' with the trade to cross-sell multiple products.
Campbell Soup	Food growing and processing know-how, such as its flavor adding technology.	A company-wide focus on performance encouraged by a 'pay-for-performance' system that is ingrained from the Board of Directors down to the supervisory level. Ability to transfer this 'pay-for-performance system' to international acquisitions.	

Okidata	Strong technical research and engineering in Japan.		Close relationship with distributors obtains customer information feedback and provides market access.
Lockheed Martin	Systems engineering and aerospace, composites, and microelectronics expertise.	Record of mission success. Reach to access resources anywhere to execute on time and on budget projects that have never been done before.	To satisfy its customers' needs, the firm has also developed closer relationships with suppliers, domestically and internationally.
Crown, Cork and Seal	Tooling investment and know-how to cut metal and reduce material and handling of cans.	Culture of cost reduction manifested in its management, structure, operations, and design of cans. Ability to transfer its cost reduction practices to over 20 acquisitions.	Leverages its close customer relationship across plastic and metal packaging, filling machinery, domestically and internationally.
National Starch and Chemicals	Expertise in both natural and synthetic polymers.	Seamless coordination between research, development, and technical services.	Close relationship with customers leads to customer-driven R&D.
HCL	Expertise in UNIX based software systems where it was an early entrant before it became the global industry standard.	A reliable system of providing offshore outsourcing of software development using the large, low-cost, computer-skilled professionals in India.	Close relationships with clients help to develop customized computer hardware and software solutions and provide servicing.
Inductotherm	Induction melting technology.	Reliability of its furnaces, arising from its integration at the factory instead of customer location, its large installed base, and round-the-clock global servicing.	Its open relationship with vendors generates ideas and components that it integrates into its new products.

The CEO of National Starch, a producer of specialty chemicals, noted that the firm has a core competence in its expertise in both natural and synthetic polymers, two upstream disciplines that are used in diverse end products and markets. The firm was originally in the chemicals business but obtained the expertise in natural polymers unintentionally through an agricultural division that was part of a larger acquisition it made decades ago. Its competitors have expertise in either natural polymers or synthetic polymers. The combination of expertise in natural *and* synthetic polymers gives National Starch a larger "toolbox" to work on the diverse needs of its industrial customers. For example, one of its customers is a manufacturer of body lotions that desired a certain "feel" in a new lotion. National Starch was able to meet this customer's need by drawing on its expertise in both kinds of polymers.

The global context provides various opportunities for developing and leveraging superior technological know-how. The special capabilities of diverse countries can be sourced in developing technological know-how. Larger international sales can fund and amortize greater R&D expenditures.[7] Superior technological know-how gives foreign firms a lever to enter foreign markets and compete with local firms that may better understand the local context. Since countries vary in their infrastructural context and development, opportunities exist for transferring and extending the life of older technologies to developing countries as newer technologies emerge in industrial countries.

RELIABLE PROCESSES

A reliable process delivers an expected result quickly, consistently, and efficiently, with the least inconvenience or disruptions to customers. A reliable process can involve the decomposition, re-integration, or transfer of skills across functions, currencies, or countries. It can also be the ability to combine various inputs to customize a product to meet a customer's particular needs. Reliable processes can occur in the research and development of new products, in zero-defect manufacturing, in consistently obtaining rapid regulatory approvals, in international sourcing without disruptions, in executing cross-border transactions efficiently without snags or losses, and in transferring an operating system or organizational culture internationally or to an acquired organization. Reliability is important because customers increasingly consider the total cost of a product over its life, not just its initial purchase price.

Merck has a reliable process competence in the development of new drugs. This reliable process is due to various factors. Its researchers are prominent in their fields and employ higher professional and ethical standards in their research than other pharmaceutical firms. Merck has stringent internal controls to prevent the release of a drug prematurely that are enforced both domestically and in its international affiliates. Employees go through training programs where safety is emphasized. In the testing stages, Merck employs more stringent tests than what is required by the Food and Drug Administration (FDA). For example, company executives noted that while the FDA typically required a sample of 1,500 patients in the phase three stage testing of a new drug, Merck employs a sample of 5,000 patients. This added testing increases the reliability of claims about a drug's efficacy and reduces the chances of unknown side effects. The added testing need not slow down the introduction of the drug to market.

Merck compensates for more stringent testing by committing more resources to R&D than its competitors, which speeds up the development process. The well-known reliability of Merck's development process helps to obtain faster approval from the FDA. Further, Merck maintains an in-house manufacturing capability in chemicals that enables the firm to quickly ramp up quality production of a new drug upon FDA approval.

A reliable process is valuable when conducting business in a global context. Being able to offer a reliable process is valued by customers since international transactions are subject to great uncertainties and disruptions because of transportation, communication, and customs delays, cultural differences, or red tape. Countries also vary in their production capabilities and desires for a customized product. Few companies have the ability to effectively break up a design or production process internationally and combine various inputs to meet a specific customer's needs.

Citicorp has a reliable process competence in providing multiple financial services through its own global network to its 100 million customers worldwide. It aims to provide its customers "any banking service, anywhere, anytime, in any currency in any way they choose" without losing transactions and without bureaucratic delay. It is able to provide these cross-border transactions efficiently because of over 100 years of foreign exchange experience. Its presence in some countries with few banking restrictions gives the firm operational flexibility. Citicorp also has a reputation with customers for executing cross-border transactions. Citicorp has been ranked the world leader in foreign exchange trading sixteen years in a row by Euromoney. Citicorp's organizational structure assigns customers a single contact person to enhance the customer confidence in these cross-border transactions. Competitors do not have such a reputation and may have different organizational structures. They also cannot offer such reliable services because they have a more limited network of their own affiliates abroad and have to rely on correspondent banks, creating seams between organizations and increasing costs in the process.

An example of this reliable process capability is reflected in Citicorp's "Globe Deposit Account" that is targeted to ethnic market retail customers in many countries. Potential account holders are offered a choice of 15 currencies in which to hold their deposit, which is held by Citicorp in Singapore, where there are few banking restrictions. Citicorp allows depositors the option to change the currency of their deposit every week and in increments of $1,000 of their total deposit. Further, in order to improve communication, each depositor is assigned a relationship manager who may also be from the same ethnic community. Customers obtain the potential benefits of being able to choose their currency exposure and take advantage of relative shifts in currencies.

CLOSE EXTERNAL RELATIONSHIPS

A close relationship with suppliers, regulators, professional organizations, distributors, and customers yields several benefits. The firm and partner can identify opportunities for mutual benefit (such as joint cost reduction by removing purchasing and sales functions or off-peak scheduling). Suppliers can suggest ideas for new product development or execute rapid design changes needed in parts. Professional organizations can provide superior talent. Regulators can facilitate and hasten product or manufacturing quality approvals. Distributors can provide market access and customer information. Customers can suggest new competencies that the firm should develop.

Inductotherm is the global market leader for induction furnaces that use electric current to create a magnetic field which, in turn, creates an electric current to heat and melt a target metal. Henry Rowan, its CEO and founder, noted that he constitutes the bulk of the R&D effort within the firm. In addition, the firm relies on close, open relationships with vendors for R&D by welcoming them instead of screening them out. These vendors expose the company to new ideas and components that Inductotherm then integrates into its own product development instead of developing new products and components from scratch, which would be slower and more costly. Not being tied to an internal technology gives Inductotherm the flexibility to innovate with lower financial investments and to provide customers continuously improved products.

Developing close relationships is important in the global environment. Firms can leverage their international distribution reach. In some industries, developing a relationship with a local partner can help to defuse protectionism. In cultures with long time frames, firms seek to develop relationships before conducting business. Relationships are particularly useful in reducing opportunistic behavior in countries that are less legalistic than the United States. A strong relationship with a local partner can be used to leverage a firm's other assets internationally. Relationships are useful to buffer the inevitable disruptions and uncertainties that characterize international business. Firms can also reduce their financial foreign investment outlays by conducting international business through close relationships with other organizations instead of through creating and operating subsidiaries abroad.

In the defense aerospace business, Lockheed Martin has close relationships with its defense agency customers. Its managers call this competence "customer intimacy" and it involves satisfying not only its own objectives, but those of its customers. Its deeply shared motto is: "The customer's mission is our mission!" The close relationship with the customer enables Lockheed Martin to understand and satisfy the varied needs that exist in the client organization: it gauges and tries to satisfy the different needs of politicians in the capital, of military generals in the defense department, and of technicians in the field. Further, as part of the long-term relationship the firm provides not only the purchased product, but the on-going servicing and support. Consequently, Lockheed Martin strives to reduce the customer's total project cost, which is quite different from the initial purchase price.

Siemens produces large capital equipment goods such as power generation, telecommunications, and transportation equipment. Siemens markets these high-ticket items in over 120 countries. Historically, German companies have had close relationships with German banks. Siemens, in particular, has had a close relationship with Deutsche Bank, with executives sitting on each other's boards. This close relationship with a major German bank provided Siemens with ample, low-cost financing for its customers, enabling the firm to make international sales to many countries. Siemens's international competitors based in other countries may not have this close relationship with their banks and cannot exercise such a financial advantage.

DYNAMICS OF COMPETENCIES

Table 3 reports the factors mentioned by executives that contributed to development of the three types of competencies. (In parentheses is the number of firms in which

• TABLE 3 •

How Firms Developed the Three Types of Competence (number of firms in which ??? emphasized in interviews)

Technological	Reliable Process	Close External Relationships
Exposure to a demanding technical, operating, or economic environment where firm is located (6)	Use of corporate culture that abhors waste, operating controls, and expected standards to reduce disruptions (5)	Use acquisition of other firms to obtain their relationships (4)
Defy prevailing assumed technical or operating limits (4)	Conduct analyses to identify activities that should be outsourced as well as to identify most reliable suppliers (4)	Market firm's international reach to develop relationships across countries (4)
Use magnitude of development task and deadlines to motivate employees (4)	Use of logistical innovations to improve communication and customer response (3)	Use of compelling technical and/or reliable process competencies to forge external relationships (4)
Commit resources early (4)	Utilization of experience associated with having a large installed base (1)	Use of an existing relationship with one party to develop relationships with others (3)
Commit substantial resources to an area (3)	Use of personal contacts and audit teams to monitor and facilitate coordination (2)	Understand and satisfy various needs by implanting a high-level team in partners (2)
Use of scope economies to justify resource commitment (2)	Use of a company-wide rewards and incentive system to promote firm efficiency and avoid waste (1)	Cross-sell multiple new products using an umbrella brand name (2)
Use of early reputation and talent to continuously attract quality resources (2)		Use of increasing firm size to develop large, efficient, mutually beneficial, long-term agreements (2)
		Use of early entry and longer time period to build a relationship (1)

each factor was emphasized in interviews.) Clearly, different approaches and multiple methods are needed to develop each type of competence.

DEVELOPING A TECHNOLOGICAL KNOW-HOW COMPETENCE

With regard to developing a technological competence, the most common factor emphasized in the interviews was exposure to a demanding technical, operating, or economic environment. Often, the firms have combined upstream technologies that were accessible where it was located or home-based. Managers operating in such an environment have defied the prevailing assumed limits and pushed the performance boundaries beyond what was commonly deemed possible. They often use a demanding deadline to emphasize the magnitude of the development task and thus motivate employees. Resource commitment is important for developing expertise in a subject area, particularly if the commitment is made early on. With an early commitment, competitors may not yet exist and the firm has a longer time frame in which to accumulate expertise. It also helps if the resource commitment is substantial, which can be encouraged by scope economies. Further, the resource commitment should be continuous to maintain forward momentum and to avoid the dysfunctional effects of stops and starts in development.

Merck provides an example which illustrates the roles played by these factors in the development of a technological competence. In 1933, George Merck set up a lab in New Jersey and hired prominent researchers in chemistry and biology. The existing chemical and health care industries in the New Jersey/Philadelphia region provided a rich base from which to draw talent. Research at the intersection of these two upstream disciplines helped to develop various pharmaceutical products, such as vitamin B-12, cortisone, and streptomycin. The combined research approach also contributed to the synthesizing of chemical compounds that block the formation of disease enzymes rather than just treat disease symptoms.

Merck was still primarily a research organization, licensing out many of its patents to other companies for royalties. Despite having prominent scientists, Merck fell behind other companies in introducing drugs to the market. This prompted Merck to become more proactive and it began to improve on competitors' drugs and license technologies from foreign drug companies. It also acquired Sharp and Dohme, another pharmaceutical company, whereby it obtained an extensive drug marketing and distribution network that could better commercialize new drugs.

In the late 1980s, Merck's CFO Judy Lewent persuaded then-CEO Roy Vagelos to sharply increase R&D expenditures, arguing that they would translate into a disproportionate increase in pioneering new drugs and firm profitability. By the late 1980s, Merck's stepped-up research program accounted for 10% of the industry's total R&D expenditures. The firm adopted a policy of hiring the top 10% of scientists and of "sparing no expense" to recruit top talent. The stature and competence of Merck's functional specialists helped to recruit and train the next generation of specialists. Within a decade, these steps resulted in Merck doubling its sales, tripling profits, and achieving the highest ratings in industry surveys, all of which catapulted the firm into becoming the undisputed leader in the pharmaceutical industry.[8]

DEVELOPING A RELIABLE PROCESS COMPETENCE

Firms utilize a mix of informal corporate culture and formal operating controls and standards to develop a reliable process. The informal corporate culture minimizes waste and delivers customer value. The formal operating controls and standards reduce the number and extent of deviations in the process. Some firms seek to minimize disruptions by analyzing what activities should be performed in-house versus outsourced, and then they conduct a rigorous analysis of supplier reliability before they select suppliers. The use of logistical innovations to improve communication and transportation (such as satellite links, common software platforms, or private jets and airfields) can also improve the firm's operational reliability and response. Diverse other methods are used by companies to enhance reliability, such as using personal contacts to achieve coordination, using analysis of a database on the firm's installed products to identify weak spots and design them out, or using a rewards and incentive system to promote efficiency.

Despite its historic competence in the design and production of airplanes, Boeing was facing both increasing competition from Europe's Airbus and rising labor costs in the United States. Airbus is state-owned and the bulk of their planes are produced in the four member countries: France, Germany, Spain, and the United Kingdom. International cost-conscious customers, such as Japan Air Lines, were increasingly demanding local sourcing in return for plane orders. Top management at Boeing reasoned that international sourcing could provide a competitive edge if it could better satisfy customer needs and if overseas production reduced production costs, and if Airbus, being state-owned and confronting stronger unions, did not have the flexibility to engage in international sourcing.

To develop a reliable process for international sourcing, however, Boeing first had to determine which items of the plane should be outsourced and which should be kept in-house. Boeing decided to retain in-house wing design and production because it was a critical component (affecting safety, lift, efficiency, strength) and one in which it had accumulated substantial expertise.

Boeing also had to determine which suppliers could be counted on. Boeing's existing technological competence in plane design and production proved useful in setting technical standards for potential suppliers. It developed a detailed, hierarchical protocol for evaluating suppliers with regards to the design team (the prospective supplier's ability to meet the needed technical specs), project management (the supplier's ability to execute projects on time), procurement (the supplier's ability to meet cost budgets), and top management (the supplier's history with other projects).

After choosing suppliers, Boeing developed an audit procedure to check not only the end-products, but the process through which they were produced at the suppliers. This audit involved weekly visits to some of its suppliers. Suppliers had to develop a planning system for their projects and had to adhere to a protocol for safety and configuration management (how proposed design changes were to be managed and communicated). Suppliers were required to provide extensive documentation to Boeing. Electronic mail was not used for communication because of potential piracy. To facilitate communication and coordination, all suppliers were placed on a common software platform developed by Dassault and a computer-aided design package that allowed concurrent three-dimensional interactive design capability.

DEVELOPING A CLOSE EXTERNAL RELATIONSHIP COMPETENCE

Firms can use early acquisitions to buy relationships that would be time-consuming and prohibitively expensive to develop from scratch. Firms that develop relationships from scratch can offer potential partners their capability to serve international markets. They can use an existing relationship to develop a relationship with another party. Their existing competencies can be offered in a prospective relationship or the lack of a competence can be the motivator to form a relationship to attract the needed resources.

In order to effectively build a relationship, firms make a commitment to understanding and satisfying the various needs that exist in their partner's organization. This commitment can involve creating a team led by a high-level sales manager personally responsible for serving larger partners' accounts. This team can be implanted in the partner's organization to identify its various needs and better satisfy them. As firms increase in size, they can seek to broaden and deepen relationships with suppliers and buyers through, for example, longer-term contracts, purchasing economies, or joint research and development. Being an early entrant also gives the firm more time under less competition in which to build relationships with potential partners.

Citicorp's origins can be traced back to 1791. As early as 1890, its President James Stillman articulated a vision to provide numerous special services as a partner to big business. By 1921, this vision of becoming the first full-service bank to businesses was accomplished. Citicorp then expanded its vision to encompass individuals as well, who up to that time had been handled by a separate set of savings banks.

Citicorp grew through several acquisitions both domestically and internationally. These early acquisitions gave it not only a quick national and international presence, but brought with it numerous relationships with the clients of the acquired banks. Access to these clients would have been time-consuming and costly to develop from scratch. The international acquisitions also gave Citicorp the opportunity to devote its energy to cementing relationships with new clients rather than to the lengthy process of trying to gain approvals for entering into foreign markets.

Innovation at Citicorp generated many new products that were used to obtain new clients and to cross-sell to existing clients. Citicorp was the first bank to introduce: travelers' checks; interest-bearing savings accounts that individuals could open with as little as one dollar; negotiable CDs (certificates of deposit); ATM teller machines; credit cards with revolving credit, photo identification, risk-adjusted pricing; and worldwide consumer banking that enables customers to make deposits in a choice of countries and currencies. The bank employed the umbrella brand name prefix "Citi" with its new products (e.g., Citicard, CitiTeller). This practice branded generic products and showed customers that Citicorp provided an innovative, one-stop shopping service for all their needs that could be reported on one unified financial statement. The proliferation of ventures into new products and markets was encouraged by the bank's emphasis on revenue growth over profitability.[9]

A DYNAMIC SHIFT IN COMPETENCE TYPES

Table 4 reports the frequency of existing competence types across all firms as well as the new competencies being planned for the future. A fundamental finding is that these firms, though they may be leaders in their field, are not standing still or resting on their prior competencies. Leading firms are constantly being challenged by ascendants. Consequently, those leaders are changing by developing new competencies.

A new emphasis is emerging on external relationship competencies. These new relationship competencies can complement a firm's traditional competencies and enable it to cope with the demands of globalization, mass customization and higher quality, and shorter product cycles. Relationship competencies help firms extend their traditional technological and reliable process competencies to worldwide markets that they may not be able to reach on their own. Closer relationships among buyers and suppliers help to customize products and improve quality. Finally, closer relationships help firms source new ideas and technologies to develop the next generation of competencies in a world of rapid product and process change.

The development of multiple types of competencies bestows various advantages over competitors. Multiple competencies are more difficult for competitors to imitate than a single type of competence. Multiple competencies allow the option of an interactive effect that is greater than each effect alone. In the accumulation of multiple competencies, firms can develop a new competence that is needed for a changing era, enhancing their adaptability and long-term survival.

Crown Cork and Seal provides an illustration of how a company transitioned from the technological to the reliable process to the closer external relationship competencies.

In the early days after its founding in 1927, Crown Cork and Seal's technological competence stood out. The firm had a patent on crowns for cans and expertise in the efficient manufacturing of three-piece steel cans. This technological competence resulted in the firm's early introduction of the crown, the aerosol can (including the improved version that did not propel fluorocarbons into the atmosphere), and the pull-tab opening can.

• TABLE 4

DYNAMIC SHIFT IN COMPETENCIES (TOTAL NUMBER OF EXISTING PLANNED COMPETENCIES BY TYPE)

	Type of Competence			
Time Period	Technological Know-How	Reliable Processes	Close External Relationships	Total
Existing	21 (42%)	16 (32%)	13 (26%)	50 (100%)
Planned	1 (9%)	2 (18%)	8 (73%)	11 (100%)

When John Connelly became President in 1957, however, the firm was on the verge of bankruptcy and lacked strong leadership. Connelly was an "ultraconservative, tight-lipped, and tight-fisted" boss who saved the firm from bankruptcy by cutting overproduction, unprofitable product lines (such as ice cube trays), and headquarters' overhead (by laying off 25% of the staff and managers). Unlike other can producers, he stayed away from the introduction of the two-piece aluminum can because it would have entailed substantial retooling costs, research and development expenditures, and exposure to a limited number of large aluminum producers that could control raw material costs. Connelly stayed with the three-piece steel can but devised a welding process instead of the traditional soldering to counter growing health concerns about solder poisoning. In contrast, competitors that ventured into the two-piece aluminum can were weakened financially and later sought to diversify out of the canning industry.

The reliable process competence became pronounced in the early 1990s. William Avery, Connelly's successor, embarked upon an ambitious acquisition campaign to buy struggling can producers at bargain prices. In a short five-year period, Crown Cork and Seal made over 20 acquisitions of canning companies and plastic packagers, becoming the world's largest packaging firm. After each acquisition, Crown Cork and Seal reliably transferred its production and headquarters cost-reduction know-how to the acquiree. Crown Cork and Seal reduced the ratio of SGA as a percentage of sales of the acquired companies, typically around 8%–10%, to its own benchmark of 5%.

Currently, Crown Cork and Seal is developing closer external relationships with customers and suppliers: The numerous acquisitions expanded the firm's national and international reach and broadened the firm's product scope to include plastic and metal packaging, as well as the package-filling machinery and the imprinting color lithography on packages. With this broadened scope, Crown Cork and Seal seeks to develop closer relationships with larger customers by providing a one-stop shopping service for all their international packaging needs. It also plans to offer its larger customers a joint research and development service. At the same time, the firm now plans to exploit its larger size with suppliers: it will pool the purchasing needs of its acquisitions to obtain purchasing economies by developing closer relationships with fewer suppliers.

CONCLUSION

The study of these leading companies has several implications for strategists. Leading companies do not stand still and rest on their traditional competencies. Instead they develop new competencies that respond to or anticipate emerging business conditions. A shift is occurring in relative emphasis from internal technological and reliable process competencies toward external relationship competencies. Having multiple competencies can make it that much more difficult for competitors to imitate. It also increases the adaptability of the firm and should promote long-term survival.

Notes

1. C.K. Prahalad and G. Hamel, "The Core Competence of the Corporation." *Harvard Business Review* (May/June 1990) 79–91.
2. J. Quinn and F.G. Hilmer, "Strategic Outsourcing," *Sloan Management Review* (Summer 1994).
3. B. Wernerfelt, "A Resource-Based View of the Firm," *Strategic Management Journal,* 5/2 (1984): 171–180; L. Dierckx and K. Cool, "Asset Stock Accumulation and Sustainability of Competitive Advantage," *Management Science,* 35 (December 1989): 1504–1511; D.J. Collis and C. Montgomery, "Competing on Resources," *Harvard Business Review* (July/August 1995): 118–128.
4. Prahalad and Hamel, op. cit.; J.B. Barney and M.H. Hansen, "Trustworthiness as a Source of Competitive Advantage," *Strategic Management Journal,* special issue on Competitive Organizational Behavior, 15 (Winter 1994): 5–9; D. Levinthal and J. Myatt, "Co-Evolution of Capabilities and Industry: The Evolution of the Mutual Fund Processing," *Strategic Management Journal,* special issue on Competitive Organizational Behavior, 15 (Winter 1994): 45–62; H. Rao, "The Social Construction of Reputation: Certification Contests, Legitimation, and the Survival of Organizations in the American Automobile Industry, 1895–1912," *Strategic Management Journal,* special issue on Competitive Organizational Behavior, 15 (Winter 1994): 29–44; R. Henderson and I. Cockburn, "Measuring Competence? Exploring Firm Effects in Pharmaceutical Research," *Strategic Management Journal,* special issue on Competitive Organizational Behavior, 15 (Winter 1994): 63–84.
5. The outstanding firms studied have multiple competencies. The median number of competencies per firm is four, with the minimum being two and the maximum being five. Marino observed a similar number of competencies in the firms he studied. Multiple competencies can provide more sources of customer value and competitive advantage than a single competence. K.E. Marino, "Developing Consensus on Firm Competencies and Capabilities," *Academy of Management Executive,* 10/3 (1996): 40–51.
6. Prahalad and Hamel, op. cit.; Marino, op. cit.; M. Treacy and F. Wiersema, *The Discipline of Market Leaders* (Reading, MA: Addison-Wesley, 1995); Henderson and Cockburn, op. cit.; Collis and Montgomery, op. cit.; Levinthal and Myatt, op. cit.; Barney and Hansen, op. cit.
7. R.E. Caves, *Multinational Enterprise and Economic Analysis* (Cambridge, UK: Cambridge University Press, 1982).
8. A.D. Gasbarre, "Merck & Co, Inc.," in T. Derdach, ed., *International Directory of Company Histories* (Chicago, IL: St. James Press, 1996), pp. 289–291; "Merck Wins the Hearts and Minds of Physicians' Most Admired," *Medical Marketing & Media,* January 22, 1997.
9. E.M. Hedblad, "Citicorp," in T. Derdach, ed., *International Directory of Company Histories* (Chicago, IL: St. James Press, 1996), pp. 123–126.

INTERNATIONAL MARKETING—AVOIDING THE SEVEN DEADLY TRAPS

Kenneth Simmonds

An international strategy extends a firm's home market strategy to include its plans for other markets. The first focus of any international strategy is on the timing and mode of entry into new markets, as well as the emphasis to be given to each. Inevitably, however, international strategies evolve to include changes in basic marketing actions that are critical to a firm's performance in markets in which competitor actions and customer wants differ from those in the home market. International strategies quickly elide into a complex international pattern of adjustments to keep the firm gaining on competitors, who themselves are doing different things in different markets.

New competitive attacks may emerge in any of a firm's markets and take a different shape from prior competition in the home market. Furthermore, competitors that feel the impact of a firm's international expansion may decide that their best strategy is to attack its home base. Even a successful strategy in a firm's home market therefore may need to be changed as a result of its own international moves.

Most firms that expand successfully in international markets first will have developed a winning strategy at home and been highly profitable well before they began significant international expansion. McDonald's Corporation, for example, was profitable and beating its competition when it had only a few Midwest outlets in the early 1960s. Large billboards proclaimed McDonald's success by announcing the millions of hamburgers sold to date. Investors soon recognized the profit potential in McDonald's marketing formula of speed, quality, service, and price, and share prices hit stratospheric price–earnings multiples well before McDonald's international expansion.

Early investors in a growth firm selling at a high multiple, such as McDonald's recorded, are backing not only the existing home market strategy, but also their belief

---

Kenneth Simmonds is professor of marketing and international business at the London Business School.

that the firm will be able to adjust its strategy successfully in international competition. The investors are not buying the present value of gains from global scale; they are buying the present value of future successful international adjustment to what is currently a local marketing strategy. To investors, ultimate globality is an outcome of a successful international marketing strategy, not the cause of success.

McDonald's justified its early investors' confidence in its ability to pursue a successful international strategy. It moved into markets outside the United States with a finesse that enabled it to develop the McDonald's concept even where the American hamburger had not been a standard meal. Today, golden arches appear globally. In some markets, McDonald's has emerged as even stronger than in its home market.

On the surface, the international expansion of McDonald's may look like an extrapolation of a single formula. Closer examination of the process, however, shows many differences. For example, when McDonald's first moved into the United Kingdom in the 1970s, it established quite basic outlets in Edgware Road and Baker Street in north central London and moved out from there. These sites were not in the midst of Ronald McDonald-Happy Birthday households. The outlets had no drive-ins and no parking. They were not in the center of tall office blocks or in the main tourist center. Until there were more outlets, London television advertising was too expensive, so door-to-door mailers and local newspaper inserts were needed to establish the McDonald's hamburger idea among the surrounding population of city dwellers and day workers. Few had any prior idea of what a golden arch might mean. Two decades years later, when McDonald's moved into Moscow at the beginning of perestroika, it took a different tack. There was a dramatic opening in Red Square, amid a blaze of international publicity, of an outlet of such size and impact that eventually it recorded the highest volume of any McDonald's outlet in the world. Again, however, its positioning was far from the average family-with-children segment so evident in McDonald's U.S. outlets. It was catering to the emerging middle class. Today, new Eastern European outlets are changing again. At the McDonald's in Khreschatik Street in Kiev, there appear couples, ranging in age from their 20s to their 50s, dressed in their best outfits for a meal out.

Despite the adaptability of McDonald's, its continued success is not guaranteed. Firms whose evolving strategies have made them global are not immune from successful competitor attack simply because they are global. There are many examples of once-global firms that have weakened and even died. British Leyland retrenched from country after country until it finally disappeared. Volkswagen and Philips were European-domiciled global firms whose value sank when Japanese firms emerged with more successful strategies, and both took further hits when the Korean chaebols undercut them in many markets. The United States' ITT Corporation withdrew entirely from its global telephone equipment position when more innovative firms surpassed it. Today, Kodak is weakening under a global attack from Fuji.

For every already global firm that fails, however, there are many more that fail to evolve from a successful domestic strategy into global achievement. Somewhere in their international expansion, they take a turn that stunts their growth. Although international expansion is unlikely ever to save a firm with poor home market performance, a bad international move can choke outstanding home performance. One poorly designed step into a new market can jeopardize all future expansion and produce losses that drain the home market.

THE SEVEN TRAPS

There can never be absolute rules for a perfect international strategy, because strategies always face the reactions of competitors striving to survive. There are, however, common traps to avoid. This article examines seven of these traps. Firms stumble into any one of these at their peril.

The first trap is the common mistake of ranking foreign markets on the basis of size or growth of demand for the firm's products or services. Whatever the size or growth rate of a market, competitors are already present. The market's strategic attractiveness does not lie in its size but in the likelihood that the firm's entry strategy will switch market share to the firm, thus beating even competitors that make their best effort to defend their position. Markets therefore should be ranked in terms of the penetration the firm's strategy will bring.

The second trap is to underestimate foreign competitors. The existing competitors in any market are, after all, the survivors. What some of them are doing must have been enough to defeat attacks in the past, and actions probably are being adjusted continually to keep as close as possible to customer motivations. Be warned. Even foreign competitors sense attacks and retaliate.

Different customer motivations in foreign markets open up the third trap. Blindness to customer motivation leads firms to use their home market formula without adjustment, perhaps by spending in an effort to change customers to fit the formula. In a global village, a single formula might work, but the real world is not a global village. Customer motivations in each country must be known, understood, and appealed to.

The fourth trap is choice of the wrong entry price. A successful firm usually will have reduced its real price gradually in the home market as the market matured. In new markets, the process may need to be restarted at a previous stage. Entry into markets that do not understand the firm's offering may require heavy promotion to gain even a small number of sales to early buyers. Low price may leave too little room for promotion, and without promotion, there are few sales. Then again, the relative effectiveness of price reduction versus spending on promotion can differ markedly from country to country. For some products, instead of establishing a brand through promotion, an equivalently lower price may provide much greater penetration. What is clear is that the home country price is not an automatic indicator of an effective price for entry into new markets.

Any international strategy based solely on an approach that achieves early sales in a new market is likely to topple a firm into the fifth trap. Survival in a market requires adjustment as the market matures. Firms that fail to prepare for future adjustments are almost certainly going to take a position that circumscribes the adjustment process at some stage. Inflexible commitment to distributors or channels that should be only temporary liaisons are common mistakes.

Choice of incompetent partners is the sixth trap. Implementation of any strategy requires partners that can determine what must be done and who will do it. A firm entering a new market must check whether a potential partner will know what to do and act accordingly. Finding this out before any commitment requires more than checking credit references and building a working relationship. Firms must find out whether a foreign partner knows what good marketing really is.

Finally, the seventh trap addresses how protection of the brand becomes much more important when a firm moves onto an international stage. When the brand is positioned at one level in one country and at a lower level in another, the entire market perception can gravitate to the lowest positioning. Going for volume in one market can erode brand premiums in others. When lowered, perceptions of a brand usually stay lowered.

When outlined in a few sentences, these seven traps seem easy to avoid. Yet they do not come with clear warning labels, and many firms with previously successful strategies will fall into one or another. Most firms do not make it to the global "realms of gold." Studying each trap in more detail will perhaps demonstrate where firms may be heading into danger.

ENTERING MARKETS IN ORDER OF SIZE OF DEMAND

It is an inviting trap for a firm to enter first those markets in which size and growth are greatest. The trouble is that such an approach assumes that market attractiveness exists independently of the firm's competitive strategy. It does not. Market attractiveness can only be measured relative to a strategy. Put simply, a firm should attempt to go where its strategy will work best.

Suppose an automobile insurance firm is considering in which countries it should expand. Its business strategy must rest heavily on how it will reach new clients. Does it work through membership in automobile associations? Does it use bank branches, real estate agencies, or direct mail and telephone quotation? Perhaps its strategy is to persuade motor vehicle manufacturers to offer free or reduced insurance packages. The effectiveness of implementing its chosen attack in a particular market becomes far more important than any statistics on the number of cars in that market or the number of existing or new insurance covers required.

A classic case involves consultants confronted with grouping foreign countries into four sets of decreasing attractiveness to a firm selling a successful brand of jeans. The firm developed its home market position through building a chain of independent jeans boutiques, then moving into national chains, and subsequently reinforcing its competitive position through national advertising. When a group studies this case, there is usually a great deal of discussion before it reaches the consultants' conclusion that the way to determine the attractiveness of a market is to assess how well the same process would work in that market. Because the strategy already has worked once, it certainly should be tried in preference to any attempt to enter a new market with actions currently required in the home market. The firm should enter markets by starting as it did before. Furthermore, the grouping of countries into four sets also makes sense only with respect to the specific strategy. The sets are groupings for which similar actions to achieve the strategy are appropriate for countries within the set, such as immediate entry with full development of a chain of independent outlets or entry at a slower pace by adding outlets only when they meet specific criteria.

During group discussion of this case, the idea of intrinsically attractive markets often is argued strongly. Some cling to the idea of markets in which youth have more to spend or cowboy or James Dean images are held most strongly. There may even be some who believe that the best markets are those in which more people wear trousers or gross national product per capita is highest.

Another example of the role of strategy in classifying markets comes from the international marketing of a slotted steel angle for storage systems. After much discussion, research, and quantification, the most profitable markets for entry proved to be those in which the firm could gain effective control of an accessible distribution point and establish its image as the supplier of standardized storage in the minds of local architects, builders, and those specifying storage systems. Again, with this strategy, the attractiveness of markets did not equate to their size, their level of industrial development, or the cost of local production of slotted steel storage systems.

UNDERESTIMATING EXISTING COMPETITION

Most demand already is created. Other firms already are supplying it. Competing firms will know immediately of a new success because it will be made at the expense of their own sales. Some will hit back hard and fast. In the past, German and Japanese firms have been particularly likely to do so to protect their home markets. They have taken the stance that the best defense is to strike before the opponent is established. Toeholds should be eliminated before they become footholds. Entrants, therefore, could expect competition to the death. Chloride Plc, battery supplier to the United Kingdom and British Commonwealth, was hit hard by competitive retaliation from Varta, the German market leader, on three attempts at entry into Germany. Only after the third failure did Chloride finally accept that the problem was not simply due to inadequate promotion and distribution of its product when it launched an entry.

Penalizing reaction by entrenched firms also can emerge in developing countries. When a firm from a developed market examines a developing market, it may conclude that, because its product is superior to the local producer's and its marketing approach is better, direct entry is the answer. However poor a local producer's marketing, though, it seldom will face extinction without a fight, and poor competitors can still ruin a market. When the French firm Danone entered central European markets, local yogurt producers were hit hard. Danone's heavy promotion costs using local television, however, required higher prices. These, in combination with outlets willing to carry the old local brands and established customer buying habits, switched most of Danone's initial gains back to the local producers. Furthermore, these producers were cooperatives, and farmers continued to supply milk to them even at penalizingly low prices. They were almost bound to survive at any price.

Capital goods firms entering China in the past few years have tended to underestimate the determination of local suppliers to copy their installations. Turbine and generator firms have seen their projected market decrease rapidly as local competitors have moved to copy them at much lower costs.

EXPECTATIONS THAT CUSTOMER MOTIVATIONS AND BENEFITS WILL BE SIMILAR WORLDWIDE

For almost every product or service, however basic, motivations vary tremendously. Food and drink, for example, play remarkably different roles in different societies. What firm outside the United States would expect that 65% of U.S. ovens are not used in any one year?

Every customer durable, however small, has its own cultural positioning. A person's first electric razor is universally a gift. In many ways, the gift is a modern coming-of-age rite. Who actually gives the razor and on what occasion? Is it a mother, father, brother, uncle, friend, or someone else? The occasion and the giver will determine how the razor is packaged and displayed; the outlets used; and the timing, placing, and message of its promotion. If women are the majority of gift givers, should razors for men be advertised in women's magazines?

As telecommunication products multiply rapidly, differences in national attitudes toward communication are becoming crucial elements in determining global strategies. In countries in which personal space is scarce, portable telephones become a liberation. If a family can always overhear a conversation on a fixed line, a portable spells personal freedom from oversight. Portables appeared everywhere in Hong Kong with great speed. In other countries, where isolation and risk are concerns, portable telephones are adopted as a means of staying in contact, hence the common argument that women driving alone should be equipped with a portable.

Blockbuster, the video rental chain, pulled out of Germany in 1997, two years after entry. Germany was the fourth-largest video market in the world, but it differed from the U.S. market in that pornographic titles accounted for one-third of German video rentals. Blockbuster refused to carry pornography, but all German video stores had become stigmatized as places children should not enter. Against this preestablished image, Blockbuster could not build in Germany the family-oriented image it had in the United States. Moreover, Blockbuster made the mistake of locating in downtown shopping areas, whereas most video stores were in residential neighborhoods. As a result, its outlets did not get the customer traffic or the rentals per customer they needed for success.

Even minor product differences based on misunderstandings as to different customer attitudes can have a major impact on sales. The ratio of manual to automatic transmissions in European automobile purchases, for example, is approximately nine to one. In the United States, it is approximately one manual to six automatics. Clearly, customers have different attitudes toward their personal involvement in driving. It is not surprising, therefore, that most Europeans do not want or expect coffee cup holders in their vehicles. In the United States, however, they are essential. European models costing $50,000 and more even have been described widely as marketing failures in the United States because they contain no cup holders.

ENTERING MARKETS AT THE WRONG PRICE

Many firms have made the mistake of pricing either too high or too low when they enter new markets. Often, they simply translate their price from the home market, even though this has emerged after many changes as the product's adoption has diffused through the home market.

For some products, the home market price would leave an inadequate margin for promotion in a new market. When potential customers are unfamiliar with the product or brand, initial sales response to promotion is likely to be small. Either the firm must invest in higher advertising expenditure than initial sales will justify, or it must enter at a higher price to make more margin available for promotion. As familiarity grows, so will volume, and price reductions may be increasingly possible while maintaining a fixed amount of promotion. It is not unusual, therefore, to encounter the introductory prices of such American brands as Timberland and Tommy Hilfiger at 30%–40% higher than the U.S. price.

High entry pricing, however, is not without its problems. The product can become trapped in a foreign market positioning of high price and low volume, in which any attempt at price reduction is interpreted as a decline in quality and volume does not respond to offset the price reduction. Sales of British Jaguars in Japan were caught in such a trap. Each one sold was, of course, highly profitable, but penetration was infinitesimal. BMW and Mercedes cars in the United States were similarly overpriced relative to the German market, hence the popular visit to Europe to pick up a model at European prices. Foreign markets have become skim markets for some branded consumer luxuries, such as Limoges or Wedgwood, and even basic consumables, such as foreign tea brands. These firms find it difficult to build up significant penetration of foreign markets.

For other products, the home market price may be too high for entry into a new market. High home market prices with extensive promotion margins have become a significant trap for consumer durable firms that concentrated their early expansion on the most developed countries. Sony is an example. It carefully nurtured a quality image in developed markets with heavy promotion and high prices. In less developed economies, it maintained a similar image and price level. As a consequence, Sony built itself into the top end of these markets. Developing countries, however, tend to have a much higher price elasticity of demand than do developed countries. When prices are dropped to some point, the product becomes affordable, and there is a rapid escalation in demand. By maintaining a price higher than this level, Sony left the way open to competitors, principally the Korean chaebols LG and Samsung. It was no coincidence that these companies built up their huge sales volumes in developing markets. In recent years, for example, LG has taken over 85% of the Egyptian television market, selling approximately 500,000 sets annually. To protect itself, Sony could have either launched a developing market brand or reduced its price worldwide to maintain volume leadership. It may be too late. Without separate brands, two levels of prices are difficult to maintain. Arbitrage from one market to another can become significant when there is more than a 10% price difference.

MARKET ENTRY WITHOUT PLANNING THE EXPANSION PROCESS

Penetration of a new market by a product or service is not a single step. If a firm does not plan second and third steps, it will likely box itself into the wrong representation, the wrong channels, and inappropriate agreements. An example is a firm that had patented a new wire connector for joining fencing. It had planned to have an exclusive distributor per country and was looking for importers of similar products for farmers. The strategy finally chosen was to grant one local wire manufacturer an exclusive right for a limited period to apply the connector to its wire and thus gain an advantage over other local wire manufacturers. At the same time, a merchandising distributor that had experience in promoting new products was sought. A distributor that could position the connectors in a wide range of channels and then monitor those channels was wanted. Whereas the wire manufacturer was intended to create basic awareness and sell more wire, the distributor's role was to develop connector sales to users for repairs. Similar to screws and bolts, many connectors are kept in barns and sheds for emergencies. An exclusive distributor chosen from among existing importers of farming supplies would have provided neither the instant awareness that the wire manufacturer could provide by attaching connectors to new wire nor the skill of a creative marketer who knew how to manage multiple channels.

Many products go through multiple stages in the channels they require for most effective marketing. Consequently, great flexibility in channel arrangements is needed. The experience of computer firms is a case in point. In the early stages, the firms that excelled were those that bundled with their hardware a full advisory service about computer use, installation, initial operation, and full maintenance. As time progressed, the business advisory service gradually withered, and computer firms sold only the programming and maintenance service along with the computer. The next step was to drop software. Then performance switched to offering a quality computer on its own and as rapidly as possible. Now, the move for some is to sell a communication system, with computers simply part of the network. Different national markets are at different stages along this chain of development. Computer firms must be careful to adjust what is offered to each country's stage of development and think ahead to the changes that will be demanded in local distribution.

ASSOCIATION WITH POOR PARTNERS

There has been much discussion of strategic alliances, but less has been said about strategic misalliances. Yet it is much more likely that partners' interests are not optimally aligned than that there is a perfect meshing of interests.

Some capital goods firms create impediments to future global expansion simply by entering into joint ventures or part ownership arrangements in individual countries. Heavier capital equipment for steel, chemical, food, or pharmaceutical plants, for example, generally will be required by only a few customers in any one country. A supplier's next sale is invariably in another country. At the same time, detailed knowledge of customer businesses and how the plant is used is crucial to further technical development and future sales. Engineers and sales staff who have contact with customers are needed to take their expertise sequentially from one country to another. On the one hand, if they are employees of a joint venture in a single country, this international flexibility is hampered. On the other hand, if all the technical and sales expertise is provided from the center, much of the margin going to a joint venture is unjustified, and the entire business becomes noncompetitive.

The most common mistake is the appointment of a "dead distributor"—a foreign partner that has no intention of marketing actively. The way to avoid this mistake is quite simple: Ask the distributor for a marketing plan. If the plan is not satisfactory or the distributor refuses, find someone else. Years ago, global consumer firms such as Coca-Cola wrote the requirement for annual marketing plans into their distributor agreements. If the plans are inadequate, the distributorship can be cancelled before damage has occurred.

Local "producer partners" can be equally deadly. If a firm's strategy is to control distribution while obtaining low-cost local production, producer partners may facilitate neither. A producer may have no contribution to make to distribution and no incentive to keep production cost to a minimum. Supply competition vanishes. Furthermore, the international firm may have to subscribe half the capital investment for production.

"Line-competing" distributors also can be problematic partners. An international marketer is heading for trouble with a distributor that wants the product as a high-end prestige item or a short-term gap plugger. The international marketer must be precise about the desired positioning of the product in each foreign market and choose a distributor that will deliver that positioning. Any distributor with a commitment to some other product for that position should be avoided. Car distributors that position the foreign brand above the local brand, for example, may end up taking the bulk of their volume in sales of the local brand, using the foreign brand to raise their own image.

Finally, the "order-taker" distributor should be recognized from the start and avoided. Order takers are particularly troublesome for suppliers of intermediate goods or services to other businesses. Industrial suppliers need distributors that can sell the value of the purchase. What they should offer is a means of achieving the customer's own strategy. To express an offer in these terms requires the distributor to have a good understanding of the customer's business. Distributors of communication equipment with sales staff who know about equipment but not about users' business communication needs are a common example of the wrong sort of representation. Order takers do not, and cannot, sell by showing customers how an order will help the customer's competitive performance.

Capital goods firms that rely on order-taker distributors in foreign markets are likely to find that their sales volumes lag those of competitors with distributors that are prepared to understand their customers' business. Even products of mediocre technical performance can produce customer value, and they will sell if the customer is shown the value.

LOSING BRAND EXCLUSIVITY

The need for legal protection of a name and a logo in foreign countries is obvious. Protection of the mental image of the brand in customer minds is more difficult. Many firms allow their actions in foreign countries to ruin their brand images.

Retaining the exclusivity of a brand is always a problem. Exclusivity and ubiquity are unlikely partners. Going global means high sales volumes and worldwide exposure. Customers find the same thing everywhere. So do competitors, and they often match it closely. When American Express became universally available, usable everywhere, and used by more and more travelers, it became hard to justify its premium charge to service establishments. After all, most card users were not the very rich and often did not buy expensive products. Other cards provided the same service at a lower charge. American Express was forced to lower its charges to service establishments and redirect its membership advertising to those with higher net worth.

Protecting exclusivity requires detailed control in every market. The classic example is the French firm Lacoste and its crocodile-branded clothing in the United States. Determined to make the most of its license and a sudden growth in popularity for crocodile-emblazoned shirts, the U.S. licensee flooded the market and dropped prices to move large volumes. After several years of depreciation of its brand value, Lacoste had no alternative but to buy back its license and withdraw from the United States for several years. It then returned with quality French production and high prices in selected high-end outlets. Overpricing of a brand, however, can be almost as bad as underpricing. The customer may perceive inadequate value for the money.

The customer image of local outlets and the ways in which outlets serve customer wants also may be important to brand performance worldwide. Better products are not associated with poor outlets. It may be good practice to limit supply to outlets that can deliver an image of success while keeping a short-order book and fast delivery. It is hard to maintain an image of exclusivity if good outlets cannot supply and if the only sources for the customer are discount stores.

CONCLUSION

A winning international strategy must remain just that. It must get the firm ahead and keep it there. The international strategist must manage to win while playing multiple games against many of the same competitors on a stack of country game boards. There are no simple rules, because the games are not simple. They are games to the death. This article points out seven common traps, but clever competitors will never run out of new attacks to survive. Firms must think clearly before each step and as far ahead as they can.

TEN STEPS TO A GLOBAL HUMAN RESOURCE STRATEGY

John A. Quelch and Helen Bloom

The scarcity of qualified managers has become a major constraint on the speed with which multinational companies can expand their international sales. The growth of the knowledge-based society, along with the pressures of opening up emerging markets, has led cutting-edge global companies to recognize now more than ever that human resources and intellectual capital are as significant as financial assets in building sustainable competitive advantage. To follow their lead, chief executives in other multinational companies will have to bridge the yawning chasm between their companies' human resources rhetoric and reality. H.R. must now be given a prominent seat in the boardroom.

Good H.R. management in a multinational company comes down to getting the right people in the right jobs in the right places at the right times and at the right cost. These international managers must then be meshed into a cohesive network in which they quickly identify and leverage good ideas worldwide.

Such an integrated network depends on executive continuity. This in turn requires career management to ensure that internal qualified executives are readily available when vacancies occur around the world and that good managers do not jump ship because they have not been recognized.

Very few companies come close to achieving this. Most multinational companies do not have the leadership capital they need to perform effectively in all their markets around the world. One reason is the lack of managerial mobility. Neither companies nor individuals have come to terms with the role that managerial mobility now has to play in marrying business strategy with H.R. strategy and in ensuring that careers are developed for both profitability and employability.

Ethnocentricity is another reason. In most multinationals, H.R. development policies have tended to concentrate on nationals of the headquarters country. Only the brightest local stars were given the career management skills and overseas assignments necessary to develop an international mindset.

The chief executives of many United States-based multinational companies lack confidence in the ability of their H.R. functions to screen, review and develop candidates for the most important posts across the globe. This is not surprising: H.R. directors rarely have extensive overseas experience and their managers often lack business knowledge. Also, most H.R. directors do not have adequate information about the brightest candidates coming through the ranks of the overseas subsidiaries. "H.R. managers also frequently lack a true commitment to the value of the multinational company experience," notes Brian Brooks, group director of human resources for the global advertising company WPP Group Plc.

The consequent lack of world-wise multicultural managerial talent is now biting into companies' bottom lines through high staff turnover, high training costs, stagnant market shares, failed joint ventures and mergers and the high opportunity costs that inevitably follow bad management selections around the globe.

Companies new to the global scene quickly discover that finding savvy, trustworthy managers for their overseas markets is one of their biggest challenges. This holds true for companies across the technology spectrum, from software manufacturers to textile companies that have to manage a global supply chain. The pressure is on these newly globalizing companies to cut the trial-and-error time in building a cadre of global managers in order to shorten the leads of their larger, established competitors, but they are stymied as to how to do it.

The solution for multinationals is to find a way to emulate companies that have decades of experience in recruiting, training and retaining good employees across the globe. Many of these multinational companies are European, but not all. Both Unilever and the International Business Machines Corporation, for example, leverage their worldwide H.R. function as a source of competitive advantage.

Anglo-Dutch Unilever has long set a high priority on human resources. H.R. has a seat on the board's executive committee and an organization that focuses on developing in-house talent and hot-housing future leaders in all markets. The result is that 95 percent of Unilever's top 300 managers are fully homegrown. Internationalization is bred into its managers through job content as well as overseas assignments. Since 1989, Unilever has redefined 75 percent of its managerial posts as "international" and doubled its number of managers assigned abroad, its expatriates, or "expats."

I.B.M., with 80 years' experience in overseas markets, reversed its H.R. policy in 1995 to deal with the new global gestalt and a new business strategy. Instead of cutting jobs abroad to reduce costs, I.B.M. is now focusing on its customers' needs and increasing overseas assignments. "We are a growing service business—our people are what our customers are buying from us," explained Eileen Major, director of international mobility at I.B.M.

When managers sign on with these companies, they know from the start that overseas assignments are part of the deal if they wish to climb high on the corporate ladder. These multinational companies manage their H.R. talent through international databases that, within hours, can provide a choice of Grade-A in-house candidates for any assignment. Even allowing for company size, few United States-based multinationals come close to matching the bench strength of a Unilever or Nestlé. The Japanese multinationals are even farther behind.

This article outlines a global H.R. action agenda based on the approaches used by leading multinational companies. The goal is to build sustainable competitive advantage by attracting and developing the best managerial talent in each of your company's markets.

The strategy demands global H.R. leadership with standard systems but local adaptation. The key underlying ideas are to satisfy your company's global human resources needs via feeder mechanisms at regional, national and local levels, and to leverage your current assets to the fullest extent by actively engaging people in developing their own careers.

Implementing these ideas can be broken down into 10 steps. By taking these steps, a company should be able to put into place an effective global human resources program within three to four years.

1. BREAK ALL THE "LOCAL NATIONAL" GLASS CEILINGS

The first, and perhaps most fundamental, step toward building a global H.R. program is to end all favoritism toward managers who are nationals of the country in which the company is based. Companies tend to consider nationals of their headquarters country as potential expatriates and to regard everyone else as "local nationals." But in today's global markets, such "us-versus-them" distinctions can put companies at a clear disadvantage, and there are strong reasons to discard them:

- Ethnocentric companies tend to be xenophobic—they put the most confidence in nationals of their headquarters country. This is why more nationals get the juicy assignments, climb the ranks and wind up sitting on the board—and why the company ends up with a skewed perception of the world. Relatively few multinational companies have more than token representation on their boards. A.B.B. is one company that recognizes the danger and now considers it a priority to move more executives from emerging countries in eastern Europe and Asia into the higher levels of the company.
- Big distinctions can be found between expatriate and local national pay, benefits and bonuses, and these differences send loud signals to the brightest local nationals to learn as much as they can and move on.
- Less effort is put into recruiting top-notch young people in overseas markets than in the headquarters country. This leaves fast-growing developing markets with shallow bench strength.
- Insufficient attention and budget are devoted to assessing, training and developing the careers of valuable local nationals already on the company payroll.

Conventional wisdom has defined a lot of the pros and cons of using expatriates versus local nationals. But in an increasingly global environment, cultural sensitivity and cumulative skills are what count. And these come with an individual, not a nationality.

After all, what exactly is a "local national"? Someone who was born in the country? Has a parent or a spouse born there? Was educated there? Speaks the language(s)? Worked there for a while? All employees are local nationals of at least one country, but often they can claim a connection with several. More frequent international travel, population mobility and cross-border university education are increasing the pool of available hybrid local nationals. Every country-connection a person has is a potential advantage for the individual and the company. So it is in a multinational company's interests to expand the definition of the term "local national" rather than restrict it.

2. TRACE YOUR LIFELINE

Based on your company's business strategy, identify the activities that are essential to achieving success around the world and specify the positions that hold responsibility for performing them. These positions represent the "lifeline" of your company. Typically, they account for about 10 percent of management.

Then define the technical, functional and soft skills needed for success in each "lifeline" role. As Ms. Major of I.B.M. notes, "It is important to understand what people need to develop as executives. They can be savvy functionally and internationally, but they also have to be savvy inside the organization."

This second step requires integrated teams of business and H.R. specialists working with line managers. Over time, they should extend the skills descriptions to cover all of the company's executive posts. It took 18 months for I.B.M. to roll out its worldwide skills management process to more than 100,000 people in manufacturing and development.

A good starting point is with posts carrying the same title around the globe, but local circumstances need to be taken into account. Chief financial officers in Latin American and eastern European subsidiaries, for example, should know how to deal with volatile exchange rates and high inflation. Unilever circulates skills profiles for most of its posts, but expects managers to adapt them to meet local needs.

Compiling these descriptions is a major undertaking, and they will not be perfect because job descriptions are subject to continuous change in today's markets and because perfect matches of candidates with job descriptions are unlikely to be found. But they are an essential building block to a global H.R. policy because they establish common standards.

The lifeline and role descriptions should be revisited at least annually to ensure they express the business strategy. Many companies recognize the need to review the impact of strategy and marketplace changes on high-technology and R&D roles but overlook the fact that managerial jobs are also redrawn by market pressures. The roles involved in running an emerging market operation, for example, expand as the company builds its investment and sales base. At I.B.M., skills teams update their role descriptions every six months to keep pace with the markets and to inform senior managers which skills are "hot" and which the company has in good supply.

3. BUILD A GLOBAL DATABASE TO KNOW WHO AND WHERE YOUR TALENT IS

The main tool of a global H.R. policy has to be a global database simply because multinational companies now have many more strategic posts scattered around the globe and must monitor the career development of many more managers. Although some multinational companies have been compiling worldwide H.R. databases over the past decade, these still tend to concentrate on posts at the top of the organization, neglecting the middle managers in the country markets and potential stars coming through the ranks.

I.B.M. has compiled a database of senior managers for 20 years, into which it feeds names of promising middle managers, tracking them all with annual reviews. But it made the base worldwide only 10 years ago. Now the company is building another global database that will cover 40,000 competencies and include all employees worldwide who can deliver those skills or be groomed to do so. I.B.M. plans to link the two databases by 2000.

Unilever has practiced a broader sweep for the past 40 years. It has five talent "pools" stretching from individual companies (e.g., Good Humor Breyers Ice Cream in the United States and Walls Ice Cream in Britain) to foreign subsidiaries (e.g., Unilever United States Inc. and Unilever U.K. Holdings Ltd.) to global corporate headquarters. From day one, new executive trainees are given targets for personal development. Those who show the potential to move up significantly are quickly earmarked for the "Development" list, where their progress through the pools—company, national, business group and/or region, global, executive committee—is guided not only by their direct bosses but by managers up to three levels above. "We want bigger yardsticks to be applied to these people and we don't want their direct bosses to hang on to them," explains Herwig Kressler, Unilever's head of remuneration and industrial relations. To make sure the company is growing the general management talent it will need, the global H.R. director's strategic arm reaches into the career moves of the third pool—those serving in a group or region—to engineer appointments across divisions and regions.

To build this type of global H.R. database, you should begin with the Step 2 role descriptions and a series of personal-profile templates that ask questions that go beyond each manager's curriculum vitae to determine cultural ties, language skills, countries visited, hobbies and interests. For overseas assignments, H.R. directors correctly consider such soft skills and cultural adaptability to be as important as functional skills. The fact that overseas appointments are often made based largely on functional skills is one reason so many of them fail.[1]

4. CONSTRUCT A MOBILITY PYRAMID

Evaluate your managers in terms of their willingness to move to new locations as well as their ability and experience. Most H.R. departments look at mobility in black-or-white terms: "movable" or "not movable." But in today's global markets this concept should be viewed as a graduated scale and constantly reassessed because of changing circumstances in managers' lives and company opportunities. This will encourage many more managers to opt for overseas assignments and open the thinking of line and H.R. managers to different ways to use available in-house talent.

Some multinational companies, for example, have been developing a new type of manager whom we term "glopats": executives who are used as business-builders and troubleshooters in short or medium-length assignments in different markets. Other multinational companies are exploring the geographical elasticity of their local nationals.

To encourage managerial mobility, each personal profile in your database should have a field where managers and functional experts assess where and for what purposes they would move. When jobs or projects open, the company can quickly determine who is able and willing to take them.

Managers can move up and down a mobility pyramid at various stages of their career, often depending on their family and other commitments. Young single people or divorced managers, for example, may be able and eager to sign up for the glopat role but want to drop to a lower level of the pyramid if they wish to start or restart a family life. Or seasoned senior managers may feel ready to rise above the regional level only when their children enter college.

I.B.M. uses its global H.R. database increasingly for international projects. In preparing a proposal for a German car manufacturer, for instance, it pulled together a team of experts with automotive experience in the client's major and new markets. To reduce costs for its overseas assignments, I.B.M. has introduced geographic "filters": a line manager signals the need for outside skills to one of I.B.M.'s 400 resource coordinators, who aims to respond in 72 hours; the coordinator then searches the global skills database for a match, filtering the request through a series of ever-widening geographic circles. Preference is often given to the suitable candidate who is geographically closest to the assignment. The line manager then negotiates with that employee's boss or team for the employee's availability.

The shape of a company's mobility pyramid will depend on its businesses, markets and development stage and will evolve as the company grows. A mature multinational food-processing company with decentralized operations, for example, might find a flat pyramid adequate, whereas a multinational company in a fast-moving, high-technology business might need a steeper pyramid with proportionately more glopats.

5. IDENTIFY YOUR LEADERSHIP CAPITAL

Build a database of your company's mix of managerial skills by persuading people to describe the information in their c.v.'s, their management talents and their potential on standard personal-profile templates. Jump-start the process by having your senior managers and those in the lifeline posts complete the forms first. Add others worldwide with the potential to move up. Include functional specialists who show general management potential.

Require over time that every executive join the global H.R. system. This makes it harder for uncut diamonds to be hidden by their local bosses. Recognizing that people's situations and career preferences shift over time, hold all managers and technical experts responsible for updating their c.v.'s and reviewing their personal profiles at least once a year.

Companies should make it clear that individual inputs to the system are voluntary but that H.R. and line managers nevertheless will be using the data to plan promotions and international assignments and to assess training needs. Be mindful of the personal privacy provisions in the European Union's new Data Protection directive and similar regulations forthcoming in Japan that basically require employee consent to gather or circulate any personal information.

6. ASSESS YOUR BENCH STRENGTH AND SKILLS GAP

Ask each executive to compare his or her skills and characteristics with the ideal requirements defined for the executive's current post and preferred next post. Invite each to propose ways to close any personal skills gaps—for example, through in-house training, mentoring, outside courses or participation in cross-border task forces.

Compare the skills detailed in the personal assessments with those required by your business strategy. This information should form the basis for your management development and training programs and show whether you have time to prepare internal candidates for new job descriptions.

Unilever uses a nine-point competency framework for its senior managers. It then holds the information in private databases that serve as feeder information for its five talent pools. The company thoroughly reviews the five pools every two years and skims them in between, always using a three- to five-year perspective. In 1990, for example, its ice cream division had a strategic plan to move into 30 new countries within seven years. Unilever began hiring in its current markets with that in mind and set up a mobile "ice cream academy" to communicate the necessary technical skills.

I.B.M. applies its competency framework to a much broader personnel base and conducts its skills gap analyses every six months. Business strategists in every strategic business unit define a plan for each market and, working with H.R. specialists, determine the skills required to succeed in it. Competencies are graded against five proficiency levels.

Managers and functional experts are responsible for checking into the database to compare their capabilities against the relevant skills profiles and to determine whether they need additional training. Their assessments are reviewed, discussed and validated by each executive's boss, and then put into the database. "Through the database, we get a business view of what we need versus what we have," explains Rick Weiss, director of skills at I.B.M. "Once the gaps are identified, the question for H.R. is whether there is time to develop the necessary people or whether they have to be headhunted from the outside."

7. RECRUIT REGULARLY

Search for new recruits in every important local market as regularly as you do in the headquarters country. Develop a reputation as "the company to join" among graduates of the best universities, as Citibank has in India, for example.

The best way to attract stellar local national recruits is to demonstrate how far up the organization they can climb. Although many Fortune 500 companies in the United States derive 50 percent or more of their revenues from non-domestic sales, only 15 percent of their senior posts are held by non-Americans.

There may be nothing to stop a local national from reaching the top, but the executive suite inevitably reflects where a company was recruiting 30 years earlier. Even today, many multinational companies recruit disproportionately more people in their largest—often their longest-established—markets, thereby perpetuating the status quo.

To counter such imbalances, a multinational company must stress recruitment in emerging markets and, when possible, hire local nationals from these markets for the middle as well as the lower rungs of its career ladder. Philips Electronics N.V., for example, gives each country subsidiary a target number of people to bring through the ranks for international experience. Some go on to lengthy international careers; others return to home base, where they then command more respect, both in the business and with government officials, as a result of their international assignments.

8. ADVERTISE YOUR POSTS INTERNALLY

Run your own global labor market. In a large company, it is hard to keep track of the best candidates. For this reason, I.B.M. now advertises many of its posts on its worldwide Intranet. Unilever usually advertises only posts in the lower two pools, but this policy varies by country and by business unit.

Routine internal advertising has many advantages in that it:

- Allows a competitive internal job market to function across nationalities, genders and other categories.

- Shows ambitious people they can make their future in the company.
- Makes it harder for bosses to hide their leading lights.
- Attracts high-flyers who may be ready to jump ship.
- Helps to break down business-unit and divisional baronies.
- Reduces inbreeding by transferring managers across businesses and divisions.
- Gives the rest of the company first pick of talent made redundant in another part of the world.
- Solidifies company culture.
- Is consistent with giving employees responsibility to manage their own careers.

There are also certain disadvantages to this practice: Line managers have to fill the shoes of those who move; a central arbiter may need to settle disputes between departments and divisions; and applicants not chosen might decide to leave. To prevent that, disappointed applicants should automatically be routed through the career development office to discuss how their skills and performance mesh with their ambitions.

I.B.M. used to hire only from the inside, but five years ago it began to recruit outsiders—including those from other industries—to broaden thinking and add objectivity. Unilever is large enough that it can garner a short list of three to five internal candidates for any post. Yet it still fills 15 percent to 20 percent of managerial jobs from outside because of the need for specialist skills and because of the decreasing ability to plan where future growth opportunities will occur.

9. INSTITUTE SUCCESSION PLANNING

Every manager in a lifeline job should be required to nominate up to three candidates who could take over that post in the next week, in three months or within a year, and their bosses should sign off on the nominations. This should go a long way toward solving succession questions, but it will not resolve them completely.

The problem in large multinational companies is that many of today's successors may leave the company tomorrow. In addition, managers name only those people they know as successors. Third, the chief executives of many multinational companies keep their succession plans—if they have any—only in their heads. This seems to overlook the harsh realities of life and death. A better approach is that of one European shipping magnate who always carries a written list with the name of a successor for the captain of every boat in his fleet.

10. CHALLENGE AND RETAIN YOUR TALENT

Global networks that transfer knowledge and good practices run on people-to-people contact and continuity. Executive continuity also cuts down on turnover, recruitment and opportunity costs. As international competition for talent intensifies, therefore, it becomes increasingly important for companies to retain their good managers. Monetary incentives are not sufficient: the package must include challenge, personal growth and job satisfaction.

A policy should be adopted that invites employees to grow with the company, in every market. In addition, a career plan should be drawn up for every executive within his or her first 100 days in the organization. And plans should be reviewed regularly to be sure they stay aligned with the business strategy and the individual's need for job satisfaction and employability.

Overseas assignments and cross-border task forces are excellent ways to challenge, develop and retain good managers. They can also be awarded as horizontal "promotions." This is particularly useful since the flat organizations currently in fashion do not have enough levels for hierarchical promotions alone to provide sufficient motivation.

Unilever has long had a policy of retentive development and manages to hold on to 50 percent of its high-flyers. As an integral part of its global H.R. policy, it develops the "good" as well as the "best." Unilever reasons realistically that it needs to back up its high-flyers at every stage and location with a strong bench of crisis-proof, experienced supporters who also understand how to move with the markets.

Unilever bases these policies on three principles:

1. Be very open with people about the company's assessment of their potential and future.
2. Pay people well—and pay those with high potential really well, even though it may look like a distortion to others.
3. Don't hesitate too long to promote people who have shown ability.

Sometimes this policy involves taking risks with people. But the point of a good system is to enable a company to place bets on the right people.

MAKING IT WORK

The 10-step global H.R. framework has the potential to affect every executive in every location. This scale of culture change has to be led by a company's chief executive, with full commitment from the top management team. A task force of H.R. and business strategists will be needed to facilitate and implement the program, but its success in the end will depend on line managers. As Rex Adams, former worldwide director of human resources at Mobil Oil, has commented, "The development of jobs and the people who fill them has to be the prime responsibility of line managers, supported by H.R. as diagnosticians and strategists."

Line managers will have to be won over to the business case for a multicultural mix, trained seriously for their career-development roles and offered strong incentives to implement world-class H.R. practices.

MANAGING OVERSEAS POSTINGS

Overseas assignments are an essential part of the 10-step program. Yet the track record at most United States-based multinational companies is poor. One study found that up to 25 percent of United States expats "black out" in their assignments and have to be recalled or let go. Between 30 percent and 50 percent of the remainder are considered "brown-outs": they stay in their posts but underperform. The failure rates for European and Japanese companies were half those of American multinational companies.[2]

Finding exciting challenges for returning expats is another problem. About 20 percent of United States expatriates quit their companies within one year of repatriation, often because their newly acquired overseas experience is disregarded.[3] A 1992 study revealed that only 11 percent of Americans, 10 percent of Japanese and 25 percent of Finns received promotions after completing global assignments, while 77 percent of the Americans, 43 percent of the Japanese and 54 percent of the Finns saw themselves as demoted after returning home.[4]

Although the average annual cost of maintaining a United States employee abroad is about $300,000, and the average overseas assignment lasts about four years, United States multinational companies have been accepting a one-in-four chance of gaining no long-term return on this $1.2 million investment.[5] The way around this problem is to manage an expat's exit and re-entry as you would any other major appointment by adopting these strategies:

- Accord overseas postings the same high priority as other important business assignments.
- Match the candidates' hard skills, soft skills, cultural background and interests with the demands of the post and location. An American manager who studies tai chi and Asian philosophy, for example, is more likely to succeed in China than one who coaches Little League.
- Give internal applicants the edge, with personal and company training if needed.
- Spend on some insurance against blackouts and brownouts, especially with medium- to long-term assignments in the company's "lifeline." Send the final candidates to visit the country where the post is based, preferably with their spouses, and give the local managers with whom they will work input into the final selection.
- Give the appointee and his or her family cultural and language-immersion training.
- Assign a mentor from headquarters who will stay in touch with the manager throughout the posting. Ideally, the mentor will have similar overseas experience and can alert the appointee to possible pitfalls and opportunities.
- Set clear objectives for the appointee's integration into the local business environment. I.B.M., for example, traditionally expects a country general manager

to join and head the local American Chamber of Commerce and to entertain a government minister at home once a quarter.

- Continue developing the manager while he or she is overseas. Do not make it an "out of sight, out of mind" assignment.
- Discuss "next steps" before departure and again during the assignment.

Unilever used to have big problems with expat appointments and would lose 20 percent to 25 percent on their return. The problems occurred partly because executives who could not make it in the most important markets were sent on overseas assignments. According to Mr. Kressler of Unilever: "When they were ready to come back, nobody wanted them. It took two years to get the message out that we would not post anyone who wouldn't have a fair chance of getting a job in-house on their return. Now, our rate of loss is well under 10 [percent]."

Unilever's overseas postings now have two equally important objectives: to provide the local unit with needed skills, technical expertise or training and to develop general management talent. Unilever prefers to have its foreign operations run by local nationals, supported by a multinational mix of senior managers, so most expats report to local nationals. Only 10 percent are sent to head a unit—either when no local national is available or when the assignment is important to a manager's career development.

A manager who is sent on overseas assignment remains linked to a company unit that retains a career responsibility for him or her. The unit must include the manager in its annual performance reviews and career-planning system. Responsibility is given to the unit rather than to an individual manager to provide continuity and is included in the performance assessment of the unit and its director.

Career development is a factor in managerial bonuses in emerging markets, where Unilever is trying to train and develop local people, and in established markets, which help supply young expatriate managers to emerging markets.

HOW LONG IS ENOUGH?

The duration of any overseas appointment has to make sense for the individual, the company and the country. Three-year assignments are typical for the regional and global levels on the mobility pyramid, but they are not always enough. The cultural gap between a Western country and Japan, for example, is especially large, so a Westerner appointed as country manager will probably need to stay six years to make a significant impact.

Even when the culture gap is narrower, three-year assignments may be too short, except for the skilled glopat. Usually the first year is spent unpacking, the third year is spent packing up and anticipating the next move, leaving only the second year for full attention to the job. Most Unilever expat assignments last three to four years, although Mr. Kressler believes four to five years would be preferable in many cases.

Unilever now gives managers international exposure through training courses and career development at younger ages than in the past. "We do this because younger people today have a far greater international orientation—command of languages, experience of travel—than their peers of previous generations. We want these people in Unilever and they want to work for an organization that can offer international assignments early on."

MATCHING COMPLEMENTARY SKILLS

One caveat—overemphasizing individual development planning can lead to trying to turn every executive into a superman or superwoman. In fact, organizational effectiveness depends mainly on leveraging complementary skills of team members. The mobility pyramid can be a great advantage here. Using a variety of information technology groupware and mobile assignments, companies can partner managers from domestic and international markets in complementary and mutually supportive assignments to transfer ideas, skills and technology.

This is done particularly in high-technology industries, where it often takes time and training to bring newly hired local nationals up to speed on highly technical product lines. In such cases, an experienced manager can be sent to the market on a short-term assignment both to build initial sales and to train the local nationals while learning about the local market from them. I.B.M., for example, uses this approach to build a more integrated network of local nationals.

Given the shortage of true glopats, many multinational companies find it useful to pair a headquarters-oriented executive from outside the market with an executive familiar with the local market as the two most senior managers in an operating subsidiary. These two often have complementary skills, and their pairing permits a "good cop, bad cop" approach to certain customers. The expat knows the product line and company well, and his or her lack of detailed knowledge about the local culture can actually help provoke a fresh and open approach to local obstacles. The insider then provides the well of country knowledge and connections for the expat to draw upon.

Once a beachhead is established, further penetration of the local market favors the executive with local knowledge. The outsider can then mentor from behind the scenes, staying in touch with headquarters to guarantee the transfer of good ideas. Motorola has used this approach very successfully in Russia.[6]

In the event of a financial crisis, the home office often elects to tighten controls and appoint a financially savvy general manager with strong ties to headquarters. A major strategy change or acquisition may also require such leadership to implement it. Once the situation is under control, however, leadership may revert to a manager with deep local knowledge.

CONCLUSION

Most multinational companies now do a good job of globalizing the supply chains for all their essential raw materials—except human resources. Players in global markets can no longer afford this blind spot. Competition for talent is intensifying, and demand far outstrips supply. To have the multicultural skills and vision they need to succeed, companies will have to put into place programs that recruit, train and retain managers in all their markets.

If companies are to handle the challenges of globalization and shift to a knowledge-based economy, they must develop systems that "walk their talk" that people are their most valuable resource. The purpose of a global H.R. program is to ensure that a multinational company has the right talent, managerial mobility and cultural mix to manage effectively all of its operating units and growth opportunities and that its managers mesh into a knowledge-sharing network with common values.

Notes

1. Kevin Barham and Marion Devine, "The Quest for the International Manager: A Survey of Global Human Resource Strategies" (Economist Intelligence Unit, 1991).
2. J. Stewart Black, Hal B. Gregersen and Mark E. Mendenhall, "Global Assignments" (Jossey-Bass Publishers, 1992).
3. "International Assignment Policies: A Benchmark Study" (Arthur Andersen, 1996).
4. J. Stewart Black, Hal B. Gregersen and Mark E. Mendenhall, "Global Assignments" (Jossey-Bass Publishers, 1992).
5. Hal B. Gregersen and J. Stewart Black, "Antecedents to Commitment to a Parent Company and a Foreign Operation," *Academy of Management Journal*, March 1992, pp. 65–90.
6. "Who's the Boss?" *The Wall Street Journal*, Sept. 26, 1996, p. 15f.

PETROZUATA: A CASE STUDY OF THE EFFECTIVE USE OF PROJECT FINANCE

Benjamin C. Esty

Companies are increasingly using project finance to fund large-scale capital expenditures. In fact, private companies invested $96 billion in project finance deals in 1998, down from $119 billion in 1997 largely due to the Asian crisis, but up more than threefold since 1994 (see Table 1). The decision to use project finance involves an explicit choice regarding both organizational form and financial structure. With project finance, sponsoring firms create legally distinct entities to develop, manage, and finance the project. These entities borrow on a limited or non-recourse basis, which means that loan repayment depends on the project's cash flows rather than on the assets or general credit of the sponsoring organizations. Despite the non-recourse nature of project borrowing, projects are highly leveraged entities: debt to total capitalization ratios average 60–70%, but can reach as high as 95% in some deals.[1]

The interesting question here is why firms use project finance instead of traditional, on-balance sheet corporate finance. While recent research has made progress in answering this question, confusion and misconceptions remain. Indeed, many of the reasons for using project finance cited in textbooks, by practitioners, and by academics alike are incomplete, if not wrong. For example, people claim that project finance allows firms to isolate project risk, to increase equity returns, to preserve (or expand) debt capacity, and to mitigate sovereign risk.[2] Upon closer examination, it is not difficult

Ben Esty is Associate Professor of Business Administration at the Harvard Business School.

Author note: I would like to thank Teo Millett for research assistance with this paper and the original case study, and executives at Conoco, Citicorp, CS First Boston, PDVSA, and S&P (though the opinions expressed herein and all remaining mistakes are mine exclusively). I would also like to thank Dwight Crane and Tom Piper for helpful comments, and acknowledge the financial support provided by Harvard Business School's Division of Research.

• TABLE I •

Total Project Finance Investment: 1994–1998*

	Project Finance Investment ($ billions)				
	1994	1995	1996	1997	1998
Debt Financing					
Bank loans	$13.7	$23.3	$42.8	$67.5	$56.7
Bonds	4.0	3.8	4.8	7.5	9.8
Equity Financing (estimate)[a]	10.8	18.9	29.4	44.2	29.4
Total Investment	28.5	46.0	76.8	119.2	95.9
Average Debt to Capital Ratio	62%	59%	62%	63%	69%
Number of projects					
with bank financing	n/a	n/a	341	407	419
with bond financing	n/a	22	19	25	43

SOURCE: Project Finance International.
*Some of the growth in total investment may be attributed to improved data collection methods.
a. Based on the average debt/equity ratios for a subset of new projects.

to see the shortcomings of each supposed benefit. The first benefit, isolation of risk, is similar to the "free lunch" fallacy surrounding the use of convertible debt: sponsors benefit when a project succeeds, but are protected when it fails. Yet this argument neglects the benefits of "co-insurance" that takes place among a firm's different business units under conventional corporate finance. Similarly, the claim that project finance increases equity returns, while true, neglects the negative impact of increased leverage on equity risk. The last two benefits—expanded debt capacity and reduction in sovereign risk—require explicit assumptions that are rarely stated. The benefit of expanded debt capacity results from a change in asset composition, improved corporate governance, and improved efficiency. Finally, the benefit of reduced sovereign risk occurs not because the debt is broadly syndicated (in fact, corporate debt is also widely syndicated to international banks), but rather because the project's highly-leveraged, stand-alone structure increases the likelihood that sovereign interference will result in default and value destruction. By making the project more vulnerable to default, this structure, somewhat paradoxically, deters expropriation in much the same way high leverage deters unions from expropriating corporate wealth. The involvement of bilateral and multilateral agencies further mitigates sovereign risk by providing a mechanism for retribution against expropriating nations.

Given the limited understanding of why and how project finance creates value, the purpose of this article is to analyze the costs and benefits of project finance and to show how properly structured deals can lead to superior financial execution and greater value creation. In a recent article in this journal, Richard Brealey, Ian Cooper, and Michel Habib (1996) argued that project finance creates value by resolving agency problems and improving risk management.[3] I agree with their hypotheses in principle. But, like another article published over 10 years ago in this journal (by John Kensinger and John Martin),[4] I take a more general view of the problem. Briefly stated, my argument is that, in the right settings, project finance allows firms to minimize the *net* costs associated with market imperfections such as transactions costs, asymmetric information, incentive conflicts, financial distress, and taxes. At the same time, it allows firms to manage risks more effectively and more efficiently. These factors make project finance a lower-cost alternative to conventional, on-balance sheet, corporate finance.

Instead of presenting a theoretical argument, I illustrate the effective use of project finance by means of a detailed case study of Petrozuata, a $2.4 billion oil field development project in Venezuela.[5] Petrozuata is a joint venture between Conoco, then part of DuPont, and Maraven, a subsidiary of Petróleos de Venezuela S.A. (PDVSA), Venezuela's national oil company. It is the first in a series of development projects that are aimed at "re-opening" the Venezuelan oil sector to foreign investment. When the deal closed in July 1997, it set numerous precedents in the bank and capital markets. For these achievements, virtually every publication covering project finance declared it "Deal of the Year" and one of them recognized it as "Deal of the Decade."

Although this deal, like most project financings, has its idiosyncrasies, it is nevertheless representative of modern project finance transactions and illustrative of the benefits of using project finance. In the end, what emerges is not only a case study of an extremely well-crafted and well-executed deal, but frameworks for cost/benefit and risk management analysis in a project setting. While neither the cost/benefit analysis nor the risk management analysis provides boilerplate answers for structuring future transactions, they should provide some guidance to the process.

BACKGROUND ON THE PROJECT

In 1976, the Venezuelan government nationalized the domestic oil industry and established Petróleos de Venezuela S.A. (PDVSA) as a state-owned enterprise to manage the country's hydrocarbon resources. Twenty years later, PDVSA had become the world's second largest oil and gas company, ranking behind Saudi Aramco and ahead of Royal Dutch Shell, and the 10th most profitable company in the world. PDVSA embarked on a major strategic initiative called "La Apertura" (the opening) in 1990. In reality, this initiative was a "reopening" of Venezuela's energy sector to foreign investment and a way to raise some of the $65 billion needed for investment.

Petrozuata, a joint venture between Maraven and Conoco (with approximately equal ownership) was created in 1993 as part of this initiative to develop the Orinoco Belt, the largest known heavy oil field in the world. Table 2 provides a financial overview of the project sponsors (Maraven and Conoco) and their parent companies (PDVSA and DuPont). The project consists of three components: a series of inland wells to produce the extra heavy crude, a pipeline system to transport the crude to the coastal city of José, and an upgrader to partially refine the extra heavy crude into syncrude. Once refined, the syncrude would be sold at market prices to Conoco under a DuPont-guaranteed off-take agreement. At the end of this 35-year purchasing agreement, Conoco will transfer its shares to Maraven at no cost.

• TABLE 2 •

1996 Financial Summary of Parent Corporations and Project Sponsors ($ Billions)

	Parent Corporations		Project Sponsors	
	DuPont	PDVSA	Conoco	Maraven
Sales	$43.8	$33.9	$20.6	$5.5
Operating Profit	20.0	18.1	1.8	3.6
Net Income[a]	3.6	4.5	0.9	1.1
Assets	38.0	45.4	13.0	10.8
Depreciation, Depletion, and Amortization	2.6	2.7	1.1	0.9
Capital Expenditures	3.7	1.9	1.6	0.6
Reserves (billions of barrels)	1.0	72.6	1.0	24.8
S&P Debt Rating	AA–	B	not rated	not rated

SOURCES: DuPont 1996 Annual Report, PDVSA 1996 Annual Report, and Maraven.
a. The reported statistic for Conoco and Maraven is after-tax operating income.

The sponsors agreed to use $975 million of equity (40%) and $1.45 billion of debt (60%) to finance the project's $2.425 billion total cost (see Table 3 for a description of the sources and uses of funds). The financial advisors, Citicorp and Credit Suisse First Boston, used a multi-pronged financing strategy to raise debt from commercial banks, development agencies, and bond investors. In the end, the sponsors raised $450 million in bank finance and $1 billion in Rule 144A bonds, all of which was non-recourse to the sponsors following completion of the project.

The decision to finance this deal on a project basis was actually a dual decision regarding both financial and organizational structure. Although it is not the focus of this article, it is worth mentioning briefly the rationale for choosing the organizational structure they did. Instead of entering into a joint venture with Conoco, PDVSA could have built the project alone and relied on spot market transactions to sell the syncrude. But the specialized assets needed to extract and upgrade syncrude would have left PDVSA vulnerable to opportunistic behavior by downstream customers; that is, once the facility was constructed, such customers could extract "quasi-rents" by offering to pay variable costs only. Alternatively, Conoco, with downstream refining capacity, could have built the project itself. Yet Venezuelan law prohibits foreign ownership of domestic hydrocarbon resources. And so, they created a joint venture with a long-term off-take agreement as a way to encourage investment in specialized assets, limit *ex post* bargaining costs, and deter opportunistic behavior. Joint ownership ensures that both sponsors have the incentive to act in the project's best interest, particularly in areas where contracts would have been costly or impossible to write.

Structured in this fashion, Petrozuata had the three hallmarks of project finance deals: it was an economically and legally independent entity; it was an operating company with limited life (35 years); and it was funded with non-recourse debt for at least part of its life. These three characteristics distinguish project finance from traditional

• TABLE 3 •

TOTAL SOURCES AND USES OF FUNDS ($ MILLIONS)

USES OF FUNDS		
Capital Expenditures		
Oil-field Development	$449	18.4%
Pipeline System	216	8.9
Upgrader and Loading Facilities	928	38.3
Contingencies	177	7.3
Other Costs		
Financing Costs and Fees	354	14.6
Legal and Advisory Fees	15	0.6
Debt Service Reserve Account	81	3.3
Other (net working capital, cash)	205	8.5
Total	$2,425	100.0%
SOURCES OF FUNDS		
Commercial Bank Debt	$450	18.6%
Rule 144A Project Bond	1,000	41.2
Paid-in Capital (incl. shareholder loans)	445	18.4
Operating Cash Flow	530	21.9
Total	$2,425	100.0%

SOURCE: Petrolera Zuata, Petrozuata C.A. Offering Circular, 6/17/97.

corporate finance as well as other forms of off-balance sheet financing such as securitization. Having provided background information on the project and its organizational form, I now turn to the benefits of using project finance as a means of resolving market imperfections and managing risk.

MINIMIZING THE NET COST OF MARKET IMPERFECTIONS

The starting point for analyzing how project finance creates value is Modigliani and Miller's capital structure irrelevance proposition. According to M&M, firm value should not depend on how a firm finances its investments; thus whether it uses corporate or project finance to raise funds should be a matter of indifference to shareholders. The M&M proposition is based on a series of assumptions that are referred to collectively as "perfect" capital markets. For example, there are no taxes, transactions costs, or costs associated with companies in financial distress. The real world, of course, is not perfect by this definition; it contains "imperfections." Besides taxes, transactions costs, and costs of financial distress, there are costs stemming from asymmetric information between corporate insiders and outsiders, and from incentive conflicts among managers, shareholders, and creditors. In this section, I argue that project finance creates value by minimizing the *net* costs associated with these market imperfections.

PROJECT FINANCE INCREASES TRANSACTIONS COSTS

In their classic 1976 paper on agency costs, Michael Jensen and William Meckling defined an organization as "the nexis of contracts, written and unwritten, among owners of factors of production and customers." Nowhere is this definition more true than in project finance. Negotiating the deal structure, including the financial, construction and operational contracts, is extremely time-consuming and expensive. It is, in fact, the biggest *disadvantage* of using project finance. Conoco and Maraven spent more than *five years* negotiating this deal and paid more than $15 million in advisory fees (see Table 3). This sum represents 60 basis points of the $2.43 billion deal value and is approximately the same amount firms would spend on advisory fees in a merger of equal size.[6] It does not, however, include the professional time and expenses for their own employees working on the deal. In addition to the structuring expenses, there were financing and issuance costs totaling approximately $17 million ($12.5 million for the bond issue and $4.5 million for the bank financing including underwriting, commitment, and participation fees).[7] These costs, which total $32 million, represent a lower bound on the benefits of using project finance instead of internally generated funds; $15 million is the lower bound if project finance is used instead of traditional, corporate debt.

The fact that many of these costs are relatively fixed in nature implies that it makes sense to use project finance only for large projects. But this is not always true; simple projects and those with established technologies such as power plants require less negotiation and, therefore, can be financed economically on a smaller scale.

PROJECT FINANCING REDUCES INFORMATION COSTS

Typically, insiders know more about the value of assets in place and growth opportunities than outsiders. This information gap, when combined with incentive conflicts discussed below, creates adverse selection problems—notably, a tendency for firms to raise capital when they are overvalued—and increases the cost of raising capital.[8] These information-related costs increase with both the type (equity is more costly than debt) and amount of capital raised, and partially explain why firms rarely finance projects with external equity and why they may find it uneconomical to finance large projects with corporate debt. The costs also appear to be more important in emerging markets like Venezuela than in developed markets like the United States.[9]

The project structure is most commonly used with tangible and, therefore, relatively transparent assets. The separation of projects from the sponsoring firm or firms facilitates initial credit decisions. Instead of analyzing Petrozuata and its sponsoring organizations as a pooled credit, the creditors can analyze the project on a stand-alone basis. With a small lending syndicate and extensive negotiations, it is relatively easy to convey information that would either be more difficult with a larger group of creditors or undesirable for competitive reasons.

The transparent nature of projects also makes it relatively easy to monitor construction and development.[10] This feature distinguishes project finance from other start-up financing such as venture capital, where it is extremely difficult to monitor development. For similar reasons, it is easier to monitor a project's on-going performance. With segregated cash flows and dedicated management, there is little room for the kind of intentional or judgmental misrepresentation that is possible with diversified or consolidated firms. These improvements in transparency can lower a project's cost of capital.[11]

PROJECT FINANCE REDUCES INCENTIVE CONFLICTS

Despite the time and effort spent on structuring deals, there are always contingencies that are either unforeseeable, or uneconomical to negotiate. This inability to write "complete" contracts, combined with the fact that it is costly to monitor and enforce contracts, creates the potential for incentive conflicts among the various participants. One of the most important reasons for using project finance is to limit the costs imposed by these conflicts.[12]

Most of these conflicts relate to investment decisions or operating efficiency. The investment distortions in particular fall into one of four categories: overinvestment in negative NPV projects (known as free cash flow conflicts); investment in high-risk, negative NPV projects (known as risk shifting); underinvestment in positive (even riskless) NPV projects (known as debt overhang); and underinvestment in risky, positive NPV projects due to managerial risk aversion.[13] Studies of conglomerates suggest that inefficient investment appears to be quite common, destroys significant amount of value, and may well explain the 10–15% conglomerate discount observed in the market.[14]

Project finance helps eliminate all four investment distortions that would otherwise plague *sponsoring* organizations using corporate finance. It reduces overinvestment in negative NPV projects by requiring firms to raise external funds from independent third parties—Conoco had to raise $1.4 billion from bank and bond investors rather than funding the project internally. At the same time it reduces underinvestment due to debt overhang by assigning project returns to new investors rather than existing capital providers. To illustrate, assume that Conoco had already made full use of its existing debt capacity and, because of a downturn in oil prices, considered itself to be somewhat overleveraged. In such a case, Conoco's management might forgo a positive NPV project because covenants are likely to prevent it from issuing senior securities and because investors might not invest in junior securities (equity or subordinated debt) since they effectively transfer wealth to more senior creditors. Project finance solves this problem by assigning project returns to a new set of claimholders.[15] Finally, the project structure solves the problem of underinvestment in risky, positive NPV projects by isolating project risk and so reducing the probability of risk contamination. By risk contamination I mean the possibility that, under a conventional corporate financing, subsidiary losses would cause financial distress or even default by the parent.

The project structure also minimizes investment distortions at the *project* level. In contrast with sponsoring organizations, projects require relatively little investment once complete. With little value associated with future growth options, the danger of underinvesting is low. Far more important are the overinvestment problems that could arise under corporate finance because projects generate large cash flows; they have very low variable costs and tend to be low-cost producers. The use of high leverage in project finance, however, forces managers to disgorge free cash flow in the form of interest and principal payments thereby limiting their ability to invest. Although it solves the free cash flow problem, high leverage exacerbates the risk shifting problem. But here, too, the project structure is designed to minimize value destruction. A trustee allocates cash flows according to a predetermined "cash waterfall," leaving little room for managerial discretion.

Besides investment decisions, there are important incentive problems that relate to managerial effort: do managers act to maximize value? When one or more of the sponsors is a government-owned entity, one of the major benefits of project finance is the substitution of private-sector for public-sector management. The superiority of private-sector management is well documented in the cases of privatized companies.[16] As residual claimants with concentrated ownership claims, the sponsors have the incentive to maximize value even in the absence of complete contracts. For example, Conoco has an incentive to supply the appropriate amounts of intangible inputs such as refining technology and project management expertise. Both sponsors have an incentive to manage the risks they control efficiently (a subject I return to in the next section). To ensure managerial efficiency, there is a small board of directors comprised of two directors from each sponsor, and there are compensation contracts for managers that are linked to project performance. This combination of concentrated equity ownership and direct control prevents a wide range of incentive problems that destroy value in diversified companies.

PROJECT FINANCE REDUCES THE COSTS OF FINANCIAL DISTRESS

The cost of financial distress is an *expected* cost equal to the probability of distress times the costs associated with distress. Project finance adds value by reducing the probability of distress at the *sponsor* level and by reducing the costs of distress at the project level. I begin by comparing the probability of distress for a firm using conventional corporate finance with that of the same firm using non-recourse project finance to fund a new investment. If the firm uses corporate finance, then it becomes vulnerable to risk "contamination"; that is, the possibility that a poor outcome for the project causes financial distress for the parent. Of course, this cost is offset by the benefit of coinsurance whereby project cash flows prevent the parent from defaulting.[17] Thus, from the parent corporation's perspective, corporate finance is preferred when the benefits of coinsurance exceed the costs of risk contamination, and vice versa for project finance. Risk contamination, and hence the use of project finance, is more likely when projects are large compared to the sponsor, have greater total risk, and have high, positively correlated cash flows.[18] Petrozuata fits all three criteria. It is large relative to either sponsor (the $2.4 billion cost represents 19% and 22% of Conoco's and Maraven's identifiable assets, respectively), is very risky (as discussed below), and is likely to have cash flows that are highly correlated with its sponsors.

With regard to the costs of financial distress, sponsors use project finance in situations that have low costs of distress. Projects typically consist of economically independent, tangible assets that do not lose much value during default or following restructuring. Because the assets have few alternative uses, an efficient restructuring is more likely than an inefficient liquidation. The recognition that projects consist primarily of going concern value makes even senior claimants prefer speedy restructurings over delayed negotiations and uncertain outcomes. A final reason for low distress costs is the fact that project output is either a commodity that holds its value through restructuring or, as was the case with Petrozuata, a more specialized product that the off-taker will still want to buy. Even in a default situation, Conoco would want access to low-cost syncrude to keep its Lake Charles refinery running at full capacity.

Moreover, the structure of the project can also be designed to reduce the costs of distress. At least in developed countries, projects have relatively simple capital structures—often with a single class of bank debt—which tends to facilitate debt restructuring.[19] In contrast, projects in developing markets have significantly more complicated capital structures—in part because, as I suggest below, the presence of more participants is one way to mitigate sovereign risk.

In sum, the combination of lowering the probability of default and lowering the actual costs of default facilitates the use of high leverage. High leverage, in turn, creates further value by reducing incentive conflicts and by increasing interest tax shields.

PROJECT FINANCE REDUCES CORPORATE TAXES

The creation of an independent economic entity allows projects to obtain tax benefits that are not available to their sponsors. For example, Petrozuata will pay reduced royalty rates on oil revenue and income tax rates in exchange for using Venezuelan "content" (jobs, suppliers, contractors, etc.). Had Maraven financed the project on-balance sheet, it would have been subject to income tax rates of 67.7% and royalty rates of 16.67%. In contrast, Petrozuata will pay income taxes at the rate of 34%, and royalties at the rate of only 1% for the first nine years of operations, and no municipal taxes.[20] A 1% reduction in either the income tax rate or the royalty rate is worth approximately $4 million of incremental after-tax cash flow. Tax rate reductions and tax holidays are fairly common in project finance deals and illustrate how sponsors can capture some of the social benefits created by their project. Another tax advantage of the project structure is the incremental interest tax shields. Assuming the 60% leverage ratio is twice as high as either sponsor could have achieved under corporate financing, the incremental tax shields are worth approximately $140 million when discounted at a weighted-average cost of debt of 8.0%.[21]

Petrozuata's structure does, however, have one tax disadvantage. Because it was structured as a corporation and not as a pass-through entity such as a partnership, it pays taxes at the project level. As a result, it must use early net operating losses (NOLs) to offset future income rather than using them in the year incurred. In some cases, this loss in time value can be significant even though operating expenses are low.

In conclusion, sponsors use project finance in situations where high leverage is appropriate (i.e., with projects that have predictable cash flows, low distress costs, and minimal ongoing investment requirements) and where the structure can reduce the costs associated with market imperfections. Indeed, the size of the transactions costs incurred in structuring deals suggests that the benefits from reducing information asymmetries, incentive conflicts, taxes, and distress costs must be significant.

MANAGING PROJECT RISK

The second way project finance creates value is by improving risk management. Risk management consists of identifying, assessing, and allocating risks with the goals of reducing cost and of ensuring proper incentives. The identification of project risks and the assessment of severity are typically done by the sponsors in conjunction with their financial advisors. Then, to add credibility to the process, the key assumptions are verified using independent experts. In this case, the sponsors hired three independent consultants to analyze the oil reserves, project design, construction schedule, operating costs, syncrude demand, and syncrude prices. The sponsors also reviewed various deal structures with the ratings agencies in an attempt to garner an investment grade rating for a possible bond issue.

The next step is to allocate the risks to the parties that are in the best position to influence or control the outcome. When it is possible and cost effective to do so, these risks should be allocated contractually. Even when it is impossible or too costly to write complete contracts, the same principle holds: allocate residual risks and returns to the party best able to influence the outcome. By thus joining risks and returns, you increase the probability that parties will act in ways that maximize efficiency. This disaggregation and allocation of project risks and returns, particularly the residual risks and returns, distinguishes project finance from corporate finance.

The purpose of this section is to analyze how the sponsors allocated both contractual and residual risk in the Petrozuata deal. To facilitate this analysis, I classify the risks into four general categories: pre-completion risks, operating risks, sovereign risks, and financing risks. Table 4 presents a comprehensive risk management matrix that identifies the risks and who bears them in this deal.[22]

• TABLE 4 •

Project Finance Risk Management Matrix

Stage and Type of Risk	Description of the Generic Risk	Who Bears the Risk in This Case
PRE-COMPLETION RISKS		
Resource Risk	Inputs are not available in the quantity and quality expected	Sponsors (suppliers)
Force Majeure	"Acts of God" such as earthquakes or political risks such as war, terrorism, or strikes affect completion	3rd party insurers
Technological Risk	The technology does not yield the expected output	Sponsors (contractors)
Timing or Delay Risk	Construction falls behind schedule or is never completed	Sponsors (contractors)

(continued)

• TABLE 4 • continued

Project Finance Risk Management Matrix

Stage and Type of Risk	Description of the Generic Risk	Who Bears the Risk in This Case
Completion Risk	The combination of technological and timing risks	Sponsors (contractors)
OPERATING RISKS (POST-COMPLETION)		
Supply or Input Risk	Raw materials are not available in the quality or quantity expected?	Sponsors (suppliers)
Throughput Risk	Output quantities are too low or costs are too high	Sponsors
Force Majeure	See above	3rd party insurers or Sponsors
Environmental Risks	The project fails to comply with national and international environmental regulations	Sponsors
Market Risk: quantity	There is insufficient demand for the output	Conoco (off-taker)
Market Risk: price	Output prices decline	Sponsors (creditors)
SOVEREIGN RISKS		
Macroeconomic Risks		
1) Exchange Rates	Changes in exchange rates reduce cash flows	Sponsors Venezuelan government
2) Currency Convertibility	Inability to convert and repatriate foreign currency proceeds	Sponsors Venezuelan government
3) Inflation	Nominal contracts become vulnerable to price changes	Sponsors Venezuelan government
Political and Legal Risks		
1) Expropriation	Government seizes the assets or cash flows directly or indirectly through taxes	Sponsors Venezuelan government
2) Diversion	The government redirects project output or cash flows	Sponsors Venezuelan government
3) Changing Legal Rules	The government changes legal rules regarding contract enforceability, bankruptcy, etc.	Sponsors Venezuelan government
FINANCIAL RISKS		
Funding Risk	The project cannot raise the necessary funds at economical rates	Sponsors/Creditors
Interest-rate Risk	Increasing interest rates reduce cash flows	Sponsors/Creditors
Debt Service Risk	The project is unable to service its debt obligations for any reason	Sponsors/Creditors

PRE-COMPLETION RISKS

Pre-completion risks include all of the risks up to the point when a project passes a detailed set of completion tests. For example, resource, *force majeure*, technological, and timing risks are all important pre-completion risks. The risk that a key resource does not exist in the expected quantity or quality is known as resource risk. Both Conoco and PDVSA conducted initial tests to confirm the presence and quality of the oil in the Orinoco Belt, tests that were subsequently verified by an independent consultant. Based on the conclusion that Petrozuata would extract only 7% of proven reserves, analysts saw this as a development, not an exploration, project.

Force majeure risks include both "Acts of God" such as earthquakes and political risks such as war or terrorism. Acts of God, which by definition are not under any party's control, are best allocated to third-party insurers with large, well-diversified portfolios. To that end, the sponsors purchased a \$1.5 billion "all-risk" insurance policy during construction, and agreed to purchase property insurance as well as business interruption insurance during the operating phase. With regard to the political risks, the sponsors did what they could through project design to mitigate these risks: the pipelines were underground and the loading facilities were underwater. As a further measure of protection against terrorism, Venezuelan troops guarded the project during construction.

Next there is the risk that the project does not work or does not meet scheduled completion, which are known as technology and timing risks, respectively. The sponsors took several steps to mitigate both risks. They selected only *proven* technologies: horizontal drilling wells were currently being used in the Orinoco Belt and elsewhere; conventional diluted oil pipelines were common; and Conoco's coking technology was used in refineries around the world. Timing risk was an even bigger concern given the project's 37-month construction schedule. Because the project involved the three distinct components, the sponsors were unlikely to find a general contractor willing to sign a fixed-price, date-certain, turnkey contract for the entire project. As a result, Petrozuata itself became the general contractor. Both Conoco and PDVSA felt comfortable bearing this risk because both firms had experience managing large oil-field development projects in emerging markets. Conoco had recently completed the \$440 million Ardalin project in Arctic Russia and the \$3.5 billion Heidrun project in Norway; PDVSA had recently completed the \$2.7 billion expansion of its Cardón refinery. Where possible, the sponsors planned to use sub-contractors subject to fixed-price engineering, procurement, and construction (EPC) contracts to shift some of the completion risk to other parties. To protect against other shortfalls, they incorporated two contingency funds into the budget representing approximately 9% of upstream (wells and pipelines) and 15% of downstream (upgrader) construction costs (which are shown in Table 3 earlier).[23]

Despite these features, debtholders still wanted some guarantee that the project would be completed on time and on budget. These concerns were not unreasonable. According to one study of 230 greenfield projects in developing countries, 45% of them had cost overruns.[24] To address these concerns, Conoco and Maraven severally guaranteed to pay project expenses, including any unexpected cost overruns, prior to completion.[25] The parent corporations, DuPont (rated AA−) and PDVSA (rated B), guaranteed these obligations. The guarantees remain in effect until the project successfully passes six completion tests, three of which must be approved by an independent engineering firm. The most restrictive test requires the project to produce syncrude at pre-determined quantities and qualities for a period of 90 days.

Given the difference in ratings between the two sponsors, this guarantee structure was unique. More typical completion guarantees involved either a letter of credit covering the lower-rated sponsor's obligation or a *joint* guarantee with a fee paid by the lower-rated to the higher-rated sponsor. One reason for structuring a several guarantee was that PDVSA saw itself as a strong credit despite its B rating. In fact, according to one company official, "PDVSA would have a AAA rating if it were located in the U.S.; but because it was in Venezuela and its lone shareholder was the Venezuelan government, it's rating was capped by the sovereign's rating." Although Table 5 shows there is some merit for this view, based solely on recent financial ratios relative to other major oil companies, the rating agencies still considered PDVSA's B rating as a "weak link" in the project.

The completion guarantee ensures that the sponsors bear residual completion risk. This allocation makes sense given their position as the *general* contractors, their construction experience, their knowledge of refining technology, and their position as equity investors. Rather than trying to specify every possible construction contingency, which would have been prohibitively expensive if not impossible, the sponsors elected to assume completion risk themselves as the low-cost alternative.

Because they are residual claimants in the project, one can assume they will develop the project optimally, particularly with regard to the project's embedded optionality. Like all development projects, the developer has the option to defer, change, and/or abandon the project. While a complete real options analysis of this project would be helpful and interesting, it is beyond the scope of this paper. Instead, I simply note that

• TABLE 5 •

1996 Debt Ratings and Financial Statistics for Integrated Oil Companies

Company	S&P Rating	Country	Country Rating	Debt to Total Capital	Pre-tax Interest Coverage	Operating Income/ Revenue	Revenue ($ billions)
Amoco	AAA	US	AAA	27%	13.1×	18.9%	$32.2
Chevron	AA	US	AAA	32	9.9	16.9	37.6
Exxon	AAA	US	AAA	21	10.3	13.8	116.7
Mobil	AA	US	AAA	33	11.7	11.9	71.2
Texaco	A+	US	AAA	39	5.7	10.1	44.6
Shell (CN)	AA	Canada	AA+	21	6.6	19.7	5.1
PDVSA	B	Venezuela	B	15	32.3	48.7	33.9

SOURCES: S&P Global Sector Review and Bloomberg.

the abandonment option is quite different in the context of large-scale project development.[26] Staged investment, which is common in venture capital, is not as valuable in this context because most projects have low salvage values and intermediate stages of completion do not reveal much about underlying demand.[27] Moreover, sponsors have limited ability to change scale or technologies once construction has begun given the specific nature of the projects. This lack of flexibility presents a significant impediment to project sponsors and helps explain why many projects have poor financial returns—witness the bankruptcies of EuroTunnel, EuroDisney, Iridium, and ICO Communications.

OPERATING OR POST-COMPLETION RISKS

Once a project has successfully passed its completion tests, then input, throughput, environmental, and output risks become relevant (*force majeure* risks are always present). Input or supply risk refers to shortfalls in the quantity or increases in the price of critical raw materials. Petrozuata's primary input is crude oil which, as discussed earlier, was in plentiful and inexpensive supply. Other raw materials, including labor, water, electricity, and gas, represent a small fraction of total costs and, with the exception of labor, are produced by the project itself subject to long-term contract.

Given appropriate inputs, daily operations are then subject to throughput and environmental risks. The ability to produce syncrude at projected costs and qualities is known as throughput risk. Once again, an independent consulting firm verified the operations prior to construction. It concluded that the system, with proper maintenance, would produce syncrude at expected costs for the life of the project barring *force majeure* events. Similarly, the project was reviewed carefully to ensure compliance with all applicable domestic and World Bank environmental standards. The sponsors play an important role in mitigating operating risks, a role they take seriously given their status as junior claimants. They are responsible for maintaining the equipment, operating it efficiently, and complying with environmental regulations.

Finally, there are the risks that the demand or price of syncrude falls. Conoco assumed the demand risk through the off-take agreement guaranteed by DuPont. Having a AA-rated entity such as DuPont guarantee demand made Petrozuata look like a utility with a guaranteed market, and reduced a key determinant of cash flow variability, something the rating agencies would expect in an investment-grade project. From a risk management perspective, Conoco was an ideal party to bear the quantity risk because it needed feedstock for its Lake Charles refinery in Louisiana. In addition, Conoco, as one of the major competitors in the developing market for syncrude, was likely to know more about the developing syncrude market than most other firms.[28]

One of the most curious aspects of this tightly structured deal is the fact that the sponsors chose not to fix the price of syncrude, particularly given the historical volatility of Maya crude prices, the marker for setting syncrude prices. (Figure 1 shows Maya crude prices since 1983.) Failure to lock in a price exposed the project to not only price risk, but also to a form of basis risk in the event that syncrude traded at an increasing discount to other crude oils. One alternative was to fix the price in the off-take agreement, but Conoco did not want to assume this risk. A second alternative was to fix the

• FIGURE 1 •

MAYA CRUDE OIL PRICES

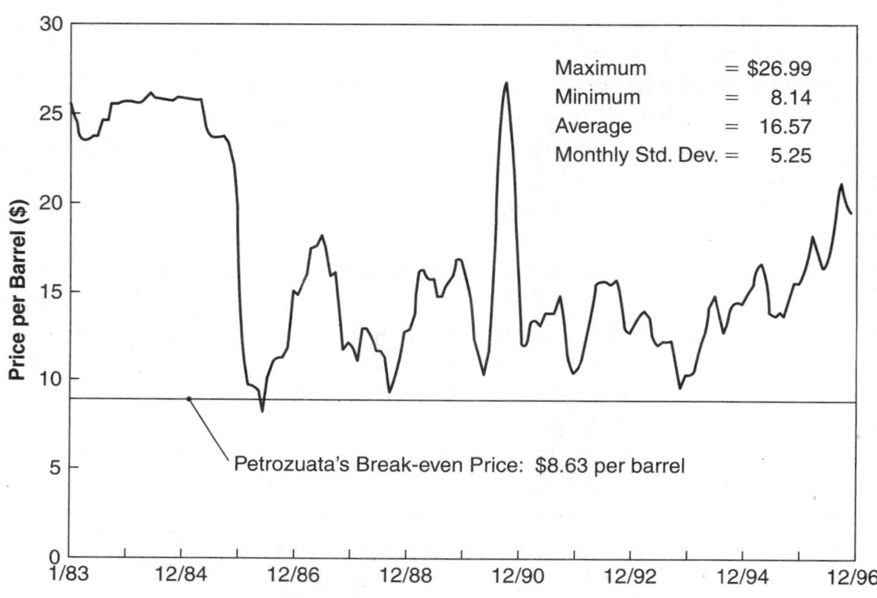

SOURCE: Energy Information Administration.

price using derivative instruments, but the sponsors rejected this alternative as being too expensive given the absence of long-term futures contracts for Maya crude—and too risky given the need to use an imperfectly correlated hedging instrument.

The final, and chosen, alternative was to let the sponsors bear this risk, which they agreed to do because of a number of mitigating factors. First, an independent consulting firm confirmed that the pricing projections were both reasonable and consistent with market expectations. Second, Petrozuata was a low-cost producer: its break-even price was well below the industry average, which meant it could still operate profitably even if prices fell dramatically.[29] And third, the financial advisors conservatively assumed a 1996 syncrude price of $12.25 per barrel compared to a current Maya crude price of over $15.00—and even though they believed that syncrude would trade above the Maya price. Thus, there was significant leeway for price declines. In fact, the nominal price of Maya crude had fallen below Petrozuata's break-even price of $8.56 per barrel only once since 1983, and even then it remained below the break-even price for only a month or so. After subjecting the project to this "backcast" of oil prices, and seeing it could survive, the sponsors agreed to accept the price risk. The expectation of increasing oil prices and, therefore, higher equity returns were enough to offset this risk.

SOVEREIGN RISKS

While mitigating completion and operating risks is important, project finance is most valuable as an instrument for mitigating sovereign risks. Indeed, it is the one feature that cannot be replicated under conventional corporate financing schemes. Sovereign risk was one of the biggest concerns about the Petrozuata deal because of Venezuela's historical macroeconomic and political instability. The bolivar had depreciated dramatically over the past few years; the government had restricted currency convertibility between 1994 and 1996, causing several firms to default on foreign currency obligations; and inflation was running rampant (see Table 6). Venezuela had also experienced more than a decade of political turmoil, including two failed military coups, a presidential impeachment, and a banking crisis. This level of uncertainty plus the history of nationalization in the 1970s made investors leery of investing in Venezuela.

In referring to this situation, one analyst referred to Petrozuata as "a great project in a bad neighborhood." Table 7 shows sovereign credit ratings for various North, Central, and South American countries. Venezuela's sub-investment grade ratings—B by S&P and Ba2 by Moody's—reflected this concern. Venezuela was also the only South American country to be downgraded by both S&P and Institutional Investor during the prior two years. Given the perception of sovereign risk, PDVSA, as a state-owned entity, had its rating capped at the sovereign B rating. The logic for capping corporate ratings is based on historical data; S&P, for example, reported finding that 68% of private sector defaults were triggered by sovereign defaults.[30]

Although the deal had many features to mitigate sovereign risks, one of the key features was the decision to keep oil revenues out of the country. Conoco as the purchaser would deposit U.S. dollar proceeds with a trustee in New York who would disburse cash according to the "waterfall" described earlier. An added benefit of this structure is that it effectively eliminated exchange rate risk because the revenues and debt

• TABLE 6 •

Venezuelan Macroeconomic Data: 1990–96

Year	Real GDP Growth	Gov't Surplus as % of GDP	Oil Exports as % of Total Exports	Oil Exports as % of GDP	Unemployment Rate	Inflation Rate	Long-Term Debt Rates	Exchange Rate (Bolivar per $US)
1990	7.5%	(2.1%)	80.0%	29.2%	11.0%	40.6%	20.1%	50.38
1991	10.1	(1.4)	81.1	23.1	10.1	34.2	27.1	61.55
1992	7.4	(3.8)	79.0	18.7	8.1	31.4	31.7	79.45
1993	(0.6)	(2.5)	74.7	18.0	6.8	38.1	41.0	105.64
1994	(2.5)	(6.8)	72.7	20.2	8.9	60.8	54.7	170.00
1995	3.7	(4.6)	74.4	17.9	10.9	59.9	53.4	290.00
1996	(0.4)	0.2	80.4	26.7	12.3	99.9	49.9	476.50

SOURCES: Inter-American Development Bank and the International Monetary Fund (IMF).

• TABLE 7 •

Sovereign Credit Ratings*

	Standard & Poor's		Moody's		Institutional Investor[a]	
Sovereign	12/94	12/96	12/94	12/96	9/94	9/96
NORTH AMERICA						
Canada	AA+	AA+	Aa1	Aa1	81.3	79.4
Mexico	BB	BB	Baa1	Baa1	46.1	41.6
United States	AAA	AAA	Aaa	Aaa	90.8	90.7
CENTRAL AMERICA						
Costa Rica	n/r	n/r	n/r	n/r	30.3	33.9
Panama	n/r	n/r	n/r	n/r	24.3	28.5
SOUTH AMERICA						
Argentina	BB−	BB−	B2	B1	37.3	38.9
Bolivia	n/r	n/r	n/r	n/r	21.4	25.4
Brazil	B+	B+	B1	B1	30.3	38.3
Chile	BBB+	A−	Baa2	Baa1	54.9	61.2
Colombia	n/r	BBB−	n/r	Baa3	44.4	46.7
Ecuador	n/r	n/r	n/r	n/r	24.5	26.4
Peru	n/r	n/r	n/r	B3	21.0	30.0
Venezuela	B+	B	Ba2	Ba2	36.0	32.0

SOURCES: Bloomberg; and "Country Credit Ratings," *Institutional Investor*, March 1995 and September 1996.

*Ratings are an assessment of the government's capacity and willingness to repay foreign currency denominated long-term debt. n/r = not rated.

a. *Institutional Investor's* "Country Credit Ratings" are based on a survey of 75 to 100 international banks. Bankers are asked to grade each country on a scale from 0 to 100 with 100 representing the least chance of default.

service were both denominated in dollars. It also helped justify the inclusion of a provision for international, not Venezuelan, arbitration for disputes.

An equally important factor was the decision to make the Venezuelan government, through PDVSA and Maraven, a project sponsor. The Venezuelan government has more influence over political and economic factors than any other entity. Accordingly, it should bear responsibility for mitigating sovereign risk. If the government fails to mitigate these risks, then it will lose the monetary benefits from taxes, royalties, and dividends as well as the accompanying benefits of increased employment and access to refining technology. In the extreme, Venezuela could lose access to foreign investment for another 20 years. In the presence of the country's $65 billion oil-field development initiative, Petrozuata can be seen as a strategic asset that the country could not afford to lose. Nevertheless, the risk of expropriation would rise significantly once the other Orinoco Belt projects were complete.[31] For this reason, the rating agencies were unlikely to give the project a high investment grade rating.

Investors and creditors could draw further comfort from the fact that PDVSA was more vulnerable to retaliation in 1996 than in 1976. Approximately 20% of its assets (worth $8 billion at book value) were located outside of Venezuela, including CITGO Petroleum Corporation, its retail gas distribution network. Even if retaliation were unlikely, the Venezuelan government would have trouble finding buyers for syncrude. Only a handful of refineries could process this type of heavy crude, none of which existed in Venezuela. The only refineries that could process it economically were located on the Gulf Coast of the United States, and they would be unlikely to participate in processing diverted or expropriated crude.

Finally, the project structure itself offers advantages in sovereign risk mitigation that are not available under corporate finance structures.[32] As highly leveraged, nonrecourse entities, projects are vulnerable to adverse sovereign acts, even partial acts of expropriation such as increased royalty rates. The object is to structure the project in such a way so that such acts result in default, inflict losses on creditors, and cause a significant reduction in project value (i.e., the loss of critical management expertise). In contrast, a corporate-financed project might survive an act of partial expropriation due to co-insurance from the parent corporation. The use of high leverage also ensures that there is little cash left in the company to attract unwarranted attention. Researchers have advanced similar arguments to explain why unionized companies have higher debt ratios than non-unionized companies.[33] The final reason why the project structure helps mitigate sovereign risk is that it facilitates participation by local governments, local financial institutions, multilateral agencies like the International Finance Corporation (IFC), and bilateral agencies like the U.S. Export–Import Bank.

FINANCIAL RISKS

There are three primary financial risks: interest-rate risk, funding risk, and credit risk. Initially, the sponsors hoped to finance 70% of the project with either fixed-rate bonds or bank loans with interest-rate swaps to deal with interest-rate risk. The idea was to transfer interest-rate risk to insurance companies and other investment fund managers that could use the fixed-rate bonds to offset long-term liabilities. (As shown in Table 8, the major investors in the bond tranches were insurance companies and other money managers.) Other advantages of bond finance include fewer covenants, greater economies of scale in issuance, and possibly better equity returns.

While these benefits were attractive and were the reasons why the sponsors chose to issue bonds, there are disadvantages of using bonds. One disadvantage is negative arbitrage. In contrast to bank facilities that can be drawn on as needed to match construction expenses, bonds are issued in lump sum. The interest cost on unused funds invariably exceeds the interest income. A rough estimate of the negative arbitrage cost in this case is $10 million. The use of bonds can also result in diminished monitoring; a large group of well-diversified bondholders is a less effective monitor than bankers and is potentially less effective at reducing sovereign risks.[34] And, in the event of financial trouble, reorganizing bondholders' claims is likely to be a more costly and time-consuming process than gaining agreement among a group of banks. A third, and potentially more serious, risk of using bond finance is that the bond market, particularly

• TABLE 8 •

PETROZUATA DEBT FINANCING

	BANK FINANCING		BOND FINANCING		
	TRANCHE A	TRANCHE B	SERIES A	SERIES B	SERIES C
Amount (billions)	$250	$200	$300	$625	$75
S&P Rating			BBB–	BBB–	BBB–
Tenor/Maturity (years)	12	14	12	20	20.25
LIBOR Margin (bps)	113–150[a]	125–200[a]			
Bank Loan Rates	7.94%[b]	7.94%[b]			
Benchmark Treasury			10 year	30 year	30 year
Spread over Treasuries (bps)			120	145	160
Bond Rates			7.63%	8.22%	8.37%
Average Life (years)	8	10	9.7	16.5	bullet
Investors (% by series)					
Investment Advisors			53.4%	50.4%	11.3%
Insurance Companies			32.3	37.0	79.3
Banks/Trusts			4.7	4.9	2.7
Mutual Funds			4.0	4.8	6.7
Other			5.6	2.9	0.0

SOURCE: Presentation by Jonathan Bram, CS First Boston, at the Emerging Markets Investor Conference, 11/18/97.

a. The margins vary because the bank loans have step-up pricing through time.

b. Bank loan rates are the weighted average step-up coupon (fixed equivalent) for both tranches.

the market for developing country bonds, is very fickle. It can quickly turn "cold," forcing sponsors to resort to alternative financial structures in spite of months or years of preparation. The inability to raise funds on an economic basis and in a timely manner is known as funding risk, a risk the sponsors managed by executing a multi-pronged financial strategy. The financial advisors held simultaneous meetings with commercial banks, development agencies, and bond investors to ensure they had alternatives in the event one source or another became unavailable.

One reason why funding risk occurs is that it is very costly, if not impossible, to issue sub-investment grade project bonds. Through the course of a series of meetings with the ratings agencies, the sponsors adjusted deal terms until they created an investment-grade structure, all the while being cognizant of their equity returns. First, they discussed whether to use 60% or 70% leverage. They chose 60% leverage to show their commitment to the project and to improve the project's minimum debt service coverage ratios (DSCR).[35] To provide further safety to the debtholders, the sponsors also created a debt service reserve account (DSRA) equal to six months of principal and interest on the senior (bank) debt. Next, they discussed the completion guarantee; should it be several or joint? And finally, they altered the regulations governing the distribution of proceeds to include a "cash trap." This feature prevented cash distributions to equityholders if the project did not have a trailing and leading 12-month DSCR of more than 1.35.

This negotiation process between the sponsors, rating agencies, various types of debt providers, and other deal participants helps explain why it can take up to five years and $15 million of advisory fees to structure a deal. What makes this process especially time-consuming is the fact that small changes in deal structure ripple through and affect other participants in possibly major ways. With as many as 15 or more distinct entities involved, each having distinct preferences and risk/reward trade-offs, it is somewhat surprising they ever reach agreement.

BETTER FINANCIAL EXECUTION

The time and energy spent structuring the deal was rewarded when financing closed in June 1997. The sponsors achieved high leverage ratios, attracted new sources of capital, and obtained better pricing than previous deals. The project's 60% leverage ratio was well in excess of either parent corporation's leverage ratio: PDVSA and DuPont had book value debt to total capital ratios of 16% and 45%, respectively. The fact that a sponsor with 16% leverage could finance an asset with 60% leverage and get a higher rating is often asserted as evidence that project finance expands a firm's debt capacity. Project finance expands debt capacity because it represents a superior governance structure that results in greater efficiency and value. This creation of value occurred not because PDVSA invested in Petrozuata, but rather because it structured Petrozuata as a project.

Petrozuata was also able to attract new sources of capital. The project raised $1 billion in Rule 144A project bonds in an offering that was oversubscribed by more than *five* times! The bonds received an investment grade rating from each of the major rating agencies: Baa1, BBB−, and BBB+ from Moody's, S&P, and Duff & Phelps, respectively. Astonishingly, this transaction pierced the sovereign ceiling by five notches—Petrozuata's BBB− project rating as compared to Venezuela's B rating. Only a few prior deals, notably Ras Laffan, have managed to pierce the sovereign ceiling, though Ras Laffan did it in an investment grade country (Qatar) and by only one notch. The Petrozuata financing received recognition as the highest-rated Latin American project bond, the largest emerging market bond offering from a sub-investment grade country, and the second largest emerging market financing in history after Ras Laffan.

Petrozuata also achieved better pricing and longer maturities than previous deals (Table 8 provides highlights of the financing). The project bonds had the tightest spreads and longest maturities (25 years) of any Rule 144A project bond while the bank debt had the tightest spreads and the longest tenor (14 years) of any uncovered (without political risk insurance) bank financing. In the beginning, the sponsors thought they would need covered bank loans. Yet in the end, they had commitments for $5 billion in *uncovered* bank financing, of which they chose to use $450 million to minimize the effects of negative arbitrage and to familiarize bankers with PDVSA for future deals.

Taken as a whole, the project structure permitted far superior financial execution than had previously been achieved in the project finance market or could have been achieved using corporate finance. Virtually every major business publication covering project finance, including *Institutional Investor, Corporate Finance, Global Finance, Latin Finance,* and *Project Finance International,* selected this transaction as "1997 Deal of the Year"—and one of them, *ProjectFinance,* selected it as "Deal of the Decade." Here are three examples of what analysts had to say about the deal:

> *This project is a stunning achievement for the sponsors and for Venezuela.*[36]
>
> *Scores of bankers not even involved in the deal refer to it as the best ever been done in the project finance sector. And for good reason.*[37]
>
> *Petrozuata's feat in raising funds is nothing short of amazing. In terms of the amounts taken from both the bank and bond markets, the tenors achieved, pricing, and the structure of the project itself, the package has no parallel.*[38]

Based on Petrozuata's success, PDVSA has financed several other projects in the Orinoco Belt. In June 1998, it financed the $1.7 billion Cerro Negro project; in August 1998, it financed the first round of the $4.6 billion Sincor project. After the emerging markets crashed in August 1998, however, PDVSA canceled additional rounds of financing for Sincor and a fourth project known as Hamaca. A few months later, in December 1998, S&P downgraded Petrozuata to BB+ citing schedule delays, lower than expected early production revenues, cost overruns totaling $430 million (as of October 1999, the project is $553 million over budget but is on schedule), falling crude prices, and political uncertainty surrounding the presidential elections—a former coup leader was the leading candidate. Conoco and Maraven have agreed to fund the cost overruns with additional equity as required by the completion guarantee.

CONCLUSION

Petrozuata is an example of the effective use of project finance for several reasons. First, the analysis shows a typical setting where project finance is likely to create value, that of a large-scale investment in greenfield assets. Although Petrozuata involves a collection of assets (wells, pipelines, and upgrader) that is somewhat unique, the collection still represents a stand-alone economic entity. Given the nature of this investment, one can think of project finance as venture capital for fixed assets except that the investments are 100 to 1000 times larger.

Besides highlighting the types of assets appropriate for project finance, the analysis illustrates the sizeable transactions costs associated with structuring a deal as well as the full range of benefits accruing to project sponsors. The structure allows sponsors to capture tax benefits not otherwise available, lowers the overall cost of financial distress, and resolves costly incentive conflicts. Further analysis of the explicit contractual terms reveals a careful allocation of project risks in an attempt to elicit optimal behavior by each of the participants. In his 1996 book on project finance, John Finnerty aptly describes this process as "asset-based financial engineering."[39] In the end, this process of financial engineering resulted in superior financial execution and increased value for the sponsoring organizations. One achievement in particular, the sponsor's ability to issue a $1 billion bond for a project in a developing country, is both an example of and a testament to the innovation taking place in this field.

The adverse circumstances following financial closure provide further evidence of the durability and merits of the project structure. As designed, the costs are falling on the parties most responsible for influencing the events or dealing with their consequences. The sponsors bear the risks of cost overruns and declining oil prices; the Venezuelan government is responsible for increased political risk. Chávez's election as President and his attempts to consolidate power have instituted a renewed level of uncertainty that is scaring off foreign investment and may prevent further investment in the Orinoco Belt. Adebayo Ogunlesi, CS First Boston's global head of project finance, commented on the ability of projects to withstand adversity:

> *Consistently, project assets outperform sovereigns in crises. Paiton bonds declined much less than the Indonesian sovereign issue did. TransGas and Cenralgas performed better than the Colombian sovereign.*[40]

Another way to judge the merits of this deal in particular and of project finance in general is to ask whether an alternative structure would have generated the same level of benefits, but done a better job of handling adversity. I think the answer to this question is quite clearly no, which helps explain why firms invested almost $100 billion in project finance deals last year and are likely to invest even more in the years ahead.

Notes

1. For an overview of the project finance market including an analysis of funding sources, leverage, investment location, and industry, see B.C. Esty, S. Harris, and K. Krueger, 1999, "An Overview of the Project Finance Market," Harvard Business School draft case study #N9-299-051, 6/4/99.
2. These four arguments, among others, are made by P.K. Nevitt in *Project Financing*, 4th edition, Euromoney Publications Ltd. (London, 1983).
3. R.A. Brealey, I.A. Cooper, and M.A. Habib, "Using Project Finance to Fund Infrastructure Investments," *Journal of Applied Corporate Finance,* Vol. 9 No. 3 (Fall 1996): 25–38.
4. J. Kensinger and J. Martin, "Project Finance, Raising Money The Old-fashioned Way," *Journal of Applied Corporate Finance* (Fall 1988), 69–81.
5. This article is based on B.C. Esty and M.M. Millett, "Petrolera Zuata. Petrozuata C.A.," Harvard Business School case study #N9-299-012, rev. September 23, 1998. Other information is from public sources only. A similar analysis of Freeport Minerals Company's investment in the Ertsberg project is presented by William Fruhan in Chapter 5 of *Financial Strategy: Studies in the Creation, Transfer, and Destruction of Shareholder Value* (Homewood, IL: Irwin, 1979).
6. McLaughlin (1990) finds that M&A advisory fees average 60 basis points for over $1 billion. See R.M. McLaughlin, "Investment Banking Contracts in Tender Offers," *Journal of Financial Economics,* 28 (1990): 209–232.

7. These calculations are based on the ProjectFinanceWare term sheet #3164 from Capital DATA, ltd.
8. For a description of the "lemons" problem of adverse selection in asset sales, see G.A. Akerlof, "The Market for 'Lemons': Quality and the Market Mechanism," *Quarterly Journal of Economics,* 84 (970): 488–500. For a discussion of how asymmetric information inhibits equity financing and causes underinvestment, see S.C. Myers and N.S. Majluf, "Corporate Financing and Investment Decisions When Firms Have Information That Investors Do Not Have," *Journal of Financial Economics,* 13 (1984): 187–221.
9. For a discussion of the incentive and information problems in emerging markets and how institutions often replace markets in these situations, see T. Khanna and K. Palepu, "Why Focused Strategies May Be Wrong for Emerging Markets," *Harvard Business Review* (July/August, 1997), 41–51.
10. The tax advantages of R&D limited partnerships are analyzed in J. Kensinger and J. Martin Kensinger, "An Economic Analysis of R&D Limited Partnerships," *Midland Corporate Finance Journal,* (Winter, 1986), 4:46. The authors refer to these structures as project finance, but recognize that the partnerships do not use non-recourse debt, a feature that I believe defines project finance.
11. For a model of capital market equilibrium with incomplete information that shows that firms can reduce their cost of capital by removing information asymmetries, see R.C. Merton, "A Simple Model of Capital Market Equilibrium with Incomplete Information," *The Journal of Finance,* 42 (1987): 483–510.
12. Brealey, Cooper, and Habib (1996) argue that the *primary* reason for using project finance is to control these costly conflicts.
13. For the seminal discussion of free cash flow theory, see M.C. Jensen, "The Agency Costs of Free Cash Flow," *American Economic Review* (1986). For the theory of risk shifting, see M.C. Jensen, and W.H. Meckling, "Theory of the Firm: Managerial Behavior, Agency Costs, and Ownership Structure," *Journal of Financial Economics,* 3 (1976): On debt overhang, see Myers and Majluf, (1984). For a discussion of managerial risk aversion, see C.W. Smith and R. Stulz, "The Determinants of Firms' Hedging Policies," *Journal of Financial and Quantitative Analysis,* 20 (1985).
14. For discussions of inefficient internal capital markets, see O. Lamont, "Cash Flow and Investment: Evidence from Internal Capital Markets," *The Journal of Finance,* 52 (1997): 83–109. R. Rajan, H. Servaes, and L. Zingales, "The Cost of Diversity: The Diversification Discount and Inefficient Investment," *Journal of Finance,* forthcoming; and D.S. Scharfstein and J.C. Stein, "The Dark Side of Internal Capital Markets: Divisional Rent-seeking and Inefficient Capital Investment," National Bureau of Economic Research, working paper #W5969, March 1997. For a study that documents the conglomerate discount, see P.G. Berger and E. Ofek, "Diversification's Effect on Firm Value," *Journal of Financial Economics,* 37 (1995): 39–65.
15. Stulz and Johnson (1985) make this argument for the use of secured debt while John and John (1991) make this argument for the use of project finance. See R.M. Stulz and H. Johnson, "An Analysis of Secured Debt," *Journal of Financial Economics,* 14 (1985): 501–521; and K. John and T. John, "Optimality of Project Financing: Theory and Empirical Implications in Finance and Accounting," *Review of Quantitative Finance and Accounting,* 1 (1991): 51–74.
16. For a review of the research on privatization's impact on economic performance, see J.D'-Souza and W.L. Megginson, "The Financial and Operating Performance of Privatized Firms During the 1990s," *The Journal of Finance,* 54 (1999): 1397–1438.

17. Brealey, Cooper, and Habib (1996) show how the use of project finance re-arranges the states of nature in which default occurs.

18. For a presentation of the model of the benefits of project finance illustrating the importance of project size, total risk, and correlation with sponsor returns, see my working paper, "Why Do Firms Use Project Finance Instead of Corporate Finance?" Harvard Business School working paper. For a study that shows that the use of project finance is positively correlated with relative project size (project size/sponsor assets) and with sovereign risk, see S. Kleimeier and W.L. Megginson, "An Economic Analysis of Project Finance," University of Oklahoma Working Paper, November 1996.

19. For a study showing that having fewer classes of debtholders facilitates restructuring, see S.C. Gilson, K. John, and L.H.P. Lang, "Troubled Debt Restructurings: An Empirical Study of Private Reorganization of Firms in Default," *Journal of Financial Economics,* 27 (1990): 315–353.

20. Standard & Poor's, 1997a, Petrozuata Finance, Inc., in Global Project Finance, September, 1997, p. 239.

21. When capital structure is pre-determined and not adjusted as a function of firm value, then the appropriate discount rate for interest tax shields is the cost of debt.

22. For good overviews of project risks, see R.F. Bruner and J. Langohr, "Project financing: An economic overview," Insead-Darden case study, #295-026-6, 1992; and Chapter 4 of International Finance Corporation (IFC), *Project Finance in Developing Countries,* Lessons of Experience Number 7, Washington, DC., 1999.

23. Sponsors typically sign engineering, procurement, and construction (EPC) contracts containing liquidated damages to cover cost overruns and delays. These guarantees cover from 15–40% of costs depending on the type of project.

24. IFC (1999), pp. 43–44.

25. Under a several guarantee, each sponsor is responsible for its share of total costs based on ownership, but is not liable for its partners' shares. In contrast, a joint guarantee means that each party is potentially liable for the entire amount.

26. For a discussion of how to value the abandonment option, see S.C. Myers and S. Majd, "Abandonment Value and Project Life," *Advances in Futures and Options Research,* 4 (1990): 1–21.

27. For an analysis of the staging of investment in venture capital organizations, see W.A. Sahlman, "The Structure and Governance of Venture-capital Organizations," *Journal of Financial Economics,* 27 (1990): 473–521.

28. For a discussion of how vertical integration provides information that helps firms make better capacity and production investment decisions, see K.J. Arrow, "Vertical integration and communication," *The Bell Journal of Economics,* 6 (1975): 173–183.

29. Standard & Poor's (1997a), pp. 242–243.

30. Standard & Poor's, Understanding Sovereign Risk, Standard & Poor's Credit Week, 1/1/97, p. 3.

31. For a discussion that refers to the increasing probability of expropriation due to the declining benefits accruing to a sovereign nation as the "obsolescing bargain," see R. Vernon, *Sovereignty at Bay: The Multinational Spread of US Enterprises,* (Basic Books, New York, NY, 1971).

32. Kleimeier and Megginson (1996) show that the use of project finance is strongly positively correlated with country risk scores.
33. For a study showing how leverage can be used to protect shareholder wealth from the threat of unionization, and presenting empirical evidence consistent with their theory, see S.G. Bronars and D.R. Deere, "The Threat of Unionization, the Use of Debt, and the Preservation of Shareholder Wealth," *The Quarterly Journal of Economics* (1991) 232–254.
34. For a model of financial intermediation that explains the role of banks as delegated monitors, see D.W. Diamond, "Financial Intermediation and Delegated Monitoring," *Review of Economic Studies,* 1984, 393–414.
35. For a discussion of how equityholders can signal project quality by increasing their investment in risky projects, see H.E. Leland and D.H. Pyle, "Information Asymmetries, Financial Structure, and Financial Intermediation," *The Journal of Finance,* 32 (1977): 371–387.
36. *Oil and Gas Journal,* 2/23/98, p. 50.
37. *Euroweek,* 1/98, p. 312.
38. *IFR,* "Review of the Year," 1997.
39. J.D. Finnerty, *Project Financing: Asset-based Financial Engineering,* (New York: John Wiley & Sons, 1996).
40. "The New Paradigms of Project Finance," *Global Finance,* August, 1998, p. 33.

PART FIVE

Organization and Implementation

THINK LOCAL, ORGANIZE...?

Ingo Theuerkauf, David Ernst and Amir Mahini

METHODOLOGY

This article is based on a survey of chief executive officers of leading consumer companies in the United States. The objective of the survey was to answer two questions. First, how successful are these US consumer companies in their international businesses? Participating companies were classified as more or less successful compared to their specific industry average, using publicly available data on international sales and profit growth over the period 1986–1991. These are clearly not the only criteria that can be used as a measure, but the two factors were ranked by participating CEOs as the most important indicators of success. Second, what organizational patterns do internationally successful companies typically follow, and how do these compare with the most common initiatives undertaken by companies in general? The findings are based on publicly available information on international performance as well as on detailed responses by survey participants regarding:

- the characteristics of their current organization;
- international decision making;
- major international opportunities and challenges over the next five years;
- organizational changes underway or planned.

The sample comprises 43 US consumer companies which responded to a detailed questionnaire. Some of the comparative analyses were based on fewer companies because of limitations in the data available. All responses are from the largest 120 consumer companies in the United States, measured by total sales in 1991, and they represent a broad set of consumer industries, including food, beverages and tobacco; general merchandise; non-food grocery and health care; and consumer services. Two-thirds of the

• FIGURE 1 •

RESEARCH CONCEPT

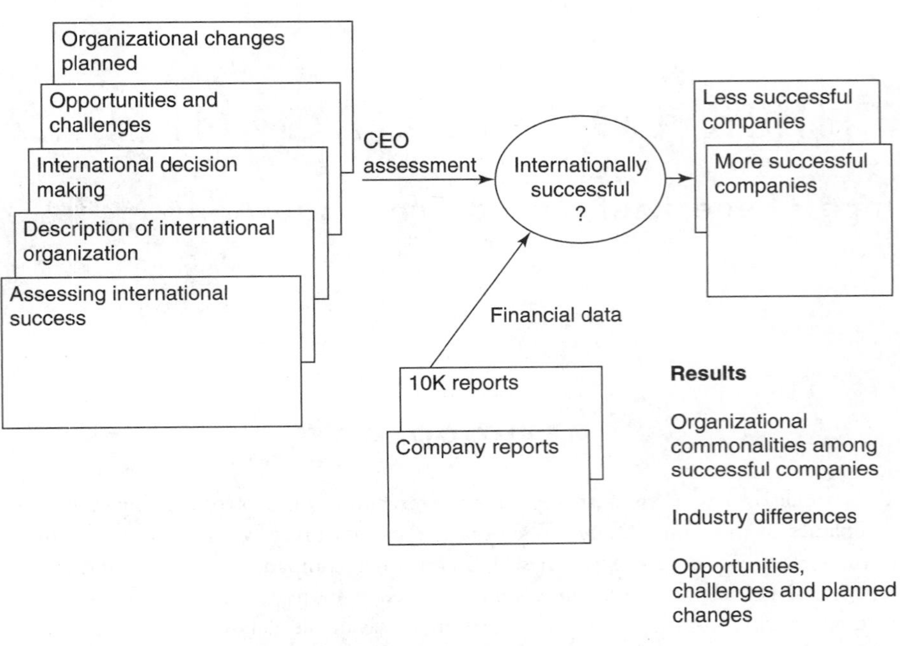

questionnaires were completed by the chairman or CEO, the remainder by senior managers. Only 34 companies were included in the comparisons between successful and unsuccessful companies, since international sales and profit growth data are lacking for privately held and/or diversified companies. The data collection process is summarized in Figure 1.

Some CEOs lack a clear and objective view of their company's international standing. Most companies in the survey—77 percent—rated themselves as successful in global markets and over half reckoned they were superior to their rivals. But comparisons with industry averages revealed a perception gap. When companies' self assessment was compared with actual performance, 35 percent of the respondents overestimated their international performance.

RESULTS

CEOs are firmly of the opinion that growth in international markets is increasingly the key to their companies' success as shown in Figure 2. Looking forwards, these

• FIGURE 2 •

CEOs Stating that Overall Success Relies Heavily on International Growth

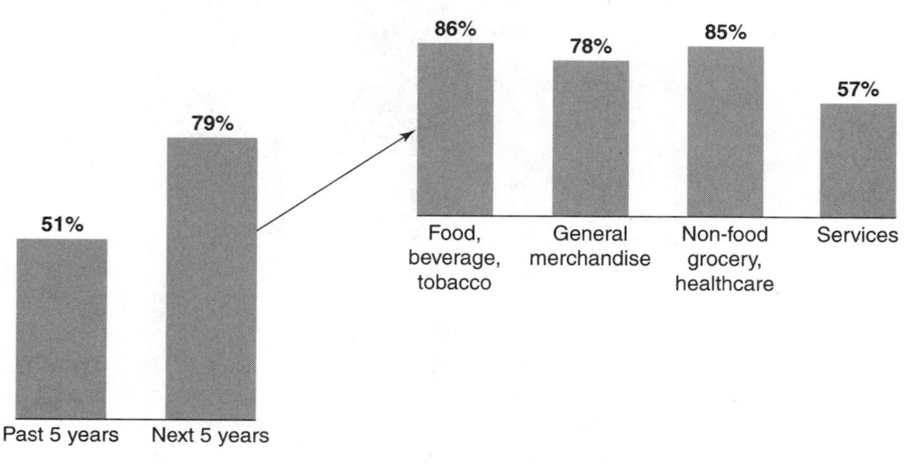

companies expect international sales to grow at twice the rate of US sales in the future. US markets were expected to grow at a rate of 5 percent from 1991 to 1996, while respective growth rates for certain markets were considerably higher. For example, eastern and central Europe was expected to grow at 18 percent, Asia (including Japan) at 15 percent, and western Europe at 9 percent. NAFTA (North American Free Trade Agreement) market's growth was estimated at 9 percent.

Many CEOs, however, question whether their organization in its current form is suited to the challenge of achieving their strategic objectives in overseas markets. A full 40 percent of the respondents felt that their organization was unsuitable for international success. The trend in organizational structures seems to be shifting away from a traditional "United States plus international" structure and towards more global alignments, for example, matrix structures. The current organizational structures as well as plans for the future are summarized in Figure 3.

Based on the survey results, 11 distinctive traits emerged to correlate heavily with high performance in international markets. They are summarized in Table I.

Many companies are planning specific organizational initiatives, aimed at strengthening their international base. Evidence suggests, however, that some of these initiatives are not linked to the factors that distinguish internationally successful companies. As a matter of fact, of the 137 specific changes planned by companies, only 23 percent of this type of changes correlate with international success. For example, while a substantial number of companies are planning structural change as shown in Figure 4, there is no clear link between organizational structure and international success.

• FIGURE 3 •

PRIMARY ORGANIZATION STRUCTURE (NUMBER OF COMPANIES)

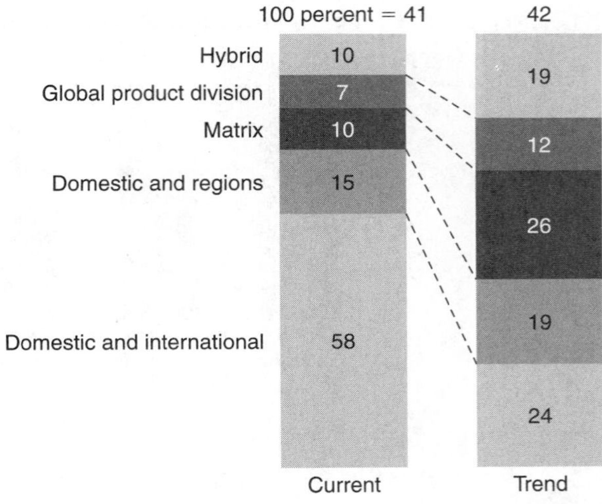

• TABLE 1 •

SUMMARY OF MOST SIGNIFICANT DIFFERENCES BETWEEN MORE AND LESS SUCCESSFUL COMPANIES[a]

SUCCESSFUL COMPANIES	PERCENTAGE POINT DIFFERENCE[b]
1 Have less difficulty integrating international acquisitions	35
1 Let subsidiary product managers report to the country general manager	35
3 Have worldwide management development system in place	34
4 Take advantage of global electronic networking capabilities	32
5 Tie overall company success to international growth	29
6 Treat country subsidiaries in differentiated way based on importance and skills	28
7 Make international experience a condition for promotion to top management	21
7 Have research centres outside US	21
7 Plan major change in international organization over the next five years	21
8 Have close network among their top 200 managers worldwide	16
8 Have a more multinational management group	16

[a]Total number of variables tested = 300

[b]Percentage incidence among international successful minus percentage incidence among international unsuccessful companies

• FIGURE 4 •

CURRENT ORGANIZATION STRUCTURE (NUMBER OF COMPANIES)

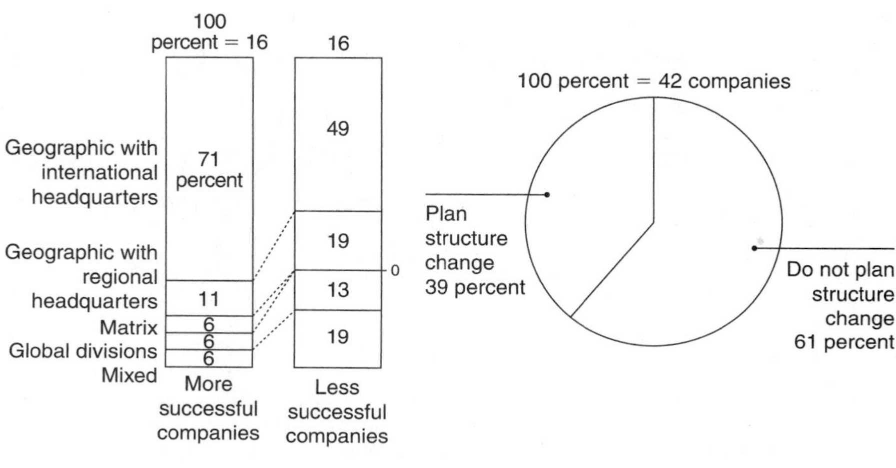

Some organizational initiatives have been quite popular in the recent past. The top six such initiatives are listed in Figure 5. Many of these initiatives are popular; for example, 91 percent of all companies have either implemented or plan to implement

• FIGURE 5 •

COMMON ORGANIZATIONAL FEATURES PLANNED BY MAJORITY (PERCENTAGE OF COMPANIES)

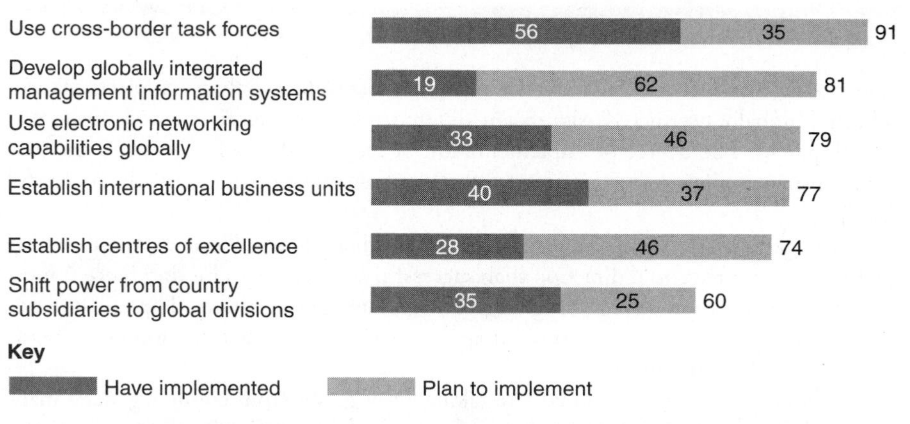

• FIGURE 6 •

INTERNATIONAL DECISION MAKING: MORE VERSUS LESS SUCCESSFUL COMPANIES

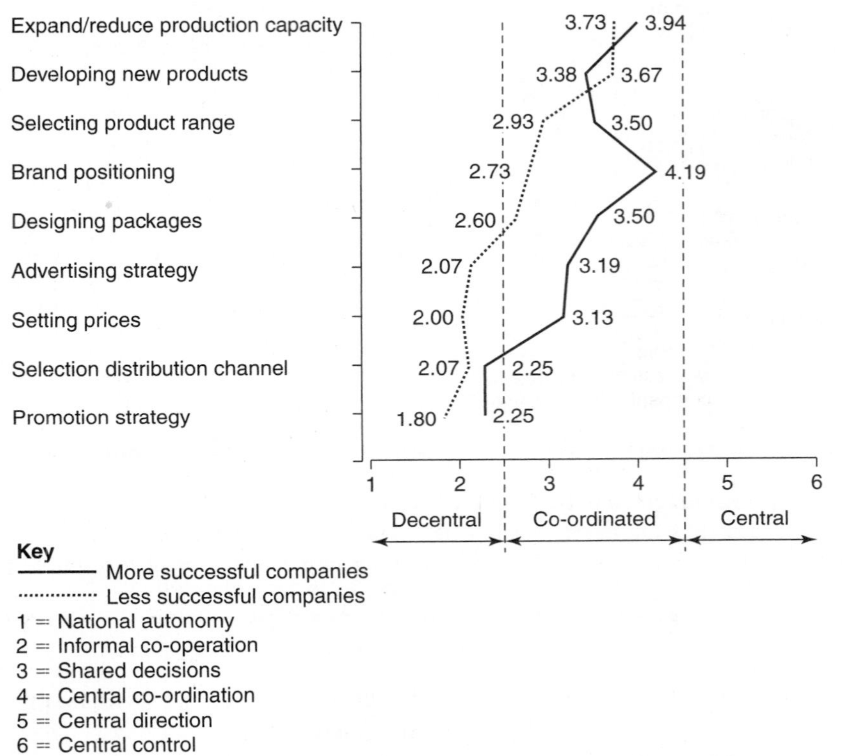

cross-border task forces, but of the six initiatives mentioned, only using electronic capabilities globally produced a significant difference between successful and unsuccessful companies. The degree of implementation of cross-border task forces and international business units is actually higher for the unsuccessful companies than the successful ones.

In general, successful companies co-ordinate their international decision making globally, with more central direction than successful competitors. This difference is most marked in brand positioning, designing packages and setting prices. There is one notable exception in a more decentralized approach to new product development. These results are highlighted in Figure 6.

Although many multinationals are taking away power from country general managers, most successful companies have the product managers in their subsidiaries reporting to the country general managers. A significant difference between successful and unsuccessful companies is evident in their human resource policies. Successful companies are more likely to have a worldwide manager development programme in place and are also moving towards requiring international experience as a condition for promotion to top management.

LOOKING TO THE FUTURE

Successful companies are unanimous that their success over the next five years will depend on international growth. Their international effectiveness goes hand in hand with an undivided focus on overseas markets. This raises an interesting question: Does the mere focus on the international lead to success? Finally, internationally successful companies do not stand still, or rest on past achievements. They are more likely to embrace further organizational change and continuous self-renewal.

GLOBAL TRANSFER OF CRITICAL CAPABILITIES

Henry P. Conn and George S. Yip

In the last decade or so, multinational companies from around the world have eagerly embraced globalization and have striven to develop and implement worldwide strategy. By now we all know how difficult this process is. Numerous barriers stand in the way of successful globalization. Some companies, however, have been spectacularly successful in taking their proven approach and replicating it across a range of markets. Examples include Toyota and Motorola worldwide, Disney in Japan, and, more recently, IKEA in Europe and the United States. Some companies have kept certain core aspects of their approach and significantly modified other aspects to suit local positioning; McDonald's in Asia Pacific (with common business systems but cuisine adjusted to local tastes) and Sears, Roebuck & Co. in Mexico (upscale image relative to mass merchant positioning in the U.S.) attest to this. Nevertheless, the business press is replete with examples of companies that have stumbled badly in transferring an approach proven in one market to other markets—Disney in Europe, Volkswagen in the U.S., and numerous companies in Japan, to name only a few.

Establishing, supporting, and leveraging foreign ventures is the essential building block in the globalization process. Yet failure can be more common than success, particularly in really tough markets such as Japan and China. In this article, we report that the effective international transfer of critical capabilities constitutes the single most important determinant of foreign venture success. We draw this conclusion from a study of the experiences of 35 major multinational corporations (MNCs) in establishing 120 foreign operations. We also discuss the means for achieving successful transfer of critical capabilities, focusing mainly on the role of global human resource processes.

Henry P. Conn is a vice president of A.T. Kearney, a global management consulting firm based in Chicago, Illinois. George S. Yip is Adjunct Professor at UCLA's Anderson Graduate School of Management. This article reports on a study conducted by A.T. Kearney. The authors thank the many companies who participated in the study, and the many A.T. Kearney staff members, as well as Professor Phil Smith of Michigan State University, who worked on it.

Much has been written about how to go about developing and compensating managers to compete globally. Our study is, however, one of the first to make the statistical link between effective global human resource processes and superior corporate performance.

VARIATIONS IN THE PERFORMANCE OF FOREIGN OPERATIONS

What causes some companies to succeed in globalization and others to fail, particularly at the level of foreign operations and subsidiaries? To investigate this and other questions, we structured our research using the framework in Figure 1. Industry globalization drivers, such as internationally common customer needs, global scale economies, barriers to trade, and global competitive threats, influence the worldwide strategy companies try to implement, as well as the organizational structures they adopt to enable that strategy. The automobile and computer industries, for example, face much stronger globalization drivers than most segments of the food or apparel industries. And strategy and organization reinforce each other in their effects. Witness Asea Brown Boveri, whose acclaimed use of global strategy depends on its careful structuring of head office and subsidiary roles.

But however good the strategy and organizational structure, other key factors—particularly critical capabilities, people, management processes, and culture—intervene

• FIGURE 1 •

GLOBALIZATION FRAMEWORK

to affect implementation. The path to superior performance lies through these gatekeepers, which can accelerate, slow, or even derail the journey.

THE ROLE OF CRITICAL CAPABILITIES

We suspected that the effective transfer of critical capabilities would be a major contributor to success. These capabilities (sometimes called core competencies) are now widely recognized as essential to competitive advantage. In globalizing, therefore, MNCs need to be able to transfer the most critical capabilities within and between their networks of international operations.

McDonalds' tremendous overseas success has been built on the corporation's ability to rapidly transfer to foreign entrepreneurs the capability of operating the entire, complex McDonald's business system. Hong Kong's luxury hotel chains—The Peninsula Group, The Regent, and Mandarin Oriental—are in the process of a similar transfer as they expand globally. Although the hotels have attained success in the rest of Asia rather quickly, winning over the United States has been tougher. But at least one transfer has succeeded: In fewer than four years since start-up, the Peninsula in Beverly Hills, California, has established itself as perhaps the premier hotel in all the Los Angeles area. This success springs in great part from the Peninsula's ability to transfer the right critical capabilities, especially its immaculate service, while adding other local requirements, such as a "stare-and-be-stared-at" swimming pool setup complete with cabanas for Hollywood negotiations.

In the automotive sector, exchange rate volatility and local content considerations have driven many Japanese manufacturers to push once "sacred" value-added design/development activities into their foreign market subsidiaries. Nissan, Toyota, and Honda have all pursued strategies whereby major elements of vehicle development are performed by in-country design teams. For those procedures that remain centralized, such as body engineering, there is heavy cross-fertilization of ideas resulting from temporary staff transfers as well as shared computer databases and telecommunications linkages.

In much the same way, aerospace manufacturers Boeing and McDonnell-Douglas have increasingly shifted value-added design and manufacturing work to "alliance" partners. This process, known as "offset" (in which partner design/manufacturing resource expenditures are offset, or used as payment for project equity commitments), is largely the result of efforts by the airframe manufacturers to defray the enormous expense of developing new aircraft and to favorably influence potential foreign customers (hoping, for instance, that JAL, ANA, and JAS will be more inclined to purchase from them if Kawasaki Heavy Industries has a significant level of design and manufacturing effort in the project). Typically, the foreign venture partner is most interested in receiving exactly the critical process/technology skills that a company such as Boeing designates as proprietary. However this issue is resolved, the success of the project rests on Boeing transferring the required skills and process knowledge to the foreign partner.

DEFINING CRITICAL CAPABILITIES

In our experience with clients and research participants, we have found the concept of "core competencies" to be ill-understood in practice—despite extensive academic discussion on the topic in recent years. Are core competencies "things we do well"? Activities that are unique to the company? Sources of competitive advantage? Some examples can illustrate the difficulties faced by companies trying to align their organizations on solid definitional ground.

General Motors, Toyota, and Volvo all know how to set up distributorships in markets outside their home base of operations, so none can claim a core competency in this regard. However, the lack of an effective distribution network could well be a significant source of competitive disadvantage. Accordingly, as a "thing we do well," the ability to define, structure, and manage distribution networks effectively across multiple country markets in the automotive industry is a "cost of doing business" activity, albeit a highly important one.

Likewise, the mere "uniqueness" of an activity clearly provides insufficient grounds for supporting a designation as a core competency. Companies and entire industries—food service, data management outsourcing, contract inventory replenishment—have been founded with the intent to off-load "non-core" activities that, although potentially "unique," do not pass a value threshold of an activity in which the company must invest its own resources.

Finally, a source of "competitive advantage," though important to maintain and develop, may have little actionable value for the thousands of employees comprising the global organization. Coca-Cola's manufacturing infrastructure in Southeast Asia, funded by the U.S. government and later turned over to the company, provided Coca-Cola with a significant cost advantage in this region. However, this asset is region-specific and therefore of limited relevance to other country operations. It is also lacking in "animation," or the intrinsic ability of a process/knowledge "asset" to be nurtured, redefined, extended, transferred, and so on.

By definition, the term "critical capability" conveys that we are dealing with capabilities (discrete, meaningful, actionable, animate) that are critical (providing sustainable advantage, highly leverageable) to the corporation. Throughout our research, we have spoken to companies about critical capabilities as defined by their business and organizational competencies as well as various forms of intellectual property, such as patents, trademarks, software technology, and other non-patented but exclusive technological products and processes. Superior value is created when the business, organizational, and technological skills of a company are enhanced by or interwoven with key asset "nuggets" (such as brands, patents, and the like). In this regard, some examples of critical capabilities might include:

- Image branding/high-end merchandising
- Rapid commercialization of new technology
- System-wide franchise quality management
- Design for low-cost manufacturing

COLLECTING AND ANALYZING THE DATA

To investigate our framework, we developed a questionnaire structured to collect data from three levels of a company—the corporate CEO, the head of a line of business, and the heads of foreign operations or subsidiaries. Figure 2 summarizes the topics we addressed at each level. We then recruited 35 major MNCs from North America, Europe, and Asia Pacific (listed in Figure 3), and asked each company to select two lines of business and identify three diverse countries it had entered within the last 5 to 15 years for each line of business. The country operations also had to vary in performance and be continentally or regionally dispersed.

The companies responded by identifying 120 foreign operations. About 70 percent of these operations were in developing markets in Asia, Latin America, and Eastern Europe, and the rest were in the United States, Canada, and Western Europe. On average, the companies had nine years of experience in these overseas ventures, and in total we collected more than 600,000 data points.

We measured the transfer of critical capabilities and most other variables, such as the effectiveness of the global processes for human resources, by asking respondents to rate these variables on a scale from 0 (not at all effective) to 10 (completely effective). To supplement the data collected from the questionnaires, we conducted personal

• FIGURE 2 •

STRUCTURE OF QUESTIONNAIRE

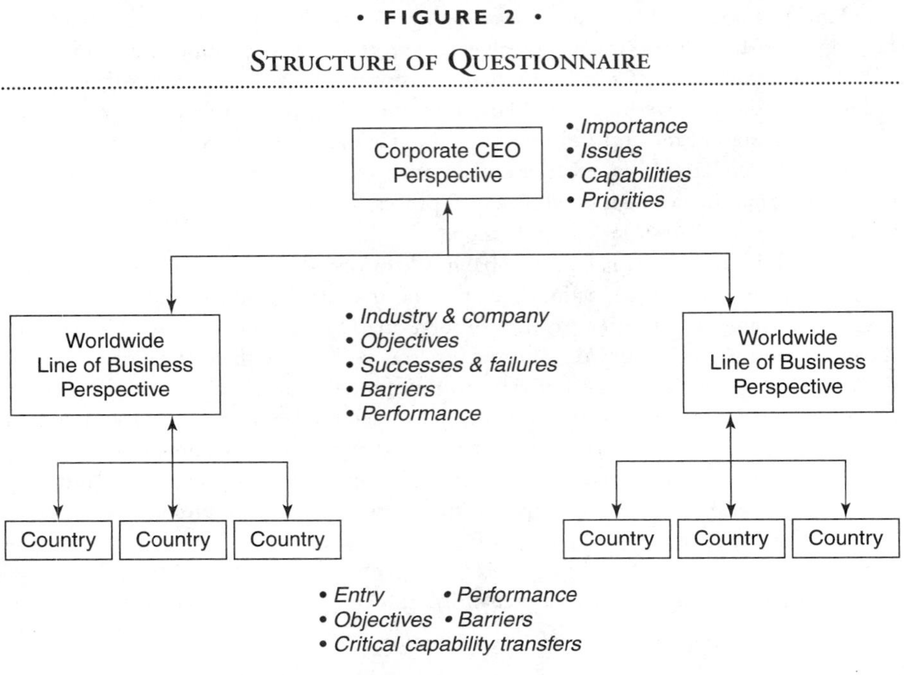

• FIGURE 3 •

COMPANIES IN THE STUDY

NORTH AMERICA HQ	EUROPE HQ	ASIA-PACIFIC HQ
Amoco	Altana	BHP
Amway	Ansaldo	Canon
AMP	Barilla	National Australia Bank
Baxter International	Danfoss	Telstra
Dow Chemical	Fiat	TNT
Du Pont	Finmeccanica	
Eaton	Jotun	
Federal Express	Kværner	
FMC	Lafarge Coppée	
General Motors	Montedison	
Molex	Olivetti	
Pittston	Pirelli	
PPG	Volvo	
Rockwell		
Tektronix		
Tenneco		
Xerox		

interviews with 16 CEOs and 22 senior executives at the line of business head offices and country operations. We used correlation coefficients and multiple regression to estimate the relationships between variables. We also compared the characteristics of foreign operations that were "winners" with those of the "losers."

HOW THE FOREIGN OPERATIONS PERFORMED

One primary measure, Expected versus Actual Performance, was obtained by asking each Line of Business (LOB) head to rate the company's performance in each country relative to the firm's expectations at the time of entry. A rating of 100 meant that expected performance was equal to actual performance. This measure allowed direct comparison of performance across industries and countries, and correlated highly with such traditional measures of performance as sales growth and market share.

The foreign operations varied greatly. Fewer than half had performed satisfactorily relative to expectations at the time of entry. Moreover—and not surprisingly—the spread in performance decreased with the years since entry. This was because the poorest performers were closed down and the companies had time to fix other poor performers.

SUCCESSFUL TRANSFER HAS THE STRONGEST EFFECT ON INTERNATIONAL PERFORMANCE

We examined a wide range of factors that might affect the success of foreign ventures. These included the extent of globalization strategy, the fit of this strategy with globalization drivers, organization structure, barriers to entry, entry objectives and strategy, use of performance measures, human resource practices, and localization of strategy and management. But the effectiveness in transferring critical capabilities was far and away the most important in affecting performance. On average, a 20 percent improvement in transfer effectiveness was associated with a better than 7 percent improvement in performance.

In addition, high performers (the upper third of our sample) scored 22 percent better than low performers (the lower third of our sample) in transfer effectiveness. If the average performer were able to improve its capacity to transfer critical capabilities to the level of the highest performer in our study, the performance improvement would exceed 15 percent. Average transfer capability among all participants was 6.8 on a scale of 0 to 10.

Several of the comments made in the interviews were:

- "If only we knew what the company knows" (a country manager).
- "What parts of the past do we want to use as pivots of the future?"
- "The firm does practice the shared services concept in North America, but not in Europe, though we are looking at this now."

CEOS WANT TO IMPROVE CRITICAL CAPABILITIES

As could be expected, the CEOs repeatedly identified critical capabilities as being among the issues for which their companies most needed improvement. These are shown in Figure 4. As one CEO put it, "It is still a matter of debate, inside and outside our group, as to whether a large company can be effective in leveraging its critical capabilities when entering a market like, say, China." Another CEO saw no easy solution:

> In terms of leveraging our knowledge across and around the Group, we do not have any simple solutions. We try and get our people around the world to work on common problems. . . . [T]hese may be common issues or ones common to a business across countries.

A third said, "We are mediocre, though improving in the exchange of know-how and best practices in manufacturing processes." The CEOs also recognized the

• FIGURE 4 •

IDENTIFIED AREAS MOST IN NEED OF IMPROVEMENT

Strategic capabilities
- Fully exploiting worldwide capabilities
- Acting on changing globalization drivers
- Making moves against competitors around the world

Organizational capabilities
- Developing talent and leadership for innovation and renewal
- Leveraging global capabilities effectively
- Structuring for optimal global performance

Management process capabilities
- Nurturing global management talent
- Transferring best practices
- Stimulating transfer of critical capabilities

competitive imperative to strengthen critical capability transfer. As one stated, "Early on, [our competitor] globalized their R&D capability, giving them a serious advantage."

But some CEOs are beginning to find solutions. Said one of our respondents, "(We are) establishing a more comprehensive and practical 'Corpus of Doctrine' reflecting the Group's experience in, and approaches to, strategy, marketing, operations, analysis, and reporting . . . to facilitate know-how transfer."

MANY CRITICAL CAPABILITIES IDENTIFIED

Figure 5 summarizes the critical capabilities identified by each level of management. CEOs in particular identified the general categories of new product development and technology as their companies' most critical capabilities. Aspects of these included design for manufacturing, time to market, patents and intellectual property, and technology in general. Other critical capabilities, in order of frequency, included partnering and alliance skills, low-cost manufacturing, customer service, product life cycle management, hiring and developing international managers, information technology, speed and flexibility, and quality management. Many of these capabilities were related to each other. One CEO said, "We have three interlinked capabilities: negotiating, developing contracts, and building relationships."

LOB heads were proportionately less concerned about new product development, but it still topped their list. Predictably, they saw operational issues as relatively more important, including capabilities in low-cost manufacturing, marketing, customer service, quality management, sales management, brands and products, channel

• FIGURE 5 •

TYPES OF CRITICAL CAPABILITIES IDENTIFIED AND PERCENTAGE OF RESPONDENTS LISTING EACH

CEO	Line of Business	Country
		Sales management—41%
Product development—67%	Product development—53%	Product development—39%
Brands and products—33%	Low-cost manufacturing—53%	Low-cost manufacturing—32%
Partnering skills—30%	Marketing—29%	Marketing—20%
Low-cost manufacturing—29%		Brands—20%
		Channel—20%
Customer service—22%	Customer service—29%	Customer service—9%
Sales management—13%	Sales management—26%	

management, product life cycle management, and hiring and developing global managers. The critical capabilities can also be very specific to individual industries. An LOB head of a mining company said, "Our critical capabilities are the ability to estimate the prospects for significant reserves and the ability to correctly assess political risks in the regions in which we operate."

The trend toward operational concerns was even more marked for country managers, although new product development was still a major concern. Other critical capabilities at country level were similar to those of the LOB heads.

The dispersion of activities in Figure 5 is noteworthy. Although differences in industries, product markets, and other factors clearly account for some of this spread, there still appears to be widespread confusion around what constitutes a critical capability. For example, "new product development" is defined at too high a level to be meaningful and actionable. Better definitions might be "rapid commercialization of new technologies" or "industry-leading styling."

MISMATCH BETWEEN MANAGEMENT LEVELS

Within individual firms, the level of alignment was less than might be expected from the above picture. CEOs and LOB heads were each asked to identify six critical capabilities. On average, and even with a generous interpretation of similarity, only 2.1 of their selections matched. When country heads were asked to name three critical capabilities, on average only 1.6 of these could also be found in the LOB list. Given this low degree of alignment, it is not surprising that these firms had difficulty determining exactly what critical capabilities to transfer.

Although the respondents did not agree on what comprised critical capabilities in their companies, we were able to establish that the transfer of those capabilities was the most important factor in the success of foreign operations through the statistical analyses relating such transfer to performance. In other words, we did not have to ask respondents directly whether they thought critical capabilities affected performance, but could deduce that from correlation and regression analysis.

HUMAN RESOURCE PRACTICES AS THE KEY METHOD FOR ENHANCING TRANSFER

Certain human resource practices, we found, had a high correlation to the successful transfer of critical capabilities: global compensation systems, transferring managers from country to country, and having worldwide training systems. A 20 percent increase in the effectiveness of each of these processes may lead to an increase of 3 to 5 percent in the effectiveness of critical capability transfer (Figure 6).

At the same time, the use and effectiveness of these processes were all relatively low—in the 3 to 6 range out of a possible 10 (Figure 7). Companies faced many problems in this area. One CEO commented, "People from central 'X-state' [location of company HQ] are very loyal, but they do not like to move." Another CEO said, "I have worked in the international area for almost 40 years. There is no greater need than identifying and nurturing talent for local markets. All U.S. corporations have the same problem."

Some firms were beginning to force international experience. "To reach a certain management level," said one CEO, "it is mandatory to have 'out of country' experience." Other firms were working hard on the problem; one was putting together a skills matrix across its global operations and addressing how to take "a 25-year-old and develop him (or her) into a global manager [via, e.g.,] three functional careers, three geographic careers, and at least two business unit careers." Summarizing this

• FIGURE 6 •

GLOBAL HUMAN RESOURCE PROCESSES HELP CRITICAL CAPABILITY TRANSFER

HR Processes	*A 20% increase in the effectiveness of the HR process may lead to an increase in the effectiveness of critical capability transfers of . . .*
Global compensation systems	5%
Global transfers	3%
Global training	3%

• FIGURE 7 •

AVERAGE RATINGS OF THE USE AND EFFECTIVENESS OF GLOBAL HUMAN RESOURCE PROCESSES

Global HR Process	USE	EFFECTIVENESS
Transferring	5.4	6.0
Training	5.2	5.7
Compensating	5.0	5.6
Evaluating	4.8	5.3
Promoting	5.1	5.3
Hiring	3.6	4.4

Rated on a 0 to 10 scale, in which 0 = "Not used at all/Not

issue, another CEO said, "My top globalization issue is people development and building a learning organization."

The low degree of global coordination of HR processes is not surprising, because country managers have the greatest autonomy in this area. The respondent country managers had more local autonomy in decisions about human resources (7.9 out of 10 overall) than about physical assets, technology, or capital (Figure 8). Among different types of HR processes, country managers did indeed have the lowest autonomy in transferring personnel (6.5). But this relative lack of autonomy was more than offset by very high levels in training (9.0) and evaluating (8.9).

• FIGURE 8 •

DEGREE OF DECISION-MAKING AUTONOMY

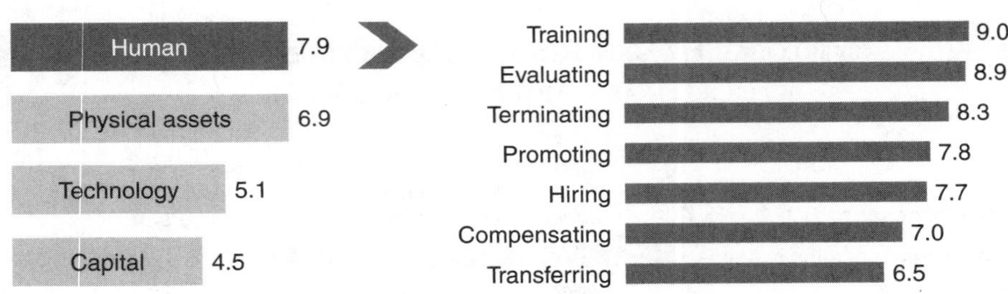

Rated on a 0 to10 scale, in which 0 = "No autonomy" and 10 = "Total autonomy"

Consequently, head office managers can exert only limited influence on global strategy execution and capability transfer when most types of HR decisions are beyond their control. Again, MNCs face the dilemma of a need for local autonomy versus a need for global coordination.

NEED FOR MORE GLOBAL MANAGERS

The companies surveyed certainly recognize the need to change their HR processes. For instance, they all plan to increase the use of global managers relative to local managers (shown in Figure 9). The executives we interviewed made many telling comments:

- "We have to find a way of managing the free flow of talent and necessary skills around the world with the objective of building a competence-based organization."
- "The single most important issue is creating internationalists."
- "The limiting factor for our growth is human capital."
- "How do we seed the samurai, and how should we manage the development and transfer of excellence?"
- "[The company] now insists that its top 50 managers have both international and cross-functional experience."

• FIGURE 9 •

FREQUENCY OF USE OF LOCAL, REGIONAL, AND GLOBAL MANAGERS

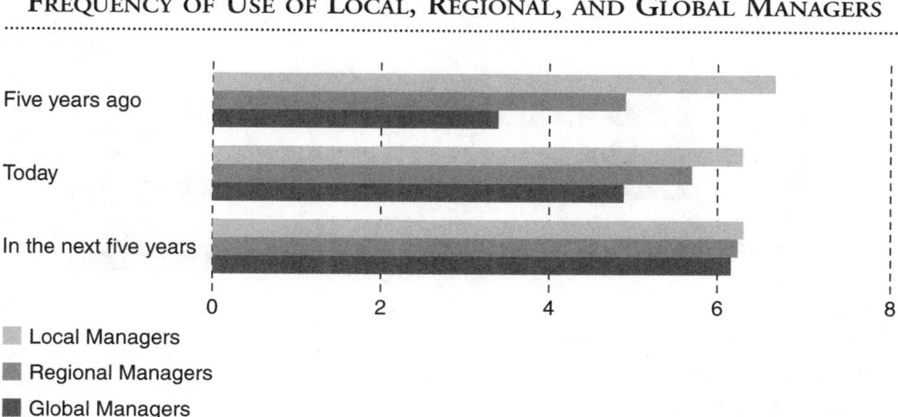

0 to 10 scale (0 = "Not at all," 10 = "Completely")

GLOBAL MANAGEMENT PROCESSES ALSO HELP MAKE THE TRANSFER

In addition to international human resource processes, global management processes in general helped the transfer of critical capabilities. Overall, a 20 percent increase in the use of global, as opposed to regional or local, management processes may lead to a 3 percent increase in the effectiveness of critical capability transfer. The use of global management processes is relatively low today. But companies plan to do much more in this regard and lessen their use of local management processes (Figure 10).

In commenting on the problem, one CEO said, "We fragment the understanding, focus, delivery, and leveraging of our critical capabilities through our information systems, patterns of communication, career paths, management reward systems, and processes of strategy development." Proposing a solution, another CEO said, "We need to weave our critical capabilities into the corporate strategic themes for, and across, each of our business's plans and budgets."

GLOBAL CULTURE PLAYS KEY ROLE

Having a global company culture, rather than regional or local cultures, also plays a powerful role in the transfer of critical capabilities. We found that a 20 percent increase in the extent of having a global culture may lead to a 4 percent increase in the effectiveness of critical capability transfer. Several quotes highlight this effect:

• FIGURE 10 •

FREQUENCY OF USE OF MANAGEMENT PROCESSES

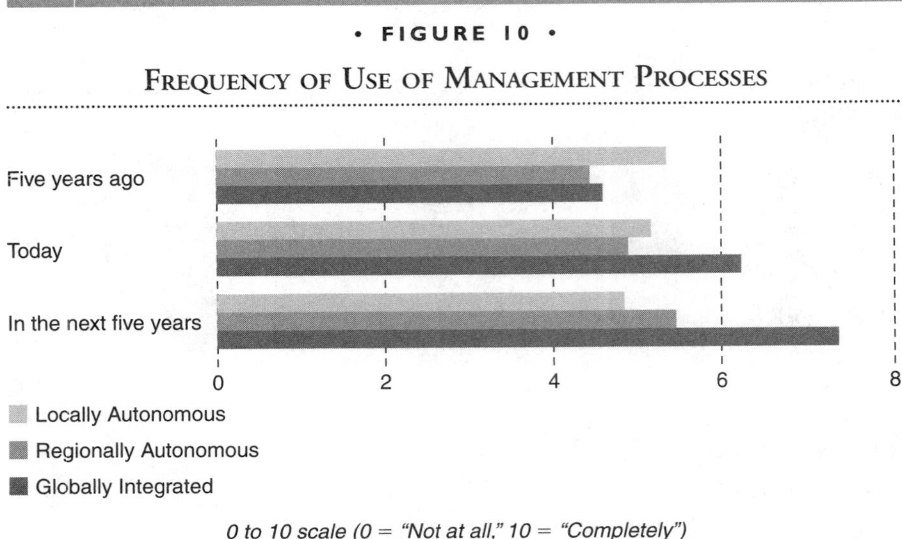

0 to 10 scale (0 = "Not at all," 10 = "Completely")

• FIGURE 11 •

GRADUAL SHIFT TO GLOBAL CULTURE

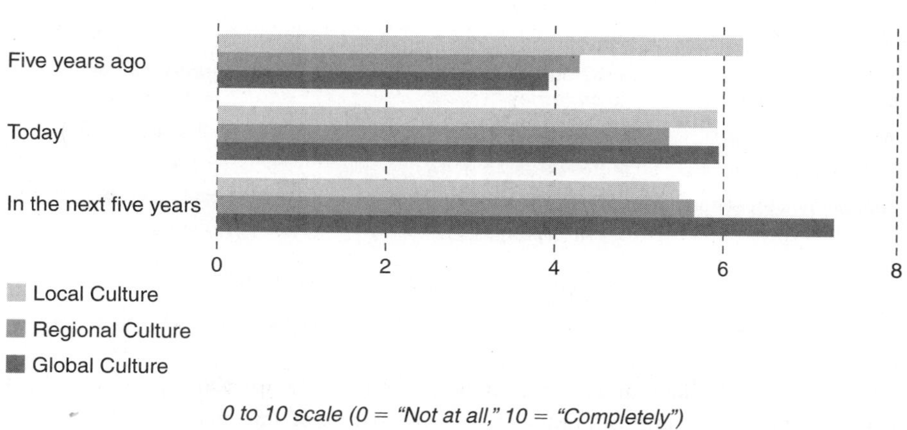

- "A global culture is denationalizing operations and creating a system of values shared by managers around the globe."
- "Culture is the value-setter and lubricator."
- "We get what we measure. We need to change our performance measuring and compensation systems to encourage sharing and teaming."
- "Establishing a common culture across the division is also a key globalization factor."
- "We are more transnational or global than [our competitor] because we grew up as a result of many acquisitions, each with its own culture."

As with global human resources and other management processes, the companies were gradually shifting from a local orientation to more of a regional and international orientation. Within the next five years, and compared with five years ago, the companies planned to reverse the dominance of local culture relative to global culture (Figure 11).

OTHER METHODS OF TRANSFER

We also asked country managers about three key methods for transferring critical capabilities: rotation of staff, dedicated global teams, and management meetings. As shown in Figure 12, these methods averaged a rating of only 5.2 (on a scale of 0 to 10) in use for transferring critical capabilities from headquarters or other units to a country operation. They rated an even lower average of 4.4 for transfer from country operations to headquarters or other units.

• FIGURE 12 •

USE OF TRANSFER MECHANISMS LOCALLY TO GLOBALLY AND VICE VERSA

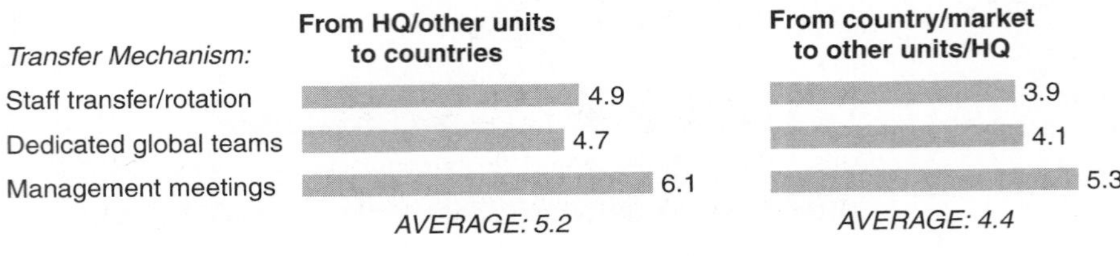

0 to 10 scale (0 = "Not at all" and 10 = "Completely")

When asked about other methods of transfer, the country managers identified many different mechanisms. Some entailed the sharing of information: written communications, memos to share lessons, newsletters and magazines, release of information, data transfer, and information technology. One CEO said, "Designing and installing an effective global IT network is critical if we are to keep in touch, share, and deliver the best—internally and to our customers." But technology will not be the sole answer. Another CEO commented, "I do not see a cybernetic revolution ahead in addressing the issue of knowledge (including best practice) sharing."

Other transfer mechanisms related to training and education, and included training at home country operations, business academies, dedicated courses, and top-down training and implementation. Coordination mechanisms comprised cross-sector umbrella teams, a global executive committee that met monthly, application segment teams, and a global customer management process. As one CEO put it, "We have started the formation and use of 'Country Councils' whereby they bring the managers of the different businesses in a country together to share views but without getting tangled up in the details of each other's business."

Direct involvement by HQ also was cited. This took the form of strategy reviews, country visits, and central and regional control. Both technical support and head office support in general were also mentioned. Centers of excellence are also being used. One CEO mentioned. "We may try and use a 'Centers of Excellence' approach for technology and best practice." Finally, simply having a customer focus or market focus could also be of help.

INCENTIVES FOR ADAPTING OR SHARING CRITICAL CAPABILITIES

Some companies provided incentives for adapting or sharing critical capabilities. Rewards to local managers for adapting corporate critical capabilities to the local market included:

- management incentive programs and other financial rewards;
- recognition programs such as corporate quality awards; and
- praise and recognition in performance appraisals.

One company went so far as to have specific performance objectives defined for implementing capabilities worldwide. Similar, though fewer, rewards were given to local managers for sharing capabilities from their country with headquarters or other units. Being recognized for their local capabilities seemed to be particularly motivating.

Many firms, however, had no specific incentives. And many local managers recognized the operating and strategic benefits of adapting corporate critical capabilities without additional reward. In actuality, there may often be significant disincentives to transfer, such as when a disproportionate level of resource investment must be borne by the capability "source" unit vis-à-vis the "recipient," or in the midst of political concerns about helping a future rival for promotion.

METHODS OF GAINING COOPERATION

Many companies used direct mechanisms not only for the transfer of critical capabilities, but also for gaining the cooperation of country managers in global and regional strategies. Of the methods we asked about, approval of local budgets was at the top of the list—rating 8.0 in the extent of its use (Figure 13)—followed by compensation for job performance, evaluation of job performance, allocation of production capacity and volume, and financial contribution from headquarters. Executives also mentioned various other methods, some of which were formal (global policy directions, strategy integration systems, approval of strategic plans, capital authorization, global customer management, business management councils, international project organization, personnel selection) and some informal (training and follow-up, seeding personnel, esprit de corps, personal contact and relationships, and constant international networking).

• FIGURE 13 •

HQ Ways of Gaining Local Cooperation

Extent of use of . . .	
Approval of local budgets	8.0
Compensation for job performance	7.6
Evaluation of job performance	7.5
Allocation of production capacity/volume	4.8
Financial contribution from HQ	4.7

0 to 10 scale (0 = "Never used" and 10 = "Always used")

These direct and indirect methods of headquarters control can be seen as counterweights to the autonomy enjoyed by country managers. Percy Barnevik, the CEO of Asea Brown Boveri (not a participant in this study), frequently proclaims the high degree of autonomy given to local managers in his company. Less publicized is the fact that ABB's head office managers use the allocation of production volume as a powerful weapon to gain compliance. Most of the industries, such as power generation systems, in which ABB's businesses participate suffer from excess capacity. Moreover, in a given line of business, ABB usually operates factories in more than one country. Getting a production order thus makes a huge difference in whether a local ABB manager will make his or her budget for the year. So ABB's head office may speak softly but it carries a very big stick! Most MNCs have similar secret weapons for influencing the hearts and minds of their local managers.

If you truly want to be successful at globalizing your company, you need to establish permanent mechanisms for the transfer of critical capabilities. Start with understanding what is critical in your industries and lines of business. Then create and improve those capabilities, identify and recognize the sources and carriers, identify which types are needed in which countries, transfer and adapt them there, and embed them into your foreign operations.

Of course, a continuing feedback and learning loop is essential; Figure 14 summarizes this process. Many of the executives in our study have pointed out what is needed:

- "We know our critical capabilities but have not done a good job in defining, communicating, and installing them."
- "We must be more explicit, exhaustive, and rigorous in communicating, educating, and practicing our critical capabilities."
- "Developing the understanding of how to transfer the lessons learned from one market to another [is crucial]."
- "View the company as a competence-based organization that delivers highest market impact through leveraging best practices worldwide."

• FIGURE 14 •

ESTABLISHING PERFORMANCE MECHANISMS FOR TRANSFERRING CRITICAL CAPABILITIES

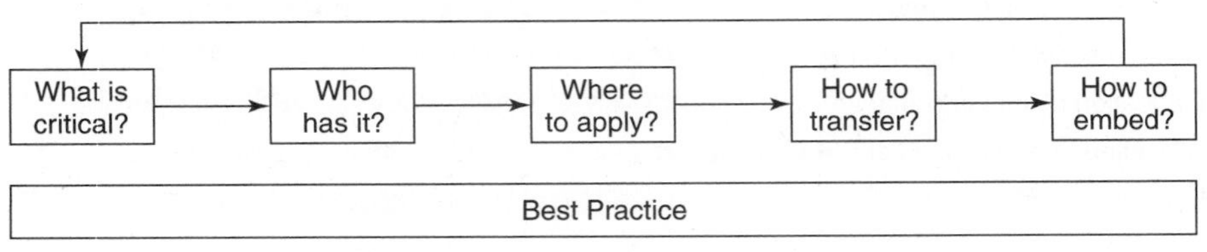

You also need to recognize that HQ is no longer the owner of critical capabilities. Instead, it is increasingly a facilitator of their transfer. Critical capabilities may be created, adapted, and transferred by many different units: headquarters, line of business, country operation, business process, centers of excellence, teams, or a shared service center. Putting it all together can mean creating a multilevel spider web of transfer capabilities. As the CEOs put it:

- "We have now decided to change from informal networking to a formal comprehensive way of capturing, measuring, and installing best practices around our world. . . . In fact, it's not a choice, but a *must* if we are to be a leader."
- "In terms of leveraging our knowledge across and around the Group, we don't have any simple solutions. . . . [W]e try to get people from around the world to work on common problems. . . . [T]hese may be common issues or ones common to a business across countries."
- "Our focus is on the management and development of the intellect, information, and tools for tailoring, flexing, leading, and differentiating."
- "A virtual HQ is rapidly replacing a 'solid center HQ' as competence centers and responsibilities are spread across the network into the operating units."

Returning to the overall framework for this study, we can see that the global transfer of critical capabilities constitutes an essential step in moving from globalization potential to realized international competitive advantage. Even in light of the many ways to effect this transfer, in every case managers will have to work very hard to make it happen.

References

Christopher A. Bartlett and Sumantra Ghoshal, *Managing Across Borders: The Transnational Solution* (Boston: Harvard Business School Press, 1989).

Andrew Bartmess and Keith Cerny, "Building Competitive Advantage Through A Global Network Of Capabilities," *California Management Review,* Winter 1993, pp. 78–103.

Joseph H. Boyett and Henry P. Conn, *Maximum Performance Management: How To Manage And Compensate People To Meet World Competition,* 2nd ed. (Lakewood, CO: Glenbridge, 1993).

Joseph H. Boyett and Henry P. Conn, *Workplace 2000* (New York, Dutton, 1991; Plume 1992).

Gary Hamel and C.K. Prahalad, *Competing For The Future* (Boston: Harvard Business School Press, 1994).

J.K. Johansson and George S. Yip, "Exploiting Globalization Potential: U.S. And Japanese Strategies," *Strategic Management Journal,* October 1994, pp. 579–601.

Michael E. Porter, "Changing Patterns Of International Competition," *California Management Review,* Winter 1986, pp. 9–40.

C.K. Prahalad and Yves L. Doz. *The Multinational Mission: Balancing Local Demands And Global Vision* (New York: Free Press, 1987).

C.K. Prahalad and Gary Hamel, "The Core Competence Of The Corporation," *Harvard Business Review,* May–June 1990, pp. 79–91.

Joseph L. Raudabaugh, "Asian Investment: Lessons From The Japanese Experience," *Planning Review,* January–February 1995, pp. 38–40.

George Stalk, Philip Evans, and Lawrence E. Schulman, "Competing On Capabilities: The New Rules Of Corporate Strategy," *Harvard Business Review,* March–April 1992, pp. 57–69.

George S. Yip, *Total Global Strategy: Managing For Worldwide Competitive Advantage* (Englewood Cliffs, NJ: Prentice Hall, 1992).

SUBSIDIARY INITIATIVES TO DEVELOP NEW MARKETS

Julian Birkinshaw and Nick Fry

In 1980, NCR's subsidiary in Dundee, Scotland, was on the verge of closure. The operation had been established as a second-source manufacturer of NCR products, but a combination of technological changes in the marketplace, along with internal problems, had caused it to shrink from 6,500 employees in 1969 to 770 in 1980. Moreover, Dundee's most promising product, the automatic teller machine (ATM), was struggling in the British marketplace because of serious quality problems.

Jim Adamson, the newly appointed general manager, had a mandate to turn the operation around—or close it. At an operational level, Adamson worked on improving manufacturing quality and restoring the confidence of major customers. At a more strategic level, he began to develop a vision for Dundee as NCR's strategic center for the ATM business. Product development responsibility officially lay with headquarters (HQ) in Dayton, Ohio, but Adamson began directing his resources toward upgrading and renewing the Dundee product line to meet the emerging demands of its key customers, the big British banks. In the face of active resistance from the development group in Dayton, Adamson pursued a delicate strategy of cooperating with people there, while continuing privately to sponsor Dundee's research program.

His persistence paid off. In 1982, Dundee launched a successful product upgrade and, eighteen months later, a next-generation ATM that set new standards in functionality, reliability, and serviceability. By 1984, Dundee had 20 percent of market share worldwide, and by 1985, headquarters officially transferred responsibility for the global ATM business to Dundee. By 1986, Dundee boasted 35 percent of worldwide shipments, surpassing competitors IBM and Diebold.

More than a good example of turnaround management and strong leadership, the Dundee success story provides insight into the changing relationship between

---

Julian Birkinshaw is assistant professor, Institute of International Business, Stockholm School of Economics. Nick Fry is a professor, Richard Ivey School of Business, University of Western Ontario.

headquarters and subsidiaries in large multinational corporations (MNCs). During a five-year period, NCR Dundee developed from being a second-source manufacturer, totally reliant on Dayton for product specifications, to a self-sufficient operation with leading-edge expertise in ATM development. More important, the turnaround went far beyond what corporate management had requested; indeed, many people in the head office had resisted Adamson's shift into product development, hanging on to their idea of Dayton as the global center for ATM development. Ultimately, it was Adamson's deliberately unconventional and somewhat subversive approach that provided the impetus for Dundee's resurgence—and led to NCR's leading position in the global ATM industry.[1]

The NCR Dundee case is typical of what we call *subsidiary initiative:* the proactive and deliberate pursuit of a new business opportunity by a subsidiary company, undertaken with a view to expand the subsidiary's scope of responsibility in a manner consistent with the MNC's strategic goals. Subsidiary initiative is important for two reasons. First, it is the principal means by which MNCs tap in to new opportunities in markets around the world. Second, it enhances operational efficiency through internal competition among units. But, at the same time, subsidiary initiative is an elusive beast. Many of the MNCs we studied actively discouraged entrepreneurial efforts in their subsidiaries, while others agreed to the concept in principle but hindered its development in practice. Subsidiary managers, it appears, need a lot of tactical savvy, persistence, and luck if they are to pursue initiatives effectively. As one manager described it, a "corporate immune system" lurks in most large organizations.[2] Its role is to kill off intruding initiatives for fear that they might infect the rest of the organism.

In this paper, we report on a four-year research study of subsidiary initiatives in five countries.[3] Our study examined the strategies that subsidiary managers use to conquer the corporate immune system, as well as the types of resistance they encountered. Our research also revealed a subtle shift in the locus of responsibility between headquarters and subsidiaries. Initiative is a sign that subsidiary managers are beginning to take responsibility for their operations' destiny, which in turn suggests the need for a more central role for subsidiary units in the implementation of corporate strategy. Initiative activity also suggests new management issues for parent-company executives, as they reappraise their innate suspicion of maverick subsidiary managers and learn how to exploit, rather than stifle, latent entrepreneurship in their far-flung operations.

TWO DISTINCT FORMS OF SUBSIDIARY INITIATIVE

Early in our research, we could see that subsidiary initiative has two forms (see Figures 1 and 2).[4] One form—which the NCR Dundee case typifies—was *externally focused.* It involved the identification of new or enhanced business opportunities through interaction with customers, suppliers, and government entities in the subsidiary's marketplace. The other form was *internally focused,* involving the identification of new business opportunities that the subsidiary could take on within the existing boundaries

• FIGURE 1 •

THE EXTERNAL INITIATIVE PROCESS

	Strategies of Subsidiary Managers	Reactions of HQ Managers	Outcome (if successful)
Opportunity identified outside the corporation, through interaction with customers, suppliers, competitors, or government bodies →	Small-scale investment, typically without blessing of HQ →	Initial ignorance	Development of new business activity
Conditions of decentralized resource allocation and high subsidiary autonomy →	Development of buy-in among customers ←	Scepticism once initiative is presented; questions regarding value of project and subsidiary's ability to pursue it	Leverage of subsidiary capabilities on an international basis
	Request for corporate investment and support once viability of project established	Competition from other units if project is attractive	

of the corporation. For example, we identified cases of subsidiaries bidding internally for planned, global-scale investments, as well as subsidiaries identifying poorly performing HQ-based activities that they could take over.

The common theme we saw in both external and internal initiatives was the entrepreneurial component. First, we saw the need for proactive, pushy, and sometimes Machiavellian tactics on the part of subsidiary managers as they sought to gain currency for their projects in headquarters. We also typically saw a skeptical reaction from

• FIGURE 2 •

THE INTERNAL INITIATIVE PROCESS

	Strategies of Subsidiary Managers	Reactions of HQ Managers	Outcome (if successful)
Opportunity identified inside the corporation: activities currently performed by other units; planned corporate investments →	High levels of selling of project to HQ managers →	Initial disinterest and scepticism	Rationalization of existing activities; removal of inefficient practices
Conditions of centralized resource allocation, low subsidiary autonomy, and strong relationships with HQ managers →	Use of personal relationships (where present) and demonstration of subsidiary's capabilities to build credibility for project ←	If project appears attractive, desire to evaluate alternative proposals	Optimal location for new investments
		Explicit process of approval by funding committee	

HQ managers, for whom subsidiary initiative was something of an oxymoron. But, in many respects, the two forms of initiative were very different. They involved distinctly different tactics, faced different forms of resistance, and had significantly different impacts on the MNC's management as a whole.

EXTERNAL INITIATIVES

External initiatives arose typically out of customers' unmet demands in the local marketplace. In the NCR Dundee case, Barclays and the other major British banks were investing heavily in ATMs. The Dundee development group worked with them to incorporate their product needs into the next generation of ATMs. We saw several variants on this theme:

- In 1991, the business development manager at GE Canada responded to a government-sponsored program seeking energy-efficient lighting in federal buildings by starting a new enterprise called GE Energy Management.[5]
- In 1992, Pharma's British subsidiary established a joint venture with a small U.K. company to develop a new technology for transmitting drugs through the skin.[6]
- Using its international industry contacts, Hewlett-Packard's Panacom subsidiary (in Waterloo, Canada) identified an emerging market for the "X terminal," a RISC-chip-based workstation, in 1989.

No less critical than the identification of an interesting business opportunity was the need for a relatively high degree of autonomy in the subsidiary. Faced with the strong likelihood of rejection if the project were presented to HQ management in its embryonic form, subsidiary managers preferred to do the initial development work with their own funds. During the 1980s, for example, Hewlett-Packard (Canada) had access to development funds for country-specific projects. Those funds facilitated development of the X terminal, as well as several other projects. Many subsidiaries didn't have this level of autonomy, however. Some were able to assemble skunk-works groups that explored the viability of their ideas on their own time, but others, because they had no access to development funds, saw their promising ideas languish.

A champion for the initiative always emerged in the early stages. Typically he or she was the individual who identified the business opportunity in the first place, although sometimes the subsidiary's general manager took ownership of the project because of its importance. Initiative champions adopted a surprisingly consistent strategy. First, they tested the idea in a small way, using subsidiary resources and without the knowledge of headquarters. Then, as the project took shape, they sought out allies—typically local customers who were interested in buying the product or service, but sometimes, also, personal contacts or mentors in the home office. Finally, once they had demonstrated their project's viability, they presented it formally to HQ managers and asked for investment funds and support. We saw this basic model in a variety of guises:

- At NCR Dundee, Jim Adamson initiated his product development efforts against the will of the R&D group in Dayton, but once Dundee's second-generation product was so obviously successful, HQ management bowed to the inevitable and transferred responsibility for ATM development to Dundee.
- In 1985, Hewlett-Packard (Canada)'s former president Malcolm Gissing funded a small development group in Calgary to develop an oil-well data management system. The group existed as an "orphan" for seven years, without a line of reporting through one of HP's business groups. It finally achieved corporate legitimacy in 1992, when it became a business unit within the Test and Measurement division.
- In 1987, a small group of engineers in Honeywell Canada bootlegged a PC interface for Honeywell's TDC3000 process control system. The system, known as PCNM, gained support quickly with a number of Canadian customers. Subsequently, the development group gained permission from HQ management in Phoenix to build PCNM as a standard product worldwide.

As these vignettes suggest, other parts of the corporation almost universally opposed the subsidiary's initiative. We termed this collective resistance the corporate immune system to illustrate its apparent intention to kill off the intruding initiative. The resistance to initiative took a wide variety of forms:

- Pharma's British subsidiary encountered outright opposition from a competing development group at headquarters. The group even vetoed the project, but fortunately the British development group was able to arrange alternative funding through the company's marketing arm.
- Two HP (Canada) initiatives, the X terminal and the Calgary development group, were challenged by U.S.-based divisions that were undertaking development work in similar areas. In both cases, the U.S. division argued that the development fell under its charter and urged that the Canadian operation be terminated.
- GE Canada's energy management business was almost closed down when its parent division in the United States, GE Supply, rationalized its operations in 1994. The problem was not that the energy management business was performing badly; the parent simply saw it as too small and too far from GE Supply's core business area to survive the rationalization.

The combination of outright opposition, internal competition, and passive indifference was a challenging set of obstacles for the initiative champions in our study. Just over half the initiatives survived this process, but that probably overstates the situation because it represents only those stories that subsidiary managers shared with us willingly. Our research focused on the latter parts of a long and mostly invisible process. Surely, many other initiatives fell at the first hurdle—or never left the starting blocks.

For those initiatives that survived, however, the rewards were impressive. NCR Dundee became a $1 billion operation; HP (Canada)'s X terminal business reached sales of $120 million four years after its inception; and GE Canada established a leading market position in the emerging energy efficiency industry. For the corporation as a whole, the rewards were multifaceted. Most obviously, NCR, HP, GE, and others gained new and vibrant businesses in emerging areas. More subtly, they also benefited from the development and maturation of one of their foreign subsidiaries. Some might view this as a mixed blessing, but if we see business as becoming ever more global, then the nurturing of new and valuable capabilities in outlying parts of the multinational network can only strengthen the corporation's global reach.

INTERNAL INITIATIVES

Internal initiatives arose from opportunities that innovative subsidiary managers identified within the corporation. The subsidiary managers in our study understood their own unit's strengths and weaknesses well and frequently were on the lookout for new activities elsewhere in the corporation that dovetailed with their capabilities. The following examples illustrate their ideas' scope:

- IBM began manufacturing PCs in Greenock, Scotland, in 1982. Toward the end of the 1980s, plant managers were looking for ways to extend the scope of their operations. In 1991, they identified a small monitor development group near London that could be a logical complement to their manufacturing and succeeded in getting it relocated to Greenock. Subsequently, they identified order fulfillment and help center functions that could cover all Europe and be centralized in Greenock. Both initiatives were successful.
- Back in 1972, as a Honeywell Canada factory manager toured the plant of a sister subsidiary in the United States that made a control switch, he saw an opportunity. He proposed to headquarters that the Canadian plant take over the manufacture of the control switch with responsibility for sales throughout North America.
- In 1991, Monsanto Canada's top management identified an interesting proposal in the corporation's long-range plan. Monsanto was developing a new formulation for its best-selling agrochemical product, with the intention of bringing it to market around 1996. Seizing the opportunity, Canadian management argued—successfully—that the investment should be made in Canada because of the country's strong agricultural industry.

Two conditions facilitated the development of internal initiatives. First, and in marked contrast to external initiatives, internal initiatives needed relatively tight integration into the corporate system. Subsidiary managers emphasized that it was important that they be tied into the corporate network, so they could hear about investment opportunities early. As one manager said, "The best way to win a competitive investment is to write the specifications." One 3M Canada manager heard about an embryonic investment plan accidentally on a routine visit to St. Paul, Minnesota. That lucky break led to a $20 million investment in Canada.

Second, the subsidiary had to have, or be prepared to work hard for, a reputation as a trustworthy and reliable operation. Typically, subsidiary managers confronted an implicit challenge: Why would we risk investing in a foreign country when we can stick with tried-and-tested solutions closer to home? Often they responded by trying to mitigate the risk by capitalizing on personal contacts at headquarters. In other cases, such as at IBM Scotland, initiative success grew after many years of manufacturing excellence. In the absence of contacts or reputation, however, a subsidiary had very limited prospects.

Unlike external initiatives, which typically avoided confrontation with HQ managers in the early stages, internal initiatives had to pursue a more orthodox line of attack through the formal lines of authority. The Monsanto Canada initiative led to the establishment of a group whose role was to assess four possible locations for the new agrochemical investment. Similarly, 3M Canada pursued several initiatives aimed at winning new manufacturing investments in Canada, each of which had to pass through two operating committees in the United States. The process was methodical and incremental, with subsidiary management gradually moving up through the corporate hierarchy, building support and commitment from all the key individuals. Frequently, this process took as long as a year. In one case, the initiative was put on hold for two years until the arrival of a new manufacturing director in the United States who was more amenable to the proposal.

We observed two additional tactics with regard to internal initiatives. One was a two-pronged approach. The initiative champion made a formal proposal through the official lines of authority. At the same time, the subsidiary president utilized his or her personal contacts at a much higher level in the home office to build legitimacy for the proposal and smooth its course through the system. The second tactic involved the use of a quid pro quo—some sort of concession by the subsidiary to compensate the losing party. The best example of this was Honeywell Canada's proposal in 1986 that it become the sole North American manufacturer of zone valves and "fan-and-limit" devices. The proposal encountered strong resistance from the plant in Minnesota that was making those products for the United States. The two parties negotiated a deal whereby the Toronto plant would swap its other manufacturing responsibilities for the exclusive production of zone valves and fan-and-limit devices. Both plants ended up shedding a few jobs, and both emerged with higher volumes and more efficient operations.

Internal initiatives were competitive by nature. Either the subsidiary was challenging other units for a new investment, or it was proposing a transfer that would leave the previous incumbent short. Resistance from the corporate immune systems was inevitable, therefore, and it took a variety of forms:

- The first line of defense was passive disinterest—If we ignore it, maybe it will go away. Honeywell Canada's initial proposal for a manufacturing rationalization came back with "superficial comments." As one manager noted, people considered it a "strategic plan for the top shelf, not something to incite quantum change."
- Skepticism about the subsidiary's abilities was the second line of defense, along with a suggestion to consider other options. Monsanto Canada faced this

reaction initially when it proposed locating the new agrochemical investment in Canada, but through an innovative design, it was able to demonstrate a superior expected rate of return over the competing location in the United States.

- Outright resistance was the third line of defense. In one case, the magnitude of the loss that the U.S. operation faced provoked strong arguments to halt the initiative. As one manager recalled, "There was an extreme amount of local resistance—marketing, engineering, everybody. How could you ship your son to the foster child, how could you do that? Look at all the things that could go wrong. We've earned the right to continue."

At first glance, the outcome from internal initiatives was less spectacular than that from external initiatives. For IBM Scotland, the result was an "extended value chain" from development to market support. For 3M Canada, it was a robust, export-oriented manufacturing operation. For Monsanto Canada, it was a significant greenfield investment in the heart of the company's large prairie market. In each case, the net impact for the corporation as a whole appeared small. No new products resulted, and no immediate new customers. The cake was simply split in a different way, with the subsidiary getting a larger slice.

But a simple analysis of the configuration of activities before and after the initiative doesn't tell the whole story. As Gordon Brown, the controller of IBM's Greenock plant commented, "By extending the value chain and linking various activities together in one location, we saved millions of dollars, improved customer satisfaction, and increased market share." In essence, the process itself created a new vitality in the initiative-taking subsidiary. Subsequent improvements in performance were often spectacular.

The enduring value of internal initiatives was more subtle. Subsidiary managers were like entrepreneurs, looking for inefficient practices within the multinational system and proposing solutions to better them. For example, companies often retain their internal sourcing relationships because they have always done things that way. But guaranteed sales can make a plant lazy, and before long the internal customer is putting up with a substandard product or an inflated price from its supplier. Internal initiatives provide a mechanism for changing inefficient sourcing relationships. And their threat fosters a more challenging environment, which keeps manufacturing operations on their toes. The same principle applies to other value-adding activities. For example, we saw several cases of product management jobs being shifted from the United States to Canada because a strong case was made that the job would be handled more efficiently there.

TOWARD A MODEL OF INTERNAL COMPETITION

Our study suggests two potentially important roles for foreign subsidiaries. The first is driven by external initiative and falls under the category of *market development.* The role is well documented in the literature.[7] The subsidiary both identifies and acts on new business opportunities in its local market. The second role is less well understood.

We call it *network optimization* because the subsidiary seeks out and eliminates inefficient activities within the multinational network. Internal initiative, of course, drives the process of network optimization. We believe that some subsidiaries, by virtue of their history, their local environment, or their management, will pursue market development roles, while others, for equally circumstantial reasons, will pursue network optimization roles. A third group might choose neither role, but we believe that many more could move toward one or the other quite successfully.

The network optimization model has some far-reaching implications. First, it suggests that many value-adding activities that MNCs are undertaking are "contestable," that is, potentially, they could be performed by a number of different units. Of course, a lot of activities are firmly embedded in their local environment, or they are so large and asset-specific that they could not be practically moved. But, in the course of our study, as we saw examples of manufacturing, development, logistics, marketing, and business management activities change locations, we concluded that much of what is done inside the MNC is neutral with regard to physical location. Moreover, increasingly, subsidiaries are seeking to "win" some of the more mobile activities that are not locked into a single location. The trend, therefore, is toward internal competition as a mechanism through which activities are allocated and reallocated within the MNC.

We don't want to overstate this point because we are aware of the inertia that inhibits a high level of fluidity within the corporate network, as well as the need for collaborative relationships among units. But we see a number of trends that will push MNCs more and more toward an organizational model based on internal competition. One is the greater globalization of business, which reduces the cost of product and capital flows across borders. Another is the growing use of internal benchmarking as a way to highlight the relative efficiency levels of different units. This trend is particularly critical in Europe, where many MNCs are still going through the painful process of rationalizing their manufacturing networks. A third is the growing level of initiative on the part of subsidiary managers, along with internal investment agencies in pursuit of "mobile" investment.

Faced with such changes, many subsidiary managers we interviewed were thinking hard about their futures. They were asking themselves, "What is my unit's unique value in this corporation? What do we do better than anyone else?" They were looking for what we might call their *sustainable competitive advantage* vis-à-vis their *internal competitors.* Two examples clarify this idea:

- Motorola's East Kilbride, Scotland, operation was one of sixteen around the world that fabricated silicon wafers for semiconductors—and one of the corporation's best performers. All the key performance measures, such as cost, service, and quality were easily compared, so obviously the company made new investments in the top-performing sites. East Kilbride's managers had a clear goal, therefore: to stay ahead of their internal competitors on the most important performance metrics. If they could do that, their operation would receive new investment when times were good and avoid closure when times were tough.
- Honeywell's Scottish subsidiary in Newhouse manufactured a range of control valves and related items for the European market. During the 1970s and early

> 1980s, control valves were mechanical devices, but Newhouse's general manager realized the impending shift toward electronic devices and invested discretionary funds in the development of an electronic manufacturing capability. When, in 1991, corporate management decided to invest in a global-scale facility for electronic fan coils, Newhouse was the obvious location because all the necessary capabilities were already in place.

East Kilbride's strategy was to be the lowest-cost/highest-quality source for silicon wafers; Newhouse chose to differentiate itself from its sister plants around the world by investing in a new technology.[8] Both strategies appeared to create sustainable positions for the subsidiary. More important, both offered clearly defined benefits to the corporate parents. When viewed this way, initiative offers a win-win solution; subsidiary growth also contributes to the MNC's competitive advantage. However, HQ and subsidiary managers' views are not always in harmony. Next we examine some perceptions—mostly those of HQ managers—which engendered uneasiness whenever we discussed subsidiary initiative, and which underlay the resistance we observed in our case studies.

THE DANGERS IN INITIATIVE: TWO CONTRARY VIEWS

In the course of our research, we observed many instances in which there were no signs of subsidiary initiative, and we heard many opposing arguments to our view that MNCs should encourage subsidiary initiative. The arguments took two basic forms.

"SOMETIMES ACCEPTABLE"

The first argument saw subsidiary initiative as acceptable under certain conditions. For example, most corporations accepted that different subsidiaries have different roles—some are strategic centers, some have contributory roles, others are just implementers of corporate strategy. Using such an approach, some people argued that only those subsidiaries at the more "evolved" end of the spectrum should take initiative. Those units, they argued, had the capabilities on which to base further development, and the management expertise necessary to drive initiatives to completion. The rest should focus on their implementational roles.

We found considerable evidence to support this perspective. Just under half the subsidiaries we surveyed claimed to have pursued some form of initiative in the past five years; the rest saw themselves as implementers. When asked why they had not pursued initiatives, typically they answered, "We focus exclusively on meeting the needs of our local customers," or "It is not appropriate for us at this stage," or "It is very difficult because of the level of centralization in the corporation." Clearly, there are fundamental differences between the two groups that are based at least in part on the level of the subsidiary's development.

But a difficult question arises: How does a passive subsidiary transform itself into an initiative-taking one? Evidently, there is a development process that subsidiaries go through over time, in which they gradually build up resources, take on more and more responsibilities, and build their credibility within the corporation. Our evidence suggests that initiative is an important step in the development process. However, HQ executives may actively resist it. Initiative, after all, is easy to view as insubordination, which is galling for a corporate parent accustomed to a more docile and obedient subsidiary.

The "growing pains" experienced by Pharma's U.K. subsidiary were typical in this regard. This subsidiary saw itself as providing strategic leadership in one area of drug development, while managers at headquarters saw it as taking a much more modest marketing and drug-testing role. As a result, the two sides clashed repeatedly during a five-year period. The subsidiary proposed a series of initiatives, and business unit managers at the home office stalled, challenged, or rejected them all. The process was "exhausting and frustrating" for both sides, and, after five years, no clear progress had been made toward a more harmonious relationship. The situation at 3M Canada was more constructive. There, management started by taking on small manufacturing operations that U.S. plants didn't want. Gradually, 3M Canada built up its manufacturing capabilities, which led to some measure of credibility south of the border. Eventually, the subsidiary had the self-confidence and legitimacy to pursue more significant initiatives.

There is another problem with an approach that sees some subsidiaries as initiative takers and others as passive implementers. If the objective of initiative is to identify and pursue new opportunities, how can corporate executives know in advance where those opportunities will arise? If the Japanese, German, and British subsidiaries are charged with market development and network optimization, what happens to the great new business opportunity that the Italian manager spots? We believe that every subsidiary needs to have a latent entrepreneurial role, so they can pursue opportunities wherever they arise. This does not mean letting every subsidiary wander off to pursue its pet project, but it does mean that corporate systems need to help long shots find their way through corporate barriers.

We want to dwell on this point a bit because it's usually the least understood. Taken to the extreme, an organizational system that encourages initiative could end up in anarchy. Initiatives could spring up in areas that lay far beyond the corporation's business domain, and head-office managers could be inundated with proposals that made little or no strategic sense. We take a more measured approach. Clearly, MNCs need control systems to constrain the number of poorly thought-out initiatives, but, increasingly, such systems should be based on the development of a shared understanding of the corporation's strategic priorities, rather than on intervention into subsidiary affairs.

The concept is similar to that of employee empowerment. The corporation gives subsidiary managers the tools they need to manage their operation effectively, along with a clear indication of the boundaries of their responsibilities. Within those limits, they have free rein to pursue opportunities as they see fit, on the assumption that they understand their operation and the local marketplace better than executives sitting in a distant head office. The subsidiary assumes new roles and responsibilities, therefore, rather than receiving assignments from above—an important distinction.[9] Control systems are necessary to make it work, but the philosophy of empowerment underlying this model shifts the headquarters–subsidiary relationship from one of mutual suspicion and interference toward one of trust and shared destiny.

"PURE OPPORTUNISM"

Another opposition to initiative that we encountered was even less accommodating. Some managers felt that subsidiary initiative was simply more trouble than it was worth. One HQ manager recounted an unfortunate episode in which a subsidiary manager in his business area had undertaken a series of investments that he insisted were necessary to build market presence, but they had led to spiraling costs and slow decision making. The HQ manager viewed that as pure opportunism and "empire building." Since then he has shifted toward a system of fairly tight control over subsidiary expenditures.

That position is difficult to counter because there are occasional cases of empire building, where the subsidiary manager's initiative is not consistent with the corporation's best interests. One can never be sure whether a subsidiary manager is acting entrepreneurially or opportunistically. The interpretation will depend a lot on whether there is a strong level of trust between the individuals in question. Unfortunately, one bad experience can jaundice an HQ manager's attitude forever.

We don't believe that all subsidiary initiatives are proposed in good faith. Most probably are, but HQ managers need to scrutinize all initiatives carefully and do their best to separate the wheat from the chaff. We do believe, though, that initiative has a critical role in the transferal of information about dispersed sources of expertise throughout the MNC. The discussions we had with one Scottish subsidiary manager—let's call him John Bryant—illustrate this point. Bryant was in charge of a large Scottish assembly operation, a long way from the head office in Boston. He saw his employees' dedication and observed the high-quality output that left the plant every day. He also knew that corporate executives had a global network of plants to manage and that they could not know in detail how each worked. He believed his operation was one of the best and, as the leader of 500 people, was concerned about their livelihood.

When we asked him about initiative—Did he actively seek new investments for his plant?—he did not hesitate. "It is my *obligation* to seek out new investment," he responded." No one else is going to stand up for these workers in the head office. They are doing a great job, and I owe it to them to build up this operation. I get angry with some of my counterparts in other parts of Scotland, who just tow the party line. They follow their orders to the letter, but when I visit their plants, I see unfulfilled potential everywhere."

CONCLUSION

Before subsidiary initiative becomes a legitimate and pervasive phenomenon in large MNCs, subsidiary and parent-company managers have to make significant, though subtle, shifts in their roles.

For subsidiary managers, we see an emerging role that is fundamentally more entrepreneurial than has been recognized historically. As one manager in our study pointed out, "No one in the head office wakes up thinking about what they can do in Canada today." That responsibility lies with the subsidiary manager. He or she has to be prepared to identify opportunities, then build support for them in the head office. But the process is difficult, and managers run the risk of wasting their efforts if their initiative is not chosen well. The following points are worth remembering:

- The magnitude of the initiative should be proportional to the subsidiary's reputation in the head office. One subsidiary management team in our study spent a decade pursuing a "big hit" investment, to no avail. Now the team is pursuing a host of smaller projects with considerable success.
- Managers must understand the reasons why they are encountering resistance and look for ways to mitigate it. If the initiative threatens to put some people out of a job, they should look for some form of compromise to create a win–win situation. If none of the HQ managers knows them personally, they should try to involve someone with whom they already have a relationship.
- Managers should not emphasize nationalistic arguments. As one person put it, "If I go there wrapped in my Canadian flag, I provoke all sorts of unnecessary challenges." Rather, they should focus on the technical or economic arguments as to why the location (which just happens to be in Canada) makes sense.
- Finally, it is important to recognize that initiatives can be either externally or internally focused, and that most subsidiaries are good at one or the other.

The emerging role for HQ managers is no less demanding. We envision a subtle shift through which executives become more open to new, challenging ideas from the periphery of the organization. This does not mean abandoning the tried-and-tested systems by which they evaluate new proposals, but it does call for a change in attitude that will encourage more subsidiary managers to bring their initiatives forward for consideration. Again, a few points to consider:

- Corporations can institute systems that encourage the flow of initiatives in a controlled manner. Some corporations send out request-for-proposal invitations whenever they plan major capital investments; others have put in place "challenge" mechanisms for changing internal sourcing relationship.
- Executives can introduce other systems to break down cross-national prejudices. Several corporations that we studied used global business teams or the sharing or transfers of senior managers, or they made a point of managing business units outside the home country. These approaches foster a more welcoming environment for subsidiary initiatives.
- HQ executives need to be clear about the difference between challenging or resisting an initiative. Challenging means seeking additional information, looking at alternatives, and coming to a decision about the initiative's merits. Resisting uses many of the same techniques, but it is fundamentally prejudiced and attaches greater importance to negative evidence.

We set out to explore the strategies that subsidiary managers used in pursuit of initiative, understand the forms of resistance they typically encountered, and assess the implications of initiative for MNC management. We believe strongly in the value of subsidiary initiative as a means for developing new markets and as a mechanism for improving the allocation of activities within the multinational. Yet there are still some strong arguments against subsidiary initiative, and subsidiary initiative remains a little-understood, risky proposition in most people's minds.

We hope we have clarified some of the mechanisms and benefits of initiative, as well as potential costs. Our research yielded some outstanding success stories, and we believe there is potential for many more. We encourage the executives of multinational corporations to consider ways to foster the changing behaviors that enable initiatives to flourish.

References

The authors thank Gunnar Hedlund. Bruce Kogut and seminar participants at the Institute of International Business, Stockholm School of Economics, for their helpful comments on drafts of this article. The research on which this paper is based appeared in two previous articles: J. M. Birkinshaw and N. Hood, "An Empirical Study of Development Processes in Foreign-Owned Subsidiaries in Canada and Scotland," Management International Review, *volume 37, number 4, 1997, pp. 339–364; and J. M. Birkinshaw, "Entrepreneurship in Multinational Corporations: The Characteristics of Subsidiary Initiatives,"* Strategic Management Journal, *volume 18, number 2, 1997, pp. 207–230.*

1. The NCR Dundee story comes from personal interviews, research by Graeme Martin at Dundee Business School and J. Kotter, *A Force for Change* (New York: Free Press, 1990).
2. The authors thank Gerhard Schmidt of Hewlett-Packard Company, who first suggested this concept of a corporate immune system. The theoretical underpinnings of the concept were developed more fully in a separate paper. See: J. M. Birkinshaw and J. Ridderstråle, "Fighting the Corporate Immune System: A Process Study of Peripheral Initiatives in Large Multinational Corporations" (Stockholm, Sweden: Institute of International Business, Working Paper 96/03).
3. The research comprised two phases. First, we conducted 132 intensive case study interviews at both the subsidiary and corporate headquarters levels in twenty subsidiaries and their parent companies in the United States, Canada, Great Britain, Sweden, and Belgium. We focused on specific initiatives that the subsidiaries had undertaken in order to understand how they came about, the resistance they faced, and their impact on parent–company strategies. The second phase, a large-sample-questionnaire study of 260 subsidiary companies in three countries (Great Britain, Canada, Sweden), sought to test empirically the hypotheses developed in the first phase. It focused on the role played by subsidiary initiative as the mechanism through which subsidiaries gained international management recognition—for example, as "centers of excellence" or through "world product mandates."
4. The Canadian study identified four types of initiative. See: J. Birkinshaw, "Entrepreneurship in Multinational Corporations: The Characteristics of Subsidiary Initiatives," *Strategic Management Journal,* volume 18, number 2, 1997, pp. 207–230. However, subsequent research

in Scotland and Sweden has indicated that a coarser distinction into two types is more generalizable.

5. This example is drawn from a teaching case. See: J. Birkinshaw. "The GE Energy Management Initiative" (University of Western Ontario, Ivey School of Business, 1994, 9-94-6005).
6. Pharma is the disguised name of a European pharmaceuticals corporation.
7. Bartlett and Ghoshal, for example, refer to contributor and strategic-leader subsidiaries, while many Canadian academics have used the concept of "world-mandate" subsidiaries. See: C. A. Bartlett and S. Ghoshal, "Tap Your Subsidiaries for Global Reach," *Harvard Business Review*, volume 64, November–December 1986, pp. 87–94; and H. Etemad and L.S. Dulude, *Managing the Multinational Subsidiary* (London: Croom Helm, 1986).
8. It should be clear that this distinction parallels Michael Porter's generic strategies as the basis for sustainable advantage vis-à-vis industry competitors. See: M. E. Porter, *Competitive Strategy* (New York: Free Press, 1980).
9. See P. Hagström, *The Wired MNC* (Stockholm: Institute of International Business, Stockholm School of Economics, 1993).

It should be pointed out that a key difference between the current work and the work of Bartlett, Ghoshal, and Nohria on the "differentiated network" is the suggestion that subsidiary units can assume roles, rather than parent companies always assigning them. See: S. Ghoshal and N. Nohria, "Internal Differentiation within Multinational Corporations," *Strategic Management Journal*, volume 10, pp. 323–337.

PART SIX

Market Specifics

THE EURO: HOW TO KEEP YOUR PRICES UP AND YOUR COMPETITORS DOWN

Johan Ahlberg, Nicklas Garemo, and Tomas Nauclér

Most companies know that the introduction of the euro in January 1999 will increase competition and level prices significantly across Europe. Yet few have changed their marketing and pricing strategies in response.

The opportunity forgone is huge. Over the next few years, it will be possible to create considerable value by carefully managing and delaying price reductions in higher-price countries and by acting to limit the fall in the average price levels of industries and companies alike.

Even before the euro's introduction, prices across Europe had been converging slowly but constantly as a result of deregulation, the removal of formal trade barriers, the harmonization of regulatory ones, and the reduced ability of manufacturers to influence retailers' prices. The euro's introduction will probably accelerate this trend. Customers will be in a better position to exploit relatively small differences in price, as well as more inclined to establish long-term sourcing agreements with foreign suppliers. Some suppliers will harmonize prices in an attempt to gain market share, and many national companies will enter foreign markets as the costs and perceived risks of cross-border trade fall.

Nonetheless, prices still have a long way to move. In the automobile market, for example, variations in market structure and competitive conduct, to say nothing of historically large currency fluctuations, have created 40 to 50 percent price differences

---

Johan Ahlberg is a principal and Tomas Nauclér is a consultant in McKinsey's Stockholm office. Nicklas Garemo is a consultant in the Gothenburg office. Copyright © 1999 McKinsey & Company. All rights reserved.

• EXHIBIT 1 •

Price Differentials across European Consumer Goods Markets

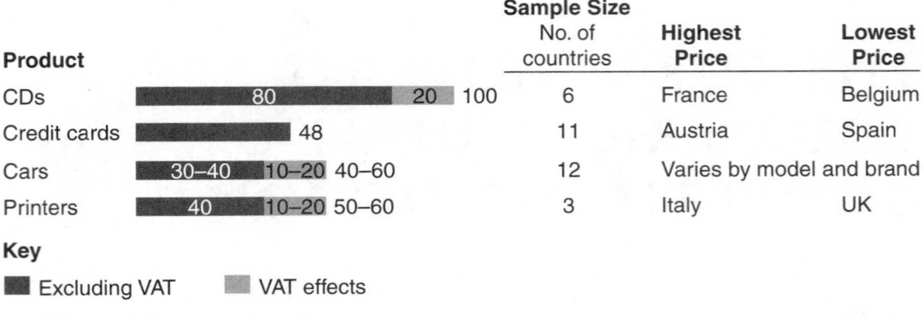

Percent difference between highest and lowest price

Product	Percent difference	Sample Size: No. of countries	Highest Price	Lowest Price
CDs	80 / 20 — 100	6	France	Belgium
Credit cards	48	11	Austria	Spain
Cars	30–40 / 10–20 — 40–60	12	Varies by model and brand	
Printers	40 / 10–20 — 50–60	3	Italy	UK

Key

Excluding VAT | VAT effects

from one country to another. The situation is similar for many consumer goods (Exhibit 1) and industrial goods (Exhibit 2). In some industries we studied, such as automotive spare parts, construction materials, and large industrial equipment, price differences often exceed 40 percent. In pharmaceuticals, country-to-country price differences are often 50 percent—and more than 100 percent for some products. Even prices

• EXHIBIT 2 •

Price Differentials across European Industrial Goods Markets

Percent difference between highest and lowest price

Product	Percent difference	Sample Size: No. of countries	Highest Price	Lowest Price
Construction equipment vehicle	30–40	12	Varies by model	
Tractor	10–20	3	UK	Germany
Automotive spare part	50–100	8	Varies by model	
Industrial pump	30–75	4	Spain	Austria
Newsprint	11	4	Spain	Italy
Pharmaceutical drug	50	4	Germany	UK

for commodities like steel and paper vary by country, although the differences are much smaller and largely reflect transportation costs.[1]

The rate at which prices converge will vary by industry, depending on the size of the price difference for a product, the price sensitivity of its customers, their buying power, its appropriateness for electronic commerce, and the degree of international presence in the market. In all likelihood, the pace will be faster in pharmaceuticals, where price differences are large and government regulations increasingly direct hospitals to choose the cheapest alternative, than in automotive spare parts, a market in which volumes per item are smaller and availability is no less important than price.

Many companies in industries ranging from trucks and construction materials to hygiene products indicate that their price levels could quickly fall by 2 to 3 percent. In different industries, such a decline would translate into a corresponding decline in operating income of 15 to 50 percent (Exhibit 3). The slippage could be considerably greater over the long term if prices fell to North American levels, which in many cases are substantially lower than their European counterparts—by as much as 15 to 25 percent for some products.

As a result, companies must immediately review their pricing strategy by product and market. To prevent arbitrage, they must even try to raise prices in lower-price markets. Without doubt, they cannot stand idly by, watching prices fall and margins erode. In the coming months, companies can move to influence the speed and effect of the decline by refining their pricing and marketing strategies, managing their international

• EXHIBIT 3 •

PRICE DROP SENSITIVITY

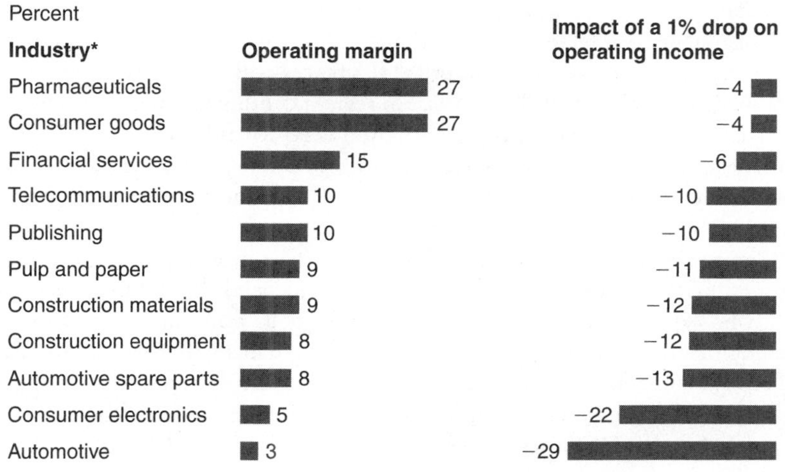

*For one company in each industry.

accounts in a more sophisticated way, managing price transparency, making it more expensive for customers to switch to other suppliers, and improving the coordination and control of their pricing.

REFINED PRICING AND MARKETING STRATEGIES

Some companies are rapidly harmonizing prices across Europe. They argue that prices will converge anyway and that harmonization is required to avoid arbitrage among countries and to gain market share by being the first to cut prices in higher-price countries. This approach may needlessly destroy value for two reasons: competitors will match these price reductions, and customers will prove to be less sensitive to prices than expected.

In fact, companies should aim to reduce prices as slowly as possible in higher-price countries, especially for less price-sensitive customers. Instead of carrying out across-the-board price reductions, suppliers should consider developing selective offers to price-sensitive customers using discounts or long-term contracts—measures that put less downward pressure on prices across the customer base.

Moreover, enhancing the perceived benefits a supplier confers on its customers—by meeting their needs on products and services more fully, for example, or by communicating the value of offerings more persuasively—can increase the supplier's penetration of certain market segments and delay price erosion in less price-sensitive ones. A steel manufacturer that provides a distinctive product and service, for instance, has achieved higher average prices across Europe than its competitors and has also been less affected by price competition. This company has succeeded in maintaining country-to-country price differences of more than 25 percent, compared with just 10 percent for its rivals.

Managing price differences across Europe will be a delicate balancing act: too rapid harmonization and excessively large price differences will both destroy value. So for each individual product, it will be critical to review, continually fine-tune, and coordinate price bands: the maximum and minimum accepted price levels in each country and the relative price difference between countries. These price bands should reflect a thorough understanding of the price sensitivity of different customer segments and of the ability of customers to exploit price differences across countries.

Of course, one of the biggest risks companies face in maintaining large country-to-country price differences is arbitrage by the independent players, called parallel traders, who exploit price differences by shipping goods from one country to another and selling them. For arbitrage to be worthwhile for parallel traders in pharmaceuticals, say, the price difference between countries must exceed 30 percent, since the trader must cover repackaging and transport, discounts to pharmacies, and the desired operating profit. In other industries, the arbitrage costs for many products are smaller, often around 10 percent.

Companies can limit the hazard of parallel traders by understanding the prices they require and their strategies in selecting products. Delaying the launch of new products in the lowest-price markets to avoid arbitrage, for example, has helped reduce the price erosion of innovative products, such as pharmaceuticals, that competitors have difficulty matching in the near term. This approach is particularly useful when lower-price countries represent only a small share of the total European market.

INTERNATIONAL ACCOUNTS

Mistakes in handling international accounts can put pressure on overall European price levels. International customers, for example, may exploit their knowledge of component prices in different countries to cherry-pick the best deals. To fight this tendency, one electronics company established a customer-specific, volume-dependent discount structure that reduced price differences among countries. Pricing was then closely controlled to ensure compliance with the volume discount structure. As a result, the prices offered to a single customer in a variety of countries could be better coordinated, and price differences could be justified as a function of volume. The company successfully avoided the convergence of prices to the levels of the lowest-price countries—which would have involved a decline of more than 10 percent.

Suppliers can often be much tougher than they are now in responding to requests for one price level across Europe. Many industrial customers, for instance, try to coordinate European purchasing by empowering a European purchasing manager or department. At the same time, however, some of these customers still have the traditional national structure, with subsidiaries in each country retaining considerable decision-making power. In many cases, the central purchasing function cannot enforce Europe-wide agreements without the explicit consent of local subsidiaries. Suppliers can take advantage of this divergence.

The following story shows how. One industrial supplier serving four of a customer's nine business units across Europe received a request for a uniform European price list, which would have cut its average price level by 5 percent. The supplier then assessed the ability of the customer's European purchasing function to enforce an agreement with the customer's local business units. True decision-making power, the analysis showed, remained in local hands. So the industrial supplier agreed to a Europe-wide arrangement but also demanded the same payment terms throughout Europe and a single shipping address for the products. In the end, the customer's centralized purchasing function failed to obtain authorization for this approach from the local units, and it eventually had to drop the request for a uniform price.

MANAGING PRICE TRANSPARENCY AND SWITCHING COSTS

Suppliers can also create considerable value by managing price transparency and switching costs to their own advantage. To do so, they should develop an understanding of which products and prices customers actually compare—list prices, for example, or invoice prices—so that price differences for these products can be reduced across countries.

Making it harder to compare prices can further reduce the risk of arbitrage. Suppliers should use discounts extensively, for instance, and in most cases avoid publishing European price lists denominated in euros. Varying terms and conditions from country to country and using pricing models based on loyalty or other drivers of profitability can reduce price transparency as well. Differentiating product features, packaging, and service levels has the same effect. In industries with complex offerings, such as construction equipment or industrial systems, bundling products and services and introducing service contracts also impedes price comparisons.

Another lever for reducing the risk of arbitrage involves raising the cost of switching for customers in higher-price countries—by introducing loyalty bonuses or long-term contracts, for example. Raising the amount of local service in product offerings may serve the same end.

PRICING COORDINATION AND CONTROL

To avoid pricing mistakes in one market that could adversely influence prices throughout Europe, successful suppliers are moving toward central coordination and control of pricing. These companies systematically track the prices they achieve in the marketplace and compare those prices with their own price bands and their competitors' price levels.

An industrial equipment manufacturer managed to raise its average European price level by 2 percent in 12 months through such steps as removing any customer that paid prices outside the determined price band for a given country. To coordinate and control prices across Europe, the manufacturer appointed a European-level pricing controller who monitored the performance of affiliates in individual countries in achieving the targeted average price.

In addition, within each country the manufacturer set a price floor that local sales managers could not undercut without their country managers' authorization. Information technology systems were established to track and evaluate list, invoice, and other prices by product and by country. These systems should help sales and country managers to detect pricing discrepancies rapidly.

Price differences across Europe are now very large, but the euro's introduction will probably serve as a strong catalyst for accelerated price equalization. On balance, average price levels will fall. If not managed correctly, the financial implications of this development could be disastrous. Companies can pull a number of levers to manage the transition toward more uniform prices and to limit the decline in average price levels. The stakes are huge, and tomorrow's winners must move quickly.

Note

1. For a discussion of the euro's impact on banking, see Jonathan A. Davidson, Alison R. Ledger, and Giovanni Viani, "Wholesale banking: The ugly implications of EMU," *The McKinsey Quarterly*, 1998 Number 1, pp. 66–81.

BYPASSING BARRIERS TO MARKETING IN JAPAN

Michael R. Czinkota and Masaaki Kotabe

The most significant market impediments to foreign firms traditionally have been unique Japanese business practices known as *keiretsu*, a term that describes the set of interlocking relationships among Japanese suppliers and manufacturers that do business with one another on a regular, and often, quite intimate basis. But our recent research indicates the situation is changing, primarily because of Japan's eight-year battle with its worst postwar recession in the 1990s, when many *keiretsu* companies saw severe asset deflation and lost their hold on member companies' shares in a tightly knit cross-shareholding relationship.

Recently, many Japanese market conditions changed. The country has been racked by low or negative economic growth rates. Major problems festering in the financial sector have brought fear and uncertainty to domestic Japanese markets and curbed consumers' willingness to spend. Few Japanese success stories are heard, even though large Japanese firms still are leading innovators and their employees continue unabated in their dedication and devotion to the tasks at hand. Talk is mainly about Japan's highest level of unemployment since the end of the war (4.4%), and the increasing

---

Michael R. Czinkota teaches international business and marketing at the McDonough School of Business at Georgetown University. He was chairman of the National Center for Export–Import Studies and held several U.S. federal government posts. He advises government agencies such as the U.S. General Accounting Office and the World Trade Organization. He's chairman of the Foundation for International Business Education and Research (FIBER) and a member of the AMA Global Advisory Committee.

Masaaki Kotabe is the Washburn Chair of International Business and Marketing and director of research at the Institute of Global Management Studies at the Fox School of Business and Management at Temple University. He's an advisor to the UNC-TAD/WTO's Executive Forum on National Export Strategies and to the Institute of Industrial Policy Studies (IPS) *National Competitiveness Report*, and is a Fellow of the Academy of International Business.

"Americanization" of Japanese corporations, which often includes major downsizing plans.

Japan's trade surplus with other countries has continued to grow. In 1998, Japan's trade surplus with the United States was $51 billion, with the European Union it came to $32 billion, and with Southeast Asia it amounted to $29 billion. Japan's overall trade relations with its major trading partners have been quite harmonious, despite some high-profile cases and actions, such as the Kodak–Fuji case at the World Trade Organization and the brief U.S. port closure to Japanese vessels by the U.S. Federal Maritime Commission in 1997. Other than in the 1980s, however, when Japan's trade performance made it the major problem child in the international trade community, Japan's export surplus in the 1990s has been met with major apathy globally.

Although President Clinton's 1999 State of the Union Address contained a brief warning to Japanese steel exporters, regular visits to Japan regarding trade issues are no longer *de rigueur* for policymakers. This could be explained by other noneconomic problems, such as the crisis in the former Yugoslavia, which are seen as more pressing. Also, non-Japanese trade matters have taken on the spotlight, particularly with the banana wars, the beef hormone dispute between the United States and Europe, and the economic malaise in Southeast Asia. Perhaps in light of Japan's sputtering domestic economy, continuing strategic importance, and influential global financial position, policymakers abroad recognize the limits of governmental capability. That theory is supported by revealing calls from the outside that Japan's government needs to take on more responsibility within the domestic economy and intervene more directly on the firm level. This sentiment is quite a contrast to the old calls for more free market activity and may indicate a return swing of the free market pendulum based on the recognition that: a) the trade playing field is not level for all players, and that b) governments can contribute to the development of economic benefits. Or perhaps it's simply the fear that an exacerbation of Japanese economic problems may place an unbearable strain on the openness of the world trading system.

In 1991 we conducted the "Distribution and Trade Relations between the United States and Japan: An Overview and Assessment" (a study published by the AMA in the book *The Japanese Distribution System*). This study, which drew on feedback from key distribution experts in Japan and the United States, offered the following perspectives: Distribution and cultural impediments such as existing close business links and high entry cost were ranked as the most important barriers, followed by government trade barriers, demanding customers, and bureaucratic practices. Except for governmental trade barriers, little change was expected in all the other areas seen as deeply rooted in Japan's political, social, and economic institutions. When asked about the primary methods that would improve foreign firms' ability to penetrate the Japanese market, respondents said trade negotiations played some role. The experts ranked as much more important, however, business strategy changes including those in market research, product adaptation, service orientation, willingness to collaborate, and long-term orientation. The experts foresaw that Japanese-type practices were likely to emerge in more countries, and that foreign direct investment mainly would facilitate entry into Japan's markets. Overall, a consensus was formed that the greatest potential for improved competitiveness would come from the corporate level. The experts recommended that international firms and governments strengthen information flows and their interactions with customers, encourage collaborative efforts, overcome export reluctance, and enhance human resources to present a level playing field for the success of international business.

The relative quiet on the policy side is contrasted by major changes within Japanese distribution systems. Foreign firms successfully are penetrating Japanese niche markets. L.L. Bean Inc., Eddie Bauer Inc., and Lands' End Inc., which began their entry into Japan through catalog mailings, now are firmly entrenched in Japan with stores. Lands' End, for example, generated $80 million in sales in Japan in 1997. On the services side, auto insurance from American International Group Inc. (AIG) now is sold directly to Japanese consumers, while McDonald's Corp., which entered the Japanese market 27 years ago, has 2,000 outlets in Japan and annual sales of $2.5 billion from the region. Morgan Stanley Dean Witter & Co. entered the Japanese financial services industry by opening retail branches in 1998, when the Tokyu Department Store Group announced the closure of its Nihonbashi store after 337 years (partially a result of Japanese consumers' increased price consciousness).

Despite improvements, many traditional barriers to entry into the distributions sector persist in Japan. Real estate prices, while lower, remain high, labor cost and freight charges are far greater than in most other nations, and a need remains to offer channel members high levels of service and substantial financing.

At the same time, new forms of doing business are becoming entrenched. Mail-order and nonstore retailing are becoming part of the daily consumer landscape. Likely to be even more prominent are the capabilities to conduct business in "market space" rather than the traditional "market place." The global emergence of electronic commerce offers alternatives that bypass many of these impediments' effects. In this area, many claim that U.S. firms are better positioned than Japanese members of the distribution system, as Japanese industry lags behind the United States in its approach to information technology (IT). But a 1999 study by the Washington, D.C.-based Council on Competitiveness (led by Michael Porter of the Harvard Business School and Scott Stern of the Massachusetts Institute of Technology) paints another picture. The study shows statistically that if current technology trends continue, the United States will trail Japan by 2005, particularly in such areas as advanced-materials science and solid-state physics because of inadequate spending on basic research and education and a shrinking percentage of technical workers—key areas to a host of information technologies. The study indicates that software is equally vulnerable. This prognosis is not difficult to understand. For example, the Japanese retail industry, still considered inefficient by many U.S. observers, has undergone a quiet revolution at the hands of major retail and convenience store chains such as Tokyo-based Seven-Eleven Japan Co. Ltd., which boast of world-class efficiency and profitability despite Japan's recession.

Corporate survival in the next century is expected to be predicated on the successful application of digital technology, and clearly, Japanese firms have some weaknesses and strengths in their technological applications. Indeed, the long-term competitiveness of Japanese firms cannot be ignored.

IDENTIFYING CHANGE

What are the changes that have taken place, and how are they affecting the Japanese distribution system and U.S.–Japanese trade relations? We addressed these issues at the 1998 AMA–Japan Marketing Association global meeting on the Japanese distribution system. After soliciting participation from business executives, policymakers, and researchers, we brought together 70 participants with a high level of expertise and interest for meetings and discussions. Talks focused on the complexity of distribution and trade practices, impending changes, and future opportunities. Participation by current and former high level policymakers, representatives of major corporations, and leading researchers ensured important discussions and insights into the process of trade and distribution policy and practice.

At the meeting's end, key participants were asked to provide their views in interviews or questionnaires to shed light on the road to change, considering the unique configuration in their expertise, diversity, and orientation. The findings reported are based on a total of 36 interviews and questionnaires. Among the respondents, 39% worked in Japan, 50% worked in the United States, 8% worked in Europe, and 3% worked in Australia. Academic researchers made up 70% of the respondents, businesses practitioners consisted of 20% of the respondents, and government officials made up the remaining 10%. Although the number of individuals involved may seem low by traditional quantitative research standards, because each respondent was one of a few global experts in the field under analysis, the collective insights obtained are meaningful.

MARKET IMPEDIMENTS

Initially, respondents identified 16 problem areas for foreign firms doing business in and with Japan. Respondents were asked to rate the importance of the problems, as well as their assessment of the improvement of those problems in the past five years, and their expected improvement in the next five years. Because we searched for the main impediments, we looked for consistency, depth, and consensus in the responses. Our analysis showed that 11 of those 16 problem areas consistently converged into four discrete categories of barriers to entry. In order of importance (as rated by our expert observers), they are: 1) unique Japanese business practices, 2) rigid quality/standard expectation and regulation, 3) high operational cost, and 4) preference for Japan-made products. Summary findings are reported in Exhibit 1.

Keiretsu are considered the most important market impediment to foreign firms. Americans, in particular, have been suspicious of the *keiretsu* groups simply because they're linked together by means that are illegal in the United States: a combination of bank holdings (banks may hold up to 5% of the outstanding stock of a company), intercorporate shareholdings, and interlocking directorates. Also, the *keiretsu* often are accused of dealing predominantly with group members, thereby denying market access to foreigners. Foreign companies complain that due to the *keiretsu* or other business

• EXHIBIT 1 •

JAPANESE MARKET IMPEDIMENTS TO FOREIGN FIRMS: THE PAST AND THE FUTURE

	IMPORTANCE (NOT AT ALL IMPORTANT = 1 5 = VERY IMPORTANT)	IMPROVEMENT IN THE LAST 5 YEARS (NOT AT ALL = 1 5 = VERY MUCH)	EXPECTED IMPROVEMENT IN THE NEXT 5 YEARS (NOT AT ALL = 1 5 = VERY MUCH)
Japanese Business Practices			
• Cultural barriers	**3.90**	3.04	**3.28**
• Close business linkages			
High Quality/Standard Expectations and Bureaucratic Practices			
• Excessive quality expectations	**3.37**	2.86	3.04
• Unreasonable standards			
• Inadequate import infrastructure			
• Delay in patent processing			
• Delay in trademark processing			
High Cost of Doing Business in Japan			
• High retail prices	3.11	3.19	**3.30**
• Lack of economies of scale			
• High entry cost			
Preference for Japan-Made Products			
• Unwillingness to purchase foreign products	**2.19**	**3.47**	**3.53**

Note: The numbers in bold indicate that responses are significantly different from a neutral response of 3.

and government relationships, a strong "buy Japanese" bias keeps out foreign products even when quality and price are competitive or superior.

Although the age-old Japanese business culture is unlikely to change drastically in a short period, our expert observers believe some improvement will occur. Change primarily will result from Japan's eight-year battle with the worst postwar recession in the 1990s, when many *keiretsu* companies experienced severe asset deflation and lost their member companies' shares in a tightly knit cross-shareholding relationship. This is a significant change, particularly as our earlier survey showed that *keiretsu* relationships were considered the most unlikely of Japanese market impediments to change.

Second, Japanese consumers' high quality and standard expectations and government's bureaucratic practices are considered somewhat important. Consumers' expectations stem from the Japanese government's high quality standard stipulated in Japan

Industrial Standards (JIS) and Japan Agricultural Standards (JAS). Yet bureaucratic red tape has increased as a result of understaffed Japanese government offices, the country's inadequate import infrastructure, and delays in processing patent, trademark, and other intellectual property rights. Consistent with our earlier survey, these market impediments are perceived to have changed little in the last five years. In our latest survey, no further significant changes are expected.

The high cost of doing business in Japan is no longer considered as important; however, our expert observers believe that the situation will improve in the next five years—primarily a result of the continued weakness of the post-bubble deflationary Japanese economy. Finally, Japanese consumers' preference for Japan-made products is considered less important—another significant change from the earlier survey results.

ELEMENTS OF CHANGE

Our respondents' optimistic perceptions could reflect some fundamental changes in the nature of the Japanese market mechanism that will facilitate foreign firms' entry. Nevertheless, consumers' high quality expectations and government bureaucratic practices appear to remain unchanged.

How, then, should foreign firms and policymakers cope with Japan's bureaucratic inefficiency and high quality expectations, among other obstacles, to improve their ability to penetrate the Japanese market? If the market does not change, do some areas exist where outside firms and governments can become active to better succeed in Japan? We asked the respondents nine questions on this issue. As shown in Exhibit 2, our

• EXHIBIT 2 •

Methods to Improve Foreign Penetration of the Japanese Market

	Likelihood of Improvement (Very low = 1 ... 5 = Very high)
Trade Negotiations	**3.33**
Business Strategy	
• Product adaptation	
• Market research	3.77
• Service orientation	
• Collaborative ventures	
• Long-term orientation	
• Personnel training	
• Information systems	
• Complaint responsiveness	

Note: The numbers in bold indicate that responses are significantly different from a neutral response of 3.

analysis suggests that two principal ways can enhance foreign firms' ability to enter the Japanese market: 1) trade negotiations and 2) better business strategy. These findings are essentially the same as our earlier study findings.

Respondents acknowledge that trade negotiations with the Japanese government may help somewhat, but they see the use of seasoned business practices as the key elements to make market penetration possible. Such practices can be foreign firms' willingness and ability to conduct thorough market research, adapt products whenever necessary, be more service-oriented, enter into collaborative ventures, have a long-term orientation, and be more responsive to changes in the market. Also important is the ability of firms exporting to Japan to develop an Export Complaint Management (ECM) system that is highly responsive to the special demands of the Japanese market. This is the case because ECM shows customers how to complain, where to complain, to whom to complain, and encourages them to complain. An ECM system captures complaints, resolves them quickly but also analyzes them to identify points of failure or opportunities for improvement in the corporation. In other words, ECM recognizes complaints as gifts from friends and uses them to progressively improve products and processes. Interestingly, these very same business practices have been a hallmark of successful Japanese companies around the world.

EXPECTED STRUCTURAL CHANGES

We've explored market impediments to trade that foreign firms face and the internal and external forces that could help mitigate barriers to entering the Japanese market. The Japanese market is changing constantly because of, or despite, the internal and external forces at play. In 1998, we asked our respondents to assess the same set of questions we asked in our earlier survey regarding the degree to which structural changes are taking place in Japan. We also asked whether those changes are attributable to Japanese or U.S. government initiatives, or to Asia's financial crisis. (Summary findings are presented in Exhibit 3.)

Significant changes have occurred in how experts see the structural changes in Japan. In 1991, they believed quite strongly that Japan would emerge as the leader of a Pacific trading bloc. An increase in Japanese imports was seen as mainly occurring through boosted import activities of Japanese firms, largely in the field of manufacturers, and to a lesser extent, in the agricultural sector. On the other hand, little expectation was expressed that the complexity of the Japanese distribution system would be reduced.

According to our 1998 survey, in reality the reverse seems to have occurred. Japan may or may not emerge as the leader in the Pacific trading bloc, and Japanese imports are not expected to increase significantly. Respondents attribute structural changes more to Asia's financial crisis than to Japanese or U.S. government initiatives. Despite U.S. government pressure on Japan to reduce its trade surplus, this imbalance is not expected to change as the Japanese tend to increase exports and reduce imports as a result of the recession in Japan. Expert observers recognize that, as a result of Asia's financial crisis and Japan's recession, Japanese firms may need to streamline their distribution systems to improve efficiency in Japan. These observations show that the market mechanism

• EXHIBIT 3 •

STRUCTURAL CHANGES IN JAPAN IN THE NEXT FIVE YEARS AND THEIR KEY CHANGE AGENTS

			CHANGE AGENTS		
	LEVEL OF AGREEMENT IN 1991[1]	LEVEL OF AGREEMENT IN 1998[1]	JAPANESE GOVERNMENT INITIATIVES[2]	U.S. GOVERNMENT INITIATIVES[2]	ASIA'S FINANCIAL CRISIS[2]
Foreign direct investment will improve market penetration	3.32	3.50	2.89	2.92	2.97
The complexity of the Japanese distribution system will be reduced	2.85 <<<	3.39	2.86	2.78	3.36
More exports to Japan will improve market penetration	2.91	3.00	2.97	3.00	3.14
Japan will emerge as the leader of a Pacific trading bloc	4.09 >>>	3.00	3.08	3.33	2.31
Japanese competitiveness will decrease	2.77	2.94	2.83	3.22	2.97
Japanese firms increase imports	3.86 >>>	2.83	3.08	3.17	3.03
Agricultural imports will increase	3.39 >>>	2.78	3.14	2.97	3.42
The Japanese trade surplus will decline	2.59	2.59	2.72	3.59	3.31

[1]Strongly disagree = 1 ... 5 = Strongly agree
[2]Not at all = 1 ... 5 = Very much
Note: Shaded areas represent particularly noteworthy changes and implications.

works better than government interventions to bring about much needed changes in the Japanese distribution system.

Along a similar vein, expert observers believe that foreign firms will improve their foothold in the Japanese market mainly through direct investment, rather than exports. Lack of such investment may serve as a self-fulfilling prophecy for a lack of success. If being there sends the signals of reliability, long-term outlook, and corporate commitment of foreign firms, than an export-only strategy may be seen as communicating the damaging obverse. Again, consistent with our earlier observation, seasoned business strategy—not government interventions—seem to help foreign firms successfully enter the Japanese market. Thanks to Asia's financial crisis and Japan's worst postwar recession, the Japanese business practices and competitive environment also are changing and becoming less culture-centric. Indeed, the famed unique Japanese business practices heralded as part of Japan's postwar economic growth may come to an end in the next five to ten years.

IMPLICATIONS

In the seven years that passed between our two conferences, experts changed their opinions about the competitiveness of Japanese firms. They once thought that Japanese firms would be invincible and that the emergence of a Japan era was imminent. Now many of the Japanese market impediments to foreign firms such as close business links epitomized by the *keiretsu*, high cost of doing business in Japan, and a "buy Japanese" attitude—all once thought to be recalcitrant—have waned considerably as a result of Asia's financial crisis and Japan's prolonged recession. The only areas expected to change minimally are the Japanese government's bureaucratic practices and Japanese consumers' high quality expectations.

Still, high customer expectations have made Japanese competitors world-class producers. And Japanese consumers' tastes and expectations are unlikely to change. Despite some fundamental shifts in the Japanese economy, the recipe for foreign firms' success in the country remains the same as seven years ago: continued trade negotiations to reduce Japan's bureaucratic impediments and sound business strategy to better cater to demanding Japanese consumers.

The effect of trade negotiations needs to be seen in a new light. Traditional trade negotiations may lead to some success, particularly if they concentrate on bureaucratic impediments directly controlled by the government. In doing so, however, they would focus mainly on issues which are of only marginal importance to overall business success in Japan. This is not to say that traditional item- or sector-specific trade negotiations have no value, but rather that they are unlikely to fulfill the expectations placed on them by the U.S. government and the public, and will not accomplish a major turnaround in the trade imbalance.

An alternative strategy could be the reorientation of trade negotiations and policy by making them more domestic. Such an approach would clearly and publicly recognize that increased global competitiveness starts at home. It also would accept that trade is only one aspect of global competitiveness, and that other approaches such as foreign direct investment, licensing, or franchising are equally important and viable, particularly if intellectual property rights can be protected. A new governmental perspective of global positioning would reduce the pressure to pry open foreign markets through politics, and would instead concentrate efforts on enhancing the strategic competence and capabilities of domestic firms. This alternative, in essence, would require foreign firms to become more Japanese in orientation and location, enabling them to compete the Japanese way by bypassing border barriers, heightening quality concerns, and strengthening information systems to respond swiftly to the everchanging needs of demanding Japanese consumers.

For example, consider the results of a U.S. Government Accounting Office investigation of wood exports to Japan. For more than a decade, the U.S. government negotiated with Japan for more market access. Building codes were revised, product certification was delegated from the Japanese government to foreign testing organizations, and tariffs were reduced drastically. In addition, the Foreign Agricultural Service spent close to $18 million to promote U.S. wood sales to Japan. The results of these U.S. government efforts were appalling. While U.S. wood exports to Japan increased minimally, Canadian lumber companies became the lead wood importers in the Japanese market. This debacle occurred because the U.S. effort was based on seeking Japanese buyers' agreement to buy U.S. products and did not provide for steps to ensure that U.S. products were tailored to the Japanese market. Japanese builders prefer post and beam construction, which requires lumber that is 4 inches by 4 inches and modules that are 3 feet by 6 feet to match the standard tatami floor mats. U.S. companies were either unaware of those requirements or unwilling to meet them. Instead, the U.S. producers focused on the standard 2-by-4 products used at home, even though only 7% of new homes in Japan actually use that standard.

Furthermore, many U.S. exporters entered the market with limited enthusiasm and commitment. In contrast to the Canadian firms, many U.S. companies paid little or no attention to product quality and appearance and did not deliver after-sales service. For example, only a few U.S. firms translated their product information into Japanese or wrote manuals describing the new type of construction. No wonder that the Japanese chose the Canadian suppliers. The lesson: Despite government efforts at deregulation and market opening, customer responsiveness and commitment remain primary to export success.

This doesn't mean the Japanese government is powerless in improving the efficiency of Japan's market. In fact, many improvements can be brought to the largely underexplored area of nonstore retailing in Japan—a form of retailing that already constitutes up to 40% of all U.S. retail sales. The expansion of television, mail-order retailing, and electronic commerce could offer significant opportunities for importers to circumvent traditional channel constraints in Japan. In 1976. Japan initiated HI-Ovis, an interactive cable television experiment. But the initial promise of this channel has not been realized, even though other nations such as the United States have achieved major breakthroughs. While shopping by TV is a multibillion dollar business in the United States, it remains only a minuscule business in Japan. Although the mail-order industry has seen substantial growth in many countries, the Japanese mail-order industry lags. Similarly, e-commerce, now already a mainstay in the United States and particularly in the business-to-business sector, remains in its incipient stage in Japan. In an era of massive geometric growth, such delays could have a deleterious effect on future competitiveness.

The lagging growth is partly the result of the Japanese government's restrictive regulations of distribution technology. While technology is quite advanced in Japan's distribution sector, advancements have occurred mainly on the industrial side of channel management through enhancements of electronic data interchange and point-of-sale (POS) systems. On the consumer side, this technology has been sadly neglected or restricted. For example, the prohibition of drug sales outside a pharmacy severely handicaps the pharmaceutical industry. Service industries such as travel and banking suffer from a Ministry of Transport prohibition on ticket sales outside a registered travel office and a Ministry of Finance restriction that limits banking business to banking hours. Similarly, local phone calls still are charged by the minute, prohibiting the unbridled use of the Internet to most consumers. Recent experience revealed that America Online charged $3.95 per hour, while the local phone call cost 10 yen per 3 minutes. This resulted in a total cost of about $6 per hour for Internet access.

Overall, some changes in the Japanese distribution system have brought new opportunities for foreigners' market entry and penetration. However, many core features of Japanese bureaucracy and distribution channels remain in place. Even with substantial corporate commitment to this important market, many restrictions and regulations of technology and industries still could inhibit importers from providing consumers with global choice. Ongoing Japanese trade surpluses are tolerated temporarily by Japan's trading partners for strategic reasons and because of a buoyant U.S. economy. Yet any sharp economic downturn in the United States surely will bring Japanese distribution issues back to the forefront of U.S. Congressional debates and action. Preparing now for such an occurrence is not just good policy, it also makes good business sense.

Additional Reading

Council on Competitiveness (1999), *The New Challenge to America's Prosperity: Findings from the Innovation Index.* Washington, D.C.

Czinkota, Michael R. and Masaaki Kotabe (eds.) (1993), *The Japanese Distribution System: Opportunities and Obstacles, Structures and Practices.* Chicago: Probus Publishing.

Czinkota, Michael R. and Jon Woronoff (1997), "Import Channels in the Japanese Market," *International Trade Forum,* 1, 8–13.

Kotabe, Masaaki (1995), "The Return of 7-Eleven . . . from Japan: The Vanguard Program," *Columbia Journal of World Business,* 30, (Winter), 70–81.

Posen, Adam S. (1998), *Restoring Japan's Economic Growth,* Washington, D.C.: Institute for International Economics.

Tomio, Tsutsumi (1998), "Future Economic Interaction between Japan and the U.S.," *Journal of Japanese Trade and Industry* 3, 28–31.

MARKETING'S CONTRIBUTION TO THE TRANSFORMATION OF CENTRAL AND EASTERN EUROPE

Reiner Springer and Michael R. Czinkota

INTRODUCTION

The transformation from planned to market economy is a worldwide phenomenon. The majority of countries in transition are former socialist nations in Europe and the successor states of the Soviet Union. Transformation means a change of systems, a paradigm change in politics and economics. The transformation process starts with a planned economy and is aimed at a market economy, but it may pass through various interim stages which vary from country to country according to historical background, concept, speed, and acceptance of transformation. All the countries started into the transformation process without an accepted and comprehensive theory of system change (Wagner, 1991, p. 17). To understand the magnitude of the scope, the tasks, and the problems of system transformation in Central and Eastern Europe, Table 1 contrasts key business dimensions of planned and market economies (Schüller, 1991; Jens, 1993).

History has proven that planned economies are less efficient than market economies. The reasons for the disintegration and collapse of the socialist system are

Reiner Springer is with Wirschaftsuniversität Wien, Vienna, Austria. Michael R. Czinkota is with Georgetown University, Washington, DC 20052; e-mail: czinkotm@msb.edu

• TABLE 1 •

Contrast of Planned and Market Economies

Criteria	Planned Economy	Market Economy
Decision making	Highly centralized, party, government, planning bureaucracy is taking economic decisions related to the macro- and micro-economic level; political–administrative dominated management of economy and companies; price regulation by the state	Autonomy of companies, limited or no interference of the state
Information gathering	Top down planning process, especially quantitative balancing of output and input on the macro and micro level	Price-market mechanism
Ownership of the means of production	State-owned companies, sometimes cooperative property	Private property
Motivation	Moral and material incentives directed at the fulfillment of national economic plans	Maximizing of profits, development of individual personality

manifold but lack of efficiency and motivation are key. Problems of motivation were mainly caused by the principle of socialist equality where everyone was to live according to his needs, not according to his own effort and contribution. The lack of efficiency resulted from the primacy of politics and dominance of national plans which prevented the development of markets as a place of exchange, eliminated the signaling function of the price mechanism, and inhibited the market orientation of companies. Marketing as a corporate strategy was undesirable since its full implementation would have strengthened the position of companies and managers and reduced the power of the party and the state bureaucracy. In terms of priorities, state control vastly outranked corporate efficiency and customer satisfaction. This choice of priorities was maintained with relative ease, since, due to a lack of democracy, customers and managers were very limited in their ability to complain effectively.

A successful transformation of planned to market economies requires the development of a market orientation in the transition countries. This affords a unique opportunity but also an obligation for marketing to help restructure society and business processes in order to improve the standard of living. Yet, there has been little established knowledge about how marketing can be used to facilitate economic transitions (Olivier, 1991). This article will assess what marketing knowledge and practice has done in the past, what marketing has accomplished during the ongoing transformation, and what it can do in the future to improve the functioning of economies in transition.

THE PAST

Marketing as management concept was not used in the planned economies of the former socialist countries for two main reasons: First, political and ideological beliefs prohibited the acceptance and use of marketing, since national economic plans rather than the market regulated and managed the economy and the economic behavior of companies, suppliers, buyers, and consumers. Some countries even prohibited the use of the term *marketing*, since it was labeled as capitalistic and therefore negative, and believed to manipulate consumers against their own will. In East Germany the term *Marktarbeit* (market work) was used. In Poland, Hungary, or Czechoslovakia the national languages did not provide an equivalent term. Secondly, markets in which demand consistently outstripped supply offered neither a basis for nor an incentive to use marketing. Virtually anything produced was sold based on a guarantee by the national economic plan and state-controlled distribution systems (Mayer, 1976; Naor, 1986, 1990; Samli, 1986).

Although the socialist economies did not permit the implementation of marketing as a management concept, companies operating in planned economies used various tools of marketing in an unsystematic way. In evaluating the role of marketing in planned economies, one can distinguish three segments of the economy: internal activities of domestic businesses, external activities of domestic firms due to international business efforts, and the internal repercussions from the export activities of foreign companies.

In their internal domestic business, firms did not aim to create customer value but rather focused on meeting quantitative targets set by the plan. In general, supply was smaller than demand, prices were set by the state, and distribution channels were fixed. Companies were production oriented and used marketing instruments only selectively. In preparing plans, market research determined the quantitative development of demand; occasionally, point of sales advertising was used to get rid of surplus stocks; fairs and exhibitions were attended to introduce new products; the transportation and distribution of products were optimized by using network planning techniques; and individual and organizational buyers learned how to develop incentives in order to source inputs in short supply. Since demand was larger than supply, consumer behavior developed buying criteria atypical for market economies. As consumers did not have a choice between a variety of offers, price and quality did not play a major role in the buying decisions. Simply to obtain a product was a major source of satisfaction.

The external efforts of domestic companies were mainly export oriented. In doing business with other centrally planned economies the need for marketing was low, since trade and product exchanges were regulated by long-term trade agreements and agreed upon pricing rules. Trade with the West required a more comprehensive use of marketing instruments. Foreign trade organizations (FTOs) were authorized by the state to handle all export and import operations. In consequence these FTOs rather than manufacturers used marketing approaches and, over time, acquired solid experience in doing business in Western markets. The marketing strengths of these FTOs were market research, channel management, use of fairs and exhibitions for introducing and selling products, adapting products to specific customer needs, competitive pricing, use of countertrade, negotiation skills, and exploiting loopholes in the import and export regulations of their target markets.

The international business activities of Western companies in planned economies were heavily influenced by the foreign trade monopoly in the East and the export control policies in the West (Czinkota & Dichtl, 1996). The inward trade monopoly limited business activities to the import of goods and simple licensing agreements. Western companies did not have access to end users and had to deal with FTOs only. Market research focused on analyzing general economic developments and economic plans to identify specific business opportunities. The participation in fairs and exhibitions played a key role in establishing business contacts with decision makers in government and party circles. Distribution was not important since the FTOs were completely in charge of domestic allocation.

In sum, there was no marketing culture and marketing based behavior of suppliers and buyers in the socialist planned economies. Due to political, economic, and systemic constraints the managerial readiness and capability to use marketing as a management concept did not exist. Manufacturers held a monopolistic position and were told by the planning bureaucracy what to produce. Therefore, they did not need marketing to determine and satisfy the needs and wants of customers. Consumers did not have buying options, and chased products rather than selecting them. Without functioning markets in planned economies, marketing as a management concept could not work.

CHANGES DURING TRANSITION

TRANSITION SHAPES AND REQUIRES A MARKETING ENVIRONMENT

Replacing the political and economic system of socialism with a new democratic and market-driven system is the objective of transition. However, the precise expectations of the new economic system vary from country to country. Most countries in transition prefer the German or Swedish type of social market economy, where markets are heavily influenced by government, to the US or British type of a less restrained market economy. This attitude may well be the result of a distrust in the invisible hand and a continued belief in government intervention by the population and is of major relevance for political and economic reforms in Central and Eastern Europe. During the introduction of a market orientation, the people of Central and Eastern Europe have both hopes and fears. On the one hand, people expect an immediate improvement in their personal economic situation. On the other hand, they fear to be without shelter, to be steamrolled by an unknown and antagonistic system. Therefore, any policy of transition has to make sure that the population accepts reforms and can endure the transformation from the old to the new system. Since the rules as well as the advantages and the disadvantages of the new system are unknown to the population, the aims, content, and mechanism of any reforms must be explained constantly to generate broad support for and acceptance of change. Differences in the explanatory success by governments may be a reason why the transition to a market economy is progressing at differing speeds and with different success from country to country. Fear and the need for popular support may also explain why the majority of countries is preferring a step-by-step transformation process. In other words, in the long run a gradual transition seems to be more successful than shock therapy.

The transition process will be a success only if the new political and economic system is accepted by the vast majority of the population, generates internal and external political and economic stability, and improves the social well-being and standard of living of the population. In the end, transition has to increase the political, economic, technological, and social proximity between the countries in transition and the countries in the industrialized West. If there is no real hope for substantial improvement in the future, then the transformation to the new system has failed.

The transition process has disbanded the bloc of socialist countries. The formerly Eastern bloc is not a bloc anymore but a group of countries with the same political past but a varying political, economic, and social future. The ongoing transition will deepen the differences between countries. Based on the speed and success in transition, countries can be clustered in progressive reformers (Czech Republic, Hungary, Poland, Estonia, Lithuania, Latvia, Slovenia), reformers on the brake (like Slovakia, Russia, Bulgaria, Romania), and late, reluctant reformers (member states of CIS except Russia).

The success of economic reforms depends heavily on comprehensive and speedy political and legal reforms. The institutional, organizational, and legal changes have been accomplished relatively fast in most of the countries in transition. But political behavior, practiced democracy, implementation of enacted laws, and legal certainty are lagging behind. A perspective of the status of system reforms by countries in transition can be gained from Figure 1.

The success of transition depends heavily on the acceptance of the new political and economic system by the elite and, even more importantly, by the whole population. According to polls taken, the acceptance of a market economy as the right way into the future differs widely between the countries in transition. Whereas in Poland and Croatia 60 percent of the people accept a market orientation, only 42 percent of the Czechs, 37 percent of the Hungarians, and 24 percent of the Russians and Ukrainians agree with this direction of transition (Business Central Europe, 1997, p. 67). These figures raise the question why, after almost 10 years of transition, only a relatively low percentage of people (and voters) have accepted a market orientation as the best way of system change. The reasons may be manifold but are basically rooted in unfulfilled expectations. People hoped for quick improvements in their standard of living, politicians promised more than they could deliver, political freedom was taken for granted and valued as an extraordinary achievement only at the beginning of the transformation process. Combined with a low readiness for hardships, the results of transition have led to disappointment and disenchantment. Many people now only remember the bright side of life under socialism and forget the dark side and the missed opportunities.

Although the transition to a new political and economic order seems to be irreversible, the establishment of a market system may take longer than expected. The process will be accompanied by developments which are not in line with market-oriented behavior and cause instability and irritation especially for outsiders. The transition from a planned to a market economy is changing the marketing environment in Central and

• FIGURE 1 •

INDEX OF ECONOMIC FREEDOM RANKING

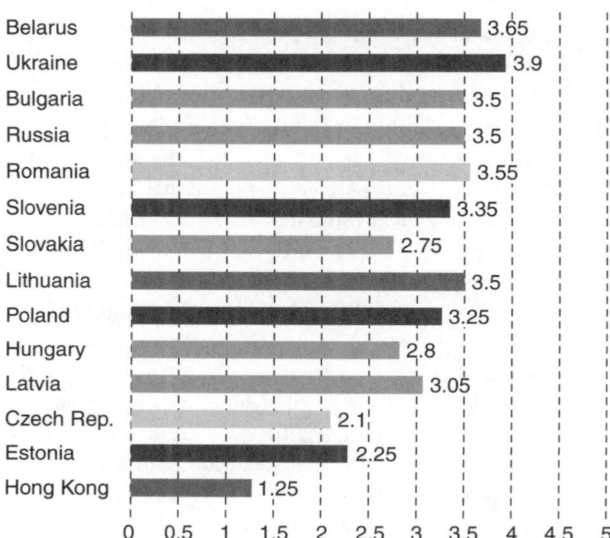

SOURCE: Transition, 1997.

Eastern Europe gradually although substantially. These changes bring about a new political, economic, financial, and legal framework for consumer behavior and doing business in the region (Huszagh, Huszagh, & Hanks, 1992; Hooley, 1993; Mueller, Wenthe, & Baron, 1993; Healey, 1994; Czinkota, Gaisbauer, & Springer, 1997). Since there is a strong interdependence between the marketing environment and the way marketing can be implemented by the players in the market, the impact of transition on consumers/customers and suppliers/companies shall be discussed next. In this context it is important to notice that the shift in marketing and managerial behavior of suppliers, customers, decision makers, and politicians is lagging behind the changes in the marketing environment. This gap between framework changes and behavioral changes may lead to conflicts, backward-oriented decisions by local politicians and managers, and an eventual slow-down in the process of transition.

CONSUMERS AND CUSTOMERS ADAPT TO MARKETING

A major feature of the marketing environment in Central and Eastern Europe is the slow and sometimes contradictory shift in the market constellation from a seller's market to a buyer's market. This shift is accompanied by long-lasting transition crises and output losses in all countries of transition. In 1997 only Poland and Slovenia surpassed or reached the GDP level of 1989, all the other countries are still below this level. Russia has reached 59 percent and the Ukraine 37 percent of the 1989 GDP (data compiled from EBRD, 1997a, 1997b). These output losses mean that there are fewer products and services available, and that both consumption and investments are decreasing. In addition some of the domestic products are in short supply or are being replaced by foreign products. With net monthly wages in manufacturing between $55 in the Ukraine and $329 in Poland (EBRD, 1996), the buying power among countries differs widely and is growing mainly in the progressive transition economies.

The transition crisis has fueled the shadow economy which may compensate at least partially for the output losses registered in the official economic sector. In 1995, the size of the shadow economy was estimated to be 19 percent of GDP in Central and Eastern Europe, 44.8 percent in the European part of the CIS, and 20.4 percent in Central Asia (EBRD, 1997a, p. 76).

Because of these economic conditions, the majority of households in Central and Eastern Europe has not yet improved its economic situation. Only 17 percent of questioned households confirm that their current economic situation is now better than under the planned economy; 46 percent of the households hope that the situation will improve in the future (Rose & Haerpfer, 1996). As a result, many people question the wisdom of transition and protest against the transition course in elections.

The general picture hides the fact that social gaps are growing and that the number of both poor and rich people is increasing. The so-called newly rich in Russia and in other countries constitute an interesting segment of customers for high-priced Western products.

The trend toward a market economy has affected the buying behavior of consumers. Limited purchasing power and the possibility of choice have led to more Western-style yet still rational buying behavior. Price and quality have become dominant buying criteria (Shama, 1992; Feick, Coulter, & Price, 1995). Consumers prepare the buying decision for long-lasting products very carefully in order to make sure that limited funds are spent wisely. Consumers demand information from suppliers to make the buying decision. Improvements in purchasing power will, perhaps, lead to more emotional buying behavior.

Country-of-origin issues have an impact on the buying behavior of consumers in Central and Eastern Europe (Papadopoulos, Heslop, & Beracs, 1990; Gajewski, 1992; Ettenson, 1993; Good & Huddleston, 1995). Immediately after the opening toward the West, consumers saw domestic products to be of inferior quality and rushed to buy foreign products to try out the unknown. In consequence, imports of Western products surged, international brands captured market share, and domestic manufacturers fired workers or even closed down. But now consumers return to local products, especially foodstuffs and low-tech products. Consumers have recognized that the quality of foreign products is not much better and that local products are much cheaper. Buying national also saves jobs. This ethnocentric buying behavior may also be partially explained by the still prevailing collectivism and national pride.

Advertising as a marketing tool is relatively new for customers in Central and Eastern Europe (Heyder, Musiol, & Peters, 1992; Church, 1992). In 1995 advertising expenditures per capita in Central and Eastern Europe were on average one-tenth of the expenditures in Austria: for instance, Poland, $24; Slovakia, $27; Hungary, $50; Czech Republic, $55; and Slovenia, $64 (Brenner, 1997, p. 47). Advertising has to reduce the information deficit of consumers with regard to goods, services, and conditions offered. It should reflect the differences in buying behavior and culture. Therefore, the style of advertising messages implemented in the East and in the West needs to differ. Eastern consumers prefer rational-based advertising which explains the features of products and provides valuable information for preparing and making the buying decision. Advertising must help the consumer navigate in an ever-broadening array of products, and develop the kind of sovereignty needed to hold his ground in an economic system which demands personal decisions. Marketing and especially advertising run the risk of being rejected if customers are misled. For example, lifestyle advertising used in the West rarely works in the East, because the lifestyles portrayed are far removed from reality. Therefore, marketing should present reliable and checkable facts to consumers in order to overcome the mistrust still emanating from their experience with ideological propaganda.

In this context branding plays a very important role. Since markets are flooded with new and very often unknown products, brands must serve as a guide through this increased offer. Customers in Central and Eastern Europe no longer consider international brands as superior per se. Sometimes they even develop brand loyalty toward local brands to protect themselves against everything foreign and to keep alive elements of the past they can personally relate to. Therefore, local brands can be as valuable as international brands, they just have to be positioned differently. In consequence, foreign companies should offer a mix of local and international brands. This will permit a much more precise targeting of various customer segments, taking into account the widespread differences in income levels and ethnocentric consumer behavior.

During the transition process, marketing has contributed by educating the consumers and helped them to develop and practice patterns of thinking and behavior based on the rules of the market economy and to cope with the challenges arising from the new economic order. Especially the buying behavior has been changed: Consumers compare and evaluate offers, demand explanations from the sellers, buy if they have a need, not if products are on the shelf, buy less frequently, and visit modern shopping facilities. Overall, consumers recognize that they are moving into a stronger position vis-à-vis the seller, and make use of a developing consumer sovereignty. By doing so, consumers gain some independence and freedom in making their own decisions.

COMPANIES AND SUPPLIERS LEARN TO OPERATE IN A COMPETITIVE SETTING

The privatization of state-owned companies in Central and Eastern Europe and the opening of the countries in transition toward the world economy have substantially changed the economic setting for corporations. The privatization of state-owned companies is a central area of economic reform in Central and Eastern Europe. In mid-1997, the share of the private sector in GDP ranged between 75 percent for the Czech Republic and 20 percent for Belarus (EBRD, 1997a, p. 14). These figures provide, at best, an indication of the change of the legal status of formerly state-owned companies. They give no indication regarding the restructuring of socialist companies into market-oriented companies. The key question in this context is whether privatization will lead to a turnaround of formerly state-owned, hardly competitive, and plan-based companies into market-oriented and competitive companies. The majority of Eastern companies are far from competitive. Labor productivity in manufacturing is around 50 percent or even lower compared to Western companies. In 1994, half of the companies were profitable (Czech Republic, 81 percent; Hungary, 68 percent; Bulgaria, 34 percent); 15 percent of all companies or fewer (Poland, 14 percent; Bulgaria, 9 percent) had a positive cash flow (EBRD 1996). Many companies lost their markets either to foreign competitors penetrating Eastern markets with Western products or because of the breakdown of trade relations with other formerly socialist countries.

What went wrong? Why have the new ownership and the prospects for profits not accomplished the necessary turnaround to a larger extent? Some of the reasons are: Privatization did not provide enough fresh capital for needed investments which delays technological restructuring. The implemented privatization schemes did not force out the old management. Many companies were privatized by changing the legal status from a state-owned company to a share holding company with the state, state-controlled banks, or investment funds as owners so that the ownership did not really change. In some instances, wild and uncontrolled privatization caused a drain on material and financial resources of Eastern companies undercutting their chances for survival. This all means that the turnaround of Eastern companies from plan-managed companies into market-oriented companies is far from complete. The transition on the company level has just started and will take years. Especially, changes in management styles and managerial behavior will progress only if a constant transfer of management know-how from the West to the East takes place.

All these developments contribute to a lack in competitiveness of the majority of domestic Eastern companies. Most of them still base their competitiveness on cost advantages, employ short-term survival tactics, and have not developed a long-term customer-oriented strategy. Such an approach works as long as competition is still underdeveloped and Eastern companies maintain a reasonable market share in a more or less protected domestic market. With progress in transition, competition will intensify and domestic Eastern companies will have to adopt a market orientation if they want to stay in the market. From a competitive perspective there are currently two segments in the transition markets: Domestic companies compete in one segment and foreign firms in the other. This is possible since the segments represent different clusters of customers being targeted by a different positioning of products and services mainly in regard to price and quality. Over time, foreign companies will be able to penetrate the segments of the Eastern companies because foreign companies have started production in Central and Eastern Europe and can therefore, due to low production costs, compete on price as well. For Eastern firms to penetrate the Western segments based on quality will be much more difficult.

An example for the two segments within the markets of Central and Eastern Europe is the retail system. Western retail chains like Auchan, Leclerc, Metro, Tesco, Carrefour,

Kaisers, Tengelmann, Billa, Meinl, and others are moving into Central and Eastern Europe on a large scale. They implement a greenfield strategy and do not cooperate with local retail systems. Western retail chains are hence competing against local retail outlets which offer a much narrower assortment, hardly carry foreign products, and provide poor facilities (e.g., no parking). Compared to Western Europe, small shops still dominate the retail system in Central and Eastern Europe, but emerging supermarkets will accelerate the concentration process in the retail system. Eastern consumers have started to accept the foreign retail outlets and no longer visit the shop around the corner several times a week. The entry of international retail chains leads to a substitution of local products by international brands. Based on buy-national attitudes, many customers complain of being forced to buy foreign products even though the Hungarian milk or apple is as good as the foreign product. Therefore, those international retailers which offer local products may have a competitive advantage over retailers who focus mainly on international products. In the long run, local retailers will survive only if they form joint ventures among themselves, open modern sales outlets, and implement a customer orientation. But already marketing has changed the retail system in Central and Eastern Europe to the benefit of the customer.

The Eastern companies competitive in Western markets are mainly those in a progressive privatization stage or joint venture companies with foreign participation (the car manufacturer Skoda/VW for instance is contributing 8 percent of all Czech exports). Eastern companies base their competition in Western markets mainly on cost advantages. They offer low-priced products at a relatively low technological level, so that a major quality gap continues to exist. A comparison of the average quality levels of products imported by Western buyers from various countries can be seen in Figure 2.

On the whole, the penetration of the markets in Central and Eastern Europe by foreign companies as exporters and investors has fueled competition and is forcing domestic companies to adapt. Even though there has been a large inflow of FDI since 1989, these cumulative FDI inflows during 1989 to 1997 are just $153 per capita (EBRD, 1998, p. 12). A comparison with the investment flows into the former East Germany lends perspective. By the end of the decade, Western Germany will have transferred $1 trillion to Eastern Germany (Czinkota, 1998). In spite of the transfer of almost $65,000 per capita, major discontent and inequity between the two German regions are likely to persist.

There are some indications that even the limited foreign investment inflows may not continue at the same speed due to political and legal uncertainties and cultural conflicts. Based on their experience, foreign companies operate more cautiously and place heavy emphasis on risk control and risk avoidance. In recent times, an increasing number of foreign companies prefers build-strategies to buy-strategies when entering Central and Eastern Europe since the turnaround of old companies is time-consuming, very costly, and much more difficult than expected. Some companies even disengage from foreign investments, especially in countries which lag behind in political and economic reforms. They find that the benefits of cheap labor and other low cost production factors are being more than absorbed by higher costs in logistics and other operating costs (Hauch-Fleck, 1997, p. 31).

• FIGURE 2 •

QUALITY GAP BETWEEN MACHINERY PRODUCED IMPORTED FROM CENTRAL AND EASTERN EUROPE AND EU AVERAGE

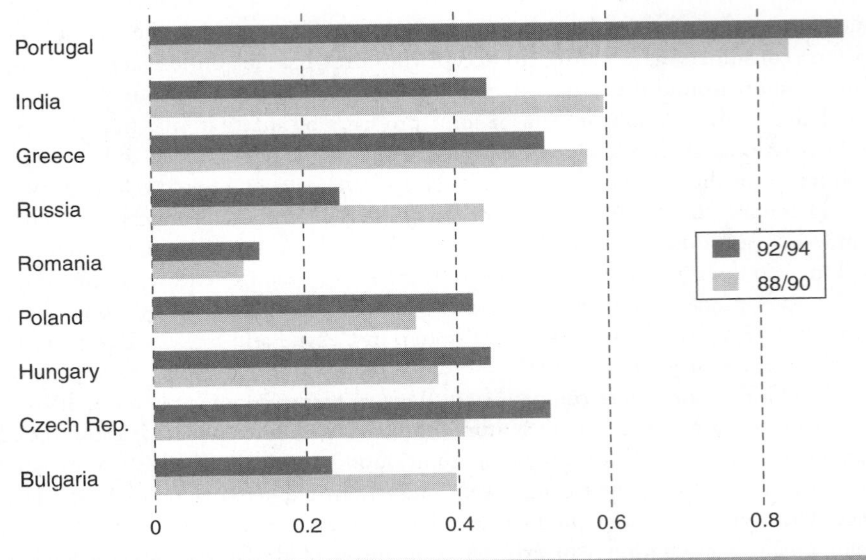

SOURCE: EBRD, 1997a.
EU average 5 1.

This may explain why contract manufacturing is a market entry mode of increasing importance since capital commitment is low, market exit is possible in a very short time, but the benefits of low cost production factors can still be exploited. More than 50 percent of all foreign contract manufacturing by German companies takes place within Central and Eastern Europe; more than 15 percent of all German imports from Central and Eastern Europe are deliveries from contract manufacturing operations (Handelsblatt, 1995, p. 16). There is a shift of contract manufacturing from Asia to Central and Eastern Europe.

In joint ventures cultural conflicts often turn out to be a reason for failure. Western companies tend to overlook that patience and thoroughness, knowledge of the country, good personal contacts, local presence of a decider from the Western partner, stable and reliable supply networks, effective and accepted organizational structures, and effective control mechanisms are key success factors of joint ventures in Central and Eastern Europe (Trommsdorff & Schuchardt, 1998; Trommsdorff, Binsack, Drüner, & Koppelt, 1995).

The marketing environment in Central and Eastern Europe is still different compared to the marketing environment in the industrialized West. This is illustrated by the fact that low purchasing power, import restrictions, low price stability, and uncertain legal conditions are major barriers for market entry into Central and Eastern Europe (Handelsblatt, 1997, p. B 5).

MARKETING MANAGEMENT WILL BE LEARNED

Management styles and managerial behavior are determined by the political and economic system and cultural values of a society. As this foundation is changing, management will change as well. Management tools can be learned in school, but managerial behavior will be learned mainly by doing. This means that as the transition progresses, the behavior of managers in the East is adjusting to the needs of a market economy (Pribova & Savitt, 1995; Tesar & Nieminen, 1994). This process takes time and the adoption of new management skills is lagging behind.

It seems to be especially difficult to give up the managerial behavior learned under the conditions of a planned economy. On the whole, managerial behavior in Central and Eastern Europe is influenced by typical cultural standards which have their roots in the socialist economic system. Using the five cultural dimensions of Hofstede (1991), one can argue that Central and Eastern Europe is characterized by high power distance, low individualism, masculinity, high uncertainty avoidance, and short-term orientation. In the planned economies managers implemented orders handed down by the national economic plan, the party, or the state planning bureaucracy. The decision process and the areas of responsibility were structured very clearly as a top-down model, so that an interaction across hierarchical borders was almost impossible. Managers and their staff were not accustomed to taking risks and postponed necessary decisions while waiting for orders from above. With the ongoing transition, companies gain autonomy and independence which requires managers to take responsibility and to prepare and implement decisions on their own. Especially middle management still waits for orders from above and demonstrates insecurity when confronted with the need for fast decision making. On the other hand, within working groups or teams, low individualism prevailed so that a we-attitude and collective pride developed in connection with solidarity among group members, which contributes to a friendly working climate and efficiency. Transition also caused a shift from a long-term orientation under the planned economy to a short-term orientation which is directed at survival.

The obvious deficit in marketing behavior in Central and Eastern Europe is the lack of customer orientation and the weak striving for customer satisfaction. With competition still underdeveloped and customers less demanding, companies only now start to care about customer needs. The necessary change toward a marketing orientation of the Eastern companies is not so much an issue of modern marketing skills, methods, and instruments but mainly a behavioral problem. Its success will require for management to grasp the meaning and the philosophy of marketing as a conceptual tool and managerial system which are instrumental to generate profits for the company and to improve the well-being of consumers and society at the same time.

The gap between existing management skills and needed management skills can be narrowed by the transfer of management know-how from West to East. For such a transfer to be successful, however, it needs to achieve a linkage between knowledge, learning, and actual change. Well-entrenched societal structures, at least in the short run, may not be overcome by learning alone. For example, in many Central European firms, a move up on the career ladder still depends on seniority, with little attention paid to capability or expertise. In order to encourage market-oriented thinking, the system needs to show that knowledge causes advancement.

But knowledge alone is not sufficient. It must be translated into changed behavioral patterns on part of all employees—the ones interacting directly with customers as well as the senior executives. Many indigenous firms face a dilemma here. In some of them, senior management has a vision of a marketing orientation, but is unable to have this vision understood or implemented by employees. In others, some employees are trying to apply new ways of thinking, but they are ignored or dismissed by their managers who are not yet ready for employees who participate or speak up. Only those firms which manage to synchronize management and labor in their thinking about a market orientation are able to achieve lasting shifts in behavior and performance. They are the ones which focus systematically on improving behavioral skills such as communication, decision making, customer orientation, and team building (Czinkota & Springer, 1997).

FUTURE CONTRIBUTIONS OF MARKETING

Marketing will evolve with the ongoing transformation. The shifts related to transition are only the beginning of a process. But the announcement of reforms and the intention to establish a market economy do not automatically result in change itself. For example, the abolition of a centrally planned economy does not create a market economy. Laws permitting the emergence of private-sector entrepreneurs do not create entrepreneurship. The reduction of price controls does not immediately make goods available or affordable. The abolition of monopolies will not lead to competition overnight. Highly prized fundamentals of the market economy such as the reliance on competition, the support of the profit motive, and the willingness to live with risk on a corporate and personal level are not yet fully accepted (Czinkota & Ronkainen, 1998, p. 776).

Transition is a learning process which needs time and requires a readiness for change on the individual, company, and societal level. Some claim that transition will be a success only when the levels of technological and economic development, income, and consumption are similar to the standards of the industrialized West. This is at least the target and promise set out by politicians in the East and West. If the GDP per capita is a valid benchmark, then it will take decades or even generations before the East catches up. As Figure 3 indicates, leading reformers like Slovenia or the Czech Republic will reach between 80 and 90 percent of the EU-average GDP per capita in the year 2010. Other countries are even further behind. Measured this way, it will take a long time to determine the degree of transition success and provide ample room for disagreements, discontent, and reversals of policies.

• FIGURE 3 •

GDP PER CAPITA IN CENTRAL AND EASTERN EUROPE COMPARED TO EU AVERAGE

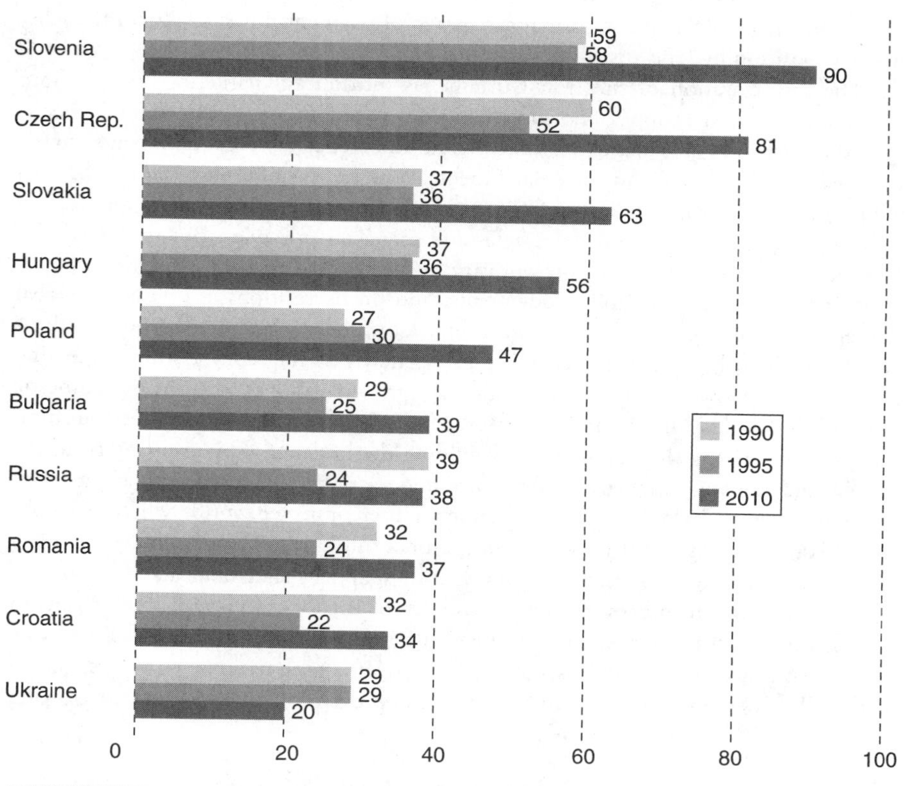

SOURCE: EBRD, 1996, 1997a, 1997b.

But perhaps the forecasts which use short-term situations and conditions to produce long-term projections are limited in their value. We believe that the success of transition needs to be measured not by any particular arbitrary outcome, but by the direction taken by an economy—a direction which attributes value to individual well-being, choice, and empowerment, but also does not neglect the importance of overall societal welfare. Marketing may not succeed in placing the primacy of consumption on the same pedestal that it has in the West. Market forces, however, are instrumental in signaling demand and in helping to determine the allocation of resources.

Nonetheless, existing social structures and expectations may result in the emergence of new marketing concepts or new marketing applications which blend the old with the new. For example, the prized marketing dimension of individual ownership of products may give way to the concept of "product use," and thus permit a more rapid increase in overall welfare levels than would otherwise be possible. A transformation of the spirit of collectivism may give unexpected rise to new concepts of voluntary individual social responsibility, or lead to consumption priorities which are more oriented toward intangibles. In such instances the implementation of marketing would shift markedly, requiring a major redesign of payment flows, product life cycles, product, positioning, and distribution strategies.

The disintegration of the Iron Curtain has introduced marketing thought into Central and Eastern Europe. The entry and presence of Western companies will continue the nurturing of a marketing system. The emergence of an economic area covering the whole of Europe and the enlargement of the European Union toward the East will promote the harmonization of Western and Eastern marketing systems and lead to some convergence of marketing strategies and management styles. But the speed and the outcome of the transformation will vary by country, based on each nation's popular aspirations, leadership, and endowments, and on its relationships with the global market. Export-influenced growth will be important. Many Western countries and firms will be surprised by and will need to adjust to newly arising competition emanating from the East. However, most of the causes for growth will be rooted in the domestic economy and its institutions and processes. Marketing can contribute to the transition process by informing the population, by guiding the leadership, by inspiring competition, by encouraging supportive global economic relations, and by offering choice. But economic interests are only one dimension in an interconnected world, which also looks toward issues such as security, peace, and personal fulfillment. As a discipline, marketing has an opportunity to assume a major role by shaping society and the future of history. However, in this process marketing will not be the focus, but rather the means to an end, the support which helps to achieve a better society. Marketing must also be ready to adapt to local conditions, to reflect newly emerging national priorities, and to offer itself to develop new economic relational approaches which will lead to growing individual and societal contentment.

References

Brenner, E. (1997). Werben oder Sterben, Gewinn, 16(3), 46–48.

Business Central Europe (1997). May.

Church, N. (1992). Advertising in the Eastern Bloc: Current practices and anticipated avenues of development. Journal of Global Marketing, 5(3), 109–129.

Czinkota, M. R. (1998). Hungary in the global economy: Strategies for improved competitiveness. European Business Journal, 10(1), 39–45.

Czinkota, M. R., & Dichtl, E. (1996). Export controls and global changes. der markt, 35(138), 148–155.

Czinkota, M. R., & Ronkainen, I. A. (1998). International marketing (5th ed.). Fort Worth: Dryden Press.

Czinkota, M. R., & Springer, R. (1997). Managementausbildung in Rußland unter den Bedingungen der Transformation zur Marktwirtschaft, der markt, 36(141), 51–62.

Czinkota, M. R., Gaisbauer, H., & Springer, R. (1997). A perspective on marketing in Central and Eastern Europe. The International Executive, 39(6), 831–848.

EBRD (1996). Transition report 1996.

EBRD (1997a). Transition report 1997a.

EBRD (1997b). Transition report update 1997b.

EBRD (1998). Transition report update 1998.

Ettenson, R. (1993). Brand name and country of origin effects in the emerging market economies of Russia, Poland and Hungary. International Marketing Review, 10(5), 14–36.

Feick, L., Coulter, R. H., & Price, L. (1995). Consumers in the transition to a market economy: Hungary, 1989–1992. International Marketing Review, 12(5), 18–34.

Gajewski, S. (1992). Consumer behavior in economics of shortage. Journal of Business Research, 24(1), 5–10.

Good, L. K., & Huddleston, P. (1995). Ethnocentrism of Polish and Russian consumers: Are feelings and intentions related? International Marketing Review, 12(5), 35–48.

Handelsblatt (1995). No. 206.

Handelsblatt (1997). No. 77.

Hauch-Fleck, M.-L. (1997). Blauäugig kalkuliert. Die Zeit, 44, 24. 10.

Healey, N. M. (1994). The transition economies of Central and Eastern Europe: A political, economic, social and technological analysis. Columbia Journal of World Business, Spring, 62–70.

Heyder, H., Musiol, K., & Peters, K. (1992). Advertising in Europe: Attitudes toward advertising in certain key East and West European countries. Marketing and Research Today, March, 58–68.

Hofstede, G. H. (1991). Cultures and organizations. Software of the mind. New York: McGraw Hill.

Hooley, G. (1993). Raising the Iron Curtain: Marketing in a period of transition. European Journal of Marketing, 11/12, 6–20.

Huszagh, S. M., Huszagh, F. W., & Hanks, G. F. (1992). Macroeconomic conditions and international marketing management. International Marketing Review, 9(1), 6–18.

Jens, U. (1993). Schocktherapie order Gradualismus? Zur Transformation einer Zentralverwaltungswirtschaft. Wirtschaftsdienst, 3, 158–164.

Mayer, C. (1976). Marketing in Eastern European socialist countries. University of Michigan Business Review, 28(1), 16–21.

Mueller, R. D., Wenthe, J., & Baron, P. (1993). The evolution of distribution systems: A framework for analysing market changes in Eastern Europe: The case of Hungary. International Marketing Review, 10(4), 36–52.

Naor, J. (1986). Toward a socialist marketing concept: The case of Romania. Journal of Marketing, 50, 28–39.

Naor, J. (1990). Research on Eastern Europe and Soviet marketing: Constraints, challenges and opportunities. International Marketing Review, 7(1), 7–14.

Olivier, M. (1991). Eastern Europe: The path to success. Columbia Journal of World Business, Spring, 10–14.

Papadopoulos, N., Heslop, L., & Beracs, J. (1990). National stereotypes and product evaluations in a socialist country, International Marketing Review, 7(1), 32–47.

Pribova, M., & Savitt, R. (1995). Attitudes of Czech managers toward markets and marketing. International Marketing Review, 12(5), 60–71.

Rose, R., & Hearpfer, C. (1996). Fears and hopes: New democracies barometer survey, Transition, The World Bank, 7(5–6), 14.

Samli, C. (1986). Changing marketing systems in Eastern Europe: What Western marketers should know. International Marketing Review, Winter, 7–16.

Schüller, A. (1991). Probleme des Übergangs von der Staatswirtschaft zur Marktwirtschaft, In Zur Transformation von Wirtschaftssystemen: Von der sozialistischen Planwirtschaft zur sozialen Marktwirtschaft. Marburg: Arbeitsberichte zum Systemvergleich.

Shama, A. (1992). Transforming the consumer in Russia and Eastern Europe. International Marketing Review, 9(5), 43–59.

Tesar, G., & Nieminen, J. (1994). Management conflict in joint ventures: A bilateral perspective. In P. Chadraba & R. Springer (Eds.), Proceedings on the Conference on Marketing Strategies for Central and Eastern Europe. Vienna.

Trommsdorff, Binsack, Drüner, & Koppelt (1995). Erfolgreich kooperieren in Osteuropa. Köln.

Trommsdorff, V., & Schuchardt, C. (1998). Transformation osteuropäischer Unternehmen. Wiesbaden.

Wagner, H. (1991). Einige Theorien des Systemwandels im Vergleich: Und ihre Anwendbarkeit für die Erklärung des gegenwärtigen Reformprozesses in Osteuropa. In K. Backhaus (Ed.), Systemwandel und reformen in östlichen wirtschaften. Marburg.

FIVE RULES FOR WINNING EMERGING MARKET CONSUMERS

James A. Gingrich

Western Europe, Japan and the United States have been the engines powering the world's economy since World War II. That is no longer the case. Emerging and developing economies, on a purchasing parity basis, now total 44 percent of the world's economy, and in the last decade, emerging nations were responsible for two-thirds of the world's economic growth. The consumer base in these economies already measures in the hundreds of millions, is young and is growing three times as rapidly as in the developed world. As recent events have demonstrated, what happens in these economies affects us all.

Given these trends, multinational corporations face profound changes in the economic landscape. Over the next 10 to 15 years, most of the total world growth in consumption of consumer goods will likely be concentrated in the largest of the developing economies. In that time span, these strategic emerging markets will grow to be comparable in aggregate size to the Group of Seven leading industrial nations (the United States, Japan, Britain, France, Germany, Canada and Italy).

The future scale and growth of global consumer businesses is dependent on their success in building strong positions in these new, challenging markets.

There are a handful of consumer goods companies that have already demonstrated the potential contained within the big, emerging markets. Companies such as Unilever, Coca-Cola, Gillette, Nestlé and Colgate-Palmolive all now capture one-third or more

---

James A. Gingrich is a vice president of Booz-Allen & Hamilton based in New York City. In his 16 years with the firm, he has specialized in assisting consumer-goods and retailing clients on issues of business building and growth, organization and operations effectiveness. Mr. Gingrich has worked throughout the Americas and Europe, and for five years coordinated Booz-Allen's consumer practice in Brazil, Argentina and Chile. He holds B.S., M.Eng. and M.B.A. degrees from Cornell University.

of their revenue from these markets, with profitability equal to, or higher than, what they achieve in developed economies. For example, the Coca-Cola Company now derives 37 percent of its revenue from Latin America, Africa and Asia, and these markets contribute a stunning 49 percent of its operating profits. Similarly, the Colgate-Palmolive Company receives 45 percent of its revenue from these same markets and nearly half of its operating income.

These pioneers have been committed to the emerging world for several generations, establishing leadership positions and brands in nearly every important emerging market. Today, in countries such as Thailand, Argentina and Indonesia, these players are identified more often as local enterprises than as foreign multinationals by their consumers. Unilever, for instance, controls nearly half of the Indian detergent market; Nestlé, 80 percent of the Chinese coffee market, and Colgate-Palmolive, 75 percent of the Brazilian toothpaste market.

Emerging market leaders are poised to ride the growth of these economies for years to come. Coca-Cola, for example, is growing at 30 percent per year in China, and its business there is fast approaching 10 percent of its total United States volume. Nevertheless, per capita consumption in China remains only about 2 percent of that in the United States, pointing to one of the reasons that Wall Street has pushed Coca-Cola's stock price to 45 times its earnings.

The success enjoyed by these pioneers, however, is not the norm. The largest group of multinationals has followed a flag-planting strategy: transplanting existing "first-world" products with minimal investment into a wide variety of new markets, without achieving significant market share in any of them. While multinationals are quick to cite the extent of their worldwide footprint, the global portfolio of most multinationals remains dominated by United States and Western European economies. The emerging markets combined in the portfolio of flag-planters are typically limited to less than 10 percent of their worldwide sales. Given their timid positions and weak understandings of these countries, the returns of those who have followed the "flag-planting" route are generally poor.

While there is a natural tendency for multinationals to build upon what made them successful in their core markets in Western Europe and the United States, it is this practice that routinely gets them into trouble. In reality, consumer goods companies cannot export their business models, products and marketing formulas wholesale from their core developed markets and expect them to work in places such as India, Turkey or Mexico. Emerging markets differ in their governmental policies, regulations and macroeconomic behaviors; in the structure of their consumer markets, distribution systems and competitive sets; in the needs and behaviors of their consumers.

Even the most experienced are not immune from making this mistake, as Coca-Cola recently found in India. When Coca-Cola went back into the market in 1993, it invested heavily behind the Coke brand, using its typical global positioning, and watched its market leadership slip to Pepsi. Recognizing its mistake, Coke re-emphasized a popular local cola brand (Thums Up) and refocused its Coke brand advertising to be more relevant to the local Indian consumer.

WINNING STRATEGIES

In 1998, Niall W.A. FitzGerald, chairman of Unilever P.L.C., summarized the challenge facing Western consumer businesses when he said, "The real action is increasingly going to be in the developing and emerging markets. Business should not be so mesmerized by the current economic difficulties in these markets that companies ignore the enormous long-term economic potential. However, realizing that potential will not be easy. It will not only require a greater emphasis on understanding what are the needs of the consumer, but a radically different way of approaching them."

What must global consumer businesses do in emerging countries that is radically different? How should consumer goods multinationals target the right markets? What sort of business model is needed for emerging markets, and how does it differ from the model to which multinationals are accustomed? What strategies and organizations work most effectively in countries such as Indonesia, Brazil, India and China?

The most important lessons for what it takes to build a large and profitable presence in emerging markets can be summarized in five rules:

1. REACH THE MASSES: MANAGE AFFORDABILITY

Consumers in big, emerging markets such as Brazil, India, Poland and China have suffered for many years under closed economies and a limited selection of shoddy goods produced by inefficient, domestic manufacturers. Now, with economic liberalization, freer trade and higher incomes, these consumers are hungry for high-quality products and are prepared to spend.

When we discuss the consumer base in emerging markets, however, we need to recognize that it is still significantly poorer than the consumer base of the Group of Seven industrial nations. Middle class in the big, emerging countries is typically a family earning $3,000 to $10,000 a year when measured in equivalent purchasing power. There is an even larger mass of the population below this income level that is also prepared to spend, albeit selectively. Only a small fraction of the population of countries such as Turkey or India are well-to-do, middle class by American standards. For example, hypermarkets in Poland have captured only about 12 percent of the market there since they cater only to the portion of the population with cars. Most retailing in Poland is still done in local shops that people can reach on foot.

Nevertheless, families in the emerging markets become active consumers at surprisingly low income levels. For example, refrigerator penetration in Mexico is roughly 90 percent. Television penetration in China's coastal cities is nearly 100 percent. However, the consumer in these markets is much more sharply balancing the price/performance equation than the Western consumer is, and so affordability becomes a key driver of marketplace development and success. Improvements in product affordability often lead to large jumps in consumption, particularly for higher value-added goods. One company recently found, for example, that a 20 percent reduction in average pricing in a frozen food category roughly doubled the category's size.

Why Are Big Emerging Markets Strategic?

Multinationals must now consider as strategic a handful—perhaps 10—emerging economies, given their size, population and prospects for growth. The combined size of these economies is nearly two-thirds of the combined gross domestic product of the Group of Seven industrial nations (the United States, Japan, Britain, France, Germany, Canada and Italy) in purchasing power parity terms. The "Big Five" emerging markets—China, India, Brazil, Mexico and Indonesia—are among the 12 largest economies in the world, with a combined purchasing power already half that of the Group of Seven nations.

In many cases, the size of the consumer markets in these countries rivals that of the developed markets. For instance, Mexico and Brazil are the second- and third-largest soft-drink markets in the world, each consuming more than Germany, France and Italy combined. China, Brazil and India are among the five largest markets for televisions and refrigerators when measured in units.

Over the past three decades, emerging markets have consistently shown growth rates well above those of more mature economies, albeit with greater levels of volatility. Looking forward, three structural socio-demographic and economic factors will ensure that consumption growth in the big emerging markets continues to significantly outpace that of the developed world well into the next century:

1. **Favorable Consumer Demographics:** With a combined 2.6 billion people, the five largest developing nations have a population that is four times that of the Group of Seven. Emerging market populations are expected to continue to grow significantly faster than those in the Group of Seven nations, many of which now have birth rates below that required to maintain today's population level.

   Furthermore, people in the developed world are living progressively longer and leaving the work force earlier. It is now forecast that by the year 2030, there will be only two workers to support the average Social Security recipient in the United States. With fewer workers generating output, and with more of the population dependent on those who do, income growth, savings levels and economic growth will all be lower.

   In contrast, the populations of emerging countries are comparatively young. For example, in the year 2010, the percentage of the population over 60 in the Group of Seven nations is expected to range from a low of 19 percent in the United States to 30 percent in Japan. Most European nations will average nearly 25 percent. In the emerging nations though, the situation will be quite different. In Brazil and India, for example, only 9 percent of the population will be elderly; in Mexico and Indonesia only 8 percent; and in China 12 percent. The working-age population in these markets—which will be the portion of the population driving economic and consumption growth—will grow at rates three to four times that of the developed world.

2. **Rising Household Incomes and Easy Credit:** The rapid economic growth in the developing world is fueling household income growth. One researcher, Jeffrey A. Rosensweig, forecasts in his book "Winning the Global Game" (Free Press, 1998) that in little more than 10 years, three out of every eight middle-class consumers will live in the developing world.

   The consumption impact of income growth is twofold. First, those who are economically active increase absolute consumption while often trading up into higher-value goods. When consumption per capita of a particular category is mapped against gross domestic product per capita, the curve is normally concave, reflecting a diminishing growth rate in consumption as incomes rise. For the majority of mid-to-higher value-added categories, the "power portion" of the consumption curve—the point at which consumption is rising most quickly—lies between $3,000 and $10,000 of gross domestic product per capita, after which consumption growth flattens. The implication is that even if there were equivalent macroeconomic growth rates, the markets for consumer goods would grow disproportionately faster in emerging markets than in the developed world.

   Second, rising incomes bring whole new waves of consumers into the market who were previously not economically active, typically at a trigger point of about $2,000 to $3,000 in annual income when expressed in equivalent purchasing power. For example, the consumption boom following economic stabilization in Brazil in 1994–1995 was driven primarily by the entry of 30 million consumers into the economy who were previously inactive.

   In many of these economies, the increased availability of credit will give a further boost to consumption. For instance, Argentina's economic stabilization under President Carlos Saul Menem suddenly made credit available to all classes of consumers. As a result, while consumption grew dramatically in packaged goods, durables such as household appliances, consumer electronics and automobiles exploded. Nevertheless, even in economies such as Argentina's, credit remains expensive. Future rate reductions should drive consumption beyond the normal "income" effect.

3. **Improving Productivity:** Surprisingly, many consumer goods are more expensive in emerging markets than in home markets. In large

measure, this can be traced to the fact that the productivity of developing countries significantly lags behind that of the developed world. The reasons for this are many—not the least of which include poor infrastructure, arcane distribution systems, lower levels of education and histories of being closed and sheltered economies.

However, productivity gains are occurring quite rapidly in these economies, and this is showing up in the form of more accessible pricing. For example, food prices in Brazil have been dropping more than 5 percent per year in real terms over the past four years, driven in part by the rapid improvements in productivity across the food supply chain. Similarly, a reduction of tariff barriers has led to rapid price declines and quality improvements in durable sectors such as white and brown goods and automobiles.

Consumer goods multinationals can build big businesses in emerging markets only if they manage affordability in a way that makes their products accessible to the masses. Roberto Goizetta, the late chief executive officer of Coca-Cola, set the objective that Coke be the same price as tea in China. C & A, the apparel retailer owned by the Dutch Brennimkmeir family, has been able to build a successful business in Latin American countries because it offers reasonable quality goods in clean, well-lit, mall settings at price points that are accessible to all consumers. C & A's philosophy is that it will offer the best $10, $20 and $30 dresses on the market. As a result, its sales span all income ranges. In Brazil, for example, about two-thirds of its sales are to families with incomes below $8,000 per year.

In contrast, consumer goods companies that attempt to sell only their "first world" products are relegated to being simply "market skimmers" and suffer from retarded category development. For a long time, the Procter & Gamble Company ran an anemic disposable diaper business in Brazil because it tried to sell only its top-end Fases diaper based on "first-world" technology.

Reaching the masses frequently means that consumer goods companies need to rethink their product lines with a sharp eye on the price/performance equation. In India, Unilever was ambushed by a local detergent maker, Nirma, that captured a substantial portion of the market with a low-cost alternative to Unilever's premium brands. Only after Unilever completely revised its product, price point, marketing strategy and distribution system was it able to come up with a viable low-cost competitor, called Wheel, priced at nearly one-quarter the price of premium brands. Today, Unilever has regained control of nearly half of the Indian market, and its sales of Wheel exceed the sales of its leading premium brand. Similarly, Procter & Gamble was finally able to drive growth in the Brazilian disposable diaper category after it introduced a less sophisticated unisex diaper that it could profitably market at nearly half the price of its "first world" product.

Structuring their product lines for the emerging-market consumer requires that multinationals challenge their product development process and investments. Mr. FitzGerald of Unilever made just this point when he said, "Consider how much of our industry's innovation is still geared to the developed world, as opposed to the great many people living in the developing and emerging markets. We are, for instance, inventing surfactants that cost many times more than those used for the basic job in the developing world—inventing them for minimal gain in the almost functionally saturated West. . . . We must shift the focus of our research and development effort to the vast numbers of consumers who in 2025 will live in the emerging markets of today."

Current research and development footprints of many consumer-product multinationals, which tend to be centralized near world headquarters, will certainly have to expand. Unilever, for one, believes its scientists need to have an intimate understanding of its consumers that can be achieved only through proximity. Its chairman asks rhetorically, "Can a United States scientist in California really understand the problems and needs of the consumers in developing and emerging markets?" Consequently, Unilever has installed a network of 68 innovation centers in 19 countries, many of which are emerging markets.

2. BE UBIQUITOUS: INVEST IN DISTRIBUTION

Distribution is one of the most challenging problems for consumer-products businesses in emerging markets. While supermarket and hypermarket retailers are increasingly present in major capital cities, consumers living on the peripheries of these cities and in the countryside continue to purchase the large majority of goods through local shops.

The tendency of new multinational entrants is to focus initially on large chains in major cities. Their strategy is to build volume quickly, without having to invest in costly sales and distribution systems. The fact that these retail chains often have familiar names such as Carrefour (of France), Wal-Mart (of the United States), Sonae (of Portugal), and Ahold (of the Netherlands) adds to their sense of comfort.

There are several difficulties with this strategy, however. The most obvious is that these manufacturers are walking away from what is typically 50 percent to 90 percent of the market. The strategy also puts them in an extremely vulnerable negotiating position with the major retailers. For instance, a local Brazilian yogurt producer distributes 80 percent of its volume to more than 10,000 small shops around the capital of São Paulo. With these small shops, the producer can command a relatively higher price, and so the company is quite profitable. As a consequence, the producer can negotiate very aggressively with the major chains in the area such as Carrefour, because the producer knows it has this profitable volume base. In contrast, major yogurt producers such as Groupe Danone (France) are much more dependent on the major chains for their volume and must be much more accommodating in their negotiations.

Failing to build quickly a broad distribution base also allows competitors to more readily combat new entrants. When Quilmes Industrial S.A., the Argentine beer leader, entered the Chilean market, it was more dependent than the local market leader, Compania Cervecerias Unidas S.A., on the supermarket channel. Consequently, C.C.U.

chose to be aggressive on pricing in this channel, while tying up the more fragmented distribution base of bars and restaurants with exclusivity agreements. As a result, Quilmes today struggles with its market share and profitability in Chile.

Finding cost-effective ways to build broad and deep sales and distribution coverage in the emerging markets is one of the most critical challenges facing consumer products companies. This can rarely be done on the cheap. Alliances with local producers that agree to provide distribution rarely work. Multinationals should also be cautious about relying too heavily on broad-line wholesalers/distributors in many of these countries; these wholesalers tend to carry only the fastest moving products, do not provide merchandising support and frequently generate their profits from speculative buying or tax evasion.

There are creative alternatives. For example, several consumer products companies have patiently developed a network of exclusive distributors to service small accounts in selected emerging countries. These exclusive distributors can operate at as little as half the cost of broader-line wholesalers, with significantly greater effectiveness.

Even when companies serve smaller shops directly, there may be creative ways to do so less expensively. In several countries, Coca-Cola, which usually visits its smallest retailers once or twice weekly, has proposed that they receive three to four weeks of consigned inventory in return for exclusivity. When Coca-Cola returns at the end of the period, the retailers pay only for the product sold during that time. For cash-strapped small shop owners, this is extremely attractive. Coca-Cola wins increased sales at the expense of displaced competition and a much lower cost-to-serve, with delivery visits cut by a factor of three or more.

Alternative channels can also be effective in emerging markets. For example, in Brazil, up to 15 percent of all apparel is sold through "sack ladies" who sell door-to-door in poorer neighborhoods. The majority of cosmetics as well as other products are typically sold through direct sales forces of hundreds of thousands of working women who pitch products to their fellow workers. As a result, multinationals such as Revlon Inc. that rely on traditional mass channels are at a distinct disadvantage.

3. CREATE DESIRABILITY: BUILD STRONG BRANDS

Interestingly, despite the limited financial means of the emerging market consumer, branding could well be more important in these markets than it is in markets such as the United States or Western Europe. In part, this is due to the aspirational attraction that strong brands have for lower-income consumers, particularly in "badge" categories. For instance, the number of lower-income consumers on the streets of São Paulo or Shanghai wearing $100 jeans, a price that represents a month's wages, is striking.

For most categories, however, the importance of branding is related to the quality guarantee that it provides. As a consequence, many producers have built brands that command price premiums in categories that to Western eyes would appear to be commodity categories. For example, the Italian multinational Parmalat S.p.A. has used a clever advertising campaign in Brazil to convey its concern for and love of babies, and in so doing, to imply a safety and quality guarantee for its products. As a result, Parmalat has been able to command a 10 percent price premium in the Brazilian milk category while building a leading market-share position, in a category previously dominated by regional milk cooperatives more concerned with volume than profit.

A fact of life in almost all emerging markets is that multinationals will face competition from local entrepreneurs whose informal operating practices, such as tax evasion or selective attention to labor laws, secures them a large cost advantage. Brand equity becomes an essential weapon in defending market position in the face of this type of competition. For instance, Frito-Lay Inc. has been able to sustain a dominant market position in Brazil by building its leading brands, such as Ruffles. Frito-Lay has invested large sums in local farmers who plant higher quality potato varieties, in the best production technologies and in a distribution system that maintains product freshness, in order to ensure a quality advantage. Simultaneously, Frito-Lay has dominated advertising spending. As a consequence, it has grown its market share despite facing a host of local competitors whose pricing can be half of Frito-Lay's.

Multinationals must remember that few emerging market consumers are global citizens, and therefore global brands may have little cachet in these markets. So overall ad spending in many of these emerging markets has exploded, and the cost of advertising has become increasingly expensive. The cost per viewer in countries such as Brazil, Argentina and Turkey equals or surpasses that of the United States. Even where the absolute cost is low (e.g., China, Indonesia, India), the effective cost is much higher after these costs are factored in by the percentage of the viewing public that is economically active.

Because the investment required to build and support a brand in these markets is high compared with the small size of many categories, companies should carefully weigh using umbrella brands in emerging markets as a means to create scale, particularly when exploring new categories. This strategy has been followed for years by local players such as Sadia and Arisco in Brazil. It is also a strategy that is increasingly utilized by experienced multinationals. Parmalat, as an example, has leveraged the success of its brand in the milk category into such diverse categories as cookies and crackers, cereals and juices.

Often the best strategy is to invest behind local brands that already have some degree of consumer loyalty, especially when targeting middle-income consumers. For example, the Whirlpool Corporation has chosen to use the Brastemp brand name in Brazil as its leading brand in that country given its preexisting equity. Danone has built a significant business in China largely through strong local brands such as Haomen Amoy. Similarly, Coca-Cola has now reversed course in India, and is investing behind the local Thums Up brand.

4. PLAY TO WIN: PICK YOUR FIGHTS WELL

Several years ago, Kraft Foods Inc. (a subsidiary of the Philip Morris Companies) entered the Brazilian food market through a sales and distribution agreement with Bunge International Ltd., a major Brazilian food company. The parties chose to import Kraft's products in order to quickly place them on supermarket shelves. Initially, products such as Philadelphia Cream Cheese were big consumer hits. Local competitors, however, soon followed with similar products at much lower prices. The Kraft/Bunge alliance, lacking local production capability, was unable to match the pricing of local players. In addition, Bunge, operating on a slim, volume-based fee, did not have the financial incentive to invest behind the Kraft products at point-of-sale. Kraft products quickly lost share and the alliance was soon dissolved.

Multinationals must play to win in the emerging markets. Too many companies fool around in the high end of these markets and remain timid about investment. Rather than shielding these companies from losses, this flag-planting strategy only exacerbates them.

Emerging markets are no different in this respect from the United States or Western Europe. Consumer goods multinationals must build leading or strong No. 2 positions in their target categories to be profitable over the long haul. Further, getting to critical mass is vital, given the sizable minimum investments necessary in brand-building and sales, distribution and production infrastructure. Scale and the demonstration of long-term commitment also create an environment that is attractive to scarce local management talent. Dabblers in these markets should either get serious or get out.

This may have been Pepsico Inc.'s attitude several years ago when it decided to make a major bet on the Brazilian soft drink market, seeking to triple its market share to 20 percent. With much fanfare, Pepsi announced in 1994 a $500 million investment to build a modern bottling and distribution network from scratch, as well as to support significant brand support activities. However, the market was already dominated by Coca-Cola and two strong, local producers, Brahma and Antarctica. Pepsi soon found itself in a war that it could not win.

Pepsi was unable to match its competitors' market coverage and reach a million points-of-sale. On one hand, Pepsi found itself being attacked aggressively in the supermarket channel on price by competitors that had a much larger customer base. On the other hand, in the small, neighborhood bars and restaurants that make up the large majority of the total market, all three of the existing market participants were also selling beer through their distribution systems. This provided them up to 10 times the scale of Pepsi in these smaller accounts, creating both the customer leverage to lock Pepsi out and the ability to serve these accounts at substantially lower cost. Pepsi, without the local market familiarity of the established players, also quickly accumulated huge amounts of uncollectible credit extended to thousands of these small customers.

Two years after Pepsi's major investment, The Wall Street Journal succinctly reported that "Pepsico's greatest expectations for growth of its soft drinks business outside the United States market have centered on Latin America. Until now." Pepsi's Brazilian bottler was in bankruptcy, its market share remained stuck below 10 percent and the corporation was forced to announce a write-down of nearly $600 million in its international beverage operations.

Equal weight should be given to choosing categories that are attractive opportunities in a given market. For example, consumers' food consumption normally follows fairly predictable patterns. Caloric intake flattens at around $5,000 of gross domestic product per capita. However, consumers steadily trade up in the types of foods they eat, moving from grains that provide basic sustenance to increasingly more value-added products. Consequently, it is often possible to identify potential category-consumption levels as an economy develops, and therefore find categories with the greatest potential for rapid growth.

Care still needs to be given to developing products that are appropriate to local markets. A jam producer studying the Brazilian and Argentine markets recently noted that the Brazilian market seemed to hold significant potential because per capita jelly and jam consumption was one-tenth that of Argentina, clearly a difference not justified by the relative income levels of the two countries. However, Argentines consume jam at "tea time," a custom that does not exist in Brazil. More importantly, Argentina's climate and soil conditions make it a major wheat producer, leading it to consume three times more bread per capita than Brazil. Brazilians simply do not have as much use for jam!

5. BE LOCAL: FOSTER EMERGING-MARKET ENTREPRENEURS

The extreme volatility and unconventional business methods in emerging markets require different management skills than are needed in mature, Western markets. For emerging market managers, raging inflation, currency swings, new taxes, continually changing business regulations and interest-rate instability are all part of the normal macroeconomic environment. For example, in the past dozen years, Brazilian governments have announced seven major economic packages (as well as several minor packages), or more than one new package every two years. The impact of these swings tends to drive disproportionate reactions in consumer consumption because a large proportion of consumption is driven by marginal consumers. In an economic downturn, these consumers either trade down in their consumption habits or drop out altogether. For instance, one department store saw its sales fall 40 percent in the early 1990s as Brazil entered a recession, only to bounce back during a currency stabilization program in 1994. Today, many categories in Southeast Asian markets have suffered similarly violent collapses. When these economies bounce back, there may be an equally severe upturn.

For managers who are unaccustomed to such an environment, the ride can be pretty wild. It can also be expensive for their parent companies. This is why the most experienced emerging market multinationals generally have strong country managers who generate significant value through their entrepreneurial spirit and intimate understanding of the local environment. They are provided with the right global support and the freedom to make decisions quickly. This ability to be more agile in the turbulent emerging-market environment is a significant competitive advantage.

Creating this level of agility may require that multinationals retool their traditional planning and budgeting systems. Coca-Cola's chief executive officer, Douglas Ivester, for one, is hoping to eventually do away with annual business plans and move to a system of continuous planning that will allow Coke's executives to respond more quickly to changing conditions. As one Coke executive commented last year in The Wall Street Journal, "Right now, if I was fixed on an annual event plan in Asia, I'd be dead in the water."

The challenges to managers in emerging markets, however, are not limited to the macroeconomic roller coaster. Managers in these countries know that their success frequently rests on their ability to compete effectively with unconventional competition such as product counterfeiters, product diverters (either within or across country borders) and informal competitors who ignore local labor and tax laws. Experienced managers also learn that what to outsiders appears to be opaque or corrupt power networks can be used to advantage once understood and properly managed.

Agility was key when Colgate-Palmolive gained 75 percent of the Brazilian toothpaste market after it purchased Kolynos. Procter & Gamble opposed the purchase on antitrust grounds, but Colgate-Palmolive was able to convince government authorities that a fair solution was to withdraw the Kolynos brand name from the market for four years. That problem out of the way, Colgate-Palmolive introduced a new toothpaste brand using the same formulation and graphics as the old Kolynos brand. Consumers understood, and Colgate-Palmolive has lost little market share.

Multinationals need to consider how they will address the unique challenges of managing in emerging markets in their organization structures and career development. Colgate-Palmolive, for one, recently grouped its geographies under two executives: one responsible for mature, developed economies and the other for high-growth, emerging markets.

21ST CENTURY GROWTH

The big, emerging markets will drive the lion's share of growth in the world's consumption of consumer goods in the next 10 to 15 years. There are a handful of consumer-products multinationals positioned well to ride this wave. Multinationals not so well positioned need to figure out quickly if they want to play and where. Those who desire to be major emerging market players are well advised to carefully reflect on the uniqueness of these markets and how their Westernized strategies and business models need to be redesigned for the emerging world.

For emerging market participants, the coming years will not be a smooth ride. In many cases, the rapid growth in the economies of the emerging nations has outpaced the required improvements in their financial and government institutions. There will undoubtedly be more bumps in the road, as the most recent economic troubles in Brazil, as well as rumblings in China, suggest. Nevertheless, for consumer businesses that aspire to grow, these markets represent an opportunity that cannot be ignored.

PART SEVEN

The Future

INTERNATIONAL BUSINESS AND TRADE IN THE NEXT DECADE: REPORT FROM A DELPHI STUDY

Michael R. Czinkota and Ilkka A. Ronkainen

INTRODUCTION

The importance and the impact of international business has become an accepted fact by practitioners, policy makers and academics alike. Executives rank globalization high on their strategic agendas [Hoffman and Gopinath 1994], governments and legislatures have dramatically increased their debate of and involvement in international trade and investment issues [Czinkota 1986b], and universities adjust their business curricula and research to address international business issues [Beamish and Calof 1989; Ball and McCullough 1993].

A unifying conclusion drawn by all observers of the international business scene is that international business causes many changes, but is itself also the subject of major transformations. As a result, it is important to anticipate such changes and to adapt to them by formulating new paradigms [Dunning 1995]. This conclusion highlights the need to investigate impending changes in the international business arena. Some scholars have taken up the challenge and conducted research designed to do so. Most frequently, investigations by the academic community have resulted in questioning the relevance of business curricula and research activities in universities [Daniels 1991]. While such investigations were initially only regionally focused, they have increasingly

Michael R. Czinkota and Ilkka A. Ronkainen are on the Faculty of Marketing and International Business at Georgetown University. They are the co-authors of several books including *International Marketing* (sixth edition), *International Business* (fifth edition) and *Global Marketing*.

become global in nature [Kwok, Arpan and Folks 1994]. Another approach has interpreted research trends of academics by analyzing the frequency of articles published in different areas of international business [Wright and Ricks 1994]. Occasionally, corporations were queried as to their future outlook and needs in international business [Hoffman and Gopinath 1994].

Several characteristics are common to all these studies. One is their primary focus on one country only when investigating a global phenomenon. Another is their concentration on only one constituency of the international business process. Even though change in international business is driven by the interaction of the business, policy and academic communities, past research typically queries only one group of these players. In consequence, the insights provided are limited to the views of the one group investigated, and do not reflect the important and possibly different perspectives of the two groups left out. This is particularly noticeable with regards to the policy community, whose views are only rarely investigated by international business scholars. A long-term analysis by Inkpen and Beamish [1994] found that, over a period of twenty-five years, only 1.9% of articles published in the *Journal of International Business Studies* had a policy-oriented focus. A final characteristic is the fact that virtually none of these studies reflected any interaction between the business, policy and research communities on the subject of trends and changes. Such interaction, however, is imperative in order to obtain a reasonably accurate forecast of impending metamorphoses.

This article presents an assessment of changes in the international business field, and does so with a broader perspective than earlier research. To trigger research ideas for academics, to assist business in preparing for impending change, and to suggest areas of importance to policy makers, this article offers insights into the thinking among the business, policy and academic communities with regards to the future of international business and trade in the major market areas of the world: the Americas, Asia-Pacific and Europe.

RESEARCH APPROACH

Various approaches can establish how pertinent constituents view the future. A broad-based content analysis of the current literature can examine trends [Naisbitt 1990; Wheeler 1988]. However, this approach is very resource intensive and, due to language limitations, possibly biased by the perceptions and interpretations of U.S.-based analysts. In addition, such an approach does not benefit from any interaction between policy makers, business leaders and academics. A second approach is the interview method, which allows for in-depth questioning. By convening a group of experts at one location and facilitating their interaction over a prolonged period, an in-depth assessment could be created. However, in order to be meaningful, such an approach requires the invitation of carefully identified and stratified experts, reflecting different types of insights and different parts of the world rather than the views of a convenience sample. Financial constraints made this approach unfeasible.

This study uses the Delphi technique, which integrates the judgement of a number of experts who cannot come together physically, but also facilitates feedback, debate and comment. The overall objective of this technique is to achieve consensus among a diverse group of participants. Past studies using such an approach have typically used thirty experts based on the finding that larger groups create few additional ideas and limit the in-depth exploration of the ones generated [Delbeq, Van De Ven and Gustafson 1975]. For the success of such a study, it is critical to secure the participation of the right kinds of experts, who understand the issues, have a vision, and represent a substantial variety of viewpoints. A research council composed of one leader each in the international policy, business and academic communities, all of them with more than twenty years of experience in their fields and very well connected to their global counterparts, identified possible participants in the study. The selection criteria were: active career in international business for at least ten years; a leadership role within the participant's professional setting; a global vision beyond local and temporary concerns; and accessibility and willingness to engage in intellectual dialogue. A list of fifty-four global experts with eighteen each in the policy, business and research fields was developed, stratified to ensure that there were eighteen representatives each from the three geographic areas chosen. The business leaders approached were typically either corporate presidents or vice-presidents for international operations. At the policy level, the representatives were current or former members of the legislative and executive branches of government. The academic participants were professors and program directors specializing in international business. Although nearly all of the experts invited to join the panel participated in the first round, duties, travel, illness, and time constraints eliminated some of them in the second and third rounds. Thirty-four experts participated in all three rounds of the study. The profile of the participants in Table 1 indicates the number, type and location of the panelists contributing to this study.

The Delphi started out with an open-ended questionnaire asking for "an identification of international business dimensions subject to change in the new millennium."

• TABLE 1 •

DELPHI RESPONSES

	NORTH AMERICA	EUROPE	ASIA	
Business community	6	3	4	13
Policy community	7	2	2	11
Academic community	4	2	4	10
	17	7	10	34

Range of Titles

Business community: Chairman, member of the board, president, executive vice president, partner

Policy community: Vice minister, ambassador, director general, executive director, division director, director, assistant secretary

Academic community: Chaired professor, professor, director

In addition, respondents were requested to "highlight the corporate responses to these changes." Issues and responses were to be rated for their impact on a ten-point scale, ranging from very low to very high. This first round resulted in eighteen pages of issues and trends. In most instances, respondents provided ratings for an issue or trend heading, and then added substantial comments that elaborated on that dimension. Based on these replies, the research council devised issue categories into which the various comments were grouped. In addition, predicted changes were linked with specific corporate responses. This consolidation of comments served to eliminate overlaps, and made the wealth of information more amenable for evaluation and discussion in the subsequent rounds.

In the second iteration of the Delphi, the panelists were presented with these categories and comments and were asked to elaborate on the statements, and to indicate their agreement or disagreement. In addition, the respondents were requested to assess the likelihood that a particular change would occur within the next ten years, and to rate the extent of the impact such a change would have on corporations. Both of these assessments were made by use of the ten-point rating scale. The third, and final round, focused on those statements for which there was disagreement between the panelists. While in the first round experts in a specific industry or sector were likely to expound on changes particular to their interests, the other panelists were able to express their agreements or disagreements with these views in the subsequent rounds, leading to the gradual building of consensus.

FINDINGS AND IMPLICATIONS

The wide variety of answers were grouped into four categories for reporting purposes: geographic issues, sectoral transformations, institutional and framework issues, and corporate adjustment strategies. Scale values were developed by multiplying perceived likelihoods of occurrence with their assessed impact on international business to derive a rank order.

THE GEOGRAPHY OF INTERNATIONAL BUSINESS

The predicted role of different regions is shown in Table 2. These predictions did not appear to be influenced by the location of the panelists. Global economic growth will be fueled to a great extent by emerging markets of the Asia-Pacific and Latin America. The speed of growth may be threatened by uncertainty in terms of international relations and by social and political tensions, arising from inequities in income distribution. Concerns were also expressed about inadequacies in infrastructure, both physical, such as transportation, and abstract, such as legal systems. The consensus, however, is that future growth will be significant and that any slowdown in growth rates will mainly be the result of the maturing of some countries' economies.

The Asia-Pacific is seen as the hot spot of interest. The area is predicted to grow into a massive economic, political and technological production power, with simulta-

• TABLE 2 •

THE GEOGRAPHY OF INTERNATIONAL BUSINESS

REGION	SCALE VALUES*	
Asia Pacific		72
China	49	
Japan	48	
Korea	45	
India	42	
Latin America		33
North America		30
Europe		26
Western Europe	27	
Eastern Europe	23	
Russia	22	
Africa		21

*Scale values were determined by multiplying the likelihood of an event or issue with its impact on international business, based on individual responses. The result was then standardized on a scale ranging from 1–100.

neously increasing regional consumer demand. For the industrialized countries, this presents significant export and investment opportunities, but also diminishes, in the longer term, the basis of their status and influence in the world economy. The Asia-Pacific region will collaborate, not in the same way as the European Union or NAFTA, but rather through trade and investment flows (e.g., Japan) and social contacts (e.g., the Chinese business community). The Asian panelists see "western compulsion for institutionalization" wrong for the region, and believe that a bloc may only emerge in reaction to perceived threats from outside forces.

China's emergence is seen as the economic event of the decade. Despite innumerable risks and significant expectations for change, experts see Chinese pragmatism prevailing and substantial opportunities for outside participation. Companies already present and those willing to make significant investments will be the main beneficiaries. The lack of predictability of Chinese demand and missing legal infrastructure will be worked out through market forces and eventual rapid development of corporate law. Long-term commitment, willingness to transfer technology, and an ability to partner either with local firms through joint ventures or close relationships with overseas Chinese firms are considered crucial for success.

Other promising emerging markets are Korea and India. Korea is likely to emerge as a participant in worldwide competition, while India is considered more important for the size of its potential market. For the Korean chaebols to emerge as global competitors, they must still improve their ability to adopt a global mindset and the quality of their products. Some experts are concerned about the chaebols' status as the Korean economy becomes more democratized. In addition, the impact of the impending reunification of the Korean peninsula on globalization efforts must be taken into account.

The considerable economic liberalization in India during the 1990s will result in major international marketing opportunities due to the country's size, its significant natural wealth, and its large, highly educated middle class. While many experts believe that political conflict, nationalism, and class structures may hamper the ability of Indian firms to emerge as a worldwide competitive force, there is strong agreement that India's disproportionately large and specialized workforce in engineering and computer sciences makes the nation a power to be reckoned with.

Japan also continues as a hot spot, leading the Asia-Pacific region through its investments. Such investments will increasingly take place closer to home, at the expense of North America and Europe. The amount of investment is also predicted to grow substantially as more Japanese firms move their production facilities to neighboring countries.

Interest in Latin America was warm. The international business climate will improve due to economic integration, market liberalization and privatization. In spite of some inefficiencies, MERCOSUR was praised for bringing countries closer together and encouraging collaboration. Due to substantial natural resources and relatively low cost of production, an increased flow of foreign direct investment and trade activity is forecast, emanating not only from the United States, but also from Europe and Japan. Some participants even felt that U.S. corporations may fall behind if they maintain their key focus on Mexico alone rather than on the entire continent.

North America also fell into the warm category. Even though economic growth was seen as only moderate, the over-proportional consumptive power of the region will continue to make North America a targeted export destination. Both Mexico and Canada were seen as continuing to depend heavily on the overwhelming dominance of the United States in their trade and investment flows. For the U.S., ongoing growth in services and agricultural exports are predicted, but, in spite of the export spurt of U.S. manufacturing firms in the past decade, the relative under-participation in exporting by the manufacturing sector was seen to continue. Design-out policies of U.S. parts and components by trading partners, due to hegemonic U.S. trade policies in areas such as export controls, were seen as contributing to the persistence of large trade deficits.

The cool spots are occupied by Europe and the Less Developed Countries in Africa. For Western Europe, some positive developments were attributed to ongoing economic liberalization and inclusion of new members, which have the potential to boost productivity and increase opportunities for global players. However, divergent nationalist pressures and conflicts on the currency front were seen as important counterweights, as was the continued high social cost of doing business. In spite of some efforts to come to grips with inflexible labor markets and extensive welfare schemes, ongoing inertia was seen to contribute in a major way to an uncompetitive cost structure and stagnant economic performance. As a result, the eventual formation of a fortress Europe was seen as a distinct possibility. Since the attractiveness of the European market is too great to ignore, the emergence of separate corporate strategies for Europe and the rest of the world was anticipated.

The countries of Central and Eastern Europe were seen to offer growing attractiveness for international business transactions due to continuing low labor cost, low-cost input factors, and large unused production capacities. This attractiveness, however, was seen to exist only for investment from Western Europe, mainly for reasons of geographic proximity and attractive outsourcing opportunities. Yet even these investment flows were seen to take place on a selective basis, resulting in very unbalanced economic conditions in the region. Export-oriented investments are likely to be restricted by the erection of trade barriers on part of the European Union, designed to prevent major economic displacements due to an onslaught of narrowly targeted competition from the region. Firms and governments from regions other than Europe were seen as much more reluctant to invest. This aversion is less driven by caution about a potential resurgence of communism or fear of economic and political instability, but mainly due to the existence of attractive investment alternatives elsewhere.

Russia and the other member countries of the former Soviet Union are seen as facing the greatest difficulties in Europe. Their economic recovery and participation in world trade is likely to be very gradual. In part, the slowness is a function of self-imposed constraints due to domestic fears of outsiders. For political reasons, financial inflows into the region will continue in the near term, yet, if these flows are to make a difference, governments need to find market-oriented ways to reduce the flight of capital abroad.

The developing countries of Africa are seen as the coolest region for international business purposes. The key reasons for such a pessimistic view are continuing political instability and the resulting inability of many African countries and firms to be consistent trading partners. In light of increased competition for scarce investment capital, these drawbacks are instrumental in holding both investment and trade down to a trickle. This starvation for funds is unlikely to be addressed by corporations or governments, although all agree that sustainable economic growth is needed for long-term global stability. More likely, the efforts of governments, multilateral institutions and Non-Governmental Organizations (NGOs) will need to be sought. In addition, the actions of committed individuals or small groups will play an important role for the region. Periodic surges in the social conscience of industrialized nations may result in debt relief measures and even targeted investments, but these are likely to be insufficient for a transformation of the economic future of the region unless accompanied by internal reform and institution building. Nevertheless, global trade liberalization may offer some hope to the region by permitting easier exports.

SECTORAL TRANSFORMATIONS

Key changes on a sectoral basis are shown in Table 3. The largest transformations are anticipated in services industries. Market openings accompanied by greater ease of reach by service providers will lead to major increases in competition. One key cause of the services transformations is the information revolution. The decreasing cost of using the information infrastructure will offer service providers new channels to communicate with customers. The ease of bridging distances will make service providers primarily

• TABLE 3 •

Sectoral Transformations

Sector	Scale Values*	
Services		48
Information		36
Financial	45	
Telecom	33	
Manufacturing		35
Biotechnology	39	
Aerospace	33	
Automotive	23	

*Scale values were determined by multiplying the likelihood of an event or issue with its impact on international business, based on individual responses. The result was then standardized on a scale ranging from 1–100.

concerned about the right to operate in a market rather than about the right to establish themselves in the global arena. Why build a large bank or insurance edifice and combat local regulations if a computer linkage will do? Service providers will also be able to develop new marketing techniques, the most important of which will be the rise of micro-marketing efforts specifically tailored to individual needs. The speed of decisionmaking will increase (together with the risk that such faster decisions may bring) and information transparency will be enhanced. In consequence, services transactions will come closer to the pure market force model.

The growing risk of information overload is likely to lead to the emergence of a new industry concentrated on the structuring of knowledge. One possible implication could be that knowledge distribution experts will form an entirely new profession with two distinct specializations: "Knowledge Focusers" will be in charge of meshing data sets and ensuring that the right kind of information is provided as parsimoniously as possible. "Knowledge Erasers" will concentrate on weeding out old or unnecessary data, in order to limit capacity constraints of information banks and to delete corporate information that may lead to future interpretation problems. Due to rising concerns in the information dissemination area, the role of privacy experts and mechanisms designed to withhold information will also be on the increase.

Two specific service industries most affected by transformations will be the financial and the telecommunication sectors. The financial sector is likely to face continuous integration leading to bank acquisitions and reduction in financial intermediaries. Customers will increasingly be able to present their needs globally and directly to financial markets. Current intermediaries will need to reexamine their niche and demonstrate their usefulness if they are not to become obsolete. Investment banks, for example, will have to find ways to survive the direct placement activities of insurance companies, pension funds and mutual funds, who will package financial assets to make them easily portable and transferable. Commercial banks will be confronted with an increasing use of electronic money, and credit activities managed by independent brokers and risk management firms such as credit agencies. On the international level, borrowers will have easy and direct access to world capital markets, which will place enormous pressure on domestic financial institutions to conform with international terms and practices. An increase in financial risks in the developing world, due to the short-term nature of its investment capital, is likely to lead to a re-establishment of the in-house risk assessment teams that were largely abandoned after 1982.

These individual teams, rather than banks, will focus on the collection, evaluation and rating of country information, and the careful monitoring of institutional exposure. Firms themselves will learn that once exports exceed 20% of sales, a key focus of the international effort will have to be on financial rather than on sales strategies, particularly since the financial support for smaller exporters is likely to decrease. As markets and their financial needs expand, there will be a great rise in the need for financing. Due to the greater mobility of capital, the world will initially be awash in money, with private sector investment flows far ahead of the international investment activities of multilateral organizations. Over time, however, poor investment choices made by overburdened financial decisionmakers, combined with the global financial absorption of the U.S. government budget deficit, the financial demands of the emerging growth markets, the needs of the Central and Eastern European economies, and the aid requirements of many developing nations, are likely to lead to heated global competition for and more cautious placement of financial resources. As a result, global real interest rates are likely to rise and remain high. An increase in the privatization of government financing programs will be accompanied by a growing need for new financial products and providers, giving rise to the growth of countertrade, self-financing programs of corporate groups, and other innovative alternative financing packages.

The international telecommunications sector will also continue to advance, requiring more corporate technology investment and ever faster response times. Since communications technology will create independent communities with significant power, it will be crucial for firms to be part of such networks. For example, participation in direct order entry networks and compatibility with large proprietary corporate logistics systems will be crucial to the survival of firms, since a lack of linkage will lead to an exclusion from any transactions.

The high cost of creating such networks will encourage strategic alliances, rapidly shifting virtual corporations, and cross industry collaborations. Communication changes will result in more efficient management operating in flatter organizations. At the same time, much effort will be dedicated to the creation of international human networks that reach beyond information technology.

Telecommunications will also have a major effect on international employment and business transactions. On the employment side, a detachment from any location will become increasingly possible, thus greatly raising the potential for productivity increases due to employment sourcing on a global level. On the transactions side, electronic forms of commerce will continue to expand, greatly augmenting the reach of any service provider, and leading to harsher competition and more consumer choice.

Manufacturing will also be strongly affected by industrial transformations. Technology innovations will precipitate an avalanche of new products. Simultaneous interactions with different parts of the world will strengthen research and development efforts. Faster knowledge transfer will allow for the concentration of product expertise, increased division of labor and a proliferation of global operations. Information shifts will allow for speedier production and product delivery, leading to a new dawn for logistics management, which will become instrumental in enabling firms to be first to market and to fortify their customer relations.

Three manufacturing sectors where change is seen as being most pronounced are the biotechnology, aerospace and automotive industries. Genetic engineering will have a major effect on the growth and supply of agricultural and piscicultural products—in spite of temporary controversies. The potential for new growing areas and increased yields is simply too important to be ignored. Major advances can also be expected in the pharmaceutical fields, driven to a large degree by the growing competition between U.S., Japanese and Western European firms. One danger that may emanate from this competition is the possibility that countries begin to compete against each other on the basis of regulatory laxness, in order to attract biotechnology industries and speed products to market.

In the aerospace sector, increasing risk and rising cost are seen as precipitating growing industry consolidation (as has already been evidenced by the merger between Boeing and McDonnell Douglas, which was announced after the input to this study was completed). Even though U.S. firms are expected to retain their global lead, stiffer competition accompanied by increased government involvement can be anticipated.

In the automotive sector, competition will remain harsh, but will shift gradually to clean car issues as environmental demands escalate. The globalization of this industry will increasingly be characterized by investment into manufacturing facilities in numerous parts of the world rather than trade. A key competitive drawback afflicting U.S. and European firms in this industry, however, continues to be labor's opposition to outsourcing, which may prevent the implementation of global best practices.

INSTITUTIONAL AND FRAMEWORK ISSUES

The key findings on issues regarding the trade framework and its institutions are shown in Table 4. The role of intellectual property was the hottest issue identified by the panelists. Given the importance of technology, creative concepts, and processes as a basis for competitive advantage, the protection of patents, copyrights and trademarks was seen as the most important asset to be safeguarded. The increasing ease with which technology can be transferred and the lack of adequate legislation and its enforcement were seen as key challenges. These problems are further exacerbated by the continuing strategy of emerging economies to achieve growth based on imitation rather than innovation. While there was unanimous feeling about the need for protection, there was disagreement whether it could be accomplished and whether there was the political will to achieve it. Multilateral agreements, especially through the WTO, and bilateral pressure were considered the most realistic public sector alternatives. Many experts felt that true protection can only come from companies themselves, by maintaining an ongoing lead in innovation and technology. The best direction for policy makers, therefore, is to provide a domestic environment which is conducive to such progress.

• TABLE 4 •

INSTITUTIONAL AND FRAMEWORK ISSUES

ISSUE	SCALE VALUES*
Intellectual property increases as a core competence and asset to be protected globally	56
Greater government use of trade rules	35
Growing role of the World Trade Organization	34
Environmental concerns by governments and customers add to producer requirements for product responsibility	27
Individualization of public policy and corporate responsibility	26
Currency stabilization efforts	19

*Scale values were determined by multiplying the likelihood of an event or issue with its impact on international business, based on individual responses. The result was then standardized on a scale ranging from 1–100.

Environmental issues, while still considered important, did not receive the same level of attention and urgency as in earlier research. Experts agreed that environmental concerns by governments and consumer groups increasingly require manufacturers to be responsible for their products from cradle to grave, but many characterize corporate reaction as lip service. Despite the prominence of environmental programs in Europe, especially Northern Europe and Germany, U.S. participants do not see European companies as having a competitive advantage in being green. Rather, global companies that are able to transfer innovations and programs between markets easily and quickly may be the long-term winners as public concern about the deterioration of the natural environment and pollution provide major new-product opportunities. Europeans are seen as having the lead in adopting the ISO 14000 standards, which focus on environmental dimensions of production. Environmental audits and "green" strategies are still seen as preliminary and used only by the leading-edge companies.

The dislocations caused by wide currency swings, triggered and magnified by speculative portfolio investment flows, will encourage governments to aim for increased currency stabilization. Such stability will be supported by the business sector as more firms become international. As a result, either the IMF or another organization sponsored primarily by the EU, Japan and the United States will become active by participating in, if not managing or even governing, global financial markets and severely affecting national monetary policies. Such a development will lead to more financing of governmental budget deficits directly on local markets, and is likely to force more fiscal discipline on nations, not dissimilar to the discipline required by states and cities in the United States.

Even though the timing of full monetary integration within the EU was subject to lively debate between the experts, there was substantial agreement that such integration would eventually take place. As a result, it was felt that while the dollar is likely to continue in an important position for international financial transactions and reserve purposes, its preeminence will be affected by the eventual emergence of a Euro regime in the European Union.

The international trade framework is seen as being strengthened by a World Trade Organization with a gradually increasing stature. Even though the forces of regionalism were seen as continuing, a growth in the enforcement capability of the WTO will provide for more consistency and stability of trade relations. Large players in the trade field, will, however, continue to be able to influence trade and investment activities on a global scale by virtue of the fact that their interpretation and application of established rules will be able to change the activities of lesser trading partners. For example, the use of labeling regulations is likely to have powerful market implications when one thinks of labels such as "made by insured workers" or "caught with dolphin protection." Combined with complex country of origin regulations, such application of existing rules will play an increasing role in the trade policies of large nations. The role of individual governments, both as customers and participants in markets, is likely to decrease in light of continued globalization. However, competition among nation-states aimed to attract investments may well increase. Such competition in turn may detrimentally affect domestic social policies, unless policy makers concentrate on offering advantages in areas such as work force education and training.

Increasingly, there will also be an assumption of heretofore sovereign policy formulation by individuals, special interest groups and corporations. For example, in the area of moral behavior, firms will be subject not just to government rules, but will also be held accountable by the public at large. There was substantial disagreement regarding the human rights dimension between American panelists and their Asian and European counterparts. While most American experts saw the issue to be of growing importance, Europeans saw it as "fading" while Asians tended to interpret it as an issue driven mainly by an American political agenda. However, there was agreement that if a firm participates in actions that are considered wrong by concerned individuals, these actions, once identified, will be communicated quickly to many interest groups and customers. Firms will then be subject to public scorn, consumer boycotts and investor scrutiny that may be much more detrimental than the sanctions of a governmental entity. In consequence, firms will increasingly recognize that an era of global communication also signifies an era of global scrutiny, and that global compliance with the expectations of consumer groups becomes a new benchmark for corporate operations. Therefore, companies are seen to invest more in community relations as a function of enlightened self-interest; i.e., these investments will not only help them gain favor in local communities but enable them to reap the benefits of an improved global image.

CORPORATE ADJUSTMENT STRATEGIES

The effects of globalization at the corporate level are shown in Table 5. Firms will need a simultaneous presence in all three major market areas of the Americas, Europe and the Asia-Pacific to respond to enduring regional preferences and to gain and ensure competitive positions. At the same time the expectation is that there will be a continuing re-engineering of companies based on core business strengths and the pursuit of

• TABLE 5 •

Key Corporate Adjustment Strategies

Adjustment Type	Scale Values*
Tactical decisionmaking more decentralized; strategic control remains global	58
Technology as an internal driver of globalization through real-time interaction	51
Organization structures flattening; focus on entrepreneurship	49
Regional integration necessitates corporate presence in all major markets	43
Economic liberalization fuels offshore investment	43
Focus on core competencies and niche markets	39
Ethnic and cultural diversity increase their impact on strategy	35
Needs of global customers lead to new systems such as global account management	35
Creativity and flexibility in recruiting and employment	34
Use of less expatriates; more need for corporate acculturation programs	24
Cultural training gains renewed significance due to diversity	22

*Scale values were determined by multiplying the likelihood of an event or issue with its impact on international business, based on individual responses. The result was then standardized on a scale ranging from 1–100.

niche strategies on a global basis. Economic liberalization is projected to increase offshore investment; competitive pressures will lead to increased overseas sourcing. Due to an increase in the number of markets entered and a strengthened feeling of ethnicity among consumers in individual markets, the effective management of cultural and ethnic diversity within a corporation will become crucial. Another driver of globalization will be the growth in the number of global organizational customers, including intermediaries. As a response, companies will have to follow them in their expansion and develop strategic responses to their needs. One example is global account management programs, which ensure the delivery of uniform products and services through one point of contact for worldwide customers.

Global strategies will have a dramatic impact on the organization of firms. The key to success will be the leverage of corporate capabilities around the world in support of operations in each country so that the company as a whole is larger than the sum of its parts. This requires a series of organizational initiatives in order to develop global strategy to its full potential and to secure effective implementation of such strategies at both the national and cross-border levels.

Key challenges will surface in the form of structures, systems, and the types of individuals who are expected to plan and implement the new global strategies. Critical will be the determination of what should and what should not be centralized and standardized. The more tactical the function, the more it should stay local; the more strategic the element, the more opportunity for cross-border coordination. The central control of strategic elements will allow for the leveraging of capabilities and company-wide use of best practice as a result of learning. For this to work without the emergence of complications, such as the not-invented-here syndrome, one of the most distinct organizational initiatives will focus on the building of networks; without the ability to exchange ideas, systems and processes across borders, the willingness to do so may be a wasted asset. Part of the need for increased interaction on all levels is to "corporatize" employees throughout the organization in the development of a common global vision. The panelists agree on an increasing emphasis on entrepreneurship in these networks. These will be manifested, for example, in centers of excellence in which a country organization may be given worldwide responsibility for a product line or a process.

Human resources management will require more creativity and flexibility in recruiting and employment to secure the type of individual needed to implement global strategies. The challenge will be to find people who either already know or are able to learn and assimilate national differences into their thinking. A shortage of such key skills requires increased investments in recruitment, training and development, as well as programs directed at retaining personnel. As the use of expatriates decreases, two types of programs will have to be incorporated more closely into the globalization effort. Corporate acculturation will have to ensure effective communication and implementation of programs across corporate units. Cultural training may also gain renewed significance to improve sensitivity to differences and to extract possible "best practices" for regional or global use.

CONCLUSIONS AND DISCUSSION

This research provided an overview of what a global panel of knowledgeable experts believe to be the most important and relevant issues in international business and trade over the next decade. What makes the results particularly interesting is its unusual nexus of insight between the business, policy and academic communities on a global level. While some of the issues presented here are already at the early stage of public recognition, many of the dimensions addressed seem to have escaped wide attention so far. Once they move to the "front burner" of business and policy concerns, the academic community needs to be ready to provide insights about alternative courses of action, since the decisions are likely to be made rapidly, with or without a sound information base. Therefore, the findings provided here can help guide academicians in both their research and teaching efforts. In particular, the forward-looking nature of this work provides an opportunity to get ahead of the power curve. Rather than being trapped in providing a description of the state of the art of business practices, the forecasts presented here may contribute to enable researchers to carry out work which is normative and prescriptive. While sectoral and regional specialists will develop their own insights from the findings presented here, we believe that there are several overarching implications for business executives, policy makers and academics. Firms may wish to concentrate their global expansion plans on Asia and Latin America, with a major emphasis on infrastructure projects. A key focus should also rest on the development of and participation in information networks, accompanied by the development of global logistics systems. It will be of major importance to understand and track the development of administrative rules, particularly in the labelling field. The development of an interface with special interest groups will also become a crucial concern.

Policy makers will need to understand the effect of Japanese competition emanating from third countries. In the United States, a decrease in the unilateralism of trade policy formulation should be sought, accompanied by support for increased enforcement capabilities of the WTO. On a global level, regulatory flexibility towards the banking and financial sector should encourage firms in these industries to adjust to rapid change. More global harmonization will be needed for regulations in areas such as biotechnology, administrative trade rules, and intellectual property rights. Trade policy formulation through the encouragement of innovation in domestic processes and technology will also need to be considered.

Researchers will continue to find fertile fields of inquiry by investigating export development processes and the role of global information structure and dissemination. Such work will be particularly useful in the context of network formation and the management of logistics systems. It will also be beneficial to explore the changes in the global financial sector, including approaches leading to the reduction of currency fluctuations, and the new role of countertrade. Of course, one may wonder about the accuracy and reliability of Delphi studies. Even though the Delphi technique was originally applied by the Rand Corporation for business forecasting purposes, it has been used as an established research tool mainly in the fields of library and information science [Buckley 1995] and in the medical disciplines [Linstone and Turoff 1975]. More recently, it has also been applied to investigate potential future developments in science and technology [Coates 1997]. In the business field, the technique has been rated highly by some as a systematic thinking tool, but has also been challenged in its ability to serve as an identifier of strategic issues [Schoemaker 1993]. Such ambivalence may be understandable in an era in which high powered quantification of business analyses is desired and admired by many. However, we believe that the study of business remains a social science, and is heavily dependent on the in-depth thoughts, evaluation and imagination of individuals. Their informed consensus is more likely to indicate future directions than the opinions of many uninformed survey participants.

To evaluate the appropriateness of the Delphi technique for business forecasting, we scrutinized two major predictive Delphi studies carried out in the business field [Czinkota 1986a; Czinkota and Ronkainen 1992]. In the 1986 study a total of seventeen key forecasts were made of which fourteen were deemed accurate five years later. In spite of this 82% "hit-rate," however, the panel did not foresee one key, world-altering event, namely the collapse of the Iron Curtain. It may well be, however, that this failure to foresee was a function of the fact that this particular study drew only on experts from one country. Input on a global level might at least have raised the possibility of such an event. In the 1992 study, which did use a global panel, a total of forty \key predictions were made, with a 1997 accuracy of thirty-two dimensions or 80%. All the inaccuracies, however, were in the form of overstatements, i.e., the anticipation of more rapid transformations than actually took place, rather than in direction. It therefore appears that the Delphi method is quite a powerful forecasting tool. Of course, the key aspect to the usefulness of this type of research will remain the selection of the participants, since their level of knowledge and degree of enthusiasm in participating in such a research venture will vitally affect the quality of the output.

It would seem worthwhile to continue research of this nature on a regular basis in order to remain aware of key impending changes. Future studies could use several Delphi panels in order to explore future developments on a regional or sectoral basis in more depth. Doing so might permit a cross-comparison of results. In addition, it would be useful to specifically address possible policy responses to change, in order to gain a more in-depth perspective of policy implications.

A few comments are appropriate regarding the execution of this research. We intended originally to conduct this research by facsimile transmission, hoping to improve on historical time delays encountered with the Delphi method. However, it was soon revealed that, due to our global approach, shortcomings in the distribution of technology did not yield the time benefits we expected. As a result, the study still took more than seven months to complete. On a regional basis it may well be possible to carry out such work in the future via the Internet and e-mail. Apart from the time dimension, the great benefit to such an approach will consist of better interaction among participants. On a global basis, however, the world is not yet ready for such a high-technology approach, if one intends to obtain input from a group of carefully selected individuals. It might also well be possible that, by making technology availability the driver for the selection of participants, the selection criterion might become a major intervening variable shaping the outcome of the study. Over time, however, it is likely that the appropriate use of more advanced technology for this type of research will improve the time factor in conducting such research, and ease the current limitation in the number of participants, therefore endowing the Delphi method with even more power and accuracy.

References

Ball, Donald A. & Wendall H. McCullough, Jr. 1993. The views of American multinational CEOs on the internationalized business education for prospective employees. *Journal of International Business Studies*, 24(2): 383–91.

Beamish, Paul W. & Jonathan L. Calof. 1989. International business education: A corporate view. *Journal of International Business Studies*, 20(2): 553–64.

Buckley, Christopher. 1995. Delphi: A methodology for preferences more than predictions. *Library Management*, 7: 16–19.

Coates, Joseph F. 1997. UK Delphi report merits study by R&D leaders. *Research-Technology Management*, 1: 5–7.

Czinkota, Michael R. 1986a. International trade and business in the late 1980s: An integrated U.S. perspective. *Journal of International Business Studies*, 17(1): 127–34.

———. 1986b. U. S. trade policy and Congress. *Columbia Journal of World Business*, 4 (20th Anniversary Issue): 71–77.

——— & Ilkka A. Ronkainen. 1992. Global Marketing 2000: A marketing survival guide. *Marketing Management*, 1: 36–45.

Daniels, John D. 1991. Relevance in international business research: A need for more linkages. *Journal of International Business Studies*, 22(2): 177–86.

Delbeq, Andrel, Andrew H. Van De Ven & David H. Gustafson. 1975. *Group techniques for program planning* . Glenview, Ill.: Scott Foresman, 83.

Dunning, John H. 1995. Reappraising the eclectic paradigm in an age of alliance capitalism. *Journal of International Business Studies*, 26(3): 461–91.

Hoffman, Richard C. & C. Gopinath. 1994. The importance of international business to the strategic agenda of U.S. CEOs. *Journal of International Business Studies*, 25(3): 625–37.

Inkpen, Andrew C. & Paul W. Beamish. 1994. An analysis of twenty-five years of research in the *Journal of International Business Studies. Journal of International Business Studies*, 25(4): 703–13.

Kwok, Chuck C. Y., Jeffrey Arpan & William R. Folks, Jr. 1994. A global survey of international business education in the 1990s. *Journal of International Business Studies*, 25(3): 605–23.

Linstone, A. & M. Turoff. 1975. *The Delphi method: Techniques and applications.* Reading, Mass.: Addison Wesley.

Naisbitt, John. 1990. *Megatrends 2000.* New York: Morrow.

Schoemaker, Paul J.H. 1993. Multiple scenario development: Its conceptual and behavioral foundation. *Strategic Management Journal*, 14: 193–213.

Wheeler, David R. 1988. Content analysis: An analytical technique for international market research. *International Marketing Review*, 4: 34–40.

Wright, Richard W. & David A. Ricks. 1994. Trends in international business research: Twenty-five years later. *Journal of International Business Studies*, (25)4: 687–701.

CREDITS

P. 11: Jane Frazer and Jeremy Oppenheim, "What's New About Globalization?" from The McKinsey Quarterly, 1997, No. 2, pp. 168–179. Reprinted by permission of McKinsey & Co.

P. 23: Jay Mazur, "Labor's New Internationalism," from Foreign Affairs, 79, January–February 2000, pp. 79–93. Copyright © 2000 by the Council on Foreign Relations, Inc. Reprinted by permission.

P. 35: Michael Czinkota, "A National Export Assistance Policy for New and Growing Businesses," from Journal of International Marketing, Vol. 2, No. 1, 1994, pp. 91–101. Reprinted by permission of the American Marketing Association.

P. 46: Michael Czinkota and Irwin Dichtl, "Export Controls and Global Changes," from der Markt, 1996, No. 3, pp. 148–155.

P. 58: Richard Brealey, "The Asian Crisis: Lessons for Crisis Management and Prevention," from International Finance, Vol. 2, No. 2, 1999, pp. 249–272.

P. 77: Martin Vander Weyer, Mark Landler and Doug Garr, "Globalism vs. Nationalism vs. E-business: The World Debates," from Strategy & Business, First Quarter 2000, pp. 63–80, Issue 18. (Part I: "Europe: Despite Unification, Local Laws Might Take the 'E' out of 'Eu'," by Martin Vander Weyer, by special permission arranged previously from Martin Vander Weyer; Part II: "Asia-Pacific: In China, Malaysia and Singapore, Freedom and Control Dance a Digital Minuet," by Mark Landler; Part III: "United States: A Presidential Campaign Tests the E-business Influence of Silicon Valley and Big Labor," by Doug Garr.) Reprinted with permission from Strategy & Business, a quarterly management magazine published by Booz-Allen & Hamilton.

P. 92: Alexander D. Stajkovic and Fred Luthans, "Business Ethics Across Cultures: A Social Cognitive Model," from Journal of World Business, 32 (1), 1997, pp. 17–34. Reprinted by permission.

P. 110: Ricky T.Y. Chan, "An Emerging Green Market in China: Myth or Reality?" from Business Horizons, March–April 2000, pp. 55–60. Reprinted with permission from Business Horizons. Copyright © 2000 by the Board of Trustees at Indiana University, Kelley School of Business.

P. 123: Anil K. Gupta and Vijay Govindarajan, "Managing Global Expansion: A Conceptual Framework," from Business Horizons, March—April 2000, pp. 45–54. Reprinted with permission from Business Horizons. Copyright © 2000 by the Board of Trustees at Indiana University, Kelley School of Business.

P. 142: Ashwin Adarkar, Asif Adil, David Ernst and Paresh Vaish, "Emerging Market Alliances: Must They Be Win-Lose?" from The McKinsey Quarterly, 1997, No. 4, pp. 120–137. Reprinted by permission of McKinsey & Co.

P. 159: Guliz Ger, "Localizing in the Global Village: Local Firms Competing in Global Markets," from California Management Review, Vol. 41, No. 4. Copyright © 1999 by The Regents of the University of California. Reprinted by permission of The Regents.

P. 181: Briance Mascarenhas, Alok Baveja and Mamnoon Jamil, "Dynamics of Core Competencies in Leading Multinational Companies," from California Management Review, Vol. 40, No. 4. Copyright © 1998 by The Regents of the University of California. Reprinted by permission of The Regents.

P. 196: Kenneth Simmonds, "International Marketing—Avoiding the Seven Deadly Traps," from Journal of International Marketing, Vol. 7, No. 2, 1999, pp. 51–62. Reprinted by permission of the American Marketing Association.

P. 207: John A. Quelch and Helen Bloom, "Ten Steps to a Global Human Resource Strategy," from Strategy & Business, First Quarter 1999, pp. 18–29. Reprinted with permission from Strategy & Business, a quarterly management magazine published by Booz-Allen & Hamilton.

P. 221: Benjamin C. Esty, "Petrozuata: A Case Study of the Effective Use of Project Finance," from Journal of Applied Corporate Finance, Vol. 12, No. 3, 1999, pp. 26–42. Reprinted by permission of Stern Stewart Management Service.

P. 249: Ingo Theuerkauf, David Ernst and Amir Mahini, "Think Local, Organize...?" from International Marketing Review, Vol. 13, No. 3, 1996, pp. 7–12. Reprinted by permission of the author.

P. 256: Henry P. Conn and George S. Yip, "Global Transfer of Critical Capabilities," from Business Horizons, January–February 1997, pp. 22–31. Reprinted with permission from Business Horizons. Copyright © 1997 by the Board of Trustees at Indiana University, Kelley School of Business.

P. 275: Julian Birkinshaw and Nick Fry, "Subsidiary Initiatives to Develop New Markets," from Sloan Management Review, Vol. 39, No. 3, Spring 1998, pp. 51–61. Reprinted by permission of the publisher. Copyright © 1998 by Sloan Management Review Association. All rights reserved.

P. 293: Johan Ahlberg, Nicklas Garemo and Tomas Naucler, "The Euro: How to Keep Your Prices Up and Your Competitors Down," from The McKinsey Quarterly, 1999, No. 2, pp. 112–118. Reprinted by permission of McKinsey & Co.

P. 299: Michael Czinkota and Masaaki Kotabe, "Bypassing Barriers to Marketing in Japan," from Marketing Management, Winter 1999, pp. 37–43. Reprinted by permission of the American Marketing Association.

P. 310: Reiner Springer and Michael Czinkota, "Marketing's Contribution to the Transformation of Central and Eastern Europe," from Thunderbird Business Review, Vol. 41 (1), January–February 1999, pp. 29–48. Copyright © 1999, John Wiley & Sons, Inc. Reprinted by permission.

P. 327: James Gingrich, "Five Rules for Winning Emerging Market Consumers," from Strategy & Business, Second Quarter 1999, pp. 19–33. Reprinted with permission from Strategy & Business, a quarterly management magazine published by Booz-Allen & Hamilton.

P. 341: Michael Czinkota and Ilkka Ronkainen, "International Business and Trade in the Next Decade: Report from a Delphi Study," from Journal of International Business Studies, Vol. 28, No. 4, 1997, pp. 827–844. Reprinted by permission.

INDEX